W9-AFE-063

DECONSTRUCTIVE VARIATIONS

DECONSTRUCTIVE VARIATIONS

Music and Reason in Western Society

Rose Rosengard Subotnik

University of Minnesota Press

Minneapolis

London

Grateful acknowledgment is made for permission to reprint from the following sources:
The Neue Mozart-Ausgabe score of Mozart's *Die Zauberflöte*. Copyright Baerenreiter
Music Corporation, by permission. Frédéric Chopin, Prelude number 7 (A-Major),
op. 28, G. Henle Verlag, Munich, by permission.

Chapter 1 appeared in revised form in *19th-Century Music* 15, no. 2 (Fall 1991):
132–50, © 1991 by the Regents of the University of California, reprinted by
permission of University of California Press; chapter 3 appeared in revised form
in *Explorations in Music, the Arts, and Ideas: Essays in Honor of Leonard B. Meyer*, ed.
Eugene Narmour and Ruth A. Solie (Stuyvesant, N.Y.: Pendragon, 1988),
by permission.

Published by the University of Minnesota Press
111 Third Avenue South, Suite 290, Minneapolis, MN 55401-2520
Printed in the United States of America on acid-free paper

Library of Congress Cataloging-in-Publication Data

Subotnik, Rose Rosengard.
    Deconstructive variations : music and reason in western society /
Rose Rosengard Subotnik.
        p.   cm.
    Includes bibliographical references and index.
    Contents: Whose Magic flute? : intimations of reality at the gates
of the Enlightenment — How could Chopin's A-major prelude be
deconstructed? — Toward a deconstruction of structural listening :
a critique of Schoenberg, Adorno, and Stravinsky — The closing of
the American dream? : a musical perspective on Allan Bloom, Spike
Lee, and doing the right thing.
    ISBN 0-8166-2197-7 (hc). — ISBN 0-8166-2198-5 (pb)
    1. Music—Philosophy and aesthetics.   2. Music and society.
3. Musical criticism.   4. Musical analysis.   I. Title.
ML3800.S898   1996
781'.1—dc20   95-13730

This book is dedicated to my husband
Dan Subotnik:
sharer of dreams,
co-conspirator in the countless projects that went nowhere,
collaborator on the few that actually worked (like the children),
and fellow phoenix.

"Age cannot wither [him], nor custom stale [his] infinite variety."

Contents

Preface

This is the second of two volumes of essays; the first, also published by the University of Minnesota Press, appeared in 1991 under the title *Developing Variations: Style and Ideology in Western Music*. The four chapters of the present volume have been ordered chronologically in terms of the periods of the works they discuss—late eighteenth century (Mozart), mid-nineteenth century (Chopin), early through middle twentieth century (Schoenberg, Stravinsky, Adorno), and late twentieth century (Allan Bloom, Spike Lee). This is not the order in which these chapters were originally written; and although they were written within a much shorter span of time than were the essays in my earlier volume, I would like here to sketch a brief history of these chapters for any reader who might want to read them in the order in which they were written. (Further particulars on the origins and earlier versions of all four chapters, as well as on the sources they cite, can be found in the Introduction.)

Of the four chapters in this book, the earliest two were written more or less simultaneously. I began writing chapter 2 ("How Could Chopin's A-Major Prelude Be Deconstructed?") in the summer of 1986. I interrupted my work on this essay to write chapter 3 ("Toward a Deconstruction of Structural Listening: A Critique of Schoenberg, Adorno, and Stravinsky") in the winter of 1986–87, then returned to work on chapter 2. A version of chapter 3 was published in *Explorations in Music, the Arts, and Ideas: Essays in Honor of Leonard B. Meyer*, ed. Eugene Narmour and Ruth A. Solie (Stuyvesant, N.Y.: Pendragon Press, 1988). Although the text and especially the notes of this essay have been revised and expanded for chapter 3 of the present volume, the numbering of the notes remains the same in both versions. Chapter 2 underwent a number of revisions and a substantial enlargement between 1987, when a relatively short version was presented at the annual meeting of the American Musicological Society, and 1994. This is its first publication.

Chapter 1 ("Whose *Magic Flute*? Intimations of Reality at the Gates of the Enlightenment") began to take shape in the spring of 1988, when it was presented at a conference at Dartmouth College entitled "The Musical and Verbal Arts: Interactions." Thereafter I revised and expanded this essay, while also designing a shorter version for publication in *19th-Century Music* 15 (1991). In this instance, many notes have been added to the longer version, so that the numbering of the notes in chapter 1 does not match that of the earlier published version.

Chapter 4 ("The Closing of the American Dream? A Musical Perspective on Allan Bloom, Spike Lee, and Doing the Right Thing") was commissioned by Wesleyan University as the annual George Jackson Memorial Lecture, for delivery in October 1989. It, too, has been considerably revised and expanded since its first presentation; this marks its first publication.

As in the preceding volume, I have provided extensive cross-references in the notes of each chapter to related material in other notes or text throughout the book; in chapter 4, this has also entailed a great deal of cross-reference within the chapter, as I explain in the Introduction. My hope here has been not only to show connections among the components of this book but also to assist readers who might wish to locate or pursue related ideas in a variety of contexts. Since I myself in reading leaf constantly through others' books to find related references, I wanted to ease this process for my own readers by going beyond the connections that an index can provide. At the same time, I should add that the index to this book has been put together with care, and that in some instances—notably where related ideas in the texts of chapters had no corresponding endnotes—the index is the only way to track down related ideas or references.

Before leaving the matter of indexes, I should like to take this opportunity to alert readers to an eleventh-hour deletion of two pages that occurred in the production of my previous book. Though no content was lost—the pages in question were blank—this change impaired the accuracy of the index. To use the index of *Developing Variations* effectively, the reader should subtract 2 from any page number that is followed by the letter "n"; that is, subtract 2 from any page reference, in the index, to the endnotes. Index references to the *body* of the text were not affected. This situation will, of course, be rectified in any future editions. It is a mark of the meticulousness of those at the University of Minnesota Press who supplied the original page numbers for the index (a truly thankless job) that this subtraction of 2 leads almost without exception to the reference desired.

R. R. S.

Acknowledgments

Rather than renaming all the people I acknowledged in my earlier volume, every one of whom retains my gratitude, I want to note here mainly those who have helped me since I completed that book and moved on to the work in the present one. Though I have tried to record these more recent debts conscientiously, the following list is not comprehensive, and I deeply regret the omissions I am bound to recall too late. A number of people, some not mentioned here, will also find themselves acknowledged in the text or notes of individual chapters. It should not be assumed that anyone I thank (with the possible exception of my mother) either endorses this book or shares its viewpoints.

Of the most immediate support to me have been the faculty, staff, and students at the Department of Music at Brown. I am fortunate to work in an atmosphere that reflects the open-mindedness and unfailing courtesy of our eminently reasonable chair, Jim Baker. Among my colleagues, junior and senior, I cannot think of one who has not given me, in the most generous spirit, extremely helpful ideas or materials, usually both. These include my senior colleagues Gerald (Shep) Shapiro, Jeff Titon, and the recently retired Ron Nelson, as well as Carol Babiracki, Arlene Cole, Fred Jodry, Henry Kingsbury, Matt McGarrell, Maurice (Moe) Methot, Paul Phillips, Nancy Rosenberg, Todd Winkler, and also the members of the Charleston String Quartet, Charles and Consuelo Sherba, Lois Finkel, and Daniel Harp. David Laurent, who retired just as I arrived at Brown, has given me numerous useful items from his own library. Matt Malsky, now at Clark, has put his expertise in both contemporary composition and computer technology at my disposal.

In a class by himself, of course, at Brown or anywhere else, is my colleague, David Josephson. Both as friend and as colleague, David has been the mainstay of my career at Brown, and the sine qua non of my career, period. For me, he has been the kind of colleague that you hope to find when you die and go to heaven.

From Carol Tatian and her assistant Sheila Hogg, at Brown's Orwig Music Library, has come a continuous stream of valuable aid, delivered always with good humor despite the ferocious pressure that is sometimes put upon them and their staff. Much the same can be said of our devoted departmental staff, Kathleen Nelson, Nancy Trudel, and Mary Rego, and of Eileen Evans, whose brief stay in the music office brightened our lives.

Among the fine students in the graduate music program at Brown, Nancy Newman, who has transferred here from the University of Minnesota, continues with her characteristic generosity to keep me in touch with the ferment of new ideas and sources at work among our younger scholars. Steve Taylor, Greg Barz, Tim Cooley, Kathy McKinley, and Christine Macmillan have also been a matchless resource, either as my assistants or in some other collegial capacity. Dan Cavicchi, an advanced doctoral candidate in American Civilization and one of Brown's teaching treasures, has given me tremendous help in the study of American popular culture; John Pitcher, a graduate student in English, has been of comparable help in the domain of literary theory. Anthony Torelli, a Rhode Island orchestral conductor, shared his musical scores, experience, and insights in ways that were of great benefit to me as well as to my students.

Of the many wonderful undergraduates I have taught, I can single out for mention here just a few who contributed more or less directly to the work in this volume (students are cited in chapters and also in the Index). Daniel D'Ordine (who puts a smile into every life he touches), Derek Donohue, and Jason Chavarria have all done a wonderful job keeping various work in order during my summers away from Providence. Jeremy Edes Pierotti has performed services for me in virtually every domain of his already versatile career. Ken Gordon took the time to introduce me to the mysteries of the electronic studio. Steve Wolford shared with me important independent research he had done on popular music. Sarah Sharpe and Alistair Newbern went out of their way to educate me about alternative popular music, as did Noel Coldiron about jazz. Andy Case told me a great deal about contemporary theater. Keith Rosen has given me ideas and materials that have palpably stretched my mind. Michael Schnall has sent me clippings of useful articles. Caren Exelbert, Eric Nelson, Ayelette Robinson, Jonathan Sadler, and Teddy Shapiro have responded graciously to a variety of questions or requests. And truly outstanding in a wide range of services was my undergraduate teaching and research assistant (UTRA) for 1993-94, William H. (Bill) Lee, whose combination of initiative and meticulousness will set a daunting standard for any research assistant I may employ in the future.

Outside of Brown, I would like to thank a number of colleagues for specific assistance or support they gave me at the time I was working on the various chapters of this book. Among those who work entirely or substantially in music these include Ruth Solie of Smith College; Richard Kramer of SUNY Stony Brook; Katherine Reeve, an interdisciplinary scholar (specializing in the nineteenth century) in Minneapolis; Willis Regier of the University of Nebraska Press; Richard Leppert of the University of Minnesota; Richard Taruskin of the University of California at Berkeley; Susan McClary of UCLA; Leonard Meyer, now retired from the University of Pennsylvania; Lance Brunner of the University of Kentucky; Fred Maus of the University of Virginia; William DeFotis of the College of William and Mary; and three faculty members of the music department at Wesleyan University, Neely Bruce, Alvin Lucier, and Ron Kuivala. Frank Retzel, a noted composer in New York, continues to keep me in touch with important contemporary currents in the arts.

Outside of music, I remain eternally in the debt of Martha Woodmansee, of the English department at Case Western Reserve University, for answering numerous specific questions for me, and more generally, for keeping me up to date with so much of her own virtuosically expanding expertise in critical theory, especially in critical and legal aspects of intellectual property. I am likewise indebted to three of my Brown colleagues, Bill Beeman of the anthropology department, Neil Lazarus of the English department, and John Lucas of the theater department, for their unusual degree of kindness in sharing research and teaching materials with me.

I am also deeply grateful to graduate students at a number of music programs around the country for supporting my work, sharing their own with me, and welcoming me into the most scintillating part of the annual meetings of the American Musicological Society, their own off-stage dialogues with one another. These students have included Mitchell Morris, Andrew Dell'Antonio, Luisa Vilar-Paya, Robert Fink, Christopher Alan Williams, and the late Greg Salmon from the University of California at Berkeley; Anthony Barone, Penny Zokaie, and Ed Thieberger (among others) from Columbia; Tom Nelson, Sowah Mensah, Andy Jones, and Christine Bezat from the University of Minnesota; and a student whose special importance to me I could never acknowledge adequately, the late David Bain of the CUNY Graduate Center. I owe special thanks to two promising scholars who both happen at present to be working on their own in Minneapolis. Sanna Pederson, who recently received her doctorate from the University of Pennsylvania, has let me use several of her papers, as yet unpublished and of extraordinary value, on nineteenth-century music and philosophy as well as on contemporary literary theory; Lloyd (Chip) Whitesell, one of my own best former students, who recently received his doctorate in musicology from SUNY Stony Brook, has sent me some equally wonderful work, on gender theory, other contemporary critical theory, and opera. Ethan Nasreddin-Longo, who received his doctorate in composition from the University of Chicago not long ago, has sent me brilliant interdisciplinary work on music and philosophy. I find astounding the degree to which this new generation has mastered the techniques, sources, and ideas of the "new musicology," as well as the speed with which young scholars like these are moving beyond my own zone of comfort. Which is (alas) as it should be.

(What is not as it should be is the dreadful prospect of unemployment facing this talented generation. Having honed their minds over long years of struggle to master an unprecedented range of material, they are coming out of graduate school to find few job openings of any kind and even fewer job descriptions calling for the kinds of competence they have sacrificed so much to attain. Music departments have little power to create new jobs in our troubled economy, but we do have some control over the relation between what we allow our graduate students to study and what we put in our job descriptions. We keep teaching these students—or at least we launch their education—and we learn an enormous amount from them that we use in our own research; but we don't hire them all that often. I know that many of my colleagues in this country share my concern about this problem, but we have not, at least to my knowledge, organized any large-scale effort to address it. While I owe an immeasurable debt to these young people, and to many others who have spoken with me or sent me samples of their work, I'm not sure how much gratitude they owe me and my peers these days.)

A special category of thanks is due those who have written either directly or indirectly in response to my previous book (or other work), sometimes to engage me in discussion, sometimes to propose the possibility of my coming somewhere to speak. It is a source of tremendous frustration to me that I have been unable for a long time, now, to keep abreast of my correspondence or to accept many speaking engagements. Someday, when I am more secure in the teaching business I was out of for so long—and when both my children are off to college—I hope to do better in both departments (if by then anyone is still interested in my work). In the present context I would like to acknowledge a few people whose invitations or letters, even when they argued with me, particularly heartened me. Among colleagues and other professionals, I am grateful to the following, whom I list in alphabetical order together with their location at the time I heard from them: Mark Everist (Department of Music, King's College London); Nicholas Marston (Department of Music, University of Exeter); James L. Martin (Cornell College, Mount Vernon, Iowa); Paul Mattick, Jr. (Department of Philosophy, Adelphi University); Thomas Nee (Director, New Hampshire Music Festival); Larry Polansky (Department of Music, Dartmouth College); Michael P. Steinberg (Department of History, Cornell University); William Thomson (professor of music theory, University of Southern California); and Leon Wieseltier (literary editor, *New Republic*).

Among those who were students when they wrote to me I would like to thank Steven Cahn (a first-rate former graduate student of mine at SUNY Stony Brook, where he received his doctorate in music); Dana Gooley (a recent graduate of Wesleyan University); Maria Harley (a doctoral candidate in music at McGill); Helen Hong (a young independent scholar in Baltimore); Basil Sachs (presumably a graduate student in Johannesburg); Yuhwen Wang (a doctoral candidate in music at Columbia); Paul Watt (a graduate student in cultural criticism from Victoria, Australia); and Jeffrey Swinkin (a graduate of Eastman and the University of Michigan). I also want to assure reviewers of my first book that I have read carefully the critiques that have come my way and deeply appreciate their largely favorable and often highly instructive evaluations. Kyle Gann's in the *Village Voice* was especially helpful since it reached beyond the usual small audience for academic books.

In putting the present book together, the staff at the University of Minnesota Press has once again been a pleasure to work with. In particular I would like to thank Biodun Iginla, my astute and understanding editor, whose tact must be counted one of the marvels of the modern world; Elizabeth Knoll Stomberg, the editorial assistant who so graciously handled the seemingly endless array of jobs that go into the preparation of a book; Becky Manfredini, my meticulous production coordinator; and my copy editor, Ann Klefstad, who brought the same high intelligence and unerring instincts to this volume as she did to the first, and whose own expression of support meant more to me than almost any other I have received.

Those fortunate enough to have read or to own copies—especially hardbound copies—of *End Product: The First Taboo* (published in New York, 1977, by the now defunct Urizen Books) will understand my indebtedness to its authors, Dan Sabbath and Mandel Hall, for having provided all academic authors with a particularly graceful example of scholarship, as well as my hope that these two authors will find a way to put their magnum opus back in print.

To function effectively in any profession, one needs the support of friends and family as well as of colleagues. In addition to the good friends mentioned in my previous volume, I would like here to thank some of the people who have welcomed my family and me so warmly to Providence: our neighbors Norman and Marika Sadler; Lorilynn, a brilliant educator of children at all the precollege levels; and Mr. Edward O. Adler, a wise man, who survived the Warsaw ghetto to become an inspirational teacher. Outside of Providence, two people require particular mention. Rabbi Albert S. Goldstein, of Brookline, Massachusetts, one of my earlier and most cherished mentors, was of help to this book in a specific way that I recount in the Introduction. Stanley Sperber, the immensely talented conductor of the Haifa Symphony Orchestra, has for more than thirty years been among the friends my husband and I value most in this world. Our discussions of music have been especially useful to me because no one understands as fully as Stanley does the idiosyncrasies of my own relationship to music.

From my family I continue to receive benefits beyond measure. My mother, Bruna Hazan Rosengard, who maintains an active interest in my work, is as generous as ever with her support, both emotional and material. My brother, Robert (Bob) Rosengard, remains the ideal sibling-colleague; and I lost something very close to that with the recent death of his dear wife, Carol. Though my father, David Eli Rosengard, did not live to see my professional reinstatement at Brown or either of my books, he along with my mother instilled the values on which all of my work rests. As a child of immigrants who became a beloved teacher and outstanding administrator in the Boston public schools, and who never compromised his integrity, my father was a man of both reason and compassion. Anyone who knew Dave Rosengard will understand why Enlightenment values, the potential goodness of the American experience, and just plain human decency turn up as themes in his children's work.

My own children have paid a high price for the ups and downs of my career—one move after another, adjustments to new schools, belongings scattered in a variety of houses, and most recently, a father working in another state, ongoing pressurized moves between Providence and Huntington (Long Island), and provisional quarters in Providence too small to accommodate comfortably both their social lives and my class preparations. I can't say that either my daughter, Eva, who is currently an undergraduate at Columbia, or my son Joseph (Joe[y]), who is currently a student at Classical High School in Providence, has been thrilled about the sacrifices exacted from them—how could they be? But both have always been understanding, helpful, and supportive, showing a deep-seated goodness of heart that matters more, in the end, than the successes they have wrested so amazingly from the chaos around them.

Finally, I want to thank my husband, Dan, a professor at Touro College of Law, who has provided the intellectual companionship, financial support, and emotional anchor I have relied on all these years to survive both personally and professionally. Like my father, Danny has keen intelligence, fierce integrity, and a good disposition; but his invariably unexpected way of thinking about things is uniquely his own. No one could go brain-dead living with Dan Subotnik. Any freshness or edge possessed by this book owes a large part of its existence to the constant vitality of my husband's presence.

Introduction

In choosing how it enters what could well be an era of post-music, contemporary music will decide whether it can rise to its own primary challenge.[1]

At the end of my previous book, contemporary Western art music was left with a difficult challenge: to merge with society, thereby giving up the distinctiveness of music as a medium, or to risk participating in its own extinction. At the time some readers found this challenge unnecessarily broad; now, only a few years later, it seems if anything too narrow.

As I write this introduction, not just contemporary Western art music but the entire field of Western musicology seems to have entered "an era of post-music." The boundaries that once circumscribed music as a discrete conceptual and social domain, epitomized by Western art music of the common practice period, are visibly eroding. Those of us who teach and study Western art music, no less than those of us who write it, face our discipline's transformation out of existence. Whether this means we are now presiding over the liquidation of an intellectual empire, or moving into a Hegelian higher stage of consciousness, nearly all of us in academic music are aware that we face some difficult challenges.

The conception of music as an autonomous domain has been wearing down in American musicology for some time. Adorno has had something to do with it. Though committed to Western art music between Bach and Webern in a passionate and exclusionary way, Adorno developed powerful methods of cutting through epistemological barriers between music and life. As those admittedly complex methods (and with them, related elements of Continental philosophy) have found their way into American musicology, the image of

Western music as a self-contained entity has become vulnerable to attack—
and to disbelief.

Closer to home, John Cage has also undermined the concept of musical
autonomy, not only through the content of his lectures and writings but also
through the shape of his career. Calling attention away from goal-oriented
musical constructions to the noises and silences of living, Cage has exerted
great influence on Western music through a career that produced relatively little of musical interest—at least in the sense of interesting music. What mattered were Cage's ideas and the critique they have fueled on old ways of separating music from life.[2]

In the five years since I have returned to work in the academy (I now teach
at Brown University), I have been especially struck by the pressures placed on
the teaching of music as a college subject by the breakdown of music as a discrete concept. Because of Brown's "new curriculum," student preferences may
contribute more directly to such pressures here than at schools where students
have less choice about what they study.[3] Informal discussions with my colleagues in the field persuade me that the changes I perceive are becoming
widespread in this country; still, I should emphasize that the remarks I make
here are drawn entirely from personal observation.

As I see things, generally speaking Western art music is beginning to go out
of fashion as a topic of study; the growth of interest in world music courses is
an important sign of this trend, but it is not the only one. To be sure, a certain
number of students accomplished in the performance of Western art music
continue to arrive as undergraduates each year. Many take music as a first or
second major; like their counterparts in the past, many still tend toward con-
servatism in their musical and academic tastes. A specialized group, often nonmajors with choral experience, always seems to take an interest in early music.
Together, these students are the musical "professionals" who keep upper-level
courses on the Western canon going. But the market for those courses remains
small at best and is probably shrinking.

In addition to these students, a respectable number of "amateurs" want to
find out something about the Western art music they have heard on various
electronic media at home and occasionally in live performances (mainly at
school).[4] These are the students who sign up for Music 1 courses as well as for
lower-level surveys of the "great masters" and repertory genres. The enthusi-
asm of these students is unforced and invigorating. But since they are not
majors and have little technical connection with music, the contact of such
students with music departments has always been limited. Just as familiarity
with Gabrieli canzonas and Beethoven quartets carries noticeably less social

cachet among undergraduates than it did thirty years ago, when I was an undergraduate, so too not all composers and genres of Western art music can count on filling classrooms. On this level as well, the study of Western art music seems to be holding on rather than flourishing.

By contrast, a large and I suspect growing contingent of students wants passionately to take courses dealing with music—but has little or no interest in Western art music. Once they have signed up for a music course, these students can be induced to develop such an interest; but left to their own devices, they will not choose a course focused on the canon. The surest way to attract them is through the promise of a chance to spend some time studying the music that nearly all students (including a substantial proportion of music majors) live with, and often make, on an everyday basis: pop music.

If Western art music generally is in decline as a topic of study, the instrumental music of that tradition is losing favor even faster. Typically, the teaching of that music in courses has involved helping students find their way through musical structures that are less than self-evident to the untrained ear. The constituency for such structural road maps still exists, but it is a minority constituency. Far more students are attracted to courses on jazz, which certainly include instrumental works, but where the approach to teaching even instrumental music is likely to emphasize social over structural parameters.[5]

Most pop music, of course, is vocal; but it is not just in courses involving popular music (or, say, the blues) that a tendency away from instrumental music has become evident. College in the age of postmodernism is a place of critical sophistication, and critical theory thrives on words. By focusing a course in critical theory on the characters, stories, costumes, stage settings, and locales of opera—using librettos, recordings, and videotapes—one can hope to draw students with a lively interest in semiotics, class structure, gender studies, the effects of imperialism, and so on, along with some intellectually adventurous music majors. Focusing the same course on the symphony is apt to scare off not only conservative music majors, who still equate music with "black notes," but also that large majority of nonmajors who cannot read music.

Here is another skill that faces obsolescence as a subject for teaching: reading music. A few years ago I was startled by an article in the *New York Times* that foretold an end to verbal literacy and writing. In time, it argued, a variety of visual symbols—international traffic signs and other pictographs, video stagings, computer graphics—would make the need to master and use written phonetic symbols obsolete. Friends whose children were older than mine warned me that videotapes of children's classics were replacing the books themselves for the younger generation. That was ten years ago; at the time I didn't believe them.

Today, a similar process is clearly under way in music. In courses and out, students are phenomenally eager to compose music. Whether the music they want to compose is pure (commercial) pop or a creative hybrid of pop and art, its sounds almost invariably involve electronic audio, and sometimes visual, media. Many students are willing to invest a great deal of time and energy mastering the complex techniques of programming, sampling, and mixing (and other modes I cannot name) that will give them the sounds they want. Large and even growing numbers still sign up for various levels of traditional courses in music theory and ear training, often in the hope of gaining some control over the sounds they want to manipulate. But many others have no interest in learning to locate pitches on a staff or even to name the intervals they hear. Why should they be, when all the sounds they want to use can be reproduced (or produced) without the intervention of paper and ink? [6]

When I can, these days, I teach courses that mix Western art music with pop music. A small percentage of music majors have always been open to experimenting in courses outside the canon; and since music majors today (unlike most in my own youth) often participate fully in the pop-music culture, they tend to take such courses along with a larger number of nonmajors. I choose the art music, the students choose the pop; through course readings and discussion we examine ways of thinking that may be useful in the study of various kinds of music. Technical terms are introduced and explained where relevant, which they often are; but I make no effort in this sort of course to teach nonmusic majors to read music or to understand Western music theory.

Whatever their backgrounds, students in these classes are required to listen to some Western art music (often including instrumental music), to read about it, and to do some of their writing about it. This last activity produces tremendous benefits, for by far the best writing about Western art music—especially instrumental music—in these courses tends to come from the nonmusic majors; the music majors freely admit it. Though the music majors are very intelligent (and on occasion are wonderful writers), they tend to have trouble breaking out of formalistic modes of thought; like a lot of academic writing, theirs, at least initially, often seems designed more to satisfy a homework requirement than to interest a reader.

By contrast, nonmusic majors, unable to write in a technical fashion about musical structures, connect what they hear with a wealth of unexpected contexts and images. They write about Western music in ways that music majors (and I) would never have imagined doing; at their best they zero in with uncanny accuracy on the stylistic character, the effect, or even the dynamic structure of the music in question.[7] Their example is wonderfully liberating. By the end of the semester, everyone has become more adventurous. Focusing less, and less narrowly, on musical structure, music students expand the contexts and images through which they look at music. They develop the nerve to criticize elements in art *and* pop music. Their writing becomes more interesting.

The history of Western art music has often been described as the movement of a pendulum back and forth between two poles: old and new, vertical and horizontal, simple and complex, textual values and musical ones. At least since 1600 or so, one could add a movement between poles of autonomous and nonautonomous conceptions of music: from the affective monody of Peri and Caccini to the trio sonatas of Corelli; from Bach's religious affect to the purely aesthetic pleasures of Rameau's clavecin; from the self-contained structure of Haydn's symphonies to the bursting content of Beethoven's; from the artistic fusions (and effusions) of Romanticism to the antiexpressive, formalistic structures of Stravinsky. It could thus be argued that the tendency I have described continues a long pattern in the history of Western music: the teaching of music has simply turned away from the autonomous Classicism of the modernists to yet another (postmodernist) version of Romanticism.[8]

Though I doubt the sufficiency of this simple explanation—almost surely, a far more comprehensive self-critique of the West is involved in current developments—it seems clear that the academic paradigm of music is moving away from autonomy. Today, much of our teaching centers on explicitly nonautonomous genres of music—vocal music, dance music, stage music, film music, even music in literature. Students can manage comfortably in many music courses without technical expertise in music—and so, for that matter, can teachers. Courses on opera, good courses, are given these days without scores, in literature departments; most courses on popular music, at least in my experience, originate outside of music departments, in fields such as American civilization and English. And by the same token, a broadening of focus is not confined to student writing about music. It can be found in many of the texts we now assign, some by scholars in other fields, and even more by people in music.

The best writing about music has probably never been technical writing, for the technical aspects of music tend to interfere with the pleasure of reading. Donald Tovey probably came closest to combining the two, and even Tovey makes better *reading* in his moments of anecdote and metaphor than when he gets down strictly to business. Most readers faced with a page full of musical diagrams and symbols grit their teeth before proceeding. They may reap wonderful rewards in musical ideas or insights, but this situation is not, on the whole, conducive to good writing.

I would argue that the best writing about music, in the last century and in this one, moved away from technical descriptions and analyses toward images and analogies and ideas. But until recently, even the most figurative of those writings worked on the basis that they were "about music." A course on European music criticism since 1800 must certainly consider decades of debates over whether or not music is autonomous; and Schumann did go so far as to suggest that poetic metaphor tells us more about music than does musical analysis.[9] In the past, however, all parties to such debates have at some fundamental level counted on the existence of some autonomous musical domain for them to argue over. This is no longer the case.

Certainly in the world of pop music today, writing about music usually means writing about everything *except* music. In the courses I have taught, this apparent evasiveness makes music majors nervous at first. At least one student is liable to speculate that pop music doesn't get written about because there *is* nothing to write about. What they mean is that there is nothing *worth* writing about; in fact, the speculation as it is worded is accurate in a more literal sense than these majors suppose. Such speculation tends to make the nonmajors, in turn, feel a little embarrassed. Though they themselves feel more comfortable discussing production values than musical style in pop recordings, they will sometimes express the wish that pop critics do some writing about the music "itself." But this last seldom happens. Instead, pop criticism offers readers an immersion in kinds of writing that really have no concept of music "itself." The quality of this pop writing varies. At its worst (at least from my perspective), it clumps together names, images, and occasional technical terms to produce a thicket of words-without-evident-verbs that is literally unreadable. I would describe it as language designed not for acceptance into the brain but for processing by a word scanner.[10]

Not all pop criticism is like this. But no matter how good the writer, after a while readers begin to lose any residual expectation of encountering music "itself" in pop criticism.[11] To an extent, this may be a matter of technological intimidation. Just as the sounds made on electronic samplers exist at a remove from any direct ability to create those sounds—most student composers could not reproduce those sounds on a desert island, or even provide instructions for reproducing them—so, too, pop criticism probably assumes that readers have no direct ability to understand music "itself." At any rate, readers of pop music criticism eventually forget about the category of music "itself"; like the patient of Oliver Sacks who could not relearn to see, readers stop looking for the category.[12] In the world of pop music criticism, music "itself" has ceased to exist.

But that is not the only world in which the notion of autonomous music is losing ground. In the new ethnomusicology, the eviction of that notion is so advanced that I have seen a dissertation proposal to study a specific non-Western repertory rejected on the grounds that its paradigm of music—in effect, a paradigm of "music itself"—was hopelessly outdated. And even in the study of Western art music, where for so long "detour[s] into critical and cultural theory [have] been interpreted by some as an abandonment of musicology," scholars are beginning to admit that, like Susan McClary, they are no "longer sure what MUSIC is."[13]

> [W]hether one regards [the] shattering of the old Great Culture paradigm as calamitous or as a cause for celebration depends quite obviously on the way in which one is positioned with respect to that paradigm. To those who were able to claim institutional privilege through the old system, much of postmodern culture appears to be utterly nihilistic. The barbarians have always been at the gates, but never before had designated gatekeepers thrown down the barriers and welcomed them in—as have certain younger composers and musicologists. All of that effort to hold onto rigorous, progressive idealism is suddenly declared null and void. This is basically the complaint in Allan Bloom's best-selling *The Closing of the American Mind.*[14]

To my mind there can be little doubt that the disappearance of "music itself" as a conceptual paradigm grew out of a massive process of Western self-criticism. The immediate target of that critique was not music; it was reason. Numerous Western schools of thought in the past two centuries have analyzed the abstract conception of reason that crystallized during the Enlightenment, and many have traced socially destructive effects to limitations of this conception. More recent critical movements such as the Frankfurt School, poststructuralism, and feminism have offered musicologists a way to reconfigure "reason" so that their field could no longer justify rejecting as "irrational" viewpoints, interests, and traditions that differed from the academic norm. Many who had been excluded from musicology on this basis had strong ties to nonautonomous conceptions of music. (Ironically, though their efforts were for a long time solidly resisted by mainstream schools of formalist and positivist musicology, their broadened definition of reason stood to elevate the standing of music itself as an academic discipline.)[15]

In American musicology, I was a relatively early participant in the critique of abstract reason. The dialectical methods of study I derived from Adorno's musical thought, and the distinctions I developed between general and particular, abstract and concrete, structure and style, logic and rhetoric, were at bottom all ways of asking my colleagues to remove stifling constraints on the ways in which musicologists were allowed to think. Aside from the damage they did my own career, my efforts did not seem to have much effect at that time. For years I had the sensation of knocking in vain on a wall of the Bastille. Shortly after I came to Brown, however, at the 1990 meeting of the American Musicological Society in Oakland, I discovered that a great number of my colleagues, especially younger ones, had knocked the wall down and run far beyond it, while I myself remained standing in a position not too far from my original point of departure.

I have no complaint about this experience, which is far from unique, nor do I regret whatever part I played in weakening the wall. The paradigm of autonomy had imprisoned musicology far too long. Change was badly needed; and now that it has come, its effects, despite some excesses, are in my judgment overwhelmingly salutary. I am far more comfortable in the new musicology than I was allowed to be in the old one; and I am especially delighted with the new opportunities that have opened to me as a teacher.

If once I was at the leading edge of new musical scholarship, I am there no longer. As a practical matter, though I have never stopped reading and writing, I lost too much ground during my nine years of unemployment to keep my place in the vanguard. But even as a theoretical matter, I was never a singleminded radical. From my earliest published piece, on Lortzing, my characteristic scholarly procedure was to set up and analyze a confrontation between an older and a new way of seeing something;[16] it was not to try and knock the older way out of commission in order to make way for the new. Thus, even if I had managed in the last decade to remain a scholarly pioneer,[17] I doubt I now would be leading any intellectual charges on musicology. My orientation has always been toward a balanced center; as in the case of many old liberals (and radicals), the world has moved to the left of me.

I am not worried that my years of disciplined training in the old musicology will go to waste in the brave new world of musicology. (To be fair to Allan Bloom, I don't think this sort of worry was his primary concern either. For what might have been, see chapter 4, note 161.) I do sometimes find myself, however, in the odd position of examining the case for skills, concepts, and attitudes that once upon a time were established in musical education to the point of monopolistic oppression but now seem destined for the landfill of history as either inconsequential or overtly harmful.

Is there a use in the new musicology for musical literacy and theoretical training? Is there a basis for preserving a special respect for the masterworks of the Western art canon, and a special role for them in musical education? Is there a benefit in keeping alive a conception of "music itself," and even of the structural criteria of value associated with that concept? And for that matter (a question I shall take up again near the close of this introduction), are there any grounds, from a musicological standpoint, for retaining the traditional Western abstract ideal of reason?

My own short answer to each of these questions is yes: every one of the items I ask about should be preserved—but not in a way that excludes other alternatives. When allowed to rule unchallenged as an intellectual standard or paradigm, each has done terrible human damage. To my own way of thinking, each of these items is best evaluated in a dialectic with alternatives. Or to draw on a powerful deconstructive image developed by Derrida, as we move away from uncritically assuming the existence of a construct such as "music itself," we might as well continue to make some provision for it, since whatever position we take toward such a construct, our language and thought will continue to preserve it, at least for the foreseeable future, "under erasure [*sous rature*]."[18] In its heyday, positivistic musicology—a handmaiden of exclusionary abstract reason—would not make any place for dialectic or deconstruction.[19] If I have been right all along in arguing that these alternative modes of reasoning do not by definition exclude the abstract mode,[20] then the new musicology has no need to repay the old musicology in kind.

In a sense, the essays in this second book can be read as the record of an ongoing struggle that preserves a place for the old paradigms. Admittedly this description—an odd one for a volume entitled *Deconstructive Variations*—reflects changes over time in my own perspective, since these pieces were certainly not designed in the first instance to effect such a preservation.

In the main, they were conceived simply to continue the kinds of inquiries I developed in my first collection of essays—inquiries primarily concerned with establishing new paradigms for the study of music. The basic themes, the images, and the attitudes in this second volume will all be familiar to anyone who has read even a portion of the earlier volume; and as in that earlier collection, readers will find that I return repeatedly within the essays here to certain issues, arguments, images, and sources—for example, in connection with trying to decipher the significance of "structural listening," to draw the consequences of Kant's critical philosophy, Hegel's *Aufhebung*, and the Enlightenment for music, or to fathom the ontological status of musical rhetoric and sound. (As the problems that bother me do not seem to get resolved, and as I find myself chewing on them again and again in different contexts, I am not sure that the avoidance of such repetitions is a realistic—or even, in all cases, a desirable—goal, at least from an author's standpoint. On the other hand, I am ruefully aware that repetitions of this kind can be wearing on the patience of the reader; and, of course, nothing puts the spotlight on such recurrences quite as effectively as collecting one's assorted works into a single volume.)

The term "deconstructive" was incorporated into the title of this second book (a title I chose when I wrote the introduction to the first) not because these later essays unravel positions taken earlier, but simply because they followed my exposure to deconstruction. Though aspects of my earlier essays unwittingly exhibited modes of deconstructionist thinking,[21] my study of this movement enlarged the dialectical framework in which I had previously moved and greatly expanded the ways in which I thought about music and organized those thoughts. Every essay in this volume, unlike any in the first, benefited at some stage in its development from my entrance into the mysteries of deconstruction.

Yet by the same token, each of these essays was designed fundamentally as an argument between two views: between views for and against the ideal of structural listening; between an Enlightenment and a Romantic reading of Mozart's *The Magic Flute*; between a high-modernist and a postmodernist reading of Chopin's A-Major Prelude; and between conceptions of reason offered by Allan Bloom and by Spike Lee. Since two views are always presented, each is in a sense preserved. As the balance now shifts in musicology from autonomous to nonautonomous views of music, and as the old hierarchical relation of the two settles into its new opposite condition, perhaps it is time yet again to deconstruct the priorities our culture takes for granted. In saying this I do refer our current situation to the trope of a pendulum used traditionally to describe earlier moments in the history (and historiography) of Western art music; but I connect it even more strongly to the imagery of infinite reversals and regress, so loved by deconstructionist thinkers as a description of the traps in which we think.

Evidence of the ways in which I have struggled to preserve two paradigms—and also of some changes that have occurred in my work since my last volume of essays—can be found in the attitude toward musical analysis taken in these essays, in the kinds of sources on which they draw, and in their written style. As in my earlier book, the essays here are divided with respect to musical analysis. There, three included it; ten did not. Here, two do ("Whose *Magic Flute?*" and "How Could Chopin's A-Major Prelude Be Deconstructed?"); the other two, both of a more philosophical character ("Toward a Deconstruction of Structural Listening" and "The Closing of the American Dream?"), do not. In both volumes, analysis is restricted to compositions by two of my favorite composers, Mozart and Chopin. In both, the writing of the essay was preceded by long and arduous efforts to analyze the piece in question fairly comprehensively. And yet there are differences, some significant.

In the previous volume, musical analysis was directed exclusively at instrumental music. Here, the objects of analysis are divided; one is instrumental music, the other an opera. In fact, this difference is not very significant. Though the characters and themes of *The Magic Flute* are important to my argument here, the very point of my analysis is to show how the music alone establishes the case for two different ways of viewing it.

On the other hand, I have placed far more restrictive formal limits on the music I examine here than I did in the earlier volume. There, I discussed some works—Mozart's last three symphonies—that were a little too large to subject to complete analytical control (though I confess I tried).[22] In another essay, I was actually able to relinquish the organic model of musical analysis sufficiently to deal with only parts of pieces.[23] My ability to surrender this much control—a feat I have not since duplicated—may have been due to the fact that when I wrote this essay, I was working as a computer programmer, and did not expect to return to musicology. By contrast, in the present volume, I have restricted my musical analyses to short numbers, in which I could pay attention to a relatively large proportion of details: three arias from *The Magic Flute* and (as in the previous volume) a Chopin piano prelude. A strong motivation behind this restriction, apart from the matter of my own control, has been to minimize the reader's need to locate musical passages not reproduced here and thereby to reduce, at least in one respect, the unpleasantness of reading musical analysis. Fully half the essays presented here include substantial musical analysis, as opposed to a far smaller percentage in the earlier work. On balance I would have to say that I have made a greater effort in this book than in the previous one to preserve the analysis of the discrete musical composition as a valued element of critical discourse.

And yet, I have included here one essay that has no counterpart in the earlier book: "The Closing of the American Dream? A Musical Perspective on Allan Bloom, Spike Lee, and Doing the Right Thing." From the title alone, it may be evident that in this essay I make no effort to address actual music, or even the existence of actual music. Offered a generous stipend by Wesleyan University to speak on any topic of my choosing—at the time, I was unemployed—I allowed myself the luxury of analyzing two nonmusical works that interested me, drawing on music only as a source of epistemological perspective. In this essay, I move well beyond the paradigm of "music itself"—though I refuse to repudiate entirely Bloom's model of abstract reason, to which that musical paradigm has close ties.

A certain logic for this polarity between detailed attention to musical analysis on the one hand, and general treatment of music as an epistemological model on the other, may be offered by the imagery of sound and silence that emerges in my chapter on Mozart and that on structural listening. The new-found emphasis on raw sound that I discern in Mozart's *Magic Flute* and the condition of silence to which I note that Adorno and Schoenberg are attracted are,[24] it seems clear, two aspects of a shift in musical paradigm that has been two centuries in the making. As abstract structure became a less persuasive basis for defining and appraising music, an inclination grew to treat music as the experience of actual sound; and such experience, with its capacity to overwhelm the perception of formal boundaries, posed an ultimate threat to the continuing existence of "music itself"—a threat that today, as I have noted, seems well on the way to being realized. Rather than capitulate to such a threat, Adorno, despite (or, perhaps, given) his philosophical aversion to states of hypostatization, still attached to old (modernist) ideals of musical autonomy, counsels a withdrawal from sound into silence. For myself, hardly more able than Adorno to resolve dialectical tensions between music as freestanding structure and as sound inseparable from an environment, giving priority to each side of this polarity in different essays—through putting either musical analysis or philosophical reflection in the foreground of my writing—has been a way to preserve the values of both.

As in my earlier work, my references in this second volume are to a mixture of scholarly and popular sources. But here the proportion of popular sources has risen substantially. In part this is a reflection of pure logistics. When you lose access to academic libraries, you rely more heavily on the books you can (afford to) buy—and you pay more attention to the popular press. By the time I arrived at Brown, moreover, the broad framework of this book was in place; and though the process of revision has taken place since then, I have not found a graceful way to refer within that framework to a number of the scholarly sources I have studied more recently. Though in some ways I regret the shift here toward the popular, I do not apologize for it. As it is, too many academic articles are designed as vehicles for writing and citing rather than for reading; in my judgment, we would be better off with fewer, to which we could give more intensive study.

Furthermore, since a primary interest of mine has always been the relationship between music and American Enlightenment traditions, I have come to appreciate the extent to which the popular press (including "Letters to the Editor") has kept me in touch with American thought. To the extent that I have moved away from scholarly sources (including foreign-language ones) to popular sources, I have clearly favored at least part of a new academic paradigm over an old one. Yet I would like to think that in my heaviest reliance on a popular source—Spike Lee's *Do The Right Thing*—I have kept some distance from a type of fawning overcomplication of the popular, fairly common in the new scholarship, that I do not much admire. Though on an ideological basis I prefer Lee's view of reason to Bloom's, a great part of my admiration for Lee's film involves an organic ideal of structure quite compatible with Bloom's paradigm, as will become clear.

The change in my sources is no doubt connected to a change in my style. When my first article, on Lortzing, appeared in the *Musical Quarterly* in 1976,[25] my father rushed to his local public library to read it, and was reasonably pleased. When my second article appeared the same year in the *Journal of the American Musicological Society*—"Adorno's Diagnosis of Beethoven's Late Style: Early Symptom of a Fatal Condition"[26]—his reaction was considerably more subdued. He warned me that if I didn't want to lose my reader altogether, I had better watch my style.

I understood his criticism but was in no position to honor it. At the time, I was engrossed in drawing from Adorno and refining a complex view of music and life that did not lend itself to plain language. In all the essays collected in my earlier volume, I labored hard over every word, sometimes taking long walks to refine a single sentence. The results were as plain as I could make them; they were not simple.

In the current book, my style has returned to a level of readability that I think would have pleased my father. Without question this simplification will provoke harsh comments from some of my critics: simpler language, simpler thoughts. I cannot prevent such criticisms; in part they may be right. Still, I do take some satisfaction in the greater degree of accessibility I have achieved in the style presented here. Perhaps the years out of academia were not altogether wasted. Yes, I am still absorbing, slowly, academic fashions that others already disregard as obsolete. And I am often writing in a manner more suited to guiding a student than to impressing a colleague. Which paradigm is this: the new paradigm of interpenetration between the academic and the popular? or the old one of Enlightenment clarity? I would like to think I have captured just a little of both. And I would especially like to thank Willis Regier of the University of Nebraska Press for assuring me, at the emotional nadir of my career, at the 1987 convention of the American Musicological Society in

New Orleans, that my relatively simple style had an important integrity as well as educational value. The largest essay in this volume is dedicated to him.

Of the four essays presented here, no fewer than three grew out of my teaching in the one year, 1986-87, I spent at the CUNY Graduate Center. Two have previously been published in some form, two have not. "Toward a Deconstruction of Structural Listening: A Critique of Schoenberg, Adorno, and Stravinsky" drew principally on a graduate course I taught that fall at Hunter College. At the end of that semester, I was asked to contribute to a Festschrift for Leonard Meyer. For me the timing was especially bad. To extend my appointment at CUNY, I had to obtain support from the music department as well as one other department; what I needed to do at that specific moment was to prepare my essay on deconstruction as a lecture to the Department of Comparative Literature at CUNY, which was favorably disposed toward me. But good as I usually am at declining the most tempting offers (the modern absence of secretarial support helps a lot here!), I could not pass up Leonard Meyer's Festschrift. I never studied with Leonard (and to me he will always be Leonard, not Meyer). I did not even meet him until I started teaching at the University of Chicago, in 1973; and by then he was severing his professional and emotional ties with Chicago. Within a year or two of my arrival—before the renewal of my contract and the birth of my first child—he had left for New York and the University of Pennsylvania. The cliché "ships that pass in the night" describes the extent of our contact rather well.

Yet in the brief time that we did spend together, Leonard spent much time and tact shepherding my first article into print at the *Musical Quarterly*— without him it would never have been published. And just about single-handedly, through a strong recommendation after he left Chicago, Leonard got me a Guggenheim Fellowship. Again, I was not his student; I was not his close friend; he "owed" me absolutely nothing. Leonard Meyer helped me because he thought I was promising—and because from Leonard Meyer's old-fashioned, liberal, humane perspective, when you think a younger colleague needs help, you knock yourself out to supply it.

So I took time off to write this essay for Leonard's Festschrift. He read it and he liked it; a few other music theorists also let me know that they liked it. In its original published version, it was edited so extraordinarily well by Ruth Solie that I might well have reprinted it intact, though in the end I did somewhat revise and update it.[27] While preparing this essay for publication, I also presented a version of it to the Department of Philosophy at CUNY, where it raised enough hackles to ensure that I did not get the joint recommendation I needed.

In spite of its sad history, I have never regretted my decision to participate in Leonard's Festschrift; nor on rereading this essay have I ever felt that it represented less than my best work. Ever since I had touched upon the notion of "structural listening" in the last essay of my previous volume,[28] I had wanted to ponder the cultural and philosophical implications of this notion. The polarities and convergences I defined between Schoenberg/Adorno and Stravinsky in the essay for Leonard Meyer gave me a congenial framework for such reflection; of particular value for my own ideas was the opportunity it gave me to distinguish between conceptions of musical autonomy as a "replete" and as a hollow condition.[29]

The second of the two previously published articles in this volume is entitled "Whose *Magic Flute*? Intimations of Reality at the Gates of the Enlightenment." Its origins lie in a course I designed, on critical theory and morality in relation to nineteenth-century German opera, and gave simultaneously at the CUNY Graduate Center and in the graduate music program at the State University of New York at Stony Brook, in the spring semester of 1987. To try and expand the ways in which the students thought about analyzing music, I drew on diverse writings by a number of scholars outside the field of music; for the purposes of that course, works by Mikhail Bakhtin and Lionel Trilling made an especially deep impression on all of us.[30]

Among the courses I taught before coming to Brown, this one stands out in my own mind, at least, as perhaps the best. During the time I spent with those students on this topic, I think most of us had the sense that something of exceptional educational value was constantly defining itself through interactions that could not be preserved. In particular I recall a moment at Stony Brook in which, after a student made a two-page oral presentation on the opening of Wagner's *Meistersinger*, I read a published commentary on the same music. The student's version brought together themes and methods from the entire preceding course; its superiority to the published commentary was so evident that we all fell silent.

A year later, in May 1988, I presented a distillation of my ideas from this course, in lectures given at Brown University (where I did not yet work) and at a conference at Dartmouth College entitled "The Musical and Verbal Arts: Interactions." Those lectures, centered on the possibility of a Bakhtinian analysis of Mozart's last opera, formed the basis for the essay "Whose *Magic Flute*?" Thereafter I expanded the lecture substantially; but because the original version had puzzled Joseph Kerman, an organizer of the Dartmouth conference, I subsequently let it drop until it was requested for a special issue (on Mozart) of *Nineteenth Century Music*.[31] Here, too, I had the good fortune to encounter an outstanding editor, Richard Kramer. In this instance, I shortened the essay, excluding some large chunks of critical and musical analysis as well as all musical examples, to meet the needs of the journal. The version here restores the deleted material but otherwise retains the strengths of Kramer's superb editing.

The year in which I wrote the *Magic Flute* essay, 1988, was an especially difficult one for me. Between the first two presentations of this paper noted above, my father died (the essay is dedicated to him since it is the last thing I wrote of which he had any knowledge). My husband and I sold our home in the Hyde Park neighborhood on the south side of Chicago, severing our ties to the only place where, in our wanderings as academic gypsies, our children had felt they were home. I had just lost an appointment at the CUNY Graduate Center under bitter circumstances, and with it the chance to live in the same house as my husband while pursuing a career in my own field. Both personally and professionally I felt close to utter defeat.

During the same year, in this country as a whole, a mood of exultation was in the air among winners who showed pitilessly little sensitivity to the less fortunate. Ronald Reagan rode out his last year in office without penalty for any of his evident deficiencies. Nancy Reagan presided to the end over a shockingly irresponsible social scene of excessive privilege. With the election of George Bush, Americans had opted for more of the same; and as my work the following year on Allan Bloom's best-seller made even clearer to me, more emphasis on the virtues of the privileged is what they continued to get.

Given the contrast of my own mood at the time with that symbolized by the White House, I wrote "Whose *Magic Flute*?" with an especially sharp sensitivity to excesses of power and wealth in this country; Nancy Reagan was very much in my mind as I thought about the attitude of the eighteenth-century aristocrat toward a character such as Mozart's Papageno. I became more intent than ever on puzzling out the connection between the obvious inequities in American society today and the ideals of equality on which the country was founded.

As a result, while working on this essay I thought a great deal about the Enlightenment, not only in Mozart's Vienna but also in my own country; and "Whose *Magic Flute*?" though less directly than my later essay on Allan Bloom and Spike Lee, concerns itself with traditions of the American Enlightenment, especially as these were affected by Protestant notions of an "Elect." At the same time, because my study of Bakhtin had drawn my attention to changes in the Enlightenment social paradigm represented by the nineteenth-century novel—and because deconstruction was now available to me as a model for making multiple readings of a single text—the essay proposes a specific strategy for "reading" *The Magic Flute* from a post-Enlightenment perspective. However one feels about the political mood behind this paper, I would be happy to think that the essay offers a useful model for the analysis of "music itself" as nonautonomous.

Of the two previously unpublished pieces here, one also stems from my stay at the CUNY Graduate Center: the long essay "How Could Chopin's A-Major Prelude Be Deconstructed?" first took shape, in a much shorter form, as a lecture to a graduate seminar I gave, at CUNY in the fall of 1986, on music and deconstruction. What I remember especially well about that first presentation is the satisfaction my students and I shared in understanding a lecture that a few months earlier would have been incomprehensible to all of us. Over the course of the next two years, in which new versions were presented at Columbia and at the 1987 convention of the American Musicological Society in New Orleans, I refined the paper and expanded it to its present length.

As by far the longest essay here, and the direct source of the title I have given this volume, this piece constitutes the centerpiece of the book and would seem to call for special comment. But since I have incorporated precisely such comment in the first two sections of the essay itself, substantially expanding it, there seems no reason to reflect at length on the essay here. Given the passing of deconstruction as a fashion in English literature, and the critical sophistication among my musicological colleagues today, I am naturally aware that a large and leisurely exposition of deconstruction as a method of musicological analysis makes an easy target at the present time for a certain kind of criticism. This doesn't unduly concern me. As I state in the essay itself, I am sufficiently skeptical about the degree to which American musicology has assimilated deconstruction to believe my essay will benefit those genuinely interested in working out the arguments of that movement—including students. (More and more as I age—and as paradigms of music shift from the isolated composition to the unrepeatable performance—I move toward the conviction that the most important measurement we face as scholars is the value of our work to our students.)[32] Of special interest to me during the summer of 1993, as I revised this volume for publication, was the extent to which some of the problems examined at length in this essay exhibited a hold over the American popular imagination, as the toddler Jessica DeBoer faced the destruction of her identity.

In all three of these essays, as in the fourth, and as in all the work I have done during and since my fellowship years of 1977-79, my single greatest intellectual preoccupation has probably remained the same. This is the gap Kant defined so reluctantly and yet so forcefully between our cognitive demands for certainty and the knowledge, aesthetic judgments, and moral principles through which we shape our lives. To put things concisely, the single biggest problem stirring up trouble today in academia, and by extension in this country at large, is the impossibility implicitly established by Kant's critical philosophy of demonstrating any particular value to be true.[33] From Kant's epistemological dilemma flow the ridiculously contorted poses of self-enlargement adopted by some advocates of the new academic paradigms in order to demonstrate their sensitivity to Heisenberg's Uncertainty Principle. From the same dilemma flow the equally ludicrous protestations of some conservatives, such as Allan Bloom, that one way (their way) must be declared (and believed) to be the right way of setting values if the very possibility of making qualitative distinctions is to be preserved.[34] I shall return to this latter point below.

I studied Kant's critical philosophy when I was in college and in graduate school. But it was not until much later, when I returned to Kant's *Critique of Judgment* as an adult scholar, that I gauged the vast import of Kant's failure to establish a universal principle of reason beyond all doubt.[35] Since rereading Kant, I have become steadily more alert to the ramifications of that failure. In the final essay of this book, on Allan Bloom and Spike Lee, I work hard to propose a strategy for accepting the unavoidability of Kant's failure without thereby accepting Allan Bloom's associated diagnosis and remedies.

Even less than Bloom himself am I a match for Kant. Should a critic decide to measure the success of this volume by the degree to which I have outwitted Kant, the verdict will of course be harsh. No one has found a cognitively ironclad solution to the dilemma brought to light by Kant; almost certainly there is none. In acknowledging this dilemma—in conceding our inability to prove the rightness of our values—we expose the reliance of our philosophy, at some level, on improvisation. Epistemologically, this is a poor solution to the problem of seeking the good life; still (whatever Nietzsche might say), it seems better to me than trying no solution at all.

Because it has never before been published, and because it takes up so many of my deepest intellectual concerns in an unconventional format, the last essay in this volume does require extended commentary in this introduction. "The Closing of the American Dream?" was originally written for the annual George Jackson Memorial Lecture at Wesleyan University. I delivered it at Wesleyan on October 17, 1989; the year of its appearance is stamped all over it.

My first idea when offered this lecture was to dig into Allan Bloom's *Closing of the American Mind*, which was still causing considerable agitation in 1989. For quite a while after the book first appeared (in 1987), I had resisted reading it or, like many academics I knew, even paying money for it. Then sometime in the fall or winter of 1988, my cousin, Paul Krinsky, who had recently become superintendent at the U.S. Merchant Marine Academy in Kings Point, New York, telephoned me to ask my opinion on the polemic against rock music that appeared in Bloom's book. No flaming radical—he was by then a rear admiral in the U.S. Maritime Service—Paul found himself skeptical concerning Bloom's opinions of popular music (among other things). This inquiry pushed me perilously close to buying the book; I wanted to see what Bloom could have written that disturbed a relatively old-fashioned liberal like my cousin. When the invitation to the Jackson Memorial Lecture was offered, I capitulated.

As I read the book, however, I did not find Bloom's attack on rock music especially challenging. Clearly indifferent to most music, Bloom showed no specific knowledge of rock music; and for all the Platonic references, his diatribe seemed little more substantial, though considerably more ill-tempered, than the complaint of my late father, another old-fashioned liberal, that popular music after the 1940s had no melody.

But two things did interest me. One was Bloom's overwhelming dissatisfaction with one aspect after another of college education. Between 1980, when I left the University of Chicago and taught a summer course at the Boston University graduate school, and 1990, when I came to Brown, I taught only a single year (1986-87). My own direct experience of the campus and of college students in the 1970s and 1980s bore no resemblance to Bloom's account. I knew only that the cultural relativists whom Bloom demonized as taking over and destroying American higher education had not had enough power anywhere to save my career in musicology from people who thought more or less as Bloom did. From my perspective, something was indeed rotten at the university—but it was a different "something" from Bloom's. In addition, Bloom's analysis of education was far from hospitable to reflection on the purposes and methods of teaching music at a university. I began to wonder: Could it be that in the very distance between Bloom's perspective and mine lay an explanation of much that seemed wrong to me in my own discipline?

The second thing that interested me—amazed me, really—was Bloom's cocksureness that he knew not only what had gone wrong at the American university but also why this had happened, and how to fix things. Admittedly, I had done my own share of preaching at the university over the years, and I had certainly run up against plenty of arrogance. But the degree of disdainful moralizing in Bloom's presentation of himself as philosopher-king was so extraordinary that at times I felt almost as if I were reading memoirs by an inhabitant of a different culture.

I say "almost" because I did have one point of comparison. The same year Bloom's book had appeared, I, like many other Americans, had been riveted to the television screen by the Senate hearings on Robert Bork's nomination to the Supreme Court—an experience that left its mark on much of what I have written in the present volume. Never had I felt simultaneously so involved in American public life and so marginal. Bloom and Bork, cultural soulmates, seemed to represent some stratum of American life in the prosperous and greedy 1980s that I, in my unemployment and depression, had apparently missed altogether. In itself, I suppose, this should not have surprised me. Despite the overweening dissatisfaction of these two men during the 1980s, the decade had been launched by the election of a national administration highly sympathetic to their dissatisfactions; in the same election year, 1980, I went from marching at the University of Chicago commencement on the Fifty-Ninth Street Midway to collecting unemployment compensation at a particularly dangerous Chicago public housing project, the Robert Taylor Homes, on Fiftieth and State. Again I wondered: Could it be that in the distance between Bloom's 1980s and mine lay an explanation of much that seemed wrong to me in my own country?

The two questions became crystallized for me during the summer of 1989, as I began to pull together my notes on Bloom for a draft of the Jackson Memorial Lecture. In 1989—the tenth year in which my husband taught summer courses at the University of Chicago Graduate School of Business—my family spent what we learned would be our last summer in Hyde Park. For the four of us, no longer in our own house, this was a painful and poignant summer, in which we all felt highly susceptible to the charged atmosphere of cultural disaffection that surrounded the University of Chicago. It was during this summer that Spike Lee's movie *Do The Right Thing* exploded into the consciousness of Hyde Park and the country.

Lee has complained that too many white people missed an essential aspect of his film by waiting until it came out on videotape so that they could watch it in the privacy (and safety) of their own homes. I myself knew white people on Long Island whose resistance to paying money to see Lee's film surpassed my resistance to buying Bloom's book.

But Lee's complaint does not fit my own encounter with his movie. My husband and I saw it early in the summer, at the local Hyde Park theater, in

Harper Court. The audience was racially mixed, and the reaction when the doors opened at the end was one of utter silence. My children saw it not long after, and were so bowled over that we all went to see it several times again. Its effect was stunning. On a structural level, it had all the earmarks of high Western art. As Professor Neely Bruce said to me at Wesleyan a few months later, "It's an old-fashioned masterpiece; it works on every level." I couldn't stop thinking about this film; and the more I thought, the more I realized it had me asking the same kinds of questions that Bloom's book provoked. I decided to bring them together; the result is the final chapter of this book.

The format of this essay is a bit unusual. In the spring of 1990, Albert S. Goldstein, rabbi emeritus of Temple Ohabei Shalom in Brookline, Massachusetts—a man by then well into his eighties who had had a deeply formative influence on my own moral development—drove out to Wellesley College to hear me give a revised version of the lecture. He listened very intently (the lecture went over an hour) and later talked to me at length about it. To him it was clear that this was a piece conceived more as a written argument than as a speech.

He was right, of course. And yet, revising the essay now for publication, I am struck by how relatively simple I kept it, after all, in order to be able to give it as a lecture. It is, I suppose, an irreducibly hybrid piece; conceived exclusively for publication, its design would have been somewhat different.

Nevertheless, I have left the text relatively simple. The struggles and complexity have been largely put into the endnotes, which take twice as much space as those for the far longer piece, "How Could Chopin's A-Major Prelude Be Deconstructed?" These notes are long and thick, but their design is not careless. For years I have been troubled by the marathon reading performances expected of academics. Like the concern Robert Winter dubbed "the Subotnik syndrome,"[36] this one no doubt stems in part from my own chronic shortage of time.[37] But in addition, as I have already suggested, the sheer number of items on which we feel compelled to draw in our scholarly publications makes close to impossible, at least for me, the intensive kind of reading with which I myself am most comfortable.

Francis Bacon may have been right that only "some few [books are] to be chewed and digested." For me this process of chewing and tasting has become more and more clearly one test of what I—unlike Bloom and many others on both sides of the political spectrum—would call authentic value. If the interest of the work holds up to that level of scrutiny—if it repays in quality intense labors to understand—then for me the book has an important kind of authentic value. No doubt this bent is largely the product of the long years in which I was trained to analyze a musical piece as if it were an organic whole—training about which I have serious misgivings, as I explain at the end of chapter 3, on structural listening. Whatever its source, the habit has stuck.

Once, much or most of my academic reading was done in the first instance as pure "research." Today most of it is done initially in direct preparation for courses that I teach (throughout my career, I have taught an unusually high proportion of new courses). But the purpose doesn't matter. Whenever I read a new academic book—or reread one after a long period of neglect—I find that whenever I can, I attack it as I would a problem for structural analysis in music. I color-code passages and make new indexes of terms and ideas that I find key. This is why it took me a year to reread Kant's *Critique of Judgment*.

My star pupil at Chicago, Lawrence J. Fuchsberg, long since gone from academia (to the irreparable loss of us all), used to urge that what we all needed was an "Evelyn Wood course in slow reading." This is how I read *The Closing of the American Mind*. As I write these remarks in the summer of 1993, I have consulted this book so many times that its pages are coming out in handfuls. Like my first copy of Kant's *Critique of Judgment*, Nietzsche's *Birth of Tragedy*, Stravinsky's *Poetics*, and a few others, my copy of Bloom's book is held together by a rubber band; next fall I shall have to unbend and buy a second copy (maybe I can find a used one) for a course I am teaching on music and the concept of authenticity. At this level, I must pronounce Bloom's book, however much past its vogue now, a work of undeniable value.

Given the way in which I characteristically work, I decided in this one chapter to try an experiment. I would see whether I could preserve in essay form something of the process of intense dialogue in which I have engaged with a book. As a consequence, instead of simply giving strings of bare page references to Bloom's book, which would make for dull reading and would have to be taken on faith as supporting my points, I have tried to provide the substance of Bloom's comments in my notes, so that readers can judge the merits of my critique for themselves. Though a list that I compiled for myself shows that I drew on a wide range of passages throughout Bloom's book, some passages are cited more than once. Rather than simply repeat exact quotations over and over, I have tried in the case of multiple citations to refer readers to a single endnote in which the cited words appear. (Occasionally, however, I have found it important to repeat the actual content of the passage when I cite it more than once.)

Most of the quotations from Bloom are incorporated into discussions that take place more or less within the endnotes themselves. In the process, I have grouped together in many of the endnotes Bloom's scattered thoughts on a specific topic that I found important. Someday, when all our books are available on line, collecting and sorting of this kind will be easy; for me, at the present time, this job required endless rereading and indexing. To make these groupings more readily accessible to the reader, especially to the many who read endnotes on a selective basis only, I have provided headings for those endnotes organized in a particularly topical fashion. Perhaps others, who work as I do, and without hypertext, will find a usable model here.

It is not just the format of this chapter that requires comment in this introduction. By sticking to sources I read in 1989, both academic and popular, and letting stand my references to issues that were current then, I have retained something of an original flavor in this essay.

But, of course, time has a way of altering how any book looks to us. In this era of multiple revisions of lectures that finally get published as retrospective collections of essays, we have all become familiar with the amplifications and modifications of perspective that affect scholarly work on a given topic. (The essay by Fredric Jameson on which I draw in "How Could Chopin's A-Major Prelude Be Deconstructed?" is by no means atypical in exhibiting at least three strata, each representing a different stage of work on the essay.)[38] *The Closing of the American Mind* has a topicality that is especially susceptible to this academic Doppler effect. To clarify my changing perspective on this book, I must return here to an issue broached earlier in this introduction, the Western self-critique of abstract reason, especially in recent scholarship.

Though the term "postmodernism" plays no evident role in Bloom's book, his argument clearly amounts to an attack on the movement now widely called by that name. More specifically, Bloom attacks the modes of thought that have coalesced around the undercutting of belief in a single standard of truth. For many years, during which Bloom built his career, nearly all American disciplines had in effect established a particular model of abstract reason as the only acceptable standard of competence in scholarly work. From this model, it was assumed, could be derived the one wholly objective and thus valid perspective on intellectual problems, and thereby the only solutions deemed sufficiently rigorous to solve those problems. Intellectual work, and consequently perspectives, derived from other models were routinely excluded as incompetent; those with academic power made no effort to clarify any distinctions between intellectual competence and ideological difference.

As different perspectives, based on different models of thought, began to find a place in academic discourse—more slowly in musicology than in most other disciplines—the American model of abstract reason became subject to a mounting critique. As I indicated earlier, my own work in the 1970s and 1980s participated in a form of critique that questioned the exclusivity of this abstract model without denying its virtues. But other critiques, again almost all outside musicology, went considerably further, rejecting notions of abstraction and objectivity even as a possible ideal of importance. These critiques constructed a world of multiple perspectives in which none is uniquely privileged; in terms of modern Western cognitive principles, it became possible to envision such a world as one where no perspective was demonstrably superior to another and where notions of standards, competence, merit, and even fact were entirely discredited in favor of the notion of ideological difference. It was this latter world, in which postmodernist epistemology has been developed to a theoretical extreme, that Bloom set out to analyze and combat in *The Closing of the American Mind*. The means by which he did so I describe in chapter 4. At this point, I need only reiterate that his fight was to restore the uniquely privileged epistemological postion of abstract reason. He saw this restoration as the only way to safeguard the very concepts of truth and qualitative distinction—concepts at the heart of the intellectual battles that Bloom's bestseller not only joined but also helped to spread.

The turmoil evident in American universities and public life during the late 1980s has broadened and intensified greatly since 1989, forming new contexts of particular pertinence to the interpretation of Bloom's book. Freespeech conflicts have proliferated with alarming speed, and bitterness has deepened, not just between conservatives such as Bloom and multiculturalists but sometimes also between the latter and traditional liberals. On campus, ideological conflicts once contained in academic journals have spilled over into everyday life; at a dinner party of college classmates I attended last year, a friendship of thirty years was very nearly destroyed by an argument between two self-designated liberals over academic "political correctness."

Again, I would not countenance efforts to restore a single abstract model of reason, even if such efforts had some hope of succeeding in practice. This point cannot be overemphasized: invoked as a scholarly standard without challenge or critical scrutiny for many years, the model of abstract reason allowed far too much intellectual and human damage ever again to lay persuasive claim to a hegemonic status. Yet on the other hand, just as I believe it wrong simply to discard old paradigms of musical autonomy and artistic value, so, too, I cannot support views that reject altogether the claims of abstract reason, even if such views have every chance of succeeding in practice.

For one thing, as Bloom understood no less well than the poststructuralists, although abstract reason cannot demonstrate persuasive grounds for its claim to constitute a single, absolute standard, neither can critiques of that claim proceed without recourse to a concept of abstract reason.[39] But even more important, a world without a powerful concept of abstract reason would be an inhumane world—a world that not only discarded the best ideals and safeguards of the American Enlightenment but also gave up on the possibility of identifying common human concerns. If I am adamant that the abandonment of a single standard of reason need not doom us to a world without qualitative distinctions—and this is a principal argument in my essay on Allan Bloom—I am equally insistent that acknowledging the multiple perspectives of every human situation does not diminish our stake in the crucial human benefits of abstract reason.[40]

Two intellectual issues that affect me personally can illustrate my reasons for fearing the dismantling of an ideal of abstract reason. One is a controversy that has surfaced both in Europe and the United States over attempts to deny that the Holocaust took place. Reviewing two recent books on this phenomenon for the front page of the *New York Times Book Review*, Walter Reich informs us that "remarkably, despite the existence of overwhelming evidence that the Holocaust really happened," deniers have published their work in a variety of places. Reich then goes on to explain:

> To some extent this success has been a product of an age that promotes the idea that every issue must have two sides, and that each side should be accorded equal respect in the marketplace of discussion. This approach to ideas is fostered by a number of current assumptions, increasingly popular in academia, regarding the indeterminacy of truth.[41]

The second controversy, less widely publicized but more typical of academia, has erupted over the use of a text entitled *The Secret Relationship between Blacks and Jews* in a course at my alma mater, Wellesley College. In a statement published in the Wellesley alumni magazine, the outgoing president of the college, the dean, and the associate dean write:

> We believe [this] book . . . is anti-Semitic in both tone and character. We believe this to be true without reference to the accuracy or inaccuracy of each specific historical contention contained within its pages. We deplore the tone and thrust of the book's generalization, which we think will strike every thoughtful reader.
>
> We are convinced that if a book comparably distorted in its attitudes toward African-Americans were to be taught in a Wellesley class, members of the

community—above all but not limited to African-Americans—would feel
justifiably outraged.

We respect [the professor's] rights through academic freedom to put this book
on his syllabus and teach it in his class. We owe it to him to tolerate his choice.
However, we owe it to ourselves and to our community to know exactly what it
is that we are tolerating

. . . We will continue to . . . explain the principles of academic freedom, and
its concomitant responsibilities.[42]

Taking the position that only one model of reason is valid, and that freedom of speech protects only expressions based on that model, Bloom would
have experienced no difficulty excluding both deniers of the Holocaust and
purveyors of certain blatant prejudices from *his* university. Unfortunately, his
position would have left intact purveyors of other, if sometimes less blatant
prejudices. But I myself see little hope for reasoned discourse at a university
that can find *no* way of invoking an ideal of abstract reason as a complement
and, at times, corrective to the results of uncensored academic speech. In particular I see no way, without recognition of some such ideal, to protect the
rights of the student who attempted an objective critique of a textbook that
expounded the professor's personal prejudices.[43] Granted, the attempt to define such an abstract ideal is fraught with epistemological as well as moral
difficulties, and at best can be neither tidy nor definitive. But experience as
well as reflection persuades me that left unchallenged by any abstract ideal,
particularistic viewpoints come to suffer from the same disease they criticize in
the old universalistic ones: they want to be the only opinion in the world—
and they don't know where to stop.

Allan Bloom, like Robert Bork and to an extent George Will, seems to have
believed that a loud supercilious offense was the only remaining defense against
the complete collapse of abstract reason. I am not ready to concede that the
defense of the best in traditional Western conceptions of reason has come
down to men of this style. But I do understand the degree to which traditional
liberal and conservative views have converged in recent years; from time to
time, now, I agree with a column of Will's, a situation I would once have found
inconceivable. Likewise, I have come to view Bloom's abstract model of reason,
which I never rejected as an ideal, as more in need of emphatic defense and
advocacy than I once did; to this end, I believe a close, critical reading of *The
Closing of the American Mind* still has something to offer American students.

In the fall of 1989, when I was deeply involved in working on the Bloom–Lee
essay, I called a former student of mine, by then a well-known writer and

editor in New York, to ask if he thought a comparison of Allan Bloom and Spike Lee had any commercial possibilities as a book. His intuitive response was to discourage my idea because one could not compare a book of high intellectual quality, such as Bloom's *Closing of the American Mind*, with a piece of popular art, such as Lee's *Do The Right Thing*. In a year or two, he predicted, people would still be reading Bloom's book, but nobody would remember Lee's film. I told him I thought he had it exactly wrong, and time seems to have sided with me. Today it is Bloom's book that has gone out of fashion. Lee remains an important and influential participant in American public discourse; and I know a fair number of people who continue to view *Do The Right Thing* as a touchstone for evaluating not just Lee's subsequent films but also a variety of other films and phenomena in contemporary American life.

Unlike Bloom's book, Lee's film continues to strike me now much as it did when I first saw it: as a masterpiece of structure—and as a potentially useful key to understanding the reasoning of others. Still, the film too presents me with more challenges today than it did the first time. Revising this piece in 1993, I found myself comparing Lee's fictional uprising in Bedford-Stuyvesant with the riots in Crown Heights, Brooklyn, in August 1991 (a report on which was made public in July 1993). In particular, I have asked myself whether the same kind of analysis can be applied to each, and whether the real-life event changes my attitude toward the film—and vice versa.

Leaving aside the distinction between life and art, the two riots do present some comparable features. Both are set off by the killing of a black youngster, though under substantially different circumstances. In life, Gavin Cato, a seven-year-old boy, was killed in an apparent automobile accident. In the film, Radio Raheem, a teenager described by Lee as "a sympathetic character . . . but . . . not an angel,"[44] is killed by the police in a choke hold. In the film, Sal, the pizzeria owner, is "basically . . . a good person, but he feels Black people are inferior."[45] Almost certainly Sal had counterparts among the Chasidim in Crown Heights. In one important sense, however, the two riots are not comparable: Lee decided early in the design of his project that no one would die in his film riot.[46]

In chapter 4 I will argue that Lee's film provides a perspective from which "it becomes possible to think of Mookie's act [in hurling the garbage can at Sal's pizzeria] as reasonable, and perhaps even as morally justified."[47] Can his film be used to justify the same perspective on the murder of Yankel Rosenbaum in Crown Heights? I believe not.

I do believe the effort to sort out modes of reasoning in Lee's film—abstract and concrete, cognitive and moral—can be helpful in understanding why the Crown Heights riots occurred and even why Yankel Rosenbaum was killed.

But the balance struck by Lee's film between the pressures of concrete existence and the claims of abstract standards is in my judgment too carefully drawn to permit justifying the murder of an uninvolved passerby as right or moral. I do not share all the sympathies and desires Lee expresses in his journal or approve of the moral direction in which all of them point. I would argue, however, that Lee imposes on the film itself a discipline remarkable for the degree in which it can contain, with humanity but without sentimentality, distinctly different moral views. To use Mookie's act to justify any remotely comparable act is to violate the complexity of both structure and content in Lee's film. Whereas in retrospect *The Closing of the American Mind* strikes me as more important than I once thought, though no less offputting, *Do The Right Thing* continues to impress me as an eloquent argument against Bloom's single abstract model of reason that is fully ready for inclusion in Bloom's sort of canon.

This introduction brings to a close the part of my career that started with my first job, at the University of Chicago, in 1973. It has been an unexpected career, and among academic survivors, odd; sad to say, the painful experiences I endured are all too common among those who did not survive, or who currently hold on with their fingernails to the eroding slopes of academia. Some of these are academic spouses, men and women, who cannot find that second job at any location, much less the humanly desired one. Too many are women whose intelligent and dedicated work is still, for all the complaints about political correctness, perceived and treated as a lethal threat. Where the gloomy prospects of even our brightest untenured colleagues and graduate students are concerned, those of us with academic security have never had more to answer for.

The twists taken by my own career have affected not only my life and the lives of my family but also the direction of my thought and scholarship. As the reader of this introduction has seen, I cannot help making connections between my experience and what I study and teach; and this process of making connections has given my written work a shape for which twenty years ago there was no paradigm. One or two reviewers of my earlier book have taken me to task for this aspect of my scholarship. In this one respect, I look forward to the day when more of my reviewers are women; for while I have received some extraordinarily generous reviews from men, and remain a great believer in the importance of staking out common grounds of academic discourse, I suspect that some of the ways in which I work are intuitively more congenial to women scholars, on the whole, than to men.

Apart from working with this consciousness of stylistic difference and taking an interest in work by colleagues and students on gender issues, in my reading and in the courses I teach, I have not yet felt impelled to address feminist questions in my scholarship. More important at least to my current concerns as a scholar is the relation of my religious and ethnic identity first to the values underlying Western art music (which largely excluded my own traditions), and second to the American context in which I have studied that music. As the preceding introduction makes clear, much of my scholarly preoccupation today is with understanding how the current renegotiation of relationships between American Jews and African Americans stands to affect the American experiment. As a scholar whose chief focus has been on the interplay of universal and particular values in music, I find it tempting to suppose that studies of past Western music and of contemporary American culture could prove mutually enlightening. As a teacher who has been affectionately accused of "raging humanism,"[48] I would like to hand on to my students a vision of music broad enough to encompass the strengths of both difference and excellence, in all of their manifestations and convergences. As an American I would like to believe that the way in which I define a relationship between music and reason could play some small part in bringing closer to realization the American ideal as Lincoln, at his best, envisioned it.

1

Whose *Magic Flute*? Intimations of Reality at the Gates of the Enlightenment

In loving memory of my father, David Eli Rosengard (1910-88)

Die Zauberflöte is one of those pieces that can enchant a child at the same time that it moves the most worldly of men to tears, and transports the wisest. Each individual and each generation finds something different in it; only to the merely "cultured" or the pure barbarian does it have nothing to say.[1]

—*Alfred Einstein*

It is by force or on occasion only that antagonistic moments will be musically identifiable in Mozart, whose music so clearly echoes the passage from enlightened late absolutism to the bourgeoisie. . . . Rather, his social aspect is the force with which his music returns to itself, the detachment from empiricism. . . . Of all the tasks awaiting us in the social interpretation of music, that of Mozart would be the most difficult and the most urgent.[2]

—*T. W. Adorno*

From the start, *The Magic Flute* appealed to an unusually diversified audience. Mozart himself called indirect attention to this phenomenon in two letters to his wife, recounting how one acquaintance showed himself "an ass" for laughing at everything in the work, and how, less than a week later, Salieri and Caterina Cavalieri pronounced the work "an *operone*, worthy to be performed for the grandest festival and before the greatest monarch."[3] In the mid-1790s, H. C. Robbins Landon tells us, "the aristocracy patronized the Italian opera, the lower classes the German opera in the suburbs, though of course everyone, and from all classes, came to see Mozart's *Zauberflöte* in the Wieden."[4] It is conceivable that *The Magic Flute* is the only Western musical work aimed explicitly at the lower levels of urban society to achieve lasting uncontested status as a masterpiece of high art.

1

A common explanation for the broad social scale of this success is that *The Magic Flute* draws upon such a wide range of musical and theatrical traditions that it presents a basis of appeal to everyone. But acknowledgment of this diversified content in turn raises questions about the unity of the work. Long-standing tradition assumes unity as a requirement for the designation of masterpiece.[5] Until quite recently, the notion that there might be chinks in the artistic unity of *The Magic Flute* has been simply unthinkable.[6] Among scholars this impression has been reinforced by the knowledge that although the hundreds of attempts at German opera that followed *The Magic Flute* in the first half of the nineteenth century were overwhelmingly heterogeneous in style, none succeeded quite so unmistakably in drawing approval across the range of social classes.[7] Even apart from the high esteem we have for Mozart's compositional abilities, we tend to assume that Classical principles provided Mozart's operas, like his symphonies, with a degree of large-scale unity that was no longer available to early Romantic music.

In what follows, I want to argue that the perception of a unity in *The Magic Flute* stems from at least two sources. Only one of these sources, a maxim, defines unity in a way that the opera could have recognized in itself, so to speak, when it first appeared. Provided this maxim is itself interpreted from an Enlightenment perspective, one can demonstrate the unity of *The Magic Flute* in a reading that takes the opera more or less at face value in terms of viewpoints proper to its own initial context.

Unity can also be said to govern *The Magic Flute* by way of a homogeneous tone, though in a far more problematical way. A reading of this second sort of unity depends on perspectives that began to develop only in the nineteenth century; it raises questions about the earlier conception of unity by exposing limitations in it. The differences between these two readings—both of which I believe the text of *The Magic Flute* allows without subjecting itself to distortion[8]—seem worth examining in some detail.

I

> It is important to separate the essential from the accidental, to conjure up the mythical Papageno and forget the actual person in the play.
>
> —*Søren Kierkegaard*[9]

From the first of my two perspectives, I believe it can be demonstrated that one conceptual principle or theme provides unity at virtually every level of

The Magic Flute, musical as well as textual. That principle could be expressed as the maxim: "Social rank does not equal human worth."

This is, of course, the explicit theme of the libretto in *The Magic Flute.* It is also one of the characterizing ideals of the European Enlightenment.[10] To the extent that this humanitarian principle can persuasively be shown to govern *The Magic Flute* on a multiplicity of structural levels, it offers insight not only into the technical unity of this work but also into the breadth of its social appeal. For if the work audibly projects this principle, it makes a persuasive claim that the unified world constructed within it is large enough for everyone, and thereby establishes the opera as a powerful metaphor for a conception of a humanity bound by universal principles.

To illustrate how the maxim just cited provides unity, I will touch briefly on three numbers: Papageno's entrance lied (the *Vogelfänger* song); the Queen of the Night's first aria; and Tamino's *Bildnis* aria. In each of these pieces, the music suggests a standard of human worth based on the relation of the character to some conception of nature.

Papageno's opening lied, together with his panpipes and stage props, presents him as a spontaneous man at one with organic nature.[11] Within his G-major world there are no signs of conflict, no threats of disorder. Orchestra and voice share the same material, the governing power of the G-major tonic (and thus of tonality more generally) is not challenged,[12] and there are no formal surprises. Papageno's world is a unified one, clear, simple, and symmetrical. From an Enlightenment perspective, his structure can readily be imagined as part of a natural order, accessible to all, without the intervention of culture or reflection, and grounded on a natural condition of reason.

For Papageno the world of his song is also a beneficent world. Sheltering him within firm frames of key and recurring material, it is repetitive to an extreme. Kierkegaard puts it: "It is the same song, the same melody; as soon as he finishes, he begins anew from the beginning, and so continuously."[13] This repetitive quality strongly suggests a characterization of time not as a finite, unidirectional force but as cyclical and unending—as a field in which the exuberance of the life force, of instinct, is continuously bubbling in an endless renewal of life.

Such cyclical characteristics link Papageno's world with the idyllic realm of the pastoral, a link that is reinforced in the emphasis on wind instruments, and explicitly signified in Papageno's pipes. And although, in terms of its typical imagery, the pastoral has been defined as a tradition in which "the universal is expressed in the concrete,"[14] pastoral nature has traditionally designated a zone apart from the real problems—which is to say, the artificially

a)

b)

Example 1. Papageno's entrance lied, measures 12-14 (a) and 22-24 (b)

constructed ones—of civilization.[15] Through his pastoral associations, Papageno is presented as existing outside of real time; his time is that of nature in its eternal aspect.

As symbolized by the orchestra material from which he takes his song, Papageno's world supplies his needs amply. Even his quest for a mate seems an aspect of this natural condition, and consequently not a matter of individual urgency. Only the chiming of his panpipes comes from Papageno himself, and at that so spontaneously that it seems almost to issue *through* him from nature. Moreover, Papageno's pipes function interchangeably in this song as consequent and as antecedent, which suggests that Papageno has no real need to ask questions; to any question he might think of posing, his world already provides the answers (Example 1).

Indeed, everything about this piece suggests that the song itself is "ready-made," from Papageno's lack of self-consciousness as he plunges into it to its stock type, its absence of individualized soloistic demands, and its appearance of familiarity—*der Schein des Bekannten*—as eighteenth-century German critics called it.[16]

Papageno's song suggests no significant distinction between nature and culture, any more than Papageno himself seems to care whether he is addressing trees on stage or people in the audience. In Papageno's song, everything is as one; despite the self-conscious critique of society that by 1791 had been developed by Rousseau, society establishes no distinctive presence here. If society is evoked at all in this song, it is as an unremarkable function of nature.

In keeping with the undifferentiated nature of his world, Papageno knows no division (or alienation) between himself and his environment. He does not sense the "differences" (in the Derridean sense) between oneself and others that typically lead people to form a social contract.[17] Or (to draw on Jacques Lacan's terms) Papageno has not experienced the gap between one's self and an object, a gap we commonly call "desire" (a notion that also figures in Kierkegaard's account of Papageno), which would impel efforts to use signs in order to communicate.[18] There is no time lag between Papageno's experience and his unquestioning sense of who he is.[19] The music of Papageno's entrance lied gives no evidence of a felt need for self-completion.

Indeed, this song suggests that Papageno is at home in nature precisely because he has no individual or socially real self. As Kierkegaard suggests, Papageno is a prereflective, preconscious creature. An instinctive life force simply issues through him. Expressed another way, Papageno's first song conveys the authenticity of what is natural, an authenticity that becomes increasingly elusive as humans identify themselves with society as a construct divided from nature. As Lionel Trilling notes of a comparably natural figure, Rousseau's noble savage, one of Papageno's defining traits is "the perfect autonomy of his consciousness."[20] In ways that Trilling's account of modern Western culture shows, such autonomy becomes extraordinarily problematical, and in actuality unattainable, once culture becomes sharply conscious of a tension between the values of existing society and those implicit in an idealized conception of nature; or as Trilling himself puts it, once a consciousness forms that "it is the social man who is the alienated man."[21]

Taken at face value, Papageno's human worth rests on his oneness with a natural world that makes no social distinctions, and that is governed by values derived ultimately from an underlying order of reason. Such values are not all that distant in spirit, despite their uncritical quality, from the principles of reason on which Kant based his account of aesthetic judgment as a universal faculty.[22] At bottom, the values of Papageno's musical world are presented as universal; and Papageno's own value derives from the universality of his status as a natural man.

Thus Papageno's social rank is of no consequence in his first song except in the positive sense that its lack of pretentiousness allows him to remain persuasively natural. Papageno's social rank has no correspondence to value except an inverse one, insofar as it implies that the socially unpretentious have direct access to a unity with nature that puts to shame the artifice of the socially privileged. Clearly, the music of Papageno's entrance lied asserts the proposition that "social rank does not equal human worth."

II

In the first two sections of her music—the recitative and Larghetto of her first aria—the Queen of the Night presents herself as perhaps the most persuasively natural character in the entire opera. Here, nature is identified with human emotion and presented as a source of suffering.

Initially the Queen presents herself as a grieving mother. To the extent that any "role" can be construed as natural, the music of the first two sections renders this one persuasively so, drawing on more or less conventional devices for depicting grief in ways that are specifically responsive to the situation in the text. Consider, first, the relation of instrumental parts to the voice. At the very opening, even before the Queen's voice enters, the syncopation, throbbing rhythms, and chromatic coloring of the orchestral parts suggest powerful and painful emotion:

Example 2. The Queen of the Night's first aria, measures 1-6

Though the initial key of the recitative is B-flat major, the major mode is rendered here with a pulsating sensuousness, and it soon gives way to the sad tones of the relative minor, G, in which the Larghetto is set.

Later, at the closing of the Larghetto section (measures 53-60), after the Queen first acknowledges that her aid for her daughter was too weak, her voice momentarily drops out, unable to negotiate anything more than a deceptive cadence on the tonic note G ("schwach," measure 56). At this point, the instruments, continuing the listless quarter-note rhythm that had previously been initiated with the voice on a diminished triad ("denn meine," measure 53), move abruptly away from the desired tonic, G minor, taking off on C minor for three measures as if they will not return to G. As the oboes nd violins suspend C over D in the bassoons and cellos, the voice reenters with a new layer of the dull rhythm, and forms its own dissonance, on a high A-flat ("Hilfe"), over G in the cellos and double basses (Example 3). More persuasive orchestral support for the text, "my help was too weak," is difficult to imagine.

In between these two moments, the sensuous power of wind color (the same colors as in Papageno's song) is used effectively as a kind of alter ego to the human voice. At times, as in the repeated phrase "durch sie ging all' mein Glück verloren" (with her all my happiness disappeared, measures 27-31), the winds precisely double the vocal line. At other moments, the

Example 3. The Queen of the Night's first aria, measures 53-60

winds offer an expanded echo or a prominent supplement to the vocal line
(as at measures 12-14, in response to "O zitt're nich, mein lieber Sohn!" [O
tremble not, my dear son]), or provide the impression of a reinforcing counterpoint (as at measures 36ff., "Noch seh' ich ihr Zittern" [I still see her
trembling]).

In the midsection of her Larghetto, moreover, starting at measure 36, as
the Queen recollects the most harrowing moments of her grief, those in
which she witnessed her daughter's terror, the strings take on a rapid rhythm
of agitation, echoing the leaps and angularity of the vocal line. Eventually
(starting at "ängstliches," measure 41, through "streben," measure 44), the
strings work in close integration with the voice, intensifying a series of
appoggiaturas and a long descending chromatic melodic line, and contribut-
ing to chromatic harmonies that include the diminished seventh and aug-

Example 4. The Queen of the Night's first aria, measures 40-44

mented sixth chords. The sensuously rhythmic and harmonic atmosphere provided by the instruments marks an extreme point of intensity in the Queen's expression of anguish (Example 4).

Within this framework, the vocal line of the first two sections shows a flexibility of style that seems simultaneously to reflect and to define an ongoing flux of emotions. The juxtaposition of relatively free rhythm in the recitative with greater rhythmic regularity in the Larghetto, while wholly conventional, corresponds to a believable change from expostulation to recollection. The shift at the end of the Larghetto, from a listless rhythm and small range in the first statement of "denn meine Hilfe war zu schwach" (for my help was too weak, measures 53-56) to an upward leap and long descending scale on the repetition of those words (measures 58-61), suggests a last gathering of energy in a context of resigned despair (see Example 3). Likewise, various alternations—of conjunct lines and leaps (for example, within the first vocal phrase of the Larghetto) and of larger and smaller ranges (the span of a ninth in the phrase "Noch . . . zittern" [A-flat to G, measures 36-38] closing down to the chromatic filling of an augmented fourth between "ihr ängstliches" and "Streben" [E-flat to A, measures 40-44])—seem to issue from a vacillation between surrender to grief and attempts at control.

Compared to the stark simplicity of Sarastro's first aria, "O Isis und Osiris," where Sarastro's bass seems almost a literal symbol of reason as the foundation of reality, the Queen's more ornate and delicate lines seem individualized and subjective—qualities traditionally credible for a sympathetic depiction of a woman's grief. At the same time, these expressions of grief are kept under control, whether by Mozart operating behind the scenes or by the Queen herself.[23] Through the largely syllabic text setting in these two sections, the Queen keeps her text clearly audible and thereby focuses attention primarily on the content of that text. The range of the vocal line does not exceed reasonable limits. Clear reference to symmetry and periodic phrasing is maintained, as are the strictures of closed form and coherent tonal logic—in the Larghetto, the tonal logic of Classical sonata structure.[24] The Queen is grief-stricken, but she is not mad.

This does not deny that the Queen gives us occasion in these first two sections to question the authenticity of her emotions, particularly as she begins moving from the tonic, G-minor, of her Larghetto to the relative major, B-flat (at the second "durch sie ging," measures 29-30). What happens from that point on invites one to wonder whether the Queen relies on the tonality of sonata to maintain her sanity or to manipulate her listeners' emotions. An almost unmistakable posturing occurs in voice and orchestra at the repeated words "ein Bösewicht" (a villain, measures 31-35). Here a sudden, convulsive, and stylized conventional rush up and down the strings, alternating with an emphatic dotted rhythm, seems more the affectation of Baroque *Affekt* than a natural expression of emotion:

Example 5. The Queen of the Night's first aria, measures 31-36

Or again, as the Queen recounts her daughter's cries for help, with two sighs in *empfindsamer Stil* on the high points of her melodic line, and two pauses ("ach helft! ach helft!," measures 46-48 [see Example 6]), she seems fully conscious of her dramatic effect. At both points, the Queen, whatever her motivation, plays a role that casts her in a particularly pathetic light; and, eventually, she does get what she wants from Tamino.

Indeed, the Queen's apparent need here to rectify a lack of harmony in her emotional life, as well as her explicit address of another individual, a person who might meet that need—so different from Papageno's unthinking self-sufficiency—both call the Queen's motives into question. It is worth noting that in each of the examples just cited, the Queen utters words twice; in a third instance, at the passage beginning "denn meine Hilfe" that closes her Larghetto (measures 53-61 [see Example 3]), she repeats not only a whole phrase but individual words within the repeated phrase. Is this the natural stammer of grief? Or a sign of duplicity? And what are we (or Tamino) to make of this melodic phrase that the Queen offers not just twice but three times? (See Example 6.)

Appearing first in the tonic G-minor, over the text "durch sie ging all' mein Glück verloren" (all my happiness disappeared with her, measures 27-29), the initial effect of this phrase is to lighten the mood just preceding. As the diminished triad on "Tochter" (measure 26) gives way to the accompaniment of a minor sixth on "sie" (measure 28, beat 1), and as oboe and bassoon are brought in to double the Queen's line, the effect is one of despair giving way to poignant pleading—or is it wheedling? This ambiguous effect is increased as the line immediately repeats itself, transposed up to modulate into the relative major (B-flat, measures 29-31). Nor is the uncertainty resolved when the phrase returns one last time in G-minor, as a kind of quasi recapitulation, over the words "Ich musste sie mir rauben sehen" (I was forced to see her stolen from me, measures 44-46). Here above all, the phrase effects a (momentary) lightening of mood, after the concentrated chromaticism and emotion at the midpoint of the Larghetto. But, again, what does this lightening signify? Is the Queen pleading with Tamino or seducing him? Is it the "nature" on which she draws the natural emotion of a grieving mother? Or is it the sensuality of (the female) sex? We are not certain of the Queen's sincerity.

In tracing the historical development of the Western concept of "self," Lionel Trilling suggests an early stage of role-playing, which could be represented by Machiavelli's *The Prince* and by Castiglione's *Book of the Courtier*, a stage often associated with villains, such as Iago.[25] Out of this stage there eventually develops an ideal of sincerity, whereby the individual seems to open up to society all that he or she is. But in actuality sincerity, by Trilling's account, is undertaken for reasons of social advancement, and thus always car-

Example 6. The Queen of the Night's first aria, measures 27-31 (a) and 44-48 (b)

ries with it the possibilities of insincerity and the concealment of what today we would call the "real self."[26]

Carried to its logical extreme, according to Trilling, sincerity involves such an overwhelming degree of concern about one's relationship to society that it may end up bankrupting the self. Rather than concealing its "true" identity, the "sincere" self may have emptied itself of all content. Such a self, in other words, may not exist at all.[27]

Example 7. The Queen of the Night's first aria, measures 61-67

The inescapability of this dilemma leads the Westerner to develop still another stage of selfhood, which Trilling calls "authenticity." By one definition that Trilling presents, a person or a character takes on authenticity precisely to the degree that he "refus[es] the commonplaces that the culture treacherously provides for his convenience and comfort."[28] To be able to mount such resistance, the representative of human authenticity takes on a certain quality of solidity. "Nowadays," Trilling writes, "our sense of what authenticity means involves a degree of rough concreteness. . . . [The authentic] person is as actual, as hard, dense, weighty, perdurable as any stone."[29] Authenticity of this modern kind comes about to erase the doubts besetting sincerity as a mode of self-definition. It is not, however, the solution chosen by the Queen to clarify the real status of her natural self. Instead, our worst fears about the Queen's insincerity, opened up when she moved to the relative major of the Larghetto, B-flat, seem to be realized as she launches into the last section of her aria (Allegro moderato, measures 61ff.) and restores B-flat as her "real" tonic.[30]

The sudden, rhythmically emphatic orchestral return to a B-flat-major tonic (in measure 62) does not seem a natural gathering of emotional reserves; it seems a thoroughly artificial recourse to old-fashioned Baroque *Affekt* (Example 7). At this moment, the Queen steps back in historical time to retrieve the privileges of rank associated with the conventions of Baroque *opera seria,* expressing only stereotyped emotions. Musical clichés abound here: simple formulaic assertions of tonality in the voice; and flourishes in the orchestra, near the end including the dotted rhythm (over "ewig," measure 97) traditionally associated with royalty.

With social privilege established, the Queen feels fully confident of her power; as the violins scramble breathlessly to keep up with her rhythmic energy, for example, at the phrase beginning "Und werd' ich dich als Sieger sehen" (and when I see you as victor, measures 74ff.), there is little doubt who is in command. And whereas her Larghetto deferred to sonata structure, in this last section she sticks very close to I, acknowledging V, the conventional "other," only in a brief half-cadence (measures 72-73).[31] Though the Queen begins the Allegro moderato by declaring "Du, du, du," the hard, bright setting of the major mode here bellows "ich."

Yet even as she demonstrates the range, speed, and sheer physical power of which her voice is capable, this display of mastery also exposes a lack of control. This is no longer a "natural" woman with whom others can reasonably be expected to sympathize on a basis of common humanity. The social decorum of periodic phrasing is pushed aside. The Queen drives ahead with a motorized Baroque energy. Her range is extreme; and the instrumental treatment of her voice seems distinctly unnatural.

As her extended coloratura passage gets under way, it becomes clear that the Queen has lost sight of her ostensible purpose in addressing Tamino. She makes quick work of Tamino's own key, brushing by E-flat in measures 80-82. Excessive ornamentation dissolves her words into inaudibility and meaninglessness; and when she is done, she cadences bluntly, without apology, on an unveiled formula. Protected by the solidity of social privilege, she no longer feels constrained to maintain a facade of naturalness and control that might ingratiate her to others; indeed, she seems oblivious to the existence of anyone else, except perhaps a collective world of subordinates for whom she postures.[32] By the end it makes no sense at all for the Queen to try to conceal her "real" motives: a character this inseparable from the trappings of power based on rank has no basis for "real" human or natural motives at all.

Critics have often treated the break between the Queen's Larghetto and her Allegro moderato as a point of troubling inconsistency between the "good" Queen and the "bad" (see note 6, this chapter). But perhaps the rupture in style that begins the final section can be associated with a consistent characterization of the Queen, albeit ambiguously, in either of two ways. Perhaps the Queen's embryonic natural self (expressed through the recitative and Larghetto, and to an extent through the key of G-minor) is too fragile to combat adversity on its own, and thus succumbs to the weaponry of established social rank. Or perhaps this natural self never existed at all; perhaps its evocation was merely a role assumed by the Queen to draw Tamino into an orbit devoted to her own self-serving power. Either her self is stillborn, or it is false. Both ways, the Queen's willingness, in the end, to identify her "true" self as this conventional monarch, safe in a social position of power and needing help from no one, makes it clear that she, like Papageno, has no individual, natural self of her own.

Where then does the Queen's human worth lie? Certainly not in the uses to which she puts her social power. Reasserting the privileges of caste, the Queen loses all connection to the rest of humanity, at least in its natural aspect. Yet to the extent that the Queen's opening sections suggest themselves as genuinely emotional, or even as the most persuasively natural moments of human expression in the opera, they point toward a capacity for human worth quite distinct from the Queen's social status. From this perspective, a queen can be taken for the most natural character in the opera, and the Queen's own human worth can be gauged as proportional to her distance from her rank. Again, the music leads us to conclude that "social rank does not equal human worth."

III

Coming between Papageno's entrance song and the Queen's aria, Tamino's *Bildnis* aria seems to mediate between the two, not only literally but also stylistically and philosophically.

Tamino's flexible, delicate, and mildly ornamental vocal line, for example, has much in common with the character of the Queen's lines in her opening sections. Likewise, from the return of E-flat at measure 45 (beginning with "Ich würde sie voll Entzücken") to the end, by way of a fleeting brush with IV ("drücken," measure 49), Tamino's repeated circlings of the tonic have an affinity with Papageno's musical irrepressibility. These examples suggest that Tamino, in his aria, shares in the most appealing natural characteristics of both Papageno and the Queen.

Tamino, like Papageno, seems natural in the sense that his melodic line remains relatively simple, without affectation. Yet his vocal line has its melismas, its chromatic tinges (the C-sharp at "nennen," measure 19, repeated two measures later, and the enharmonically equivalent D-flat at "drücken"), its peaks of range (starting with the A-flat on "Götterbild" [likeness of the gods], measure 9), its gathering of rhythmic and directional energy ("O wenn ich sie nur finden könnte" [Oh, if only I could find her], measures 36ff.). Similarly,

Example 8. Tamino's aria, measures 14-19

the orchestra in Tamino's aria provides deceptive cadences ("füllt," measure 12, the first "allein," measure 29), appoggiaturas (the ninth sounded on "Liebe," measure 28, among others), and, as happened in the Queen's Larghetto, a heightening of rhythmic and harmonic intensity at the midsection (measures 34-43); this is particularly noticeable at "ich würde" (measure 40), as Tamino, asking himself what he would do if he found the woman in the picture, grows increasingly excited. Furthermore, Tamino has access to the clarinet, an instrument Mozart always imbues with a special radiance, here especially noticeable as the B-flat section of Tamino's aria begins, just after he has cadenced on the tonic E-flat ("füllt," measure 15; Example 8).

Tamino, in the sensuousness of his music, signifies a capacity for real emotion. In this he is like the Queen. Pamina's *Bildnis* impels him to articulate the desire for another through musical language. In this he is unlike Papageno.

Yet his emotion neither escapes nor exceeds his powers of control. Never lapsing into coloratura, he keeps the text clear at all times, projecting—unlike the Queen—a steady consciousness of purpose without guile. Tamino needs no "other" for assistance in fulfilling his desire, as even the stage directions immediately preceding his aria signify.[33] Deaf to the outside world, and accompanied only by a silenced Papageno, Tamino is alone in his own world. Addressing himself only to the symbolic *Bildnis*, Tamino suggests through his music that he has it in his own power to fulfill his desire in some human way.

Tamino does not rely on stereotyped popular vocal conventions, as does

a)

b)

Example 9. Tamino's aria, measures 9-12 (a) and 51-54 (b)

Papageno. And, though a prince, he does not resort to the conventions of the aristocracy. Rather, he creates his line as it develops, consistently and audibly molding it in accordance with generally intelligible principles of structure. Its large-scale form is balanced both through the framing tonality of E-flat and through thematic recurrence; Tamino uses a melodic formula from the opening ("mein Herz mit neuer Regung füllt" [my heart fills with new stirring], measures 9-12) at the close ("und ewig wäre sie dann mein" [and then she would always be mine], measures 51-54), to round off the whole (Example 9).

Likewise, while avoiding the sectional divisions of the traditional recitative and aria, Tamino marks the middle section of his aria clearly by ceasing to sing at both its ends. During the earlier silence (measures 16-18), the clarinets enter to change the key to the dominant. The latter silence (measures 44-45), which leads into the return of the tonic, is joined by all the instruments. During the passage that immediately precedes this break, under the chromatic and rhythmic peak of his agitation, Tamino holds to a dominant pedal point (measures 34-43), which shapes his address to its logical resolution.

All of these procedures link this aria, no less than the Queen's Larghetto, to Classical sonata structure. The difference in effect can be gauged from the relation of each character to the second key area. The Queen's move toward the relative major, B-flat, in her moving Larghetto opens the suspicion that she is exploiting some preconceived sonata structure to her own ends, a suspicion aggravated by her triumphant restoration of B-flat as I and by her virtual disdain of all other keys in her closing section. Tamino's turn toward V, by contrast, generously articulated by the lyrical clarinets, and his subsequent return through adversity to I, suggest him as a person who develops sonatalike principles through a combination of feeling and discipline.

In fact, Tamino requires neither preexisting musical conventions nor the self-assurances of virtuosity because he carries within him the one tool that will give him mastery of every situation: an active faculty of reason. It is this faculty that determines the most important aspect of Tamino's relation to nature.

Tamino is not unnatural, even though his relation to nature often invites negative definition—that is, definition in terms of qualities that he does not share with other characters. From Papageno's perspective, it is true, Tamino is the very opposite of a man of nature: a man of culture. Whereas culture, represented crudely by the bird cage, constitutes a trap for Papageno, Tamino is able not only to appreciate a cultural object of beauty (Pamina's picture) but also to create one—his own aria. Whereas Papageno exists outside of time in his lied, and the Queen steps back into a historical time of artificiality, Tamino through his aria shows a capacity to control and organize time, to envision and provide for its unfolding into the future, to move forward toward the fulfillment of his ideals, and to give time a shape. In a word, Tamino is the quintessential man of culture: he is an artist.

But from an Enlightenment perspective, the man who is truest to nature *is* the man of culture; for it is civilized man who is truest to his own distinctively human nature, which is based on reason. Even Tamino's artistry is grounded on a human conception of reason. For though the notion of creativity was increasingly evoked in the late eighteenth century so as to suggest the artist as a successor to God,[34] Tamino's art adheres to an Enlightenment ideal of beauty as a condition that confirmed the universal structure of the human mind.[35] At bottom his aria presents abstract standards of rational structure as prior to the contingencies even of concrete sensuous beauty.

Through his faculty of reason, Tamino meets a high standard of human value, one that was perhaps thinkable only during the late Enlightenment and its aftermath. Encompassing within himself the capacities for both discipline and creative freedom, Tamino synthesizes the higher natural powers of both Papageno and the Queen: he becomes a fully autonomous human being, able to actualize his individuality through reliance on universally valid principles of reason.

Although by post-Kantian standards Tamino is not yet critically reflective, neither is he preconscious in Papageno's manner. He is self-determining in a way that is morally responsible; it is significant that the first emphatic leap in his aria is to a form of the word "God" ("Götterbild" [likeness of the gods], measure 9), whereas its counterpart in the Queen's aria is to a form of the word "evil" ("Bösewicht," measure 34). Through the use of E-flat Tamino possesses, literally as well as figuratively, the key that will give him entrance into Sarastro's ideal realm—a realm theoretically open to all, however few reach it in actuality. Tamino has it all—even the clarinets. By Enlightenment standards, Tamino, the man of reason, is the man of ultimate worth.

The concept of human worth proposed by Tamino in his *Bildnis* aria is a condition to which all humans can in theory aspire. The message embodied musically in this piece is that in relation to universal standards of reason, particularities of origin, social status, and cultural identity are mere accidents that have no bearing on true human worth. Like Papageno's song and the Queen's aria, but in a way that the Enlightenment would have considered especially noble, Tamino's aria musically embodies the maxim "Social rank does not equal human worth."

IV

"Wer ich bin? [für sich:] Dumme Frage! [laut:] Ein Mensch, wie du." (Who am I? [to himself:] Stupid question! [aloud:] A human being, like you.)
—*Papageno (on meeting Tamino)*

"Ein Weiser prüft und achtet nicht, was der gemeine Pöbel spricht." (A wise man tests and does not heed what the vulgar rabble says.)
—*Tamino (in the Quintet, no. 12)*

We leave now the mythical Papageno. The fate of the actual Papageno need not concern us.
—*Søren Kierkegaard*[36]

It is in keeping with the spirit of the Enlightenment to argue that *The Magic Flute* is unified by the maxim I suggested, itself interpreted to mean that considerations of social class should be excluded from our evaluations of a person's worth. But perspectives on this opera did not end with the Enlightenment. In the two hundred years since *The Magic Flute* first appeared, new perspectives have emerged that today make us doubt the validity of subsuming heterogeneity, unproblematically, under a single abstract principle. Is there perhaps another way of understanding the heterogeneity of this opera that might prove more persuasive to contemporary critical reflection?

Encouragement for an alternative reading is provided by the late Russian critic Mikhail Bakhtin, who in *The Dialogic Imagination* developed a theory of the novel that focused precisely on cultural heterogeneity as a parameter of literature open to analysis.[37] Bakhtin himself, moreover, explicitly suggested that some of his ideas about the novel might have analogues in opera, and in music more generally.[38] Although Bakhtin's ideas have particular resonance for the study of nineteenth-century Western art music, where aesthetic ideals associated with prose came increasingly to supplant values more suggestive of poetry, a passage such as the following cannot help but bring to mind *The Magic Flute*:

> The novel can be defined as a diversity of social speech types (sometimes even [a] diversity of languages) and a diversity of individual voices, artificially organized. The internal stratification of any single national language in[to] social dialects . . . present in every language at any given moment of its historical existence is the indispensable prerequisite of the novel as a genre. The novel orchestrates all its themes, the totality of the world of objects and ideas depicted and expressed in it, by means of the social diversity of speech types and by the differing individual voices that flourish under such conditions.[39]

Bakhtin takes care to distinguish the domain of the novel from the domain of poetry, which for him is characterized by, among other things, an exclusion of actual linguistic diversity and the idealization of a unitary and normative voice. By implication, poetry connotes a state of relative social isolation from concrete social concerns.[40]

For Bakhtin, the novel is characterized by its artistic representation of the diverse languages that coexist at any one time in (Western) society. The representation of these languages in a novel reflects a recognition that society *does* involve numerous subcultures (not his term), whose viewpoints and values cannot simply be ignored. Not surprisingly, the novel tends to appear in situations of social instability, such as the aftermath of the French Revolution.

Prominent in the nineteenth century, the aesthetic described by Bakhtin in connection with the novel is fundamentally concerned with the concrete conditions of social reality; and it tends toward a position of cultural relativism, which honors the differences among diverse social viewpoints while opening to question the universality of moral principles. These values differ considerably from the Enlightenment principles invoked in the reading of my maxim as a ground of unity in *The Magic Flute*.

From the perspective of the later aesthetic, it becomes possible to draw from this maxim a rather different conclusion. My earlier reading proposes an ideal of human equality based on a discounting of actual social condition. But if social rank does not determine human worth, it follows that the social conditions of the lower-class person's life are as worth examining as those of the privileged classes. According to this second way of thinking (the emergence of which can to an important extent be associated with the emergence of modernity), ideals of equality may perhaps be more effectively served by noticing social differences, in their concrete actuality, than by ignoring them.[41] From this position a growing recognition would emerge in Western culture, first of social condition as an irreducible aspect of the human condition, and second of relativity as a potentially unavoidable condition of human values.

To apply this second interpretation to my central maxim as a basis for analyzing the heterogeneity in *The Magic Flute* is to propose a deconstruction: the alternative reading threatens to unravel all that appeared true in our previous reading. At what "point of deconstruction" might such a reading begin? In his account of nineteenth-century musical realism, Carl Dahlhaus offers a helpful suggestion when he describes realism in part as "extend[ing] to areas which were previously excluded from art as 'unsuitable.'"[42] Papageno springs to mind. Let us approach this second reading through a critical reassessment of Papageno in his opening song. Do we find any inconsistency between what

Papageno appeared to signify in the Enlightenment and what to us he seems to signify in reality?

In a sense it can be said that, particularly in the case of Papageno, Mozart took an aesthetic position that opens itself to such an examination. At bottom this is the same position taken by Kant in his *Critique of Judgment*, published only a year before the appearance of *The Magic Flute*:

> The purposiveness in the product of beautiful art, although it is designed, must not seem to be designed, i.e. beautiful art must *look* like nature, although we are conscious of it as art. But a product of art appears like nature when, although its agreement with the rules, according to which alone the product can become what it ought to be, is *punctiliously* observed, yet this is not *painfully* apparent.[43]

In essence, this position valued the persuasiveness of an illusion of naturalness; and any aesthetic based centrally on the notion of illusion offers, by definition, a basis for questions about the relation of appearance and reality.

My first reading proposed Papageno as a wholly natural man, and no doubt this is how the first audiences who flocked to the Theater auf der Wieden thought of him. What they first glimpsed, however, was a character presenting a type of song they knew especially well. No more a genuine *Volkslied* than an "aria" (as it is called in Mozart's score), it was, rather, a *volkstümliches Lied*, or native folk-*like* song, a type drawn not from people of "the land" but from the urban lower classes.[44] In fact, many in these first audiences would have perceived in Papageno not a literal inhabitant of nature but a mirror image of themselves. Almost certainly, Papageno seemed "natural" because this perception of the already known or familiar (*Bekannten*) was so immediate and effortless. To paraphrase Kant, although the resemblance of Papageno's song to its *volkstümliches* model was *punctiliously* observed, it was not *painfully* apparent.

To be sure, the identity of the class represented by Papageno is itself relevant to the impression of naturalness he produced from the start. The lower classes in Mozart's audience would have failed to identify themselves with the aristocratic conventions of Baroque opera; in addition, those fundamentally ornate conventions never made any attempt to conceal their artificial character, even in contexts where they explicitly referred to nature. The relatively simple, popular theatrical genres, such as *opera buffa* and *Singspiel*, from their inception marked a movement away from the explicit artificiality of aristocratic genres, such as *opera seria*, which presented a single, normative social voice. Long before an aesthetic of realism developed in the nineteenth century, the very emergence of popular operatic genres was inseparable from a new placing of aesthetic value on the natural in art.

But it is not simply the reference to popular conventions that accounts for the impression of naturalness in Papageno's song. Not just any street or tavern song would have made Papageno persuasively natural to his original audience; paradoxically, a song lifted from the actual popular repertory of the day would have strained the ready acceptance of Papageno, through the jarring contrast of its crudely simple musical style with the rest of the opera. It is the combination of Mozart's technical competence to represent a particular social language (and this capacity for representation is crucial to Bakhtin's definition of novelistic realism) with a language distant from socially accepted artistic conventions that allows Papageno's song its instant credibility. Expending unmistakably artistic technique on the medium of Papageno's self-presentation, Mozart simultaneously rendered that artistry transparent to the projection of Papageno as natural.

In short, the fact that Papageno's audience accepted his song so readily as one of their own was due less to its actual *bekannten* characteristics than to the *Schein*, or illusion, it created of typicality. Fashioning Papageno's song to his own structural and orchestral requirements, Mozart preserved a tension between Papageno's cultural voice and his own, conferring artistic dignity on Papageno's voice while still maintaining the position of that voice as a domain of contrast. This duality of voices, so central to Bakhtin's definition of the novel as a realistic genre, begins in *The Magic Flute* to point attention in the same direction as the novel would, beyond the traditional boundaries of art toward empirical reality.

This is not to say that this dualistic technique rendered *The Magic Flute* realistic in the same degree, or even the same sense, as a nineteenth-century novel. True, Papageno's song rejects the overt artificiality of Baroque references to nature; in semiotic terms, this song, unlike an extended Baroque *Affekt*, is not offered to the audience as an explicitly arbitrary *signifiant* (signifier) designating a conventionally preassigned *signifié* (signified). Through its artful simplicity this song casts off the opaque fictionality of the Baroque "sign" in favor of projecting, through its own transparency, an illusion of the natural.

Yet, however transparent the effect of this song, its images are always to be understood as mediated rather than immediate. However seamless the (seeming!) continuity between this particular song and *volkstümliche Lieder* in the real world, there has never been a question of mistaking this stylized song for a real rather than fictional object; it does not forget which side of the footlights it belongs on.[45] Nor does this song try to persuade us that its relation to nature is real rather than symbolic. On the contrary, it refrains from defining the physical domain of nature literally, refusing either to merge itself with a surrounding domain of physical sound or to act as if it *were* nature in some ono-matopoeic sense. Maintaining the clarity both of its outer frames and of its inner organization, this song projects itself as a self-contained object, existing in a realm equivalent or analogous to those of real experience and of nature, but nevertheless distinct from them. To use another analytical category of semiotic theory, the relation of Papageno's song to the real world, whether of society or of nature, is to be understood as primarily metaphorical, or symbolic, rather than as metonymical, or literal.[46]

In this respect (along with Tamino's Act II trials by fire and water), Papageno's song defines a different attitude toward both nature and reality than did nineteenth-century German opera music such as the Wolf-Glen scene in Weber's *Freischütz*, the "fire-music" in Wagner's *Walküre*, or arguably even the gravedigging melodrama in Beethoven's *Fidelio*.[47] Unlike Papageno's song, each of the latter scenes does center (somewhat like the Baroque *Affekt*) on one or more elements of nature as its content, or *signifié*. Moreover (in contrast to Baroque practice), each seems at the same time to evoke nature in a heavily literal sense, leaning on the immediacy of physical sensation in a way that breaks through the condition of structural self-containment, fusing (or collapsing) signifier and signified into a single musical embodiment, and requiring the reaction of a physically contiguous audience to complete its structurally fragmentary meaning.[48] Even the symbolic motives of Wagner's music dramas have something of this literal quality, producing as they do the repetitive and overlapping patterns that characterize (prose) language and thought in the everyday world.[49]

To the extent that it leaned toward the very condition of realism, nineteenth-century German opera engaged in a kind of dishonesty about art that in our own century has come repeatedly under fire. Roland Barthes, in Terry Eagleton's words, characterizes "the realist" (and, for that matter, even the "representational") sign as "unhealthy . . . [in that] it effaces its own status as a sign, in order to foster the illusion that we are perceiving reality without its intervention."[50] Adorno accused Wagner's operas in particular of trying to pass themselves off as natural rather than constructed objects; in his view, these operas produced "phantasmagoria," or magic-lantern effects, which in turn promoted "the concept of illusion as the absolute reality of the unreal."[51]

In fairness, such charges of dishonesty, at least in the case of nineteenth-century German opera, require qualification. For just as it became difficult, in the wake of Kant's critical philosophy, to deny the presence in art of a mediating intelligence, so, too, nineteenth-century German opera seems to have developed an increasing sensitivity to its own epistemological precariousness.

Indeed, the movement toward a literal, physical condition of meaning in German opera can be seen as a function of this very sensitivity: the more problematic the status of art in relation to reality became, the more art tried to get around the problem by moving toward reality.[52] This situation reached an early crisis in *Die Meistersinger*, an opera preoccupied with the theme of art. Here sensitivity to the incontrovertible artificiality of music, and hence to the futility of trying to justify the presence of music on stage as natural, has become so acute that Wagner seems willing to include music at all in the opera only insofar as it serves the self-consciously "orchestrated" and signifying purposes of realistic prose[53]—or restricts itself to the figurative domain of quotation marks. (Although *Die Meistersinger* presents a voluptuous flow of music, it *admits* to the presence of music only as "music.")

How distant these epistemological scruples seem from the breeziness with which Papageno launches into his opening song! And yet how inseparable is our response to Papageno's spontaneity from an underlying recognition—our inability to forget—that such a quality comes about only by contrivance. The presentation of Papageno as natural need not be taken at face value. It can also be read as evidence that Papageno's status as a natural man is mere *Schein*—appearance, semblance, illusion, pretense.[54]

By now it should be obvious that far from being natural, Papageno is a thoroughly cultural creature, not only in the sense that he issued from Mozart's imagination but also insofar as his music mirrored lower-class urban music. Nor was the perception of Papageno as natural from a socially more privileged standpoint any less problematic. Much of this latter perception stemmed from an association of Papageno with pastoral traditions; and it is difficult to imagine conventions more explicitly artificial than those of the pastoral.[55] Furthermore, the social interests of the aristocracy during the eighteenth century were so forcefully served by idealized pastoral evocations of nature that the motives behind such evocations, and hence the validity of characterizations based upon them, became open to question.

Whether in paintings, such as Watteau's *Embarkation for Cythera* (1717), or in actuality (one thinks of Marie Antoinette's capers at the Petit Trianon), visits by the eighteenth-century aristocracy to the landscape of the pastoral imagination were often a form of what today we would call slumming.[56] Far from reflecting an interest in the lives of simpler people, such pastoral references encouraged the aristocracy in attitudes of escape, in part from the rigidities of its own social conventions but also from the actuality of the lower classes. In effect, the sentimentalized character of these references provided license for social irresponsibility. In the same way, the aristocracy stood to benefit from an association of Papageno with the eternal aspect of pastoral time. For a focus on eternity makes no room for the living of actual lives, any more than it directs attention to the possibility (or, worse, the desirability) of change.

From our own standpoint, any late-eighteenth-century aristocratic attribution to Papageno of an idealized unity with nature carries an unavoidable moral taint. For that audience, such an attribution must primarily have signified neither a literal nor an idealized interpretation of Papageno himself but rather a means of reassuring itself that Papageno occupied the bottom of a social order that remained in place. What the aristocracy meant by a unity with nature was a relegation to nature, and thereby an exclusion from society. Sentimentalizing this unity with nature, the upper classes could keep the concrete social characteristics of Papageno at a distance while disguising their actual contempt for him. For this audience, after all, to call Papageno a natural was to call him a fool.[57] Mozart himself reveals this prejudice when he relates that to keep from calling a spectator at *The Magic Flute* an ass, "I called him a Papageno and cleared out."[58]

Papageno provided comfort both to the aristocracy, through his *exclusion* from society, and to his social peers, through the *inclusion* of a part of their own culture in an ambitious musico-dramatic work. Neither was prepared to acknowledge the enormous sacrifice entailed by Papageno's seemingly special relation to nature as a lower-class character. It entailed a forfeit of nearly every characteristic of solidity that would have made him credible as an actual man—from strength of character and maturity to a concrete social identity, history, and virtually every other gratification associated with participation in culture. It entailed a lack of power and any basis for respect. It entailed the sacrifice of any real life even by the fictional standards of the musical stage.

Over the course of the opera as a whole, Papageno is consistently presented as a character who is not to be taken seriously. Enslaved by bodily needs for food, drink, and sex that are invariably treated as a cause for laughter, Papageno renounces the challenges of trial and ambition and readily admits to cowardice. In terms of material possessions, Papageno has almost nothing of his own, even in his music. What belongs to Papageno musically, apart from his pipes, are the repeated notes and nonsense syllables ("hm hm hm" in the first-act Quintet, "Pa-pa-pa-pa" in the second Finale) that make him ridiculous. The rest of his music belongs to others. Sometimes it is given to him by the orchestra, as in his opening song, or in the Trio of Act I (see measures 48ff., "Schön Mädchen jung und fein"); sometimes by another character (for example, Pamina, in their Duet). At his most serious, in his attempted suicide in Act II, his style is a parody of Pamina's pathos in her own suicide attempt, just as Papageno's entire relationship to his magic glockenspiel seems a child-like parody of Tamino's to his flute.

Rather than rendering Papageno a plausible Everyman, this chameleon-like quality suggests that he is incapable of self-determination; other aspects of his music contribute to this impression as well. His formal modes of music are repetitive and strophic; his very first song, pretending to spontaneity, makes explicit reference to perhaps the most conventional, stereotyped, and artificial genre on which the opera draws. In fact, this song turns out to be virtually none of the things that it at first projected itself as being. Nor do these gaps confer on Papageno even the dignity of questioning whether he is sincere or insincere, since from the start we assume his childish incapacity for both.

Not one of the ideals proposed through Papageno's entrance song is believably his own; and neither here nor subsequently does he dare to have any serious dreams of his own. It is not surprising that a lock is placed on his mouth.[59] As anything more substantial than a figure of burlesque, Papageno has virtually no voice of his own. He is excluded, ultimately, from Sarastro's supposedly universal temple less because he proves unworthy than because, as Gertrude Stein might have put it, "there is no *there* there" to admit.

Ironically, it would seem that the most "natural" character in *The Magic Flute* is the one least real by the standards of modern realism. Although we can see how Mozart's first audience found Papageno believably "natural," we ourselves can believe in him only as explicitly make-believe, as a puppet. From the first, Papageno plays a role in other people's fantasies. He is idealized as a natural man—but only at the cost of forfeiting serious consideration as a participant in the human drama and its social dialogue. Is this what it means to be of the lower class?

Of the pre-Enlightened Russian peasant, Bakhtin writes: "Only by remaining in a closed environment, one without writing or thought, completely off the maps of socio-ideological becoming, could a man fail to sense [the] activity of selecting a language and rest assured in the inviolability of his own language, the conviction that his own language is predetermined."[60] The poet, who by Bakhtin's account, immerses his language in the river Lethe, can be imagined as aiming at a unitary language out of an informed sensibility to the structural difficulties and value of such an achievement.[61] The peasant, by contrast, achieves such uniformity out of ignorance, based on a lack of exposure to alternative cultural possibilities. Bakhtin continues:

> An illiterate peasant . . . lived in several languages: he prayed to God in one language . . . , sang songs in another, spoke to his family in a third, and when he began to dictate petitions to the local authorities through a scribe, he tried

speaking yet a fourth language. . . . All of these are *different languages*. . . . But these languages were not . . . coordinated in the linguistic consciousness of the peasant; he passed from one to the other without thinking, automatically: each was indisputable in its own place, and the place of each was indisputable. He was not yet able to regard one language . . . through the eyes of another language.[62]

This was the pre-Enlightened peasant, who had not yet formed a consciousness of the relativity of his own language or, hence, of the social possibilities from which he was still excluded. This is also Papageno, who can take on styles that suit the occasion and parody those with whom he found himself in ensemble without acquiring substance as a member of society.

Just as Bakhtin differentiated the peasant's ignorance from the poet's informed choice, so, too, Papageno's cultural impoverishment is not to be confused with the "refus[al of] the commonplaces that the culture treacherously provides for [one's] convenience and comfort" through which the artist, as described by Trilling, may approach authenticity.[63] Lacking concrete definition, Papageno does not possess the solidity that by modern standards, according to Trilling, makes the authentic person "as hard, dense, weighty, perdurable as any stone."[64]

Nor does any other character in the opera. Tamino has enough cultural specificity to make him a tentative model for subsequent German opera composers: his music removes him from the conventionalized domain of Italian opera; and, of course, he uses the vernacular, German, rather than the cosmopolitan language of the eighteenth century, French. Yet he too lacks the solidity we associate with authenticity. As Trilling says of Rousseau's "ideal of authentic personal being," its presence, "however forcible it may have seemed to [his] contemporaries, is rather too abstract, or too moderate, to command the modern imagination."[65] Tamino is no more at home in the concreteness of history than Papageno is.

Certainly the actual future does not belong to Tamino. Although it is true that the formal design of his music projects an ability to control time, this formal control is of a symbolic rather than actual kind. And though the ideals he espouses are more progressive than those of the Queen, the nature of their force, along with Tamino's own position, calls into question the relationship between "progress" and actual time.[66] For unlike Papageno, Tamino has a stake in preserving a timeless order of eternal values in which the contingencies and changes of empirical time do not intrude.

Can an individual who stands in every sense for abstract universal values, and avoids the concreteness of an explicitly cultural definition, be thought of as acting in self-interest? This question, which is coming to polarize American

society in the 1990s, has been asked of the Classical style (as of other Enlightenment legacies) for almost two centuries in one form or another: in words, by
critics such as Adorno; and in music, beginning with Beethoven's last style
and with Romanticism.

Within *The Magic Flute* one must concede that the consequences of lacking
concrete social characteristics are considerably different for Tamino than for
Papageno. For, as many in our own society now strenuously point out, a world
of abstract definition, however idealistically conceived, does not encourage
direct attention to concrete inequities in themselves.[67] Left to itself, such a
world will favor the perpetuation of an old order, where the prince can count
on being the designated hero, and the Moor can expect, like the bastard son in
King Lear, to be the villain—in such a world, status and value are not in practice readily disentangled. All characters in this world may in theory be equal
in worth; but a lower-class figure such as Papageno will in fact remain less
equal than others.[68]

Insofar as he stood to gain the most from an infusion of historical time, and
thereby the possibility of real change, into his world, Papageno was the character of the future in *The Magic Flute*. And in a way not yet discussed,
Papageno's opening song offers a glimmer of the strong and earthy presence
that the lower classes, in their social "differentness," may once have maintained in European culture, not within some idyllic Golden Age but through
the scatological Feast of Fools.[69] I refer here to an emphasis on the physicality
of sound, represented in particular by the use of wind instruments.

V

[*Die Zauberflöte*] introduced a new sound to opera . . . In the first act it [appears
at] the beginning of the finale with the trombones, muted trumpets, sustained
notes in the woodwinds, . . . the luminous voices of the trio of boys . . . and the
invisible choir. In the second act it [includes] . . . the muted slow march of the
wind instruments to Tamino's flute.[70]

By the late eighteenth century, wind instruments had established a long-standing
pastoral association with the "natural." By contrast, the instruments that were
considered the normal carriers of the "cultural" were the strings, especially the
violins.[71] For it was the strings that formed the core of the eighteenth-century
orchestra and were called upon most typically, in nontexted music, to demonstrate the distinctly human, cultural capacity to build rational structures.

As form in instrumental music became refined and sophisticated during the eighteenth century, the violins became in effect the musical signifiers of culture in its highest form, civilization. As such they came to be construed as the quintessentially human instruments, representing that victory of reason over nature through which the Frankfurt School, for example, defines "Enlightenment."[72] Supplanting the human voice itself (and with it the verbal text), the strings came to stand for the normatively human in music. Not tied to the particularity of any spoken language, the violins came to represent humanized sound as a more or less abstract phenomenon, universally intelligible through its thematic structuring or "narrative." The concrete physical existence of violin music, along with its specific cultural identity, could be perceived as less real than its abstract formal logic.

For this very reason, the normative status accorded the violins sharpened attentiveness to the presence of other instruments, especially the woodwinds and brass, but also at times the lower strings, if used coloristically, and through an ironic historical shift of function, the human voice. Precisely because they differed from the narrative-bearing strings, other instruments could readily be heard as sources of sound in all its concrete particularity. Relative to the violin and its family, everything else signified an identity somehow "other." In maintaining this otherness, such instruments could offer recalcitrant resistance to the dominance of abstract norms, refusing to subordinate the opaqueness of color to a transparent structural capacity. Their otherness demanded to be heard.[73] The metaphorical suggestiveness of these differences for social and cultural history is self-evident.

In Papageno's song, a tension is maintained between the strings and winds, and thereby between two sets of values. On the level of sheer physical impact, surely it is Papageno's pipes, along with their antiphonal companions, the oboes and French horns, that define the most striking instrumental presence in the *Vogelfänger* song. But the strings carry nearly all the musical material in the song, and in a way that is more explicitly thematic than coloristic.

The string-dominated sections of this song have a graceful formal coherence that approaches the ideal of beauty held in the late Enlightenment.[74] The wind interludes contribute not only charm (a quality Kant contemptuously distinguishes from beauty)[75] but also a concrete distinctiveness of character. These passages do not move the song out of the domain of beauty into what Dahlhaus characterizes as the realistic domains of "the 'descriptive' and the 'ugly,'"[76] or render the song earthy. Certainly the effect of these passages is not comparable to the "raucous effects in Kaspar's drinking song [number 4 in Weber's *Freischütz*]," in which "'the greatest realism is to be noted . . . where the two piccolos trill and squeal together.'"[77] Nor are they comparable even to the rasping flute and cello solos that, along with vocal effects of laughter, make Kilian's opening song in the same opera seem almost the documentary record of a specific rural culture.

Nevertheless, the winds in Papageno's song, and above all his pipes—the one element that is clearly his own—do provide a concreteness of presence that threatens to subvert the apparent argument of this song for measuring human worth solely in terms of abstract universals. Moreover, the use of these instruments in Papageno's song seems to confirm a suggestion first made in the overture, by some pointed contrasts between the violins and flutes (as at measures 58ff.), and also by the stark contrast between the civilized fugal theme of the violins and the literally solid, athematic, so-called Masonic chord, which in its most characteristic form excludes the strings entirely.[78] That is, the winds in Papageno's song confirm the importance of concrete sound to the entire opera.

At the beginning of this essay I postulated a homogeneous tone as one of two principal unifying elements in *The Magic Flute*. The source of this tone, as I am defining it, is the uncompromising importance this opera gives to timbre. Such a tone unifies the heterogeneous differently than a maxim does. A general principle can reduce all differences to a single case through the breadth of its abstraction. By contrast, a concrete tone can confer on diverse elements a common quality of emphasis that preserves the (irreducible) specificity of their differences.[79]

By placing an emphasis on the value of concrete physical sound, Mozart achieves an effect similar to what we today would call "defamiliarization": he jostles the listener out of an unthinking acceptance of the meanings ascribed to familiar formal principles, and calls attention to the work as a distinct material structure with its own physically actual identity, in which an important layer of meaning can be discerned.

Alfred Einstein finds the tone of this opera particularly concentrated in the two finales.[80] Actually, the entire opera is pervaded by a "new sound" of emphasis on color rather than construction. Wind instruments play an especially prominent role in producing this sound. One thinks, for example, of the clarinet in Tamino's aria and in the latter part of the first-act Quintet; of the basset horns (essentially alto clarinets) coupled with high winds, in the March of the Priests; of the basset horns, bassoons, and trombones—and the absence of violins—in Sarastro's first aria; and of the contrast of flute against low colors in his second. More conventional, but explicitly associated with an otherness through the physicality of its sound, is the "Turkish" piccolo of Monostatos's aria. Then there are those characteristic solo instruments that serve as palpable signifiers: Tamino's flute, Papageno's pipes, and—not a wind instrument but most extreme in its distance from the conventions of orchestra—his glockenspiel.

The stress on color in this opera in fact involves many sources of sound besides the winds, including the strings themselves at times, as in the Queen's first recitative and Larghetto. And some of the most distinctive sounds in the opera are vocal, including the Queen's florid soprano, Sarastro's emphatic bass, and especially the timbres of the Three Ladies and of the Three Boys.

This interpenetration of instrument and voice has potentially important social implications: the pervasive emphasis on diverse timbres, which cannot be imagined through generalization but must be experienced in their particularity, gives *The Magic Flute* a hint of connection to the here-and-now.[81] Although the collective effect of its sonorous tone has often been described as "unearthly," the concreteness of its variegated sound gives it a potentially earthbound significance as well, linking it not only to the physicality of nature but also to the actuality of the voices—all different, all human—that make up society.

VI

This reading is conceivable only retrospectively, from a vantage point familiar with the diversitarian and material values that began to unfold with the Romantic "principle of plenitude."[82] A connection between material color in music and the material conditions in society would not—could not—have been perceived in the eighteenth century. Almost certainly, the sound Mozart would have expected to emerge from the diverse social voices of *The Magic Flute* was not the concrete actuality of their differences—not their multivoiced social dialogue—but their common convergence on the universal voice of abstract reason.[83] In Bakhtin's terms, Mozart himself almost certainly understood the voice of *The Magic Flute* as the unitary normative voice of poetry, not as the polyglot babble of novelistic prose. And while it seems plausible that Mozart would have acknowledged the homogeneous presence of an emphasis on concrete sound in *The Magic Flute*, we cannot suppose that he would have recognized its metaphorical support for ideals of social inclusiveness.

We cannot, for that matter, assume even that Mozart would have sympathized with such ideals. Mozart showed himself ready to reject the circumstances of birth as a measure of human worth. But it is difficult to imagine the composer of this opera in particular embracing an all-inclusive ideal of human worth based on the (mere) fact of concrete existence, without a qualifying test of merit by some plausibly abstract standard (essentially, reason).

For *The Magic Flute* is an opera in which structures idealized or even consecrated as universal remain selective and exclusionary to the end.[84] Such structures are symbolized most tellingly in the end by Sarastro's temple. Scholars have often pointed to a quasi-religious (unearthly!) character in *The Magic Flute*; Paul Henry Lang even insisted that this work was really Mozart's last mass.[85] But if this opera seems structured to embody a Catholic notion of universality—including all, but with vast hierarchical distinctions—in actuality it projects a vision of equality that does not extend beyond the limits of an elite Elect. In this sense it seems less a Catholic mass than a sacred work in the Protestant spirit.[86]

Paradoxically, moreover, *The Magic Flute*, an opera that puts particular emphasis on vocal sonorities, seems not to depend on the word in the same fundamental way as Weber's operas, and especially Wagner's operas, later would. As music in the nineteenth century moved closer to the physically and culturally specific condition of prose, the very concept of opera was altered, in the direction of greater realism, to incorporate the epistemological functions of words into music itself.[87] By contrast, almost everything *The Magic Flute* wants us to know about its characters, as the analysis in my first reading should indicate, is conveyed through music alone, without dependence on the concreteness (or multivoiced specificity) of verbal conceptions.[88]

This is true of the characters who exist in a pure sound realm: Does anyone really care what the Three Ladies or the Three Boys are saying? And it is equally true of the characters who define themselves through form. Tamino shows very little need to explain his situation through words; his aria shows his ability to control his time and destiny through purely musical means that work equally well in a Classical sonata movement. Such crossing over into the genres of instrumental music is evident everywhere, but perhaps most palpably in the opening of the Queen's first aria, which evokes two beautiful passages in the second movements from two of Mozart's last symphonies (see Example 2).[89] Maybe Mozart's last opera is "really" his last symphony!

Significantly, however, the movements I have just cited are *slow* movements. Slow movements by tradition call attention not so much to the abstract, conceptual structures of reason characteristically evinced in symphonic first movements as to contingent conditions of physical sensuousness—conditions we today find increasingly difficult to exclude from conceptions of humanity and selfhood. Second movements suggest "otherness" in a sense specifically exemplified here by the link with the Queen's first aria: in contrast to the dominating, traditionally masculine character of opening movements, they seem more pliable, more traditionally feminine. In all these respects, the second movements of Classical symphonies had more in common than first movements did with the musical Romanticism of the nineteenth century. And it is especially important to note that, at least before Beethoven, second movements traditionally had the closest link in the symphony to vocal genres such as the hymn or aria—that is, to forms of music that contained words.

It may sound odd to suggest that *The Magic Flute*, an opera, was pointing indirectly, by way of symphonic second movements, toward a need to make words explicit in music. And yet I think something akin to this dynamic is integral to our impression of *The Magic Flute*. High Classicism denied a need to "make the words explicit" in music; Romanticism, which tended toward musical prose, recognized such a need. In its emphasis on the sensuousness of sound, *The Magic Flute* may locate a door between these two worlds.

The effect of granting concrete sound a constituent role in musical construction is to increase sensitivity to the inescapable actuality, and therefore significance, of the diverse actual sounds—and words—that may be competing for admission into the musical structures now called high art. Like Wagner, we already sense something of the kind in the straining of Beethoven's symphonies toward words.[90] Romantic music, in its focus on sound and word, confirms many ways in which the formerly "closed" world of the Classical symphony would be opened up to contact with a real social environment.

Mozart himself is not yet a Romantic. Yet his inability to resist characterizing his universal ideals through the irreducible physicality of sound may be the weak point, so to speak, in his insulated musical universe of reason. The use of the sensuous clarinet in the *Bildnis* aria suggests the vulnerability to physical sound of even Tamino's world. And it is Tamino who is given the seemingly ultimate wind instrument, the magic flute.

In allowing the magic flute to function as the very title of his opera, Mozart almost certainly did not mean to impute to wind sonority the sort of interpretation proposed here. If anything, he probably intended the opposite: to symbolize in his title that the physicality of sound is finally governed by abstract reason. To be sure, in granting importance to a distinctive timbre, the title does indirectly indicate a domain beyond Tamino's musical universe: the real world to which art would open up in the nineteenth century.

Still, Tamino was no more able than Mozart himself to cross into the promised land that could be glimpsed from *The Magic Flute*. In fact, by the nineteenth century, this character and his magic instrument were perceived as clearly limited in their powers. Kierkegaard in particular was very hard on Tamino's use of the flute, finding it

> exceedingly tiresome and sentimental . . . one cannot help but think, every time [Tamino] takes up his flute and begins to play on it, of the farmer in Horace . . . , except that Horace did not give his farmer a flute for an unprofitable pastime.[91]

Referring to his conception of Tamino as abstract or theoretical, Kierkegaard goes on to assert that "Tamino . . . is entirely outside of the [realm of the] musical, just as the intellectual development [*The Magic Flute*] would realize is, on the whole, a totally unmusical idea"; indeed, "Tamino has really come so far that the musical ceases; therefore his flute-playing is only a time-killer, brought in to drive away thought."[92]

Kierkegaard explicitly sees the theoretical tendency of Tamino's flute as symbolic of the whole opera. "The fault in *The Magic Flute*," he concludes, "is . . . that the whole opera tends toward consciousness."[93] By "consciousness" Kierkegaard here means language, in its ability to conceptualize an ethical principle. But as he notes earlier in the same essay, between Mozart's time and Kierkegaard's own (his essay was published in 1843), a very different notion of consciousness had already emerged in European thought. Kierkegaard identifies this new notion with Hegel's concept of consciousness as a principle that defines itself through history.[94]

This new consciousness, perceptible in nineteenth-century music as well as prose, was essentially a modern consciousness: it became attentive to the polyphony of languages spoken, and lives lived, beyond Sarastro's hallowed halls. However great an ethical advance was marked by the triumph of reason over the bleak assumptions of the *ancien régime*, this new consciousness would have trouble honoring a strictly abstract conception of reason to the point of treating the physical and social conditions of life as unreal. It would question how an ideal could guarantee human value if it made no provision for the actuality of life; and it would attach importance to qualities of solidity through which even a Papageno might hope to attain authentic being in a changed world. It would begin to read the maxim "Social rank does not equal human worth" in an essentially modern way.

It is hardly surprising that Tamino's flute stops short of driving a chink into the abstract world idealized in *The Magic Flute. That* role is reserved for another instrument, which Kierkegaard loved without reservation, and which he came close to characterizing as truly magical, observing that "every ear has certainly felt itself moved in a strange manner by [it]."[95] The instrument in question—first heard almost immediately after Tamino asks "Wo bin ich?" (Where am I?)—is, of course, Papageno's pipes.

Ultimately, it is this unpretentious, earthy instrument that jars the illusion of a self-contained, harmonious universe in *The Magic Flute*. It is Papageno's humble pipes that delimit the claims of Mozart's mighty opera to be understood only within the terms on which it presents itself. It is Papageno's pipes that establish a basis *within the opera* for criticizing *The Magic Flute*'s reading of itself as a corroboration of Enlightenment values. Further, Papageno's pipes expose Mozart's composition itself, like the symbolical realm of the opera's story, as something other than an autonomous world that contains all the keys needed to unlock its own single meaning. They open a perspective from which a counterreading of *The Magic Flute* becomes not just possible but plausible. Sensitizing us to a tone of sensuously opaque sonority, the pipes point us toward a human world far more irreducibly diverse than Tamino's.

At the same time, the pipes alert us to the risks associated with this expanded worldview. For unlike an abstract general principle that lends itself to rational analysis, concreteness, whether physical or cultural, does have an aspect of irreducible contingency, even when it is used as a unifying principle. Hence, a world bound by a concrete tone may by definition elude control through demonstrably rational principles. In a world where solid actuality of being is a sufficient ground for inclusion, the danger arises of a radical relativism, in which all general standards for determining validity are lost. Such a world, in other words, is beset by precisely the sorts of contradictory claims that vex our own society today.

That I can see my own society reflected in *The Magic Flute* no less clearly (though less directly) than Papageno's audience saw theirs is in large part a measure of the epistemological limits that we share. *The Magic Flute* turns out, after all, to be a "text," in the poststructuralist sense, open to readings that inevitably tell us more about the reader than the work.

Nevertheless, the work remains remarkable for the firmness of the basis it offers, through a successful second unifying device, for its reading as part of the historical continuum that followed it. That Papageno's pipes constitute a point of deconstruction does not in itself distinguish this opera; every text offers inadvertent weak points in its own favored self-reading. It is the extraordinary consistency with which the opera articulates its material conception of musical sound, as well as its symbolic conception thereof, that distinguishes *The Magic Flute*. The tone of *The Magic Flute*, suggesting interrelated images and ideas that "make sense" when referred back to the particulars of the score and libretto, continues to provide unity for readings from positions well outside any scope it could initially have envisioned.[96]

Mozart's *Magic Flute* became ours once it went out into the world—a world that would soon be beyond the control even of Mozart's genius. In the end, Papageno's pipes define a watershed through musical means. They mark the point of entry by which a gathering storm of conflicting social voices would explode the self-contained musical world idealized by Classicism—even the verbal symphonic world that, in *The Magic Flute*, we still find miraculously held together, for one last time.

2

How Could Chopin's A-Major Prelude Be Deconstructed?

For Willis Regier, whose encouragement at New Orleans kept this alive.

During the fall of 1986, when I was teaching a course on music and deconstruction at the City University of New York Graduate Center, I had the opportunity of talking briefly with Jacques Derrida, the acknowledged "originator" of this movement (Derrida's own work requires the quotation marks). I mentioned that I had become engaged in an attempt to apply deconstruction to music. Derrida took this to mean that I was trying to deconstruct some musicological texts. When I told him that the text in question was actually a prelude by Chopin, he expressed surprise at the idea of applying deconstruction directly to music, and said he would be interested to see what resulted.

Derrida's surprise, at least at that time, was itself not altogether surprising. True, a few scholars associated with the poststructuralist movement, in which deconstruction took shape, had begun to make reference to music: Foucault had explicitly suggested music as a potential field for theoretical investigation;[1] Roland Barthes had written essays on music that would come to generate considerable excitement in some circles of semiotic study.[2] Both Derrida and Barthes had, of course, already directed their attention to aesthetic problems in the visual arts.[3] And I myself already had a sense at that time that some of my colleagues in American musicology shared my own growing interest in movements related to deconstruction—an interest that became evident in the structure and content of the annual meeting of the American Musicological Society in New Orleans during October 1987.

On the other hand, up to then nearly all deconstructionist criticism, even when applied to nonverbal mediums, had been thoroughly and inextricably concerned with problems of verbal language. There was good reason for this.

The entire movement of poststructuralism had developed in large part out of structuralism, a movement that in turn could be identified as an outgrowth of twentieth-century linguistics. And for most of those concerned with deconstruction, one of the central problems of critical theory was to understand the role played by verbally articulated thought in shaping the perception of any text or artifact.

Given these close links with language theory, deconstruction seemed bound to have offered itself most readily as a strategy for analyzing verbal texts. Indeed, throughout the period when they were most in fashion, the majority of essays in deconstructionist criticism were focused on such texts. Even now, well into the 1990s, whatever effect deconstruction has had on American musicology has been far less sweeping and direct than the enormous impact this school has had on American literary study during the past two decades or so.

Yet even in the latter 1980s, the obvious appeal of verbal texts for a verbally oriented critical theory did not discourage my own interest, as a musicologist, in deconstruction. Then as now, after all, virtually all critical theories depended fundamentally on verbal modes of interpreting the world. If we were to allow the comparative inconveniences posed by nonverbal mediums to restrict the scope of critical theory, we would renounce the possibility of subjecting those mediums to critical reflection. In effect, this would signify our willingness to treat all nonverbal artifacts—from hit tunes to Castro's beard[4]—as if they were immutable facts of nature rather than contingent constructs. The need to avoid such uncritical acceptance (which had been for decades the attitude of most American musicology) struck me as incentive enough to explore what value the ideas involved in deconstruction could have for the study of music.

This was not, I admit, my only incentive for undertaking the work that led to this essay. One of my strongest motivations was a simple desire to see for myself what all the fuss over deconstruction was about in American departments of literature. I was curious—still sometimes the best reason for pursuing a line of inquiry.

In addition, I was not at all sure that the technical difficulties of applying deconstruction to a nonverbal medium would turn out to be hopelessly formidable. Knowing, for example, that a school of architecture had in recent years coalesced around principles of deconstruction helped sustain my optimism that the dynamics of deconstruction could be directly employed, with useful results, within the medium of music. I realized, however, that it would be wise to acknowledge at the outset the possibility that differences between verbal and nonverbal mediums might pose theoretical problems for an attempt to deconstruct music. This I hereby do.

Yet I think it important to note that, as I worked on this essay, I came to find the theoretical importance of such differences overrated in relation to certain fundamental, though not always obvious, semiotic similarities. Unfortunately, I do not have the space (or time) to explore this impression in any explicitness or detail. Originally I had hoped in the course of this introduction to focus on such similarities as the ability of both mediums to present the ideals of a given culture as themes of a particular text. As the essay expanded, however, I reluctantly abandoned the project of including here an analysis of this theoretical issue, as well as several others that will be identified below.

Thus except on occasion, and for the most part elliptically, I shall not make any effort in this essay to identify and confront differences between verbal language and music, or to propose any theoretical framework for understanding the relationship between the two mediums. Beyond its assumption of certain general positions concerning semiotics, and any persuasiveness it may have as an example of applying deconstruction to music, this essay will make no argument for the theoretical validity of deconstructing music.[5]

My original purpose here was to give both musicologists and scholars in other disciplines a concrete demonstration of how a musical deconstruction might work. Although my concerns have expanded considerably since I started out to write this essay, this original purpose has remained central to my enterprise. In order to maintain the pragmatic aspect of this purpose, I have chosen to restrict my discussion here in a number of ways, which should be mentioned at the start.

First, I have in no way attempted to provide a full account here either of any particular deconstructionist's work or of the deconstructionist movement on the more general level that would include its history, theory, and methods as well as a documentation of its by now very extensive literature. Nor will I say much about the relation between deconstruction and the even larger movement of poststructuralism beyond noting here that the former can be thought of as offering one particular methodological approach to more general epistemological positions worked out by the latter. What I wish to present here is mainly such background material on deconstruction as would allow musicologists who are relatively unfamiliar with the movement to follow my analysis of Chopin's prelude on a need-to-know basis—and to take steps to follow it up where there is a want-to-know as well. Thus, I will not cite all of the sources I have read, and often wrestled with, in order to prepare this article;

rather, such citations will be made only to the extent that they have a direct bearing on this discussion as it develops.

No doubt this will, to some extent, turn out to be a thankless strategy. For those who know little about deconstruction, what I can provide within this restricted framework will certainly be too scarce. For those, either in musicology or in other disciplines, who may be curious about a specifically musical deconstruction but who are already at home with the theory of the movement, the information included here will undoubtedly also seem too scarce. Fortunately, for those in the first group, a large introductory literature already exists. For those in the second group I can hope only that the value of this essay as an argument compensates for its bibliographical limitations.

After initial presentations—to my class at CUNY Graduate Center and to an interview committee at Columbia—this essay was given its first large-scale public airing (in a much shorter version) at a more or less interdisciplinary session of the 1987 American Musicological Society convention in New Orleans. On the flight home from that convention I learned, quite by chance, that some of the audience considered the references to literary theories at sessions such as mine to be patronizing. These listeners seemed to have decided (or perhaps they assumed) that the primary purpose of the people giving interdisciplinary papers had been to establish the superiority of their own knowledge of literary theory to that of their audience.

Given the risks still attendant at that time on interdisciplinary excursions, I doubt that such a motivation played much of a role in New Orleans. Even now, several years later, when musicology has become incomparably more advanced in its theoretical sophistication, I feel confident that most of us in the field believe we still have something more to learn about literary theory, especially about theories that predate postmodernism. It is my impression that the great burst of theoretical energy that has occurred in our field has for the most part involved only a limited effort to go back and master movements missed the first time round, such as poststructuralism, structuralism, and Marxism. (Phenomenology seems to have fared a bit better.)

But even if most of us were already long since initiated into the mysteries of deconstruction, I would want to ask this: Is the value of a literary theory exhausted as soon as many scholars have familiarized themselves with its basic terminology? Comparative literature used to be frequently chastised for the seemingly frenzied faddishness with which it followed up one "ism" with another. "Comp lit" itself seems to be out of fashion these days, but today's information explosion exerts an escalating pressure on all of us to absorb one theoretical formulation after another. Is such speed compatible with mastery or, if that is now suspect, even competence? In our era of hypertext, occasional efforts to follow through on the promise of yesterday's theories might have a welcome steadying effect.

At any rate, I have acknowledged that my presentation here of deconstruction is in no sense definitive. I hope that my motivation for trying to keep this presentation limited and clear will not be misconstrued [!][6] By restricting the scope of this discussion I have hoped to increase my chances of drawing others into a cooperative expansion of this interdisciplinary enterprise. But these restrictions denote no underestimation on my part of either the intelligence or the knowledge of other scholars. If anything those restrictions reflect my own need, as someone who is still a newcomer to deconstruction, to proceed slowly and carefully in my efforts to understand well at least some portion of the issues raised by this movement. And I suppose my willingness to observe such restrictions reflects also a personal conviction that no thoughtful exploration of a critical method ever wholly (or merely) duplicates work that has gone before.

In addition to those already mentioned, I have placed several other restrictions on this undertaking. Besides renouncing any attempt at a systematic exposition of deconstruction, this essay will refrain from applying any systematic evaluations to this movement. It will not, for example, assess the usefulness of deconstruction in relation to other critical methods. Though, again, I had originally hoped to provide here a systematic comparison between deconstructionist criticism and Theodor Adorno's criticism, as I once did between the criticism of Adorno and Claude Lévi-Strauss, it soon became apparent that such a project would require at the very least an extended article of its own.[7] Apart from focusing in this introduction on a few points of comparison between the two that seem useful to me, I will simply suggest, as I did in the case of language and music, that Adorno and deconstruction have a good deal more in common than superficial differences between the two might initially suggest.

Furthermore, I have made no effort here to assess the internal strengths and weaknesses of deconstruction, or to single out those elements that in my judgment distinguish good deconstructionist criticism from bad. On the surface it might seem that deconstructionist theory discourages this particular sort of value judgment in any case. But even if that were so we would not be obliged, in my judgment, to accept uncritically the self-presentation offered by deconstruction any more than (as deconstruction itself would agree) we are morally limited to understanding Chopin's A-Major Prelude at what might be called "face value."[8] The importance of trying to understand an argument or style on something close to its own chosen terms need not be diminished by the recognition of other claims on interpretation as well.

Here, of course, I am already rehearsing a central issue not only of the musical analysis that follows but also of deconstruction (and poststructuralism more generally) itself. What my musical analysis does, as I can now see in hindsight, is to argue that the terms on which Chopin's prelude presents itself consist at bottom in the very urgency and privilege this work attaches to self-chosen terms as a basis for interpretation. Not only in its high degree of individualization but also in its inability to establish the possibility of meaningfulness except through the persuasiveness of that individualization, the prelude seems ultimately to argue that its very meaning is this: that it should be understood wholly and only on its own specified terms. In brief the prelude turns the claims of self-presentation into its own theme, which my analysis assesses, as it might any literary theme (such as "All men are created equal"), for its power to control the readings we may honestly make of the prelude.

This interpretation raises a line of argument that I have pursued in other writings but draw on only implicitly in the present essay. To establish the kind of meaning it wants to establish—which involves the very possibility of establishing a secure meaning—the prelude must persuade us of its status as a "necessary" structure. It exists, and has a right to exist, it tells us, not simply because it is unique but because it must be precisely as it is.[9] There is a sleight of hand visible here: from the proposed necessity of its internal connections, the prelude extrapolates the necessity of its own existence. In effect, the prelude takes advantage of the fact that the content of its theme concerns a structural condition. It turns the content of its theme into an occasion for demonstrating its own structural substantiality, which then serves to validate that content.

The usefulness of these suggestions will, I hope, become more apparent in later sections of this essay, especially when I take up the question of the prelude as a metaphor for human life. What should already be evident, however, is that I am speaking here of a very special kind of theme. For this theme is not only self-referential; it is exponentially so. (Again, one begins here to glimpse the dark image of "infinite regress" that will shadow much of the following discussion, as it does much deconstructionist writing.) This kind of theme is particularly vulnerable to a mode of criticism that asserts, in the words of Jonathan Culler, that "under exegetical pressure, self-reference demonstrates the impossibility of self-possession."[10]

It seems to have become fashionable in recent years to argue that a given poem or painting is really "about" itself, that is, "about" its own underlying structural problems.[11] Whether or not all styles lend themselves equally well to such treatment, I cannot say. But Romantic music does seem, in my judgment, to gravitate rather forcefully toward the imagery that can be associated with a self-referential theme; and thus it may offer a particularly rich field for deconstructionist investigation. It could in fact be argued that in pointing toward a theme so central to deconstructionist epistemology, Romantic music provides an explicit basis for its own deconstruction.[12] My own impression is that the frequency with which the imagery of post-Enlightenment music accommodates the paradoxes of deconstruction enhances the attractiveness of the latter as a critical method.

Having now forced this whole issue of self-conception and evaluation upon the reader in a regrettably abbreviated way (and without having provided evidence that deconstruction discourages value judgments of its own literature), I reiterate that I have avoided systematizing standards here for the evaluation of deconstructionist criticism. Without question some opinions as to this matter will from time to time, by implication or example, emerge in this essay; some already have. Nevertheless, I have always believed that my first obligation, when confronting a new way of thinking, is to see where a good-faith effort at understanding that kind of thought might lead me. Much as I may doubt the possibility of understanding any argument completely on its own terms—from the inside, as it were—I do still believe that the appropriate time for crystallizing objections to a critical theory comes after, not before, the effort at such understanding has been made. (Admittedly this is a complex and fragile observation, with implications to which I shall return repeatedly in this introduction.)

This essay, it should be said, makes no claim to lay out a doctrinally pure deconstruction. Attempts to apply the critical methods of any school in a rigidly orthodox manner almost invariably result in mechanical exercises that offer little insight into the fundamental questions that brought the school into existence. Deconstructionist analyses are often accused of being derivative; the charge may in many cases be accurate, since the well-defined themes and techniques of deconstruction do offer a strong temptation for mechanical replication. Nevertheless, the fiercely self-conscious resistance of deconstructionist theory to entrapment within any fixed doctrinal position, however futile such resistance may ultimately be, should discourage unreflective imitation as a strategy that is particularly inappropriate, on many levels, to working with deconstructionist methods.

Perhaps the greatest restriction I have placed on the following essay lies in its limited degree of attention to many of the multifaceted issues raised by exposure to the deconstructionist movement. Principal among these are the relations of deconstruction to politics and to history. The latter relationship in particular seems to me so important, and so prone to misconception, that I shall return to it several times, from several angles, in this and the following section. But I do not pretend to examine either of these relationships in a comprehensive or systematic fashion.

I have in this essay bypassed considering the degree to which deconstructionist criticism may be directed at a text in ways that reflect or even serve the critic's political convictions. That deconstruction can operate from a very deep sense of political engagement is obvious even in its tendency to equate the metaphysical convictions it distills from a text with "ideology." In terms of Michel Foucault's concept of discourse as a self-validating language system—a system that confirms the account of reality given by those who use it— "deconstructing" the language of those with power in society is obviously a political act. On the other hand, literary theorists have often criticized American deconstruction, as opposed to its French counterpart, for taking an ostensibly apolitical stance that results in the irresponsible reduction of literature to an argument for nihilism.

Within musicology, which for years denied "legitimate" scholarship any political parameter, such apoliticism may still be counted a virtue by many;[13] though ironically, some of the latter might be among the first to decry those versions of deconstruction that seem to consist in a kind of esoteric and effete game-playing for nonexistent stakes. I share the distaste for such game-playing, and would not claim an apolitical status for deconstruction or any other scholarship, including my own. Nevertheless, this essay will avoid explicit political issues.

Deconstruction, as will be shown in the following sections, characteristically works by defining and analyzing dialectical contradictions in a text. The textual contradictions that I will analyze here through deconstruction will not be used as a means of criticizing Chopin as the representative of any sociopolitical viewpoint. In this sense, clearly, my essay will differ sharply from the kind of cultural critique offered by Adorno, who also worked by way of analyzing dialectical contradictions in a text. From Adorno's perspective, structural contradictions in a composition represent artistic limitations that are inseparable from defects in the particular artist's political situation—and more often than not in the artist's political philosophy as well.[14] Deconstruction (especially European deconstruction) by no means disallows the possibility of using its methods to criticize the relation of art and politics in a specific historical context. But neither does it make itself unavailable for use *except* in terms of such criticism. Whereas it would be difficult to use Adorno's model of analysis for totally apolitical inquiries, even on a heuristic level, it has seemed possible to me, working in good faith, to draw upon the theory and methods of deconstruction in ways that are not, or at least not always, overtly political.

A good deal of the difference just cited between Adorno and deconstruction in fact centers on differences in attitude toward history. Whereas for Adorno (to put it crudely) reality is inextricable from history, deconstruction—like poststructuralism more generally and like structuralism before it—is regularly accused of being ahistorical.

Now there are, without question, a good many scholars who would charge poststructuralist *and* dialectical schools with distorting history. One important cause of such objections involves the relative lack of interest of both schools in certain kinds of individual specificities.

Such a characterization may seem odd in connection with Adorno's writing, the very soul of which cries out for individual integrity and freedom. Yet the personal as such held very little interest for Adorno—assuming that Adorno could even grant the possibility of distilling a stratum of the purely personal from a composer's biography. In actuality Adorno argued explicitly that essentially everything in a human being's personal experience is to be understood in terms of the social dynamics that have shaped it.[15]

It is well known, of course, that one simply does not turn to Adorno's studies to determine what one of my more positivistic students once called "the forty most important facts" about the lives of Wagner or Mahler. From the available data of composer's lives, Adorno attended only to those he considered to have some pressing social significance. If Adorno, like the ancient scholar Hillel, had been asked to sum up his philosophy while standing on one foot, he could have done worse than to quote this sentence from Martin Jay: "The good society [is] one in which man [is] free to act as a subject rather than be acted upon as a contingent predicate."[16] From Adorno's standpoint—and it goes without saying that I simplify here—the value of individuality, while self-evident, was unthinkable apart from the (moral) universality inherent in Kant's categorical imperative. Thus, on the one hand, individual freedom had value for Adorno only insofar as it was exercised with a degree of responsibility that made unmistakable the claim of all individuals to such a state. On the other hand, the defense of individual freedom rang hollow unless mounted as part of an attempt to change the social conditions that deprive most people of any real, meaningful freedom. In brief, what mattered to Adorno was the autonomous subject, a universal ideal, not the contingent individual as such.

For similar reasons, Adorno valued knowledge about the original performing conditions of past music only for the insight it could offer into the social pressures on composition, not for its indispensability to modern reproductions of earlier sounds in all their particularity.[17] That such reproductions might preserve, in some literal, quantifiable sense, the particulars of a composer's experience counted for nothing with Adorno, who took it for granted that whatever humane values an original configuration might once have articulated were in actuality bound to be neutralized by the interaction of an original medium with a later environment of physical conditions and cultural assumptions. Indeed, such values could be understood as compromised at the very instant of their physical articulation, through the very act of submission to a culturally determined medium.

This is because, from Adorno's standpoint, the external mediums of reproduction are too vulnerable to the contingencies of whatever social priorities may currently be in effect to advance any genuine values of individuality. For Adorno, only the structural relations of music have the capacity to define, or at least advance, the resistance to conformity to the social status quo that amounts to a meaningful condition of individual freedom. In effect Adorno postulates that using the specific materials that happen to be available in a culture, the composer shapes structural relationships that have a greater or lesser chance of pointing beyond the cultural immediacy of their embodying language toward the establishment of a moral society—a society that guarantees the universal right to individual autonomy.

Obviously, then, a composer's *structural* decisions, if made with sufficient rigor, have tremendous potential value for Adorno in all their specificity. In this respect, Adorno might conceivably have championed modern, "scientifically" rendered, critical editions of past music as the best available means of protecting a composer's structure against the unavoidable ravages of social corruption.

But, from Adorno's perspective, historical change in itself was not necessarily, at least in ideal terms, a corrupting force. True, history in practice seemed to him inextricable from social manipulation—inextricable to the point where the elimination of the latter could be imagined, within the context of Adorno's theory, as marking the end of history in an optimistic as well as a pessimistic sense. Thus, on the one hand, the end of history seemed likely, from his perspective, to occur through an increase of social corruption until it reached an apocalyptic point of annihilation; indeed, to a great extent for Adorno history had already ended in this way through the Holocaust. Yet on the other hand, Adorno's theory could also envision an end of history, with all its entrenchment in corruption, through its own *Aufhebung*, in the sense of transcendence rather than of annihilation, into utopia. (The word *Aufheben* is a prime candidate for deconstruction.)[18] From Adorno's standpoint, the rigorous structural integrity of art pointed as well as anything could to such a condition of utopia.[19]

What is important to note is that however inseparable it seemed in practice from social manipulation and corruption, history could also be imagined, from Adorno's perspective, as defining a capacity for social improvement. Indeed, from any morally responsible viewpoint, it had to be so imagined, for it offered the only framework Adorno found plausible for pursuing such improvement, that is, the only alternative to the death, in one way or another, of humane values. One could put it, perhaps, that history was the only exit Adorno could in honesty propose out of the existentialist dilemma.

This positive aspect of history had direct consequences for Adorno's music theory. If social conditions could improve, and an altered physical rendition of a past compositional structure could be drawn from a new and healthier set of performing conditions, such an altered version might conceivably represent a humane advance over an original rendition. Or, failing that remote possibility, a new rendition—by compensating for the trade-offs in humane values through which succeeding cultures alter modes of perception, and thereby maintaining cultural access to the structural integrity of a work—might at least preserve a rough continuity in the ability of the work to project humane values.

What should be clear, at any rate, is that this point of view precluded Adorno from equating historical value with antiquarian purity. From this point of view, on the contrary, antiquarian preservation vitiates the value offered by history, and is thus intrinsically antihistorical. Thus a scientific critical edition is not to be valued beyond its ability to preserve a vision of structural integrity. Certainly it is not to be valued for its ability to preserve, much less to elevate into a state of absolute inviolability, the contingencies of every decision made by a contingently existing individual.

This analysis may help clarify why traditions committed to antiquarian values (such as positivist musicology) have the impression that Adorno's work distorts history. Depending on one's own point of view, however, this analysis need not validate that impression.

The uninterest of deconstruction in particularities of individual biography may be a bit easier to summarize in ways that are understandable from a traditional American perspective. Deconstruction, like structuralism as well as poststructuralism more generally, is in some respects more concerned with the systematic than with the historical dynamics of signification. Like structuralism, deconstruction has removed the individual (including the author) from a central role in the semiotic domain that it takes to be its own principal field of study.

Unlike Adorno, deconstruction assigns no particular parameter of semiotic structures, even structure itself, to the province of individual choice and responsibility. While granting that individuals use languages in an open-ended variety of ways, deconstruction is preoccupied with the principles that link individual usages in processes of social interaction.

Thus, ultimately like Adorno, though in ways that tend to seem significantly different, deconstruction is concerned with language as a social phenomenon. Its primary interest is in elucidating the dynamics at work in discourse. As a result, the deconstructionist enterprise, like Adorno's, offers us at least a possible perspective for viewing its scholarship as a contribution to the criticism and improvement of society.

One could, I grant, argue that deconstruction points toward an ultimate condition of systematic human limitations that nothing could alter. But before we accept such an argument in its entirety, the degree to which deconstruction projects its own orientation as distinctly social, rather than as simply, abstractly, or (in Kant's sense) aesthetically structural should give us pause. Yes, deconstruction makes itself available to those who would isolate the patterns it discerns from social reality. In this respect it may seem to converge, for instance, on the New Criticism. Nevertheless—and I recognize that I am treading here on delicate methodological ground that could collapse at any moment into self-deconstruction—using deconstruction in this way seems, in my judgment, to distort the method, or at least to underutilize it without compelling justification. For such a usage requires a conscious violation of the concrete kinds of awareness that the social focus of deconstruction makes available. Even if deconstructionist theory could, at bottom, license us to abandon all hope of changing the conditions of society, its social orientation could still provide a basis for encouraging us to try to do so.

The conflicting thrusts to which I point here in fact bear a strong resemblance to the existentialist sort of dilemma that apparently confronted Adorno's notion of history and, for that matter, a good deal of nineteenth-century music, including Chopin's A-Major Prelude (as I hope to show). In none of these instances as I read them, however, is it necessary to discern an unqualified submission to the premises and implications of nihilism.

In an earlier essay, I once argued that Adorno's vision of nineteenth-century music constitutes a kind of historical structure, which Adorno put forward as primarily historical in character, but which can be also be interpreted as primarily structural (rather than historical) in its significance.[20] As I have come to see, I developed this argument by subjecting Adorno's texts to a de-constructionist sort of analysis.[21]

In a similar sense, one could argue that the interpretive structures developed by various French schools of criticism have a concrete social character that is not to be dismissed as wholly secondary. These schools would include decon-struction, though the latter would no doubt prefer to see itself as operating by way of "anti-structures" (rather than structures). If we think back to the models provided by structuralism, the structures adduced by Lévi-Strauss, for example, were saturated with details pointing to the concrete particularity of a culture.

Now it is true that Lévi-Strauss typically did not present the culture he ana-lyzed as projecting a *historical* perspective, at least in any Western sense. But within the study of modern Western societies, historical consciousness has been viewed as no less an element of cultural particularity than are elements of dress or food. Thus, at least when used in the analysis of Western culture, the concrete social character of deconstructionist constructs [!] offers a framework in which both the method and its (dialectically related) objects can be under-stood as historical. Offered as well then is at least the basis for a sensibility regarding the notion of social improvement.

This is, as I say, a delicate argument to make about deconstruction. On the one hand I am cautioning against a strategy that singles out the ahistorical tendencies of deconstruction and then applies them "against the grain" of the fundamentally social, and thus historical, concerns that shape its field of inquiry. Yet precisely such a strategy is central to the functioning of de-construction.

On the other hand, I am also defending the radical inconsistency of such a strategy on the very grounds that deconstruction insists on the recognition of such inconsistency as fundamental to all argument. In other words, I am relying on the premises of deconstruction as proof of their own validity, and, for the purpose, at that, of disproving any priority—be it historical or ahistorical—that deconstruction may seem to claim for itself.

For those whose intellectual energy may begin to wilt at this point, such an open-endedly reversible nesting of method and content within each other may well seem strong evidence in favor of the now-famous characterization, passed along by John Searle, of Jacques Derrida as "the sort of philosopher who gives bullshit a bad name."[22] (To be sure, this account is not a direct reproduc-tion of Derrida's thinking but merely my own take on it.) Still, this argument may also persuade a few readers to take seriously the epistemological limits deconstruction places on discourse, precisely by virtue of the consistency between these limits and those defined by this movement as the limits of its own field of vision. From this perspective, to use Paul de Man's term, the "blindness" shared by deconstruction with all other methods of interpretation constitutes something more akin to evidence than to *a priori* grounds for the validity of deconstructionist insights, even though at bottom such blindness understands itself as grounded on its own limitations.[23]

A definitive end to such a dynamic of infinite regress I do not feel myself able to provide. My hope is that the level of detail in which I have presented this argument will counteract suspicions of a reliance, in its construction, on the crude thematic impression (of attachment to contradiction) rather than on the logical subtleties that deconstruction evokes. What I wish to suggest is that deconstruction makes available a persuasive consideration of the logical paradoxes in discourse, and not merely a heavy-handed dependence on the qualitative confusion of paradox.

Perhaps this wish stems at bottom from an existential attraction I feel at times for the joy Roland Barthes takes in the reversals of infinite regress, in contrast to the specter Adorno conjures up of metaphysical despair.[24] Beyond such motivations, I admit, I can offer in defense of the preceding line of argument only the honesty of its efforts to address the polarity of history and structure— and my own conviction that argument can, in some plausibly rational sense, be governed, not completely but to a significant degree, by rigorously self-critical standards of good faith (no doubt this is a point of deconstruction!).

But even if one rejects the entire preceding line of argument, which extracts a historical capacity from the social character of deconstruction, the charge of ahistoricism would be simplistic. I say this not simply because deconstructionist writings tend so often, whether wittingly or not, to heighten our sensitivity to problematical and contradictory relationships between critical theory and history. I say it also in part because deconstruction insists, no less emphatically than does Adorno, on the fundamentally processive (antistructural and antimetaphysical) grounds of its own value—on grounds that resist encapsulation in any abstract, ahistorical formula for truth. And in part I say this because a notion that lies at the very heart of deconstruction seems to me so simply and profoundly historical. For if *Derrida* were now placed on one foot, he could locate the core of deconstruction in his notion of *différance*.[25] And the precise function of this notion, it seems to me, is to historicize the notion of "significant differences," which Derrida inherited, by way of structuralism, from structural linguistics.

So intrinsically historical is the notion of *différance* that it gives us unusually direct access to understanding the relation between "structure" and "history" as defined in poststructuralist theory. Earlier I argued, in essence, that

Adorno's theory of discourse is grounded on a conception of its origins in history, a conception that, in spite of itself, may in turn point to still deeper structural conditions of discourse—conditions that may not, however, be definable except indirectly, through reference to history. Conversely, the notion of *différance* gives plausibility to the argument that the deconstructionist theory of discourse is grounded on a conception of its underlying structural conditions—a conception that is itself implicitly historical, both in its formal character and in its manner of operation.

Though I am reserving a fuller exposition of the term *"différance"* for the following section of this essay, some preliminary observations may be useful in assessing the particular historical perspective I will take of Chopin's A-Major Prelude. A conscientious traditional musicologist, Leeman Perkins, once expressed reservations to me about what he saw as the anachronistic character of the readings I develop in a study such as this. If, as he assumes, these readings reflect musical understanding in my own culture rather than in Chopin's, then aren't they historically invalid? This is precisely the sort of question that Derrida's notion of *différance* sets out to address. There is an unavoidable delay in the process of signification, Derrida is arguing, that results in an unavoidable difference between the meanings initially and subsequently perceived in a text.

That my readings could not have taken their particular shape in any culture but my own seems self-evident. Yet there is no reason to assume that contemporary readings cannot simultaneously, so to speak—granted, this perception is implicitly figurative—have a basis in the music as articulated in its original context of meaning. No reason, that is, unless we are prepared (and able) to restrict the process of signification to some initial moment of emergence.[26] Arguing against the possibility of realizing such an antiquarian dream, poststructuralism, in its recognition of delay as intrinsic to signification from the very outset, defines this process as intrinsically historical. In this respect, deconstruction can be called a fundamentally historical mode of criticism.

This way of thinking by no means deprives us of a legitimate right to reject any given deconstruction as historically invalid. It merely increases the difficulty of designing criteria for such a judgment; for such a viewpoint does not measure the historical validity of a reading today by its degree of indistinguishability from readings that were, or could have been, made at the time a text came into existence, even by the original author himself or herself. Indeed, since deconstruction considers such a condition of identity an impossibility, it would interpret claims to the full achievement of such an identity as evidence of a modern critic's bad faith, precisely with respect to history.

Here again, it should be pointed out, deconstruction converges on Adorno's theory in at least two respects. First, it clearly shares his horror of hypostatization, an aversion that cannot be disentangled from fundamentally historical concerns. For both schools, though in different ways, texts are conceivable only in terms of contexts, which are continuously redefined by the flow of history. It is true that Adorno insists more emphatically on the irreversibility of that flow, whereas deconstruction calls more attention to a variety of temporal relations that can be perceived through an act of interpretation. These include the kinds of reverse chains of meaning that are established as later events alter the understanding of earlier ones, and also relations of static simultaneity that emerge when we contemplate different levels of meaning at the same time. On the other hand, the dialectical character and constant reversals of direction in Adorno's methods also entail, in effect, a temporally varied relation between the critic and history. Where both schools agree is in their common recognition of the listener, whose activities start after the speaker's, as an integral contributor to the process of signification.

In addition it can be suggested—though only in a brief and simple way— that both schools share a deep-rooted tendency to think of "being" from a specifically human perspective, as being [!] synonymous with "meaning."[27] Let me specify a bit about some of the themes and issues that can be raised by a tendency to think in this way. Humans themselves, it can be argued, tend to define their own sense of "being" through a continuous capacity for interpretation. And the claim to being human (and hence the life) of someone who lacks such a capacity—a comatose patient, a fetus, possibly even an infant—is precarious precisely because this claim depends on the willingness of others to recognize it as such.

Much the same kind of interpretation of "being" is regularly made by modern semioticians. It has become a truism of modern semiotics that conditions for which a culture has no word have not come into existence for that culture.[28] Thus, for example, the very use (or non-use) of the name "Israel" or "Palestine" confers a condition of meaning (or meaninglessness) and thereby one of existence (or nonexistence). ("Israel is real" said a pin recently fashionable in that country.) The term "rinse cycle" has neither meaning nor existence for an unliberated husband. From the perspective I am describing, in other words, something "is" only to the extent that someone (a human) puts meaning upon it.

The relation of "being" and "meaning," I need hardly say, has a long philosophical history, which took a particularly interesting turn in the work of Kant and Hegel. My impression is that analytic philosophy, for all of its concentration on the domain of language, is at bottom unsympathetic to an equation of "being" and "meaning." What Adorno and deconstruction share may be less a conviction that "being" *is* [!] "meaning" than a Continentalist sensibility concerning the persuasive aspects of such a formulation.

Certainly neither would deny the fiercely problematical implications of that formulation, some of which should become evident when I take up the relation of Chopin's A-Major Prelude to "real" and "figurative" kinds of meaning. What is important for present purposes is to note that any perspective that assigns a kind of ontological priority [!] to "meaning" acknowledges its sense, from the outset, of the historical parameters of "being."

Such a perspective is not likely to be sympathetic to a viewpoint that measures historical validity against some ahistorically pure condition of being. And whether or not such a viewpoint can be laid at the doorstep of analytic philosophy, it can certainly be associated with antiquarian schools of music history, which in effect elevate the particularities of past cultures to a position of timeless essence, beyond the contingencies of any plausibly historical condition.

But if antiquarian standards are rejected, what criterion does deconstruction offer us for measuring historical validity? As far as I can tell, simply honest judgment, impossibly problematical as that notion is. Deconstruction allows us to measure the degree to which the differences between an initial reading, both as documented and hypothesized, and a contemporary reading can persuasively be explained by a good-faith effort on the critic's part to accommodate changes in historical perspective that have developed since a text first appeared.

Admittedly, the assessment of such good faith, in a post-Kantian age, is a slippery task. Admittedly, from this viewpoint, the governing framework of interpretation is explicitly acknowledged as our own. And admittedly, the original meaning of a text is thereby conceded as lying beyond the reach of our knowledge. What we have, at best, is only an idea of that meaning, posited as an object within the limits of our own governing viewpoint. Good faith, hard work, and corroborative evidence may persuade us that we have approached very near to that original meaning. But nothing can eliminate the final gap between our idea and the thing itself, a gap that is measured quite appropriately by Derrida's notion of *différance*, and that in turn allows none of our ideas to secure indisputably safe passage beyond the epistemological domain of metaphor, or fiction.

We come here to the sticking point, at which so many efforts to retain sympathy with deconstruction seem to falter. Perhaps the most frequently leveled charge against poststructuralist criticism in general is that of disregarding the "actual" texts it interprets, either cynically or with blithe irresponsibility, for doctrinal purposes of its own. Those who make this objection would undoubtedly seize on the following statement by Roland Barthes (about paintings) as a case in point: "The picture, whoever writes it, exists only in the *account* given of it; or again: in the total and the organization of the various readings that can be made of it: a picture is never anything but its own plural description."[29]

Now I would not dispute that one could find deconstructionist analyses, perhaps many of them, that fail to establish a relationship of good faith between the critic's activities and the text the critic is examining. But need this happen? Does Barthes' insistence here that the painting can be said to exist only through the "writing" (or reception) of it *really* render unthinkable and unusable the recognition, within and through our concept of "text," of a tension between the "painting" and the "viewer"? Does acknowledging the epistemological limits on our ability to retrieve an original meaning intact really give us *carte blanche* to sever our dialogue with the past as represented by the texts that reach us? To renounce efforts at maintaining a tension, and its attendant disciplinary restraints, between the "otherness" of a text and ourselves? To construe, out of our overheated imaginations, meanings that have no plausible basis in the text they address?

Not unless we scrap Derrida's notion of *différance* altogether.[30] Precisely by insisting on the irreducible distance between initial and subsequent meanings, the notion of *différance* keeps us honest. For while acknowledging limits on what we can know, this notion also precludes us from characterizing as adequate any reading that answers solely to our own personal circumstances. (Barthes himself, in the passage just quoted, acknowledges the *plurality* of readings in which a painting can be said to exist; keeping such a notion in mind helps safeguard us from the illusion that we ourselves have a unique direct line to metaphysical truth.) In a word, by distinguishing between a speaker and a listener, deconstruction at once reminds us as listeners of our limited role in cultural discourse. By the same token, of course, it also dispels our illusion, as speakers, that we can create texts that are both impervious to the reactions of listeners and at the same time, in any meaningful sense, meaningful.

By pushing a conception of "text" based on *différance* to the center of criticism, and thereby forcing sensitivity to the problematical aspects of such notions as an "actual" text, poststructuralist movements such as deconstruction have done a good deal to encourage our integrity as critics. At the very least, these movements have made it more difficult for us to disregard the limiting effects of our own historical and cultural perspective on our access to one another's texts. At their best they have increased our opportunity to form historically persuasive relationships with the texts that have reached us from the past. Deconstruction is not by any means the first or only movement to push criticism in this direction, but it has surely been among the most influential schools of thought to do so in recent times.

Of course, the elusiveness of the differences centered in *différance* to definitive resolution does not stop with the relationship between speaker and listener. Poststructuralism goes still further by asserting that even in its initial moment of physical concretization by an author, a text is already distanced from a plethora of its own sources that leave in the text only more or less discernible "traces" of themselves.[31] Thus, even at the moment when I speak to you, my words issue from a complex of cultural, linguistic, and psychological sources over which I have only limited conscious control. And thus even if, by some epistemological miracle, you could recapture in their pristine entirety the meanings I myself could originally have retrieved, what you would possess would be no more than a fragment of the elements inscribed in my text. From this perspective, the very use of the possessive form in connection with a text ("my" text, "your" text) is understood as problematical—as is the definition of "[a] text" to mean an object, rather than a process.

Once we come to this point in our account of signification, we have two alternatives. Either we throw up our hands in despair at the impossibility of all human communication, or we resign ourselves more or less good-naturedly to what I would call the "dialectics of text." By this I mean that we accept as unavoidable the contradictory character of discourse. On the one hand we acknowledge the inconceivability of acquiring an exhaustive knowledge of the factors that initially created a text. On the other hand we accept a continuing moral obligation to engage as directly as possible with the configuration of the texts that are offered to us. And throughout the process we make an effort to penetrate each other's "otherness," even as we recognize our inability to do so except within the confines of the structuring capacities on which each of us draws to define ourselves. We open up our own modes of understanding to reshaping by someone else's construct or text; yet, as Derrrida might say, we have "always already" reshaped that text according to our own modes of understanding.

In effect, perhaps here locating the *archetypal* case of dialectics, we agree to define honest interpretation of another person's text (and ultimately even of our own) as the dogged pursuit of a will o' the wisp. We focus on each other's texts as objects (we treat them figuratively as fixed objects) through a process of interaction that excludes us from access to all texts, even our own, as objects. In doing these things, we admit our equality with each other as participants in a dialogue—and we admit to limits on even our own exceptional perspicacity as interpreters. The process is not as scientifically neat as some might like. But perhaps seeing it this way can help us avoid the kind of arrogance, and moral myopia, that Shirley Hufstedler surely had in mind when she accused Judge Robert Bork of shrinking from "the grief and the untidiness of the human condition."[32]

In the end such a dialectical vision of the interpretive process may even enhance our ability to accommodate each other's ideological differences, by serving as a model of creative tension. Let's say we can't reasonably expect everyone to agree as to which pole of the dialectical pair "method" and "object" has epistemological priority. And let's say we can't expect everyone to take a perspective that encompasses both ends of that dialectic (precisely because to recognize that dialectic is in effect to grant priority to "method"). Perhaps we can at least get the value of such a dialectic by allowing partisans of each side a real place in our discourse.[33]

Having now provided something of a theoretical context, I would like simply to enumerate a few guidelines I have used in the following analysis. First, I have made no effort to relate the prelude either to Chopin's personal experience or to the specific events in his career. Although my musical analysis presupposes a historical familiarity with the Classical and Romantic styles, and though I have found it essential to locate the prelude in a historical context of post-Enlightenment Western high art, the kinds of questions I pursue here, as in most of my work, tend more toward the generality of philosophy than toward the specificity of biography.

At the same time, however, in order to limit the number of historical variables pressing upon my enterprise, and also to honor, as well as possible, the attitude of respect that Chopin's own culture had for the particularities of "original expression"—an attitude that, in effect, constitutes the self-chosen "theme" of this prelude[34]—I have chosen to use that version of Chopin's prelude that is currently thought closest to the configuration Chopin himself had in mind. In other words, I have worked with a scholarly edition of the prelude.[35]

In the same way, I have elected to consider Chopin's prelude more or less in its entirety. (Of course, as deconstructionist thought emphasizes, no analysis can hope to be exhaustive; readers will find many relationships and parameters that my analysis overlooks or scants.) Indeed, in my attempt to apply deconstruction, I have deliberately chosen a piece short enough to be considered whole. This is not because I object on principle either to the deconstructionist rejection of organic models for the artistic "work" (i.e., the text as object) or to the preference of this school for considering only parts of works. On the contrary, I believe we have a pressing need for criticism that declines to stay within the limits of formal analysis, even of exhaustive formal analysis, and that attempts instead to form dynamic connections between one or two points in a work and elements in the world outside of that work. Moreover, as I believe my past work makes clear, I feel quite comfortable with the notion that many musical works, and certainly most nineteenth-century compositions, are more usefully construed as fragments than as complete entities.[36]

On the other hand, I see no necessary and fundamental incompatibility between deconstruction and the analysis of entire works. In fact, if deconstruction proposes to operate by exploding the unity of a work as an illusion, there is an obvious strategic benefit in beginning with a musical structure that seems to constitute such a unity. At bottom, however, this particular choice was probably made in large measure out of musicological habit. In part it was also made out of an unwillingness, at this point, to make a final judgment as to just how much of deconstructionist theory I find persuasive. And in part it was undoubtedly made on the basis of an instinctive and temperamental inability to find honest any dialectical process of interpretation that does not make every effort to honor both poles that define the tension of a contradiction. Thus, even as I find it persuasive to subsume the concept of text-as-object under a prior concept of text-as-process, I have tried to work in ways that clarify the case for the integrity of the former.

Finally, I have made no effort in this analysis to contradict the assumptions and priorities of those who defend the exceptional value of the standard Western art repertory, or what is now called the canon—a notion that could be said to stand for the concept of text-as-object on a collective scale. I could say this decision not to evaluate the notion of the canon is merely a decision of convenience. I could also say that deep down I don't really think very much of any music except that of the "common practice" repertory. Neither assertion would be true.

I do at heart believe that the human condition has little chance of improvement until most of the dogmas and value judgments that separate us into particularized subcultures are swept away. After more than three decades of limiting my listening to the Western high art repertory, I have come to acknowledge this habit as a snobbish folly no more defensible than limiting my interlocutors on matters intellectual to holders of the Ph.D. On the other hand, I am equally convinced, and will insist throughout this essay, that the concrete particularities that divide us into subcultures are as primary as they are secondary, not only to our definitions of the human condition but also to the value we impute to that condition. Along with encouraging us to broaden greatly the range of the repertories we study, respect for the concreteness of cultural particularities should encourage us to reexamine the works of the Western musical canon, not in their aspect as timeless masterpieces, beyond all possibility of criticism, but as part of an ongoing and contingently shaped human discourse. (This issue will resurface much later, p. 205.)

Again, I do not admire the cultural one-sidedness of the artistic repertories that have traditionally been taught at our universities, much less the attitude of elitism epitomized, until his death, by Allan Bloom. Yet I do not deny that some musical texts seem to me worth more of my time and attention than others. Over the years, the bases of my interest have changed and expanded a great deal, and I have become increasingly impatient with the narrowly structural standards of musical value that I learned as a student. And yet again, on the other hand, it seems clear to me that certain "canonized" texts—though *not all* and *not only such*—offer a particularly potent contraindication to metaphysical despair. In addition, it seems clear that some texts withstand far better than others perverse efforts, such as my own, to find inconsistencies in the imagery with which they tempt us to make sense of the world. Many of these are in the canon.[37]

As I was developing this introduction to my analysis, a controversy over the "Great Books" curriculum at Stanford exploded into the public consciousness, and many of the issues I address here began moving out of the academic journals into more popular publications. The broadening of this discussion, which by the early 1990s had expanded into all segments of the daily and weekly popular press, is bound to be healthy for our public discourse. On the whole—though I have come to be troubled by what I see as certain excesses and rigidities of multiculturalist schools of thought—the sensibilities calling for an expansion of the curriculum strike me as more persuasively grounded on humane concerns than those calling for its restriction to the traditional Western canon.

When one has to choose between focusing on the concrete needs of those who have previously been excluded from established discourse or on the abstract ideals of those who have mastered that discourse, it seems to me clear that we are far less likely to err morally by choosing the former. In intellectual terms, my own understanding of human expression as a process shaped by ongoing limitations of contingent history and experience persuades me of a need for constant, self-critical openness to changing circumstances and perspectives. Moreover, those who live near the front line of changing times and needs, such as the young, in a sense are always right. As reporters about what is happening now, they are right to insist on the indispensability of their reports to those of us whose modes of perceiving "what there is" were formed through an earlier confluence of conditions. But perhaps I can put this much more simply. If a choice *must* be made, the rights of those who have not yet "had"—the young, the poor, the excluded—seem to me to have a more powerful claim on our priorities than the rights of those who have already had.

But probably the best hope of solving these controversies lies, once again, in a willingness to develop a capacity for contradiction and thereby to leave these controversies unsolved. If there is no conceivable point of reconciliation between the two extremes, and almost certainly there is not, then the best alternative may be to foster a climate in which both schools of thought can flourish in a constant creative tension with each other. For this to work, however, the powers of the two schools must be brought into something like a state of equivalence. Attention must continuously be paid to the degree of power wielded by each. Whenever one side—in this case the side that conserves canonical values—has achieved an overwhelming first-strike capacity in relation to the other side, the priorities must for some period be reversed.[38] If this process leads to a new perspective, from which the differences between the two schools seem ultimately insignificant—for example, if both can be shown to represent essentially Western perspectives—which can in turn be analyzed in relation to other, non-Western perspectives, we may be better off. But even if this undercutting of divisions does not occur in the immediate future, the application of such strategies of reversal, which are essentially deconstruction-ist in character, could validate a good part of the deconstructionist enterprise in ways that directly benefit society.

It remains to be said here only that although the relationship between logi-cal and figurative language, a prominent theme of deconstructionist criticism, receives considerable attention in the analysis that follows, it is not explored as fully as it might have been. Although I am at pains to analyze this relation-ship within Chopin's prelude, I have chosen finally not to call attention to the numerous instances where I myself use the terms of logic (such as "causes," "demonstrates," "proves," "therefore," "misconstrues," and sometimes even "is") in the very development of arguments I make against the apparent force of logic in Chopin's prelude. Although I have written with a constant aware-ness of the tension between such terms and the thrust of my second reading, and with a growing respect for the ability of deconstruction to produce this awareness, I have concluded that the intricacies and length of the arguments I make in what follows are sufficient to discourage introducing this extra layer of conceptual complication.

Brief Exposition of Terms and Ideas

Deconstruction alleges that any text can be shown to maintain simultaneous contradictory positions about metaphysical reality, essentially by virtue of limitations in the way we use language to think and speak. Thus a text may appear to assume some metaphysical position by accepting some first principle or invoking what deconstructionists call a "presence," and yet simultaneously undercut that position. Or, conversely, a text may apparently try to escape some metaphysical assumption that nevertheless ensnares it, by virtue of the ways in which discourse defines itself. The goal of deconstruction is to expose the strategies through which this contradiction is maintained.

Deconstructionist analysis typically involves the dismantling of what can be called "binary oppositions," or more accurately, "hierarchical binary oppositions." Essentially these oppositions amount to conceptual polarities, that is, to pairs of opposing terms that can usually be thought of as dialectically related, and of which one can provisionally be assumed to assert priority over the other. Some commonly used examples that have particular relevance to the following analysis would include these: essential and supplemental; necessity and accident; literal and figurative; syntax and rhetoric; metaphor and metonym.

The terms "metaphorical" (used interchangeably with "paradigmatic") and "metonymical" (used interchangeably with "syntagmatic") should be understood here in the particular sense that the structuralist movement has given them. By "metaphor" is meant a symbolic relationship of analogues or equivalents that can be substituted for each other (hot dogs and hamburgers). By "metonym" is meant a contextual relationship of physical or conventional association (hot dogs and mustard).[39]

In a characteristic deconstruction of a text, the critic will set up a binary opposition, identifying the term that seems to claim priority. The critic's analysis will then try to show (1) that the inequity thus indicated should not be accepted uncritically as valid since the priority of these terms can be logically reversed, through reference to the text itself; and (2) that since the conception of each term inextricably involves reference to the other, the significance of the difference between the two terms can be undercut. To the extent that these two procedures are persuasive they suggest that the very opposition analyzed is not in any sense real, but rather only a fiction. This fictional status in turn suggests that a principal function of any hierarchical opposition proposed by a text is to support the ideological position represented by whichever term seems (in a first reading at least) to have priority. This is precisely the situation suggested in

Terry Eagleton's characterization of deconstruction as a movement that "has grasped the point that the binary oppositions with which classical structuralism tends to work represent a way of seeing typical of ideologies."[40]

Deconstruction is not the only school that develops its critical methods in terms of binary oppositions. Nor is it the only school that assumes, in effect, that to retain its capacity for meaningfulness, a text must permit a perception of one field of its components as more emphatically projected than the remainder. (By this I mean that a text that allowed no distinction between a marked foreground and an unmarked background would be as incapable of conveying meaning as would be a speech delivered in an unbroken, utterly even monotone.)[41] What seems to distinguish deconstructionist theory is its perception of a simultaneous necessity and contingency in the inequality between the two semiotic poles or fields of a text. What distinguishes this theory is its insistence on the infinite precariousness of the hierarchical arrangements that make it possible for us, at any moment, to discern meaning in a text.

Some texts seem to emphasize one side of a binary opposition unequivocally. One might suppose, then, that the ultimate aim of a deconstruction is simply to expose fallacies in assertions made by explicitly polemical texts. Certainly deconstruction can be useful for such a restricted purpose, but it would itself characterize the conclusions of any such exercise as crudely provisional. More impressive is the value deconstruction claims when it is applied more extensively, in situations far more ambiguous and subtle than the one I have just described.

Deconstruction alleges, after all, that texts characteristically maintain simultaneous contradictory positions. Another way of putting this is to say that even where a text markedly proclaims, in ways that are widely acknowledged, a preference for one position in a conflict, it necessarily, in order to define that very position, points toward the conceivability of an opposite view as well. But in thus preserving the tension between two opposite viewpoints, a text allows consideration of the position it seems to reject. In fact, deconstruction asserts that through a continuous process of reversals by the reader, texts expose the ambiguous status of their polarities at a number of levels.

At the level of explicit content or "intended" argument, for example, a text puts into question the relative merits of the two positions it simultaneously defines. On the other end, at the level of reception, texts prod the critical reader into acknowledging his or her own preference for one position or the other. In between these two extremes, the text offers what could be called the level of its own formal configuration, which could in turn be subdivided into layers of perspective represented by the characters, the narrator, the com-

poser's voice, the composer's cultural milieu, and so on.[42] And at these levels
texts very often open themselves to differences in perception as to which position in a conflict seems more emphatically marked.

Indeed, just which of the two terms in a polarity is to be initially construed
as highlighted (or preferred, so to speak) by a text, and on what kinds of evidence, is something that deconstruction already puts at issue. What matters
here is not whether the specific conclusions we might initially form about a
text in this respect are right; those conclusions are assumed by deconstruction
to be provisional. What matters is whether deconstruction provides us with
any systematic or theoretical basis for forming those initial conclusions. It
does not. A deconstruction cannot, without violating the spirit of its own
enterprise, justify its own attribution of priorities to a particular text except on
what amounts to an ad hoc basis.[43] To provide a systematic set of rules for
determining priorities would be to undercut the principal point about discourse that deconstruction wishes to make, and assign to its own perceptions a
conclusiveness that it has neither the power nor the desire to defend.

For deconstruction does not envision a text as a fixed object that, by itself,
in the absence of readers, establishes definitively, perhaps through some physical means, the identity of the values it articulates. Instead, it proposes texts as
semiotically indeterminate constructs that require the responses of readers, in
all their variability, as a fundamental condition for making sense. (For that
matter, as I hope will become clear, it proposes texts as constructs that can do
no more than approximate a condition of meaningful physical constancy.)[44]

Consequently, deconstruction is never in a position to attribute more than
provisional status to the hierarchy of values it discerns in a text—or, as is often
the case, in a group of texts that it perceives as related. At most, the critic can
try to make an assessment as to which values the text projects with sufficient
force to define an ideological foreground. But he or she can never exclude the
possibility that another critic, working with an equal sense of fidelity to the
historical significance of the text and to its formal characteristics as they seem
to present themselves, may arrive at a substantially different attribution of its
elements to a status of foreground or background.

This recognition of pluralism at such a profound level of the signifying
process might seem to some (I think again of Allan Bloom, and also of E. D.
Hirsch, Jr.) to vitiate the claims of deconstruction to moral responsibility. Yet,
like any other kind of criticism, a deconstruction can and should be called to
account for the intellectual and moral honesty of its conclusions. Now, it does
seem difficult to deny that the basis for that accounting will involve considerations that extend beyond the formal relationships within a text, such as the

critic's intuitive response to those relationships as well as the general theoretical predispositions through which those relationships are defined. Deconstruction itself argues that such considerations affect *every* act of interpretation, including those undertaken by antirelativists.

What happens if we grant some provisional validity to this position? Does it follow that deconstructionist critics are thereby absolved from maintaining the moral integrity of their own work? Not at all. Indeed, in my judgment, it is precisely those modes of interpretation that deny their indebtedness to such considerations that are least likely to provide correctives for their potential abuse. In contrast, deconstruction itself, by seeking to avoid systematic theoretical positions, and by restricting claims of validity to an ad hoc framework, actually encourages an intensity of relationship between its methods and the particular texts it studies. And clearly the very pressure deconstruction exerts in attempting to reverse hierarchical attributions offers the potentially corrective force of a dialectical process. Though my immediate intuition may lead me to identify parameter A as the foreground element of a text, and parameter B as a background element, the dynamic of continuous reversal forces me to consider a variety of perspectives from which each assertion may be persuasive. In addition, this dynamic acts as a brake on my tendency to accept the immediacy of my own intuitions uncritically. In short, this dynamic encourages attentiveness to the moral implications and effects of my own activities.[45]

In undertaking the deconstruction of contradictions "embedded" in a text, one of Derrida's own favorite binary oppositions—one that obviously articulates quite directly the viewpoint just described—is that of "essence" and "supplement." A supplement, according to Derrida, is a double-edged notion. On the one hand it is something extra or external, optional, and therefore secondary to a text. On the other hand, in the sense that a supplement is required to provide something that is missing from a text, it is integral or internal, essential, and thus primary. Or as one of Derrida's translators elegantly puts it, "It means *both* the missing piece and the extra piece."[46]

Often deconstructionists will begin an analysis by focusing on some ostensibly "supplemental" or "marginal" aspect of a text, that is, on some element that the text seems to subordinate, or minimize, or ignore, or hurry over, or push aside as secondary, exceptional, temporary, incidental, or accidental. For it is precisely such moments, in the deconstructionist view, that most sorely test the relative force with which a text supports or undermines a metaphysical position.

It is sometimes said that the difference between ordinary people and great achievers, not only in the arts but also, for example, in the business world, is that the latter pay attention to (or capitalize on) perceptions that the rest of us take for granted. Examine the point at which a writer you admire decides to begin a story. Or consider what you might have earned a few decades ago if in a hot moment you'd taken your need for fast food, or a family-style motel, or voluminous photocopying, seriously. What deconstruction calls "marginal" may well be the moments that best allow us to retrieve and capture important immediate perceptions, perceptions that most of us tend to discount and lose—like the troll in the children's story "The Three Billy Goats Gruff"—in our pursuit of "bigger game." Where deconstruction at its best often starts is at a moment that crystallizes impressions and reservations we ourselves have always had concerning a text but never bothered to articulate.

Characteristically, a deconstruction results in (at least) two coherent readings of a single text that coexist but cannot be reconciled with each other. In deconstructionist terminology, the relative weight of these two readings is "undecidable." At bottom this is in keeping with a tenet that seems central to the deconstructionist movement; it can be described as follows. On the one hand, we as post-Kantians know that the true nature of metaphysical reality is inaccessible to the human mind. And on the other hand, unable to function without *some* belief about metaphysical reality (which means, at bottom, a belief in some metaphysically grounded principle of universality that allows us to agree on "real" distinctions between the significant and the insignificant, and thereby *guarantees* the success of our communications), we choose, as Nietzsche put it, to "forget" this post-Kantian knowledge.[47] But the contingency of those positions we choose to canonize as "knowledge" reasserts its force when we are pressed to confront conflicting versions of what we "know." From this standpoint, all knowledge is ultimately acknowledged as at best a very sophisticated version of fiction, or as a metaphysical metaphor. And metaphors, by structuralist definition, are exchangeable.

Furthermore, in keeping with this undecidability as to the priority of the readings it allows, any text, including the deconstructionist's own analysis, is vulnerable to a potentially infinite series of deconstructive reversals in subsequent readings. Thus, deconstruction opposes itself squarely to the "organic" model of construing a text, even an artwork.[48] In the deconstructionist view, a text is a profoundly indeterminate construct, functioning always as part of an ongoing, open-ended process of historical discourse. No single meaning can be definitively assigned to a text. Rather, once a text takes shape in the public domains of physical and conventional articulation, "it" [!] passes beyond the control of its originator(s) and becomes accessible to as many legitimate readings as there are readers.[49]

Because this issue is so important, and so hotly contested, it may be well to reiterate at this point, in somewhat different terms, a central argument of my preceding introduction. Despite the fluidity of the signifying process as I have just described it, deconstruction need not disintegrate into a process of radical relativizing whereby respect for the discipline provided by a physically extant text gives way to irresponsible, arbitrary, and solipsistic free association by the reader.

On the one hand, the deconstructionist does understand both text and interpretation as interdependent aspects of a signifying process in which the two continuously—and dialectically—interpenetrate, affect, and modify each other. As historical events and knowledge intervene between the first appearance of a text and the act of interpreting it, it is not just interpretative concerns and methods that the deconstructionist acknowledges as changing; at the same time, deconstruction asserts, changes are effected in the kinds and scope of context that form an integral component of the text. It is precisely because analyses can focus on different moments in the historical significance of a text that numerous conflicting interpretations can insist, with equal claim to legitimacy, on their fidelity to the historical parameter of signification.

Over time, as the reader can probably verify from his or her own experience, cultural perspectives change as to which elements of a text constitute its most strongly marked or foreground components, and which constitute "mere background assumptions."[50] (Here, perhaps, is one way of seizing upon that ever-more-elusive concept of "intention." Perhaps we should equate intention with those things that seem to the historically informed reader or listener to constitute emphatically the foreground of the text that reaches us.)

Thus far, then, it seems clear, the text is characterized by deconstruction as a fluid construct—as a living, open-ended network of available meanings rather than as a fixed physical object with a fixed meaning. To test this assertion, suppose that in the Dred Scott decision Justice Roger Taney, in order to emphasize his political impartiality, had uttered the words "Justice is blind" and imagine how we would construe those words today.

On the other hand, however, working within these constraints, and in constant awareness of the fundamental contradictions between historical needs for change and the epistemological (which we experience as the existential) need for some recognizable constancy of text, responsible deconstruction tries to maintain a scrupulous responsiveness to the "existing" physical characteristics of the textual source. Indeed, for all its insistence on the vulnerability of physical texts as well as of interpretive methods to the modifying forces of dialectical viewpoints, deconstruction has more than once been defined as virtually synonymous with close reading.[51]

Another way that deconstructionists describe the historical indeterminacy of the text is by asserting that a text is never fully present as a simple identity, or "identical with itself," but is rather always divided against itself, because it is constituted by what Derrida calls *différance*, the term that he coined to signify both difference, in the conventional sense, and delay.[52]

The term "divided against itself" is used so regularly in deconstructionist literature that we could easily dismiss it as it as a cliché—as a socially neutralized phrase that has lost all substantive meaning for those who employ it. Perhaps it has for many; still, it is not (yet) meaningless. According to this formulation, every text is from the start "different from itself" in the sense that every text, even at the moment when it comes into physical existence, is a translation of countless impulses, originating outside the conscious mind, into a commonly accessible rather than personally controlled medium.[53] Thus every text, as Derrida likes to say, is "always already," on a multiplicity of levels, preformed by innumerable physically absent yet historically generative traces.

I have already suggested that, from the deconstructionist standpoint, signification is an intrinsically historical process, involving delays and differences from what Derrida calls (quite persuasively for those who don't summarily reject the value of knowledge gained from experience) the "non-originary origins" of the text.[54] From this standpoint, signification is not identical to the physical presenting of a text, any more than a text itself is identical to its own uninterpreted physical appearance. Such an appearance, to the deconstructionist, is only the immediate source of the text, not the text "itself." Texts come into existence only when they are perceived as in some sense meaningful—that is, only at the point where they enter into human discourse. Thus even if the reader or viewer or listener starts by taking in a more or less undifferentiated mass of physical data, it is only afterwards, through interaction with a reflective capacity, that the data enters fully into the condition of text.[55] Furthermore, since from the deconstructionist standpoint context figures inseparably into the notion of text, subsequent readings can themselves over time become incorporated into what is recognized as the text. Consequently, as we have already indicated in other connections (see notes 8 and 49, this chapter), an analysis has no obligation to limit itself to those interpretations that were made at the time a text first appeared.

I myself would argue that it is important that *some* scholars address themselves to this initial stage of signification. In part I would make this argument for reasons that deconstruction generally accepts: the *différance* represented by our own interpretations measures a distance that can be gauged meaningfully only in relation to other viewpoints; the latter should certainly include some starting point, no matter how distant, theoretically indeterminate, and (itself) provisional. And in part I would argue, on a basis less clearly of interest to deconstruction, that the integrity, and indeed the possibility, of human communication (and society) requires honoring the value, no matter how unattainable the realization, of attempts at reconstructing original intention [!]. In my judgment, such attempts, no less than good-faith efforts at constructing an interpretive method, are vital for maintaining the integrity of what I have earlier (p. 57) called "the dialectics of text."

Without strenuous efforts by some people in such a cause, the very possibility of human communication—and here I do agree with Hirsch (see chapter 4, note 17)—is doomed. At the same time, however, I would also stress that the importance of approaching such an asymptote varies greatly according to the kind and status of the text involved. In ordinary conversation, my failure to understand my husband's dinner plans for tonight may have trivial (or, then again, not-so-trivial) consequences. On the other hand, a comparable failure can have life-or-death consequences in an operating room, or in a courtroom, where Leo Frank, or Sacco and Vanzetti, may depend for their lives on our ability to read their texts on their own intended terms. It is to the credit of our Anglo-American traditions of jurisprudence that, at least in theory, we insist on efforts by jurors to go beyond their own stylistic prejudices by trying to distill something close to the abstract logical constants of a defendant's text.

In taking this position—and I recognize that it pinpoints the extent to which my liberalism, so recently feared as radical, has become old-fashioned— I do not advocate simply denying the existence of those stylistic prejudices. As the outcome of the so-called Rodney King trial suggests, it can be even more dangerous in a courtroom than in a classroom to confer an absolute status on the ideal of a single, abstract version of the truth, and to refuse to acknowledge the role played in practice by the concretely formed viewpoints of both speakers and listeners. The American judicial system stands to benefit from efforts now ongoing to broaden the concept of the legal text through a deconstruction of the dialectical relation between conflicting claims on that concept.

But even if we restrict ourselves to the narrower notion of text long assumed in American jurisprudence, it is apparent that our system of jury deliberations recognizes the contingent or approximate status of reading a text. If the giving and receiving of court testimony were exercises in abstract logic to which no particularities of culture or experience adhered, the texts involved at each end of the process might be considered identical. And if it were possible to establish an absolute identity between the "original" text of a crime and perceptions thereof, any single, certifiably sane judge could decide cases of fact with certainty. The presence of twelve jurors reflects a perceived need to provide correctives for the variability of perception. Through the pooling of the jurors' perceptions, it is hoped, some reasonable approximation of the "facts" can be achieved. In structuralist terms, each juror's perception can be described as a transformation, or variation, of an "original" structure of events.

Even in this case, it should be noted, the so-called original structure amounts to a fiction. It can never be assumed that any one juror knows exactly "what happened" because no object called "what happened" ever existed, in any humanly retrievable sense. As in the archetypal movie *Rashomon*, "what happened" is at the earliest retrievable point, and unavoidably, a version of those events as structured by a perceiver. In short, "what happened" is "always already" a text.

To make this point emphatic, I once gave my students at the CUNY Graduate Center a simple exercise in historiography. I asked them to tell me specifically how they would go about writing a history of the day in New York on which our class took place. Where would they start? What would they include? How would they order the telling of events that happened simultaneously? Whose viewpoint(s) would they try to project? If Joyce's account of events in Dublin on June 16, 1904, were "true," would it follow that no other "true" rendering of those events would be possible? Is a *Penelope*, for instance, a theoretical impossibility?

In the sense I am describing, poststructuralism is surely right to deny a privileged status to the construction an author puts upon his or her own text.[56] While there are many instances when efforts to retrieve such a construction are morally imperative, even an author's version of a text is, at bottom, no more verifiably "real" than any other.

Nevertheless there *are* certainly numerous situations, even outside the courtroom, where a good-faith effort to reconstruct an initial version of a text is morally crucial. As a fifty-two-year-old Jew, who might have been murdered in infancy through the legalized operation of contingent cultural preferences (if my parents had lived in Europe), I personally am grateful to be living in a country that honors, and values, essentially as a requirement of abstract, universal reason, the ideal of an original text—say, the construction my parents put upon my significance in 1943.[57]

Nor is it only in literal life-or-death situations that attempts to approximate an original text, on some idealized basis of quasi-universal reason, assume importance. When my children were younger, I sometimes played a game with them and their friends while waiting to be served at a restaurant. The game was called "Anastasia"; the idea was to put ourselves in the position of Princess Anastasia if she did indeed survive the Russian Revolution. Imagine yourself in the position of having to prove your identity to a world that will not take your word for it. Imagine that establishing even your claim to a name depended on the ability (and willingness) of others to reconstruct that claim by assembling overwhelmingly persuasive external evidence. Imagine the degree to which even a physically intact life would be sapped of vitality if your own sense of your identity could never be socially validated. This is a not uncommon tragedy, for example among people who have outlived the social recognition of their professional success.

The very notion of "tragedy" derives its power over us from our ability to *imagine* a difference between "original" and subsequent meanings of a text—in literature and in life. When Shakespeare's Anthony exclaims, "O, pardon me, thou bleeding piece of earth," he contrasts the tragic text of Caesar against an original, say, the Caesar of "we who are about to die salute thee." How else do we measure the tragedy, for example, of Alzheimer's oblivion except in reference to the patient's former self-conception? Or take the ineradicable ominous overtones we hear in the name *Titanic*. Is it sufficient to say that we hear them because we know the horrible fate of the ship that bore this name? I would say rather that we respond as we do because embedded in the name *Titanic* we hear some trace of how that word must once, before the event, have been heard. The very name, *Titanic*, for all its apparent physical constancy, has been irrevocably (and arguably even physically) altered for us because we can gauge something of the distance between its (unrecoverable) "original" and its subsequent meaning. (Its subsequent meaning is, if you will, that this meaning *is* subsequent.) Or consider O. J. Simpson.

Even apart from tragedy, moreover, the experience of life as a meaningful process seems to depend fundamentally on an ability to perceive conflict and difference. We exercise this ability on a regular, indeed, virtually continuous basis, for instance, as we struggle to maintain some sense of our own constant identity. Let me take two examples from my own experience. I myself forcibly reject the fundamentalism of Orthodox Jews. Yet I appreciate the willingness of some people to submit to the strictures of "original" Orthodox ideals because it allows my own position as a liberal, more or less secular Jew to have a measurable identity, and thus, a meaning. Likewise, following the example of my brother Bob, a high-school English teacher, when I grade papers I place more stock in the distinctiveness of a student's voice than in any standardized ideal of written English. I also recognize that my ability to articulate this value requires the willingness of others—my teacher Jacques Barzun, for example—

to maintain the tension of a different view, by holding on to "original" standards of proper English.

Or again, I admit my desire that readers of this text extend to me the courtesy of trying to understand me on my own terms, from the inside out, as it were. On the other hand, the events of my life have made clear the futility of expecting to exert an ironclad control over my own words once I release them, which would guarantee such shared, or "proper," understanding.[58] And on the third hand, as my colleague David Josephson likes to say, there is a sense in which maintaining the structural integrity of my argument, by way of precisely chosen language, matters more to me than whether I ever find a sympathetic reader.[59]

This, of course, is precisely the situation of the individualistic artist in post-Enlightenment society, as analyzed by Adorno in his critiques of Beethoven and Schoenberg. And yet here it should also be admitted that the importance of attempting to reconstruct original readings for the kinds of texts we commonly call artworks is by no means always urgent.

For one thing, even if we momentarily assume the absolute importance of the artist's own wishes, it seems clear that providing a basis for such precise reconstructions has by no means always been important, say, for Western composers. What distinguishes Romantic composers on the whole from their predecessors may well be their increasingly explicit awareness that a change or loss (of meaning) in any originally chosen detail could by definition compromise the intelligibility of their text. In earlier generations, a greater faith in the solidity of general principles seems to have limited the semiotic weight attributed to details and allowed more tolerance for variability in the process of transmission.

It could even be the case that at least some earlier composers were little more aware of variations in the performance of their works than might be the case in the transmission of an oral tradition. Some of these composers may well have subscribed to a view, also compatible with our perception of oral traditions, that constant changes are not only unavoidable but valuable—precisely for the reasons that improvisation was once considered valuable in Western art music.

Thus, the leeway that many composers before (and some after) Beethoven often left for variations in instrumentation, for the substitution of one section or number for another, for flexible starting and ending points, is hardly to be taken as evidence of mere sloppiness or uninterest in the choice of details. It may represent a vast difference in perception. The earlier composers seem to have to have taken an entirely different attitude (or nonattitude) toward the concept of structural wholeness—a concept that came to loom large in the nineteenth century, when for a variety of reasons that seemed important to composers, this concept proved a useful device for segregating certain compositions into a normative class called "art."

For that matter, even after 1800, precisely as they became more attuned to the stakes involved in "fixing" a structure into a precise, normative state, composers made many decisions that render highly problematical our efforts to reduce versions of their work to a single, authoritative one. As exemplified by the often seemingly tormented process of revision in Beethoven's sketchbooks, the very ascription of importance to the act of "freezing" a structure into a state of perfection seems to have entailed a concomitant recognition of the futility of trying to do it. Many Romantic composers left their structures literally incomplete, or completed them in ways that often seem to us contrived or otherwise unconvincing. Chopin himself is known to have continued revising his works even after they had reached the stage of publication. Or if I may deviate momentarily to another medium, James Joyce, for all the intensity he directed at perfecting every detail in *Ulysses*, seems to have left no single physical object behind that could plausibly be called THE original version.[60]

In these latter, post-Enlightenment cases, the matter of a fixed, original version does indeed seem to have constituted a matter of considerable urgency to the artists in question. All the same, they eventually deferred, happily or not, to the enormous odds against producing such a definitive structure on terms that would have completely satisfied them. And this deference should make us consider not only whether precise reconstructions in such cases are conceivable, but also whether efforts at such reconstruction help us to understand the most significant issues and values offered by these works.

So far I have questioned the urgency of reconstructing original versions of music only in terms of what we can suppose a given composer might have wanted. But there are other bases as well for entertaining reservations about that urgency. Precisely in the sense that educated Westerners have traditionally reserved the normative title of "art" for structures with a plausibly universal value, we tend (quite apart from the poststructuralist "death of the author") to assert the ability of at least certain works to withstand detachment from the explanatory presence of their authors, and to take on a valued life of their own in society. Many of the artworks that grace our lives today—and this is particularly the case with musical compositions—have established a great value to society in guises (or contexts) quite physically altered from those their authors might have anticipated. Some of us, for example, find greater profundity in full-bodied post-Romantic orchestrations of the Bach B-Minor Mass than in historically correct thinner versions. Should we reconstruct the arms of the Venus de Milo?

True, most of the Western artists we call "great" have persuaded us of their ability to fashion structures that have an exceptional degree of formal integrity. On the other hand, do we not regularly turn out articles demonstrating the formal perfection of relationships that may not be historically "authentic" in all their particulars?[61] Don't battles continue to be fought over questions of physical authenticity? And having pronounced an artwork perfect in some extant version, don't we readily shift gears to pronounce the even greater perfection of some newly authenticated version? Is my musical analysis here not vulnerable to the discovery of some older, better original?

Indeed, there are ways of thinking about art that might well persuade us of an urgency in subjecting to critical scrutiny the very values that authors themselves may have held dear. Even great authors cannot always persuade us as easily of the human value underlying their work as of its technical value. Works executed with formal brilliance may have issued from viewpoints we find morally questionable, or worse. In such cases we certainly have no pressing moral obligation to honor the reading, or even the literal configuration, of a text as its author may have wanted. If our interest is in understanding the author's relationship to his or her own text, then we will have a strong interest in recreating for ourselves that initial reading and configuration—but not in leaving them uncriticized. Our own moral responsibilities as readers will require us to acknowledge the moral problems we find, as when questionable sexual or religious attitudes are "problematized" in modern productions of Shakespeare's plays.[62]

If, in other words, we find elements of structural value, which we would like to preserve, intermingled with morally questionable attitudes, we have an obligation to make clear our objections to the "original," and often even to make changes in the configuration on which an author's own reading was based. To be sure, there is an argument to be made that giving society license to reconfigure art in every generation according to its own stylistic preferences opens up horrible possibilities of inhumane abuse. Nevertheless, there is also an argument to be made for the other side of the dialectical tension I invoke here: that certain artworks, in their earliest known form, encourage a morally unjustifiable denigration of values located outside the cultural mainstream, an encouragement that does not deserve uncritical preservation.

On the other hand, though I would not recommend this course to all critics, some of us may choose to dissociate an author's personal history and identity altogether from a text and interpret the latter in relation to some context that excludes the author. Such dissociation is, of course, encouraged by the structuralist and poststructuralist emphasis on "decentering" the author. But even apart from these schools, such dissociation, as I have tried to indicate, seems to be built into the very processes through which signification operates, as an unavoidable possibility. In fact it occurs all the time, and not just in poststructuralist analyses, wherever authorship is unknown or judged irrelevant to the significance of a text. The possibility of such dissociation could well be used to justify, for example, my own reliance in the present essay on an article by Paul de Man. What interests me about that article is the assistance its argument offers in answering my own questions about language, not its relation to de Man the particular individual. Such a position seems morally defensible to me provided the following conditions are true: (1) that we do not knowingly ignore evidence that a text, in whatever context we may examine it, points toward immoral values, which may already have led it to serve immoral purposes, and that we do not, thereby, knowingly refrain from criticizing the text on grounds of moral deficiencies that we can perceive; (2) that we do not use the apparent absence of such moral flaws in a text, *once dissociated from its author*, in order to deny, in effect by definition, that the author could have had immoral motivations for producing any text; (3) that we do not propose our own readings as definitive and complete, or deny the need for readings concerned with different contexts or problems; and (4) that we approach this sort of problem with an attitude of morally scrupulous self-criticism,[63] and do not pretend to have universal answers that would suit every case. Given these stipulations, there are innumerable situations where interpreting texts in contexts not governed by an author's own reading can have great value.

In short what I am asserting is this. Not only is the reconstruction of an author's original reading never wholly possible; in addition, neither the efforts to reconstruct such a reading nor the ideals served by such efforts are necessary, or even desirable, for all our own readings—though for some readings those efforts and ideals are crucial.

The various positions that can be taken on the importance of the concept of an original reading all figure in current battles over the teaching of the Western canon. But at issue here is not just an academic choice between preserving old texts or responding to new contexts. What is involved here is a conflict between abstractionist principles for ensuring human equality and a viewpoint that insists on attention to the concrete particularities of human experience as a requisite for establishing such equality. This is a conflict of obvious social importance.

Apart from these relatively broad social implications of the issues addressed by deconstruction, one further deconstructionist notion that will prove relevant to the discussion that follows is "transcendental signification." This notion has its origins in aspects of the term "sign" as defined in structuralist usage, which is in turn derived from the work of Ferdinand de Saussure.

Saussure argues that, at bottom, signs owe their intelligibility to what can be called the "significant differences" between signs. Essentially these are the fundamental linguistic differences (systematically described by Saussure) that allow us to distinguish between, for instance, the words "cat" and "hat." It is in the very act of grasping that these differences have significance that we understand the function of words as signs, that is, their capacity to have meaning. Anyone who has ever witnessed a baby breaking into the circle of language by making many sounds, discarding some, presumably because they elicit no gratifying response, and altering others in ways that bring increasing recognition of their resemblance to words used by their elders, has some basis in experience for appreciating the value of Saussure's conceptualization.

In effect what Saussure is doing in his identification of significant differences is to define meaning as a function of the grounds that make meaning possible. But, of course, words as they are actually used not only embody differences in potentially meaningful structures but also point to the presence of a specific content, which we commonly call "meaning." To refine this latter sense of the term "meaning," Saussure proposes understanding the notion "sign" to encompass three semiotic (significatory) units: a signifier (*signifiant*, in French, often usefully abbreviated as "*sa*"); a signified (*signifié*, abbreviated as "*sé*"); and a referent. According to this formulation, the "signifier" is a physical unit (say "dog," "chien," "Hund," or "canis") that points to a mental idea of what this physical sign is supposed to represent. This latter idea is the "signified." Both the signifier and the signified are construed as operating in a domain accessible to, and even governed by, human thought (though not in the sense that they can be fully controlled by conscious individual intention). In short, both of these terms are construed as operating on *this* side of the great metaphysical divide.

By contrast, the referent—the warm thing that cuddles on your lap, or the snarling source of the ancient caveat—is defined as the object in the real world to which the pair signifier-signified points. Because of the way in which post-Kantian epistemology defines knowledge—because of the barrier this epistemology recognizes between human knowledge and metaphysical reality (defined as reality in itself apart from the activities of the human mind)—the referent is problematical for most contemporary schools of critical theory (and, I would argue, for contemporary philosophy as well).[64]

Take, for example, structuralism (which by now seems regrettably to have been reduced in most circles to a status of pre-poststructuralism). Like Saussure, structuralists tend to emphasize the stability of a one-to-one relationship between a signifier and a signified. "Dog" means the idea of a dog. This stability allows structuralists, like Saussure, to concentrate on subsuming signs under general laws of linguistic or semiotic structure. At the same time, focusing on the relation of signifier and signified keeps structuralist analysis within the accepted domain of knowledge—that is, within the conceptual realm, on this side of the great metaphysical divide—and suspends indefinitely a consideration of the relationship between a sign and its real-world referent.

Poststructuralism, of which deconstructionism is one prominent school, is in a sense wider ranging. It focuses on the "polysemic" capacity of signs. This term indicates the ability of signs to establish numerous different meanings, first of all in the sense that one signifier can point to multiple signifieds. The word "bed," for example, can make us think of an object on which we sleep, a flower garden, the foundation of a railroad track, the bottom of the sea, the base of a fingernail, a space for a patient in a hospital, and so on. It can, of course, also make us think of certain actions, such as having sex, or putting a baby to sleep.

But these examples present only part of the polysemic capacity. One could, for example, argue, that depending on the context, a signifier points to only one signified. But even if this is so, we cannot exclude the possibility that residues or "traces" of other signifieds that we know for this word have some bearing on our formulation of the particular signified that seems to be called for. We cannot know, for example, just how much the meaning we attach to this word is affected by our subliminal awareness of its close physical similarity to many other words, such as "bad," "beg," "bet," the German *Bett*, "red," "wed," and so on. That we recognize the workings of some such effect is shown by the embarrassment we experience when we are caught in a Freudian slip.

Moreover, beyond all these semiotic relationships derived from physical adjacence in the alphabet, so to speak, the meaning of the word "bed" may also encompass numerous other words or terms that are conventionally linked with it: "double-," "kingsize-," "bunk,-" "water-," "brass-," "marital-," "hospital-," "sick-," "death-," "-room," "-chamber," "-time," "-rest," "-ridden," "-bug," "-spread," "- and board," "- and breakfast," "- of nails," "- of roses," and so on. In addition, our construction of the meaning of this word is almost certain to involve certain ideas we habitually associate with it, such as laying down our body or burdens, sinking into softness, praying, escaping, sleeping, having trouble sleeping, dreaming, snoring, waking up, making love.

And beyond these, we have numerous associations with the word derived from specific experience. On a personal level, certain beds in certain places have left a wealth of diverse sensory impressions on us. On a cultural level, the word may contain traces for us of Van Gogh's painting of his bed, of the murder scene in Verdi's *Otello*, of John and Yoko's love-in, and so on. When we consider meaning on these latter levels, we become aware not only of the experiential and cultural richness on which our words (can) draw but also of the vast potential differences between our respective linguistic domains, and hence, of the fragility of communication.

But let us for the moment stick with those resources that are more or less commonly available for meaning in a particular culture. Is there any way for us to decide, even at this relatively impoverished linguistic level, what the term "bed" *really* means in a particular context?

One strategy is to use a dictionary. If we look up the word "bed," the entry will point us to some other word as its signified, such as "furniture." But this word, too, is a signifier; and if we look it up in turn, we will find some other signified, such as "movable article."

At any, and indeed at virtually every, point, the path may branch, leading us to numerous series of signifier/signifieds, depending on which route we choose. In this sense we can envision meaning, or "polysemy," as a kind of open-ended network. At other times we can picture polysemy as circular, in the sense that some words we find en route, such as "cot," or "crib," or "bunk," will lead us back to "bed," but now as a signified, which in turn functions as a signifier. In one way, when we use the dictionary, we make no progress: to understand the signified of a signifier, it seems we must be able to understand in advance the signifier or its equivalents.

To describe such relationships, deconstruction sometimes makes reference to a metonymical chain of signifiers. This image suggests the ever-widening ramifications of meaning that result from the endless physical and conventional associations through which a word (or any sign) operates. It also suggests an undercutting of the distinction between signifier and signified. For if a signifier and a signified operated in a one-to-one correspondence, with each pointing to and exhausting the other, no chain would be formed. Each would have a distinct function in relation to the other; and this complementary relationship, like the symbolic equivalence of metaphor, would project some abstractly intelligible basis of persuasiveness—it would make some sort of sense.

Instead, poststructuralism seems to have deconstructed the polarity of signifier and signified to show that the underlying relationship between these two is at bottom metonymical. By this poststructuralism does not mean simply that all words function simultaneously in both capacities. More specifically it means that even the signifieds we find in dictionaries satisfy our demands for meaning principally through the persuasiveness of their concrete, contingent associations with the signifier we look up, rather than in their provision of a distinct yet functionally related "otherness" to which the signifier points. In short, poststructuralism suggests that the relationship between signifier and signified is characterized at bottom not by significant difference but by qualitative similarity. Though the ostensible function of a signifier may be to point to a signified, the very notion of a "signified" is understood by poststructuralism to represent one case, or function, of the notion "signifier."

From the standpoint of commonplace assumptions about how language operates, the undercutting of this distinction has implications that are quite unsettling, though in practice our culture seems, not quite knowingly, to embrace them more closely each day. On this practical level, as television ads illustrate, we have become less and less interested in meaning as the content, or signified, that signifiers purport to say, and more and more sensitive to meaning as something that occurs in the process of saying. In American culture today, we have become used to thinking of signification as a wildly contingent process. For us, as John Lennon might have put it, meaning is what leaks out of words as they try to point beyond themselves toward a meaning. This is a poststructuralist position. A Bill Clinton speech (a signifier) is less about the state of the economy (a signified) than it is, for example, "about" the state of fatigue (another signifier) apparent in his hoarseness. What we learn from "You've got the right one, baby" is the irresistible appeal of the signifier (Ray Charles), not the identity of the signified (is the right one Pepsi or Coke?).

Especially unsettling are the theoretical implications of the poststructuralist position. To question the distinction between "signifier" and "signified" is to put into question the very possibility of meaning. Terry Eagleton notes that "if structuralism divided the sign from the referent . . . [poststructuralism] goes a step further: it divides the signifier from the signified."[65] By "divides" Eagleton does not mean "differentiates"; he means "cuts off." Poststructuralism moves beyond Saussure's one-to-one correspondence of signifier and signified to consider an indeterminately expansive chain of signifiers. But if those signifiers cannot be relied on to connect us even to a signified, how can they hope to tell us anything about the "real" world beyond the sign?

These considerations may begin to make intelligible a much-noted description by Derrida of the process of signification. It appears in connection with his analysis of the relation among the signifiers for objects of desire in Rousseau's *Confessions*:

> Through this sequence of supplements a necessity is announced: that of an infinite chain, ineluctably multiplying the supplementary mediations that produce the sense of the very thing they defer: the mirage of the thing itself, of immediate presence, of originary perception. Immediacy is derived. That all begins through the intermediary is what is indeed "inconceivable [to reason]."[66]

In presenting these signifiers as a "chain of supplements,"[67] Derrida clearly characterizes their relationship as that of metonymical adjacence—a relationship by definition too contingent to serve as a secure basis of knowledge. In other words, though there are ways in which a supplement can be understood to constitute a text rich enough to serve as an equivalent to the "main body"—to constitute a countervalent force that seems equal to the task of providing real new knowledge as a signified—the completion it effects takes place fundamentally at the same epistemological level as the text, a level of association. And whether physically or conventionally determined, association is a contingent, not necessary, process. A connotes B not because it has to but because it happens to. To be sure, Derrida asserts that (in Spivak's translation) "a necessity is announced."[68] What Derrida seems to envision here, however, is not a logical necessity, or law, but the irresistible force of momentum in a contingently determined direction.[69]

Derrida's imagery here portrays explicitly the inability of language, at any point on the signifying chain, to get outside itself. Born out of the desire to (re)capture a real presence, say, the ultimate, original loved one, Rousseau's language, like all language, is itself already mediated, with no hope of retrieving its own origins.[70] Nor, no matter how far the chain extends itself, no matter how many supplements it adds, can it ever arrive at an object of desire that is indisputably real. In a sense, by Derrida's account, language takes away what it gives. Through language we acquire a sense of power to attain real knowledge, only to realize that the very force or immediacy that suggests this power is a function of the ways in which language operates by way of itself, not of an ability of language to connect us (convincingly) to metaphysical reality.

The final sentence of this passage can be read as a reference to the paradoxes of Kant's critical philosophy. Fearing the consequences of a theory that limits and relativizes the bases of knowledge, Kant devised a strategy for asserting that "*E pur*" we know. Granting the need of conscious intelligence to verify some connection between itself and the grounds of knowledge in order to trust knowledge as such, Kant produced "transcendental reason," a construct that proclaimed the universality, and hence the hardness, of at least certain kinds of knowledge. At bottom, however, Kant gives us no more than a suggestive metaphor. All the logic of Kant's internal arguments cannot compensate for our ability, if we choose, to reject the very premise of transcendental reason on imaginably plausible grounds. Kant shouts the limits of human knowledge loud enough to resound to the end of time. And yet, at a palpable qualitative level, he seems to seek to reassure us that he doesn't really mean it. Having gone to so much trouble to devise this strategy, Kant (and, at bottom, hard-core analytic philosophers) cannot quite stomach the assertion that transcendental reason, as no more than a linguistic construct, secures nothing substantial with respect to the reality of human knowledge.

It could be to Kant's transcendental universality that Derrida refers when concluding, in effect, that reason cannot finally reconcile itself to the radical provisionality of knowledge construed as always already mediated by the limiting effects of language.[71] By Derrida's account here, knowledge never exceeds the reach of the metonymical relations that can be established by, and within, language.

And yet, as the signifier-signified relationship seems to suggest, language also operates by way of metaphor. The differences between signs are not, as language is *used*, insignificant but significant. Every signifier can in some sense be construed as pointing us to a nexus of meaning—the signified—that adds something substantial to knowledge. In part this possible construction derives from the apparent power of the signified to serve as an equivalent or replacement of the signifier; Derrida himself associates supplementarity with a "play of substitutions."[72] Ultimately, such a construction probably derives from our need to invoke a symbolic, intellectual capacity in order to explain the very persuasiveness of relationships of replaceability, which do not seem to depend for their soundness on the happenstance of contiguity.

Whatever the dynamic, we can conjure up a vision of language as a metaphorical process that allows us to institute significant differences in a unidirectional and progressive series of transformations. And one of our fondest dreams, according to deconstructionist writers, is to follow such a chain of transformations until we reach an ultimate meaning that is grounded in a referent on the other side of the metaphysical divide, and that thereby reveals the true nature of reality as being meaningful or intelligible. This referent would be the "transcendental signified," and the process of reaching it would be "transcendental signification."[73]

Two Literary Models

In testing out deconstructionist method on Chopin's A-Major Prelude, I will use as guidelines two articles about literature. The first, "Semiology and Rhetoric," by Paul de Man, is something of a classic in deconstruction and will be familiar to many students of the movement.[74] The second, "The Realist Floor-Plan," by Fredric Jameson, may seem a more idiosyncratic choice since Jameson could hardly be called a card-carrying deconstructionist.[75]

In his preface to the collection *On Signs*, Marshall Blonsky characterizes the Jameson of this article as "ill at ease."[76] Whether or not Blonsky means here to describe the mood of Jameson's cultural vision or (as I suppose) his relation to deconstruction is not altogether clear. Either way, I have found it richly evocative on numerous levels for the study of nineteenth-century European music, and exceptionally useful in its attempt to integrate deconstruction with explicitly historical concerns. I have felt no hesitation about drawing selectively on de Man's analyses of Yeats and Proust. The structure of the article seems explicitly to invite this, or at least allow it. The structure of Jameson's article, on the other hand, is a good deal more complex than one might suppose on a first reading. Precisely because it attempts to make sense of intellectual history as a continuous structure, it develops subtle interrelationships between earlier and later portions of this structure. Though I believe Jameson's structure could be used in something like its entirety as a model for musical analysis, I have decided finally to focus only on those aspects of his argument that seem most directly related to an initial deconstruction of Chopin's music.

A key moment in de Man's essay comes with his proposal of two conflicting interpretations for the final line of Yeats's poem "Among School Children."[77] The line is this: "How can we know the dancer from the dance?" Ordinarily this line is interpreted as a rhetorical question, conveying a nonliteral, figurative meaning, which is this: "We can't know. We cannot know the dancer from the dance." In terms of this traditional reading, the line could be paraphrased thus: "How can we *know* the dancer from the dance? We can't. It's impossible."

But, writes de Man, if the logic of the line is taken literally as a request for information—"Please tell me, how *can* I know the dancer from the dance?"—then the poem can be read not as depreciating distinctions but as seeking to establish them.[78] And thus the logic of the previous reading can be unraveled. Through the confrontation of these two readings, de Man goes on to question the traditional conception of rhetoric, or figurative language, as "supplemental," subordinate, and opposed to logic—even as he demonstrates the dependence of his argument on logical forms of reasoning.[79]

Jameson's essay studies a short passage in Flaubert's story "Un Coeur simple," which reads in translation as follows:

> This house had a slate roof and stood between an alley-way and a lane leading down to the river. Inside there were differences in level which were the cause of many a stumble. A narrow entrance-hall separated the kitchen from the parlour, where Madame Aubain sat all day long in a wicker easy-chair by the window. Eight mahogany chairs were lined up against the white-painted wainscoting, and under the barometer stood an old piano loaded with a pyramid of boxes and cartons. On either side of the chimney piece, which was carved out of yellow marble in the Louis Quinze style, there was a tapestry-covered armchair. The clock, in the middle, was designed to look like a temple of Vesta—and the whole room smelt a little musty, as the floor was on a lower level than the garden.[80]

Jameson sets out to see whether ninetenth-century realism can be interpreted as part of an ongoing process of secularization, that is, of decoding and demystifying ancient sacred codes, a process Jameson calls "the bourgeois cultural revolution."[81] Jameson characterizes this revolution as a passage from the heterogeneity, ritual, and cyclical character of sacred space and time (presumably crystallized when Catholicism still offered the West a plausibly unified worldview) to the infinite geometric grid, the physical and measurable time and space, and the relations of homogeneity and equivalence in Descartes's scientific world, where the sensory, qualitative, and libidinal are now reduced to what Descartes would term a secondary, merely psychological status.[82]

Jameson contends, in effect, that the role of the nineteenth-century artist was to create a physical world that confirmed the contemporary, scientific belief in "'the reality of the appearance.'"[83] Flaubert's text does this in a way that to Jameson suggests bourgeois space as virtually empty and decentered.[84] Flaubert's pairs of objects lie side by side, not as meaningful polarities but as "dual inequalit[ies]," within an (essentially) atomized world of potentially "infinite fission," where everything has been decentered to the margin.[85] Flaubert solves the problem of concretely defining an empty space "in which the center is always *elsewhere*," according to Jameson, by replacing an "organic or qualitative" space with an "additive" one.[86]

Using the clock as an example, Jameson finds in Flaubert's text references to "culture" that seem to resist the scientific demystification required by the modern bourgeois world.[87] Yet this strategy "as the final Flaubertian cadence confirms, is doomed in advance to failure," in part because the cultural objects are themselves indebted to science.[88]

Only in the last sentence of Flaubert's passage is a phrase introduced that invokes a subjective human experience: "The whole room smelt a little musty." Yet the effect of this invocation, Jameson argues, is not to recenter this empty space on the consciousness of the Cartesian subject but to suggest the marginality of the new bourgeois subject, in its inability to control space, at the very moment it makes its appearance. Subjectivity enters the work here as an already absent trace. Though it constitutes "the only genuine *event* in this lengthy paragraph," according to Jameson, "this sudden and unexpected burst of 'affect' announces the fitful emergence of the subject in Flaubert's text: the 'musty smell' inscribing, with a triumphant, desolate flourish, the place of subjectivity in a henceforth reified universe."[89] This reading is confirmed, in Jameson's account, by the immediate appearance of "the seemingly aimless rationalizing and logical connective '*car*' ('as' or 'since') which offers the very symptom of a cause-and-effect logic running wild and consuming the universe."[90]

Jameson eventually proposes two "radically incompatible" readings for this passage.[91] One, moved by a "nostalgia for meaning" that Jameson calls "high modernist,"[92] tries to encompass all of the realistic details in a unified symbolic theory, and thereby to confirm the grounds for belief in "the reality of the appearance." The other, a "postmodernist" reading, sees represented in this passage a divorce of concrete reality from the possibility of a unified conception of meaning—a deconstruction by science, so to speak, of its own promise.

To articulate this interpretation, Jameson cites Barthes's attack on the concept of realism, which reads in part as follows: "We have only to recall how, in the ideology of our time, the obsessional evocation of the 'concrete' . . . is always staged as an aggressive arm against meaning, as though by some *de jure* exclusion, what lives is structurally incapable of carrying a meaning—and vice versa."[93] As summed up in this last passage, which in another context one would be tempted to identify as précis of Stravinsky's *Poetics*, this entire line of argument offers intriguing possibilities for the criticism of nineteenth-century music—particularly if one is prepared to use the term "concrete" as a kind of musical analogue for the literary term "real."[94]

A Deconstruction of Chopin's A-Major Prelude: First Reading

Although Chopin's prelude lacks the explicit semantic parameter that deconstruction, at least in its earlier stages, took for granted, it nevertheless lends itself generously to interpretation as a field in which conflicting forces of construction and deconstruction are at play (Example 1).

My immediate strategy here is to account in some measure for two conflicting interpretations, or readings, of this piece, one that of an educated layman

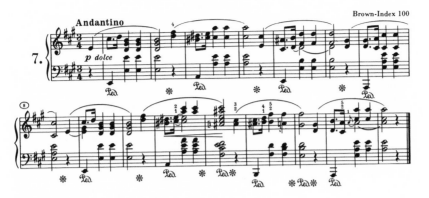

Example 1. Chopin's A-Major Prelude, op. 28, no. 7

and one my own. My husband, Dan, hears the A-Major Prelude as "happy"— as an affirmation of the possibility of establishing, in his words, "beauty and meaning in the world." From this perspective, as I understand it, the prelude expresses contentment that beauty and meaning, as defined through its own example, are real. Such an expression seems close to what Jameson calls a belief in "the reality of the appearance." Heard in this way, the prelude seems to offer a reassuring vision of humanly congenial intelligibility as a fundamental component of reality.

I, on the other hand, hear this piece not as happy or contented but as poignantly sad or resigned. Its physical concreteness seems marked by a quality of absence, by a "trace," by its evocation of something missing. To me this piece conveys a wistful sense that something once thought to be securely in its possession—let us say a belief in the inseparability of intelligibility and reality—can no longer be counted on. From this perspective, the first reading does not affirm the "reality of the appearance" but only what Jameson calls its own "nostalgia for meaning."[95]

For me it has been helpful to visualize these two readings in terms of a metaphorical or figurative device: I see them as positioned on a horizontal axis, which represents two possible ways of relating human consciousness to reality. At the center of this axis lies what could be called the field of human subjectivity, as it has been defined in a good deal of Western thought since the Enlightenment. This is the field where human consciousness, operating within the constraints of its own experience and intelligence, goes about imposing rational meaning on objective reality, by forging connections into a coherent pattern of unity.

Though I am defining this field as a figurative device, in practice it tends to be treated in Western culture as a domain, and sometimes the entire domain, of reality. For as long as the thinking subject can locate its operations with confidence in such a field, subjectivity can validate itself as a real and powerful entity. Without some such working confidence, as Kant and many subsequent philosophers have understood, modern Western thought offers little protection against metaphysical despair. Our tradition of scientific rigor cannot definitively exclude the possibility that consciousness itself is a chimera, an evolutionary excrescence engendered in a meaningless reality, to which consciousness itself provides no more access than does the upward thrust of the giraffe's neck.

Western tradition has tended to define the field in which subjectivity validates itself through a series of polarities, of which the subject-object relationship is only one. Prominent among these polarities are the principles of order and freedom. On the one hand, unable to conceptualize itself apart from a capacity to conceptualize—to proceed by constructing meanings—subjectivity regularly treats the principles of its own intelligence as sufficient to establish the ordered character of reality. It does so even if, in many cases, this entails limiting the notion of reality to what can at least be imagined as cognitively intelligible. To take the most obvious example (Kant's efforts notwithstanding), the enjoyment of its own powers to illuminate reality would be woefully hollow if modern Western science felt it had to take responsibility for the ontological status of domains evoked through religion—or for that matter through art.

Yet, on the other hand, subjectivity experiences its own reality and power not only by way of its intellectual character but also through its essentially moral capacity for free choice. Indeed, however rigorously Kant sought to validate the powers of pure (cognitive) reason in his account of practical (moral) reason (and of aesthetic judgment), his topography of reason seems to me to rest finally, in both its content and its structure, on a priority of moral, as opposed to cognitive, necessities.[96] But for those of us who have followed in Western tradition, the priority seems clearly reversed. When forced to choose [!] between characterizing reality as a meaningless principle that allows unlimited freedom of choice, or as an intelligible principle that disciplines and constrains freedom, Western thought has generally, though by no means always, opted for the latter alternative. "Morality" may in theory connote the highest human capacities; but without concessions to some cognitively demonstrable principles of order, moral systems tend to be feared, in modern Western culture, as vulnerable to irrational abuse.

On the whole, modern Western thought seems much more confident of its

ability to "capture" and "possess" reality by adducing universal cognitive principles, which would render reality intelligible, than to do so by working out
comparably universal moral principles. (Whereas I would question the
grounds for universal necessity in both realms, the scientific viewpoint—
which is no longer honored uncritically by all scientists—has traditionally
reserved its doubts only for the moral one.) Certainly the term "reason" is currently associated far more widely in the West with the cognitive than with the
moral domain. Consequently I would assume that within the polarity of order
and freedom, the former, in today's Western culture, takes precedence.

But to either of these alternatives, Western thought would prefer a conception of reality that unified the needs of cognition and morality. A subjectivity
that must explicitly choose between cognitive and moral considerations
would have difficulty establishing its claim to validity (especially to universal
validity) as a principle of reality. Thus the center of the axis I am visualizing is
caught in a tension between the priority of cognition to morality (of order to
freedom) and an ideal of unity between the two.

This idealized unity can be aptly symbolized by Chopin's A-Major Prelude
when it is itself interpreted as a persuasively unified structure. Within such an
interpretation, the prelude can be heard as an example of the internally
weighted unity—that is, of the hierarchical binary opposition between order
and freedom that persuasively demonstrates the reality and power of subjectivity.[97] Some such conception lies at the heart of those "high-modernist"
readings that, in Jameson's terms, present a unified "symbolic" theory of a text.
These would include my husband's reading of Chopin's A-Major Prelude.

Now, the force on which subjectivity tries to exert order seems quite clearly
to be that of random contingency, where the latter is taken as the fundamental principle of reality. And the force that subjectivity tries to "humanize" by
asserting its capacity for freedom is the inexorability of some absolute, deterministic law of reality operating beyond the control of human action. These
two principles—random contingency and inexorable law—seem to me to
define the extremes of human relations to reality, as conceived in modern
Western culture.

Both of these extremes seem to lie equally beyond the boundaries of any
field in which human subjectivity might affirm its reality and power. For both
define a condition of arbitrariness that makes no sense from the standpoint of
either intelligibility or rational moral choice, a condition that is thus irrelevant to any traditional concept of subjectivity.

As principles of organization, it is interesting to note, the polar opposites of
determinism and randomness have both shaped important tendencies in

Western musical composition since the onset of post-tonalism—that is, in the twentieth century. Within the history of post-tonal music as it developed, the principle of determinism, as represented by serialism, established a certain priority, both temporally and conceptually. (No one would seriously describe serialism as a response to aleatory tendencies.)

And within Western history more generally, the same hierarchy can probably be said to have characterized the value assigned to these two principles. Again, faced with the alternatives of conceding reality to be utterly random or attributing all of the apparent irrationalities and meaningless cruelties of human experience to some overarching deterministic principle, Judeo-Christian culture, at least, seems to have been more drawn from the start to the latter than to the former as a working metaphysical principle. Presumably determinism, however uncongenial its inexorability to the particularities of human experience, seems closer to the ordering principles of human intelligence than does random contingency to the exercise of free will.

At any rate, these two extremes, determinism and contingency, operating outside the domain of self-validating subjectivity, can be taken as the endpoints of the interpretational axis I have proposed for Chopin's A-Major Prelude. These endpoints will define the location for my own "second" reading, which in Jameson's terms could be called postmodernist.

Given the cultural context in which Chopin's prelude emerged, it seems to me reasonable to assume that the reading to which this piece assigns priority, and which it projects most emphatically as its foreground layer of meaning, is the first reading, the one that points toward a validation of subjectivity. For this prelude makes sufficient use of preexisting musical strategies for imposing order through unity, while also providing imagery that powerfully evokes the concept of subjective freedom, as to suggest its ongoing agreement with the thrust of preceding Western musical tradition. And certainly immediately preceding tradition, as represented in Viennese Classicism, made a powerful case for a reading of itself at the center of the axis I have described. Not only did this style, like Bach's before it, design extraordinarily persuasive models of a fundamentally intelligible reality; in addition, it bequeathed directly to Romanticism rich musical resources for symbolizing effectively the power of subjective freedom. And it did so through musical structures that have, perhaps more successfully than any others in Western history, projected themselves as fundamentally unified.

Assuming, then, the priority of my husband's reading, I would like to begin my analysis of that reading with a typically deconstructive focus on a secondary, supplemental, or marginal moment in the prelude. In a sense the most emphatically secondary moment occurs at the climax of the piece, at the big chord at the end of the sixth phrase, on the first beat of measure 12 (V of B-minor).

It may seem strange to consider a climax secondary or "supplemental." As I have indicated, this first reading of Chopin's prelude, as an affirmation of the possibility of establishing beauty and meaning in the world, involves construing the piece as a coherent, unified whole. But surely a climax must be taken for the primary center of importance in such a whole. An effective climax—and this is a very effective climax—is among the most powerful devices we can imagine for establishing the unified status of a musical structure.

Rufus Hallmark, in a letter to me, has suggested the following strategy for understanding my characterization of the climactic chord as "secondary." "Ask the reader," he suggests, "to contemplate a hypothetical version of the prelude in which phrase 6 behaves harmonically like phrase 2. . . . [H]ad Chopin left out the surprising A sharp and kept the A in the bass—in short left this phrase on the tonic—the piece would still 'work' as a musical composition. Isn't this what you mean when you say the F-sharp V⁷ chord is 'inessential'?"

Hallmark's suggestion is helpful insofar as it formulates concisely a hierarchical relation toward which this entire first reading points: the priority of tonal logic to more contingent aspects of sonorous identity, whether the latter stem from physical characteristics (including even pitch *as such*) or from what I have elsewhere called "rhetorical" techniques of emphasis.[98] By this formulation, one could imagine substituting not only a different triad but also a sonority restricted in range, fullness, or volume, without destroying the intelligibility of the work as a plausible whole. Whether the chord were on I or on V of II, the piece could still make at least overall sense tonally.

Nevertheless, Hallmark's strategy must be used with caution. In the first place, the relationship between the climactic function of this chord and the structural unity of the piece is a two-way, dialectical relationship. In other words, this climax is perceived not only as a source but also as a beneficiary of structural relationships that collectively establish a condition of unity. On the one hand, the ability of this chord to define an indisputably supreme point of climax contributes critically to our perception of the whole structure as unified. But on the other hand, this very ability depends on the density of the connections this chord establishes between itself and various other elements of the piece. The moment evokes an emotionally powerful sense of significance—indeed, it is experienced not just as a symbol but virtually as an embodiment of poignancy—precisely because of the tension it maintains between its aspects of precarious singularity and solid connectedness. Any

loud crash at this moment might well be jarring. But what if its sounds bore little or no perceptible relation (either of similarity or controlled difference) to
the rest of the piece? Unless we were to radically restructure our ways of perceiving meaning in this prelude—perhaps by putting the piece in quotation
marks and presenting it as a late twentieth-century construct (as George
Crumb does in his "Dream Images" with Chopin's Fantaisie-Impromptu)[99]—
the effect of such a sonority would not exceed that of a physically crude,
merely literal, and arbitrary contrast, to which we could attach no meaning.
Such an essentially meaningless effect would not be construed in any traditional sense as a climax.

And as I hope shortly to clarify, the specific aspects of this sonority are
bound palpably, though often subtly, to a number of other elements in the prelude. It seems quite certain, in fact, that altering the particular sonority of this
chord would drastically weaken its structural connectedness to the rest of the
prelude. This in turn would dull its effectiveness as a climax, and thereby
undermine still further the perception of structural unity.

There is another reason for caution here as well. The argument I intend to
make—that this chord functions effectively as a climax precisely to the extent
that it defines its own particular attributes as secondary in relation to other
characteristics and values in the piece—is not the same as calling the chord
"inessential."[100] Indeed, much of the reputation that Viennese Classicism
enjoys for "universality" is derived from the frequently noted ability of a composer such as Haydn to give conventionally secondary elements, such as
accompanimental patterns, an "essential" role in his musical structures.[101]

This reference to Haydn is not merely incidental to the cautions I urge in
connection with Hallmark's heuristic strategy. It will be recalled that a significant continuity between Chopin's A-Major Prelude and Viennese Classicism
is assumed in my first reading. In fact, the contradictory force of my second
reading will depend very heavily on its initial assumption of the same continuity in one important respect, namely, its basis for distinguishing between
"primary" and "secondary" characteristics in themselves.

True, my second reading (by focusing from the start on secondary attributes
in themselves rather than on their relation to primary ones) will assign structural
weight differently to the two categories. Nevertheless, in both readings, the
designation of "primary" as a qualitative attribute will be reserved for those
musical elements that, by traditional Western tonal standards, tend toward a
condition of stability. By these standards, primary characteristics are dominated, even on a perceptual level, by the constancies of tonal function, rather
than by the contingencies of a literal physical configuration. Conversely, sec-

ondary characteristics will be associated with tonal instability and a predominantly physical (or rhetorically emphatic) identity.

Now, short of disrupting the tonal intelligibility of this prelude altogether, almost any alteration we can imagine in the climactic sonority would lessen its effect of contrast. Most of these changes would increase the similarities between this sonority and the more stable primary elements of the piece.

Such homogenization, it should be stressed, would not necessarily enhance the unity of the prelude. On the contrary, it would deprive other unstable elements in the piece of a focus of unity, while also removing the element that most clearly defines a polarity of structural principles. Thus it would destroy the tension needed to establish unity; sameness is not a sufficient condition for the perception of structural unity. Such a perception, at least within the terms of Western musical convention, requires difference as well as similarity. One feels comfortable speaking of structural unity in Western music only in situations that present something to be unified.

In effect, what I have just proposed is a series of multilayered linguistic definitions and distinctions. On a fairly simple and straightforward level I have suggested a constant equation between "primary" (or, to an extent, "essential") characteristics *in themselves* and values associated with "stability," and a corresponding equation between "secondary" and "unstable" (or contingent) characteristics. Yet at the same time I have also suggested that the relation between the two groups of terms *as indicators of relative weight or structural importance* can be complex and even volatile.

For, again, though the designation "secondary" by definition assigns some sort of priority to a concept of "primary"—say to "primary" qualities in themselves, or to a level of structural significance associated with such qualities— this designation does not necessarily concede the functional role of "the secondary" as "inessential," at least in the sense of "dispensable" or "optional." In fact, my second reading will go so far as to suggest that "secondary" qualities in themselves can define a level of structural significance that is prior in some functional sense to the level defined through "primary" characteristics—that these secondary qualities define a level to which, in some ways, our interpretation assigns a more fundamental status, or relatively greater weight, than it does to the so-called primary level.

Without question, these multilayered linguistic definitions and distinctions are subtle, delicate, slippery. As the following two readings unfold, moreover, the reader will become increasingly aware, as I myself have become, of the degree to which virtually every critical term I use is from the outset enmeshed in a series of paradoxes, which can readily extend toward infinite regress. A "primary" characteristic in itself, for example, is dominated by its tonal identity. But isn't tonal identity an implicitly relational term? A tonal center offers weight and stability. But do these terms signify a substantive condition? Or a relative standard of measure? Again and again it will seem that just as I decide to take up some characteristic in its relational aspects I begin by describing its qualitative character, and vice versa. No matter what term I fasten upon, it seems to be nested within other considerations that point to a totally opposite meaning from the one I am trying to propose.

Such complexities pose formidable problems not only for the reader's understanding of my arguments but also for my own construction and control of those arguments. Yet these complexities should not on this account be dismissed out of hand as mere sophistry. They arise not from any perverse desire on my part to manipulate the reader but out of an analysis, which I have pursued as honestly as I can, of how musical as well as verbal language operates.

Take, for instance, my distinctions between "primary" and "secondary." A potential disjunction (such as will emerge in my second reading) between the inherent qualitative identity and the relative functional significance of "secondary" characteristics is allowed by the multiple meanings of the term "secondary." In our own language, for example, just as the adjective "stable" can signify either the properties of being at rest or the comparative aspects of a "fundamental" state, so, too, "secondary" can denote not only a relative but also a substantive condition. (Locke's use of the term "secondary" points to a group of definable attributes as well as to an epistemological hierarchy. One might even argue that Berkeley's epistemology concedes a functional priority to such secondary attributes.)

In a similar way, depending on its context, we can understand the term "essential" to define conditions ranging from "substantively weighty," or "stable," through "more important than something else," to "indispensable," and "first" insofar as it means "absolutely fundamental." Or even, perhaps in some abstract logical sense, "prior to time, or to the contingencies of concrete physical existence or perception." And by the same token, the term "secondary" in our language can define a state of polar opposition to any of these signified conditions.

Whether or not the semiotic systems of all cultures produce similar ambiguities is a question I am unqualified to address. What I can say with some confidence, and what I hope will be borne out here, is that nineteenth-century Western art music is itself deeply preoccupied with such ambiguities. Let us consider, for example, the concept of "weight." In ordinary usage, this term has at least two distinct meanings. On the one hand it refers to a condition of physical thickness or solidity. On the other hand, it denotes a relative degree of importance.

Consider now the general historical direction of Western tonal music. During the first stages, which we can term "Baroque," one senses a palpable delight in the growing realization that the more abstract, explicitly semiotic, intelligible, and (without doubt) figurative meanings of "weight" can be established as the primary definition of this term through musical means. This pleasure reaches a kind of zenith, in varying ways that I cannot explore here, in the music of Bach, Handel, and Domenico Scarlatti (all born in 1685), and of Haydn.[102]

Possibly this condition of delight can be made to account for our continuing perception of humor in Haydn's music. Whereas the establishment of this primary meaning is a matter of serious metaphysical significance for Bach, and a source of powerful dramatic effect for Handel, Haydn is sufficiently secure about its possibility to use it as an instrument for flexing his intellectual muscles, so to speak; that is, for reveling in the status of superiority he takes for granted as conferred by intellectual powers.[103] All these attitudes are in keeping with the rationalistic priorities that fueled the Enlightenment in its various stages.

Within the mature styles of Mozart and Beethoven, on the other hand, intellectual confidence has reached a sufficient degree of self-consciousness that it appears to pique a tendency toward individualistic challenge, and, eventually (at least in Beethoven's last style), toward experiments in what we usually characterize as "mannerism" (a term, interestingly, seldom applied to Western music history after 1600).

Compared to Beethoven, Mozart's impulse to take exception to the priorities presented by convention is more restrained, but by no means negligible. His explorations of chromaticism, and of differences in sonorous effect produced, say, through instrumentation or major-minor contrast, are not just the pleasantries of a speaker who knows that we all know what's *really* important. Though such explorations may sometimes begin in a spirit of humor, they begin to open up some serious questions about metaphysical and existential priorities.

The majority of Beethoven's compositions, and not just in the last period, ask outright, "Says who?" For Beethoven himself this question may still have had a predominantly rhetorical import. But the Romantics, in keeping with an age that conclusively established the importance of empirical investigation, took Beethoven's question seriously as the indication of a need for further information. (One sees here, already, the sort of application that de Man's interplay of real and rhetorical questions could have for the interpretation of music history.) In the Romantic style, which launched orchestration as a more or less scientific enterprise, the primary meaning of "weight" tends often toward "physical thickness," as opposed to "intellectual priority." Such a historical reconsideration of what "weight" means explains as well as anything Mahler's desperation, and Schoenberg's ultimately militant denial of despair.

Even this brief excursion into the changing musical history of what we call "weight" seems strongly to support the poststructuralist characterization of thought—or at least Western thought—as fundamentally entrapped in the multilayered and ultimately elusive paradoxes of language, in its most general sense. Many such paradoxes, it should soon be clear, come into play when I characterize the climactic moment in Chopin's prelude as "secondary."

It should also soon be clear that my analysis of the term "secondary" here comes close to articulating Derrida's more specific concept of the term "supplement." This is a concept I have found extremely illuminating—and one that I hope will disarm any lingering resistance to a characterization of the climax in Chopin's A-Major Prelude as "secondary."

Actually, the ways in which I use the notion of "supplement" as a tool for musical criticism will stop a good deal short, particularly in this first reading, of Derrida's own complexity. In analyzing the means by which the sonority in measure 12 of Chopin's prelude asserts its power as a climax, in terms of its physical identity and also of its logical function, I have come to understand this sonority as a construct that exemplifies persuasively Derrida's double-edged definition of a supplement both as extra, optional, or external, and as integral, essential, or internal to its "parent" text.

In relation to the prelude construed (in this first reading) as a coherent whole, the climactic sonority does indeed present itself as essential—but essential precisely because it is secondary. By this I mean (and clearly the word "because" is ambiguous in this context) it is essential because it is *no more than* secondary, that is, it is essential only insofar as it is secondary. Within this formulation, it should be apparent, the term "secondary" is taken to denote, chiefly, a relative degree of significance, rather than some intrinsic qualitative condition.

Let us therefore look at the relational force of the climactic sonority, first in terms of its more literal, concrete physical characteristics, and then in terms of its more functional characteristics.

In physical terms, one hears this sonority as a rupture precisely because of its singularity. This sonority reiterates the breakthrough of the top line to an unprecedentedly high point of the range, while it simultaneously breaks the pattern of repeated bass notes that ended all previous phrases in order to step downward and open out. This sonority also bridges its own outer span with a fullness of texture that is unique in the piece; and it is, apparently, the loudest moment in the prelude.

In all these respects, the chord is striking because it defines an extreme of physical possibility that is nowhere else attempted. It has an exceptional status that, precisely as such, reaffirms the superior power of the norms that it momentarily violates. One could even argue that the outer fifth established in this chord, between F-sharp and C-sharp, defines structurally prominent parallel fifths with the preceding outer E and B at the beginning of measure 10, a situation that in this stylistic context would clearly constitute the violation of an established and (at least by now) essentially sonorous or physical norm.

In turning to the relational force of the climax in terms of its functional characteristics, we will naturally [!] look first at its tonal composition. Quite clearly the basis of the climactic tonal effect produced by this chord is similar to the basis of its physical power. This chord on V of II (V of B-minor) is tonally dramatic because it is the only point in the piece where an unveiled, unambiguous reference is made to a tonal area other than the tonic, A.

This is not to argue that V of II appears out of the blue, as a tonally senseless solecism. On the contrary, it is crucially important to note that this chord clearly crystallizes other impulses of tension in the prelude. These include both movement *away from* simple reconfirmation of the tonic, as in the relatively dissonant or unstable appoggiaturas on the first beats of all the odd-numbered measures starting with 3. It also includes movement specifically *toward* the relatively distant pole of B-minor. In particular, a prominent earlier reference to B-minor occurs in the third phrase (measures 5 and 6), where the notes of the V and the I triads of this key, intensifying the passing dissonance of the preceding phrase, are superimposed over V of A, with B playing a dual tonal role (as V of V of A and as its own tonic). In the three repeated chords of phrase 3, indeed, the entire B-minor triad sounds, whereas G-sharp, the third degree of the E-major (V) triad is missing. At that moment, however, the tonal force of B-minor is very obviously secondary, since its V and I triads are wrapped within a root-position dominant seventh on E. The latter is clearly the governing chord here, both in terms of its symmetrical relation to the first half-cadence of the piece (measures 1 and 2) and of its own resolution to A.

But the power of the climactic chord, too, inheres in the force with which this sonority clarifies the secondary tonal status of B-minor, and thus confirms the governing constructive role of the tonic, A. In itself, the climactic V of II sonority sticks out as especially precarious or unstable because the music shrinks from resolving its physical fullness with an equally full, stable realization of II. Instead, the music hits the resolution on II, B-minor, more or less in passing, and immediately thereafter lowers the leading tone of B down to A-natural (measure 13), taking us irreversibly out of the B-minor domain. Thus, although the pedal (of which, more later) may momentarily protect the sound of B-minor from total dissolution—and though a subsequent effort is made, as will be seen, to reinforce the strength of this B-minor resolution—the field even momentarily governed by B-minor extends no further than the second beat of measure 13.

In short, the tonal effect of the climactic chord is to clarify its own propulsive thrust toward II (here B-minor) as an exception to a norm of I (here A). The primacy of the outer frame in A-major remains persuasively intact, even at this climactic moment. And, of course, the alternating pattern of V–I cadences in A, which has been established by previous symmetrically related pairs of phrases, is resumed in the final pair.

Symmetry, which in this piece (as in most Classical and early Romantic music) is closely intertwined with tonal structure, offers a second relational framework for defining the power of the climactic sonority. One of the most striking characteristics of this chord is its involvement in the disruption of numerous symmetrical patterns.

At the last moment in the sixth phrase, as just noted, the climax substitutes V of II for the tonic of the cadences that closed the second and fourth phrases. Likewise, this chord repeats the outer fifth that ends its own antecedent phrase (the E and B in measure 10) instead of resolving that outer interval to a more stable one, as the closing chords in all the other consequent phrases do (outer fifth to octave in the first two phrases, seventh to sixth in the second pair, and ninth to octave in the closing pair).

In fact, the substitution of instability and disruption for stability and closure at this moment tends further to undermine the symmetrical status of the sixth phrase as a "consequent," by transforming it into something more akin to another "antecedent." This latter effect is reinforced by the reappearance in measure 11 of the melodically ascending sixth, E to C-sharp, an event unparalleled in the first half of the piece. This is the same ascending sixth that initiated the immediately preceding phrase (and, of course, the opening phrase of the piece), its identity made all the more emphatic now by its rise to a higher register. This effect of transformation into an antecedent is also reinforced by the reappearance of the outer simultaneous fifth that closed phrases 1 and 5.[104]

Such disruptions of symmetry have a powerful effect. But again, the source of this power lies above all in the clear projection of such asymmetries as relatively or functionally secondary characteristics. Just as A-major never surrenders its status as the primary tonality in this prelude, so, too, the asymmetries thus far described do not supplant symmetry as a structural norm. In addition to more obvious symmetrical features, for example, the upward rupture in range at the climactic moment has a clear counterpart in the leap to the top melodic A at the end of the second phrase. Though the later gesture is physically less restrained than the earlier one (and thus in some respects, as will be seen, can be taken as the symbol of a real power to progress), the placement of each at precisely corresponding points in the two halves of the piece calls marked attention to the pervasive role of symmetry at virtually every level of this structure.

Likewise, the climactic chord itself, though in a precipitate and (as we shall see) inexact manner, establishes a general tonal symmetry between the two halves of the piece. In taking up the hints of B-minor presented earlier, it impresses upon us the momentary increase of tonal tension in the third phrases of each half. Furthermore, at the very moment of climax, the rhythm, the formal phrasing, the delineation of a cadential gesture, even the unbroken pattern of repetitions in the uppermost melodic (though not the bass) line all maintain in very literal ways the continuity of symmetrical regularity.

Still, as the terms "general" and "inexact" suggest, the normative status of symmetry is a bit more complicated in this prelude than is that of the tonic. By definition, virtually any piece that maintains a clear tonic identity does so precisely through the general grammatical device of relegating all other tonal fields to a secondary level of structural importance. One could make that point about Chopin's A-Major Prelude without referring to much of its specific musical content at all.

Such an observation does not vitiate Derrida's basic definition of "supplements." If anything, it tends to support that definition as a generally valid insight into the fundamental operation of human discourse. But the symmetrical aspects of this prelude involve a far more particularized, individualistic set of choices. One cannot safely predict the relative priority of symmetry and asymmetry here without a detailed examination of what actually happens.

In fact, the workings of symmetry in this prelude, as centered in the climactic sonority, suggest themselves very powerfully (in ways that will shortly be described) as a metaphor for free choice. But if asymmetry can be shown here to exhibit an extensive, freewheeling dominion over structure, a dominion that is nevertheless subject ultimately to still more fundamental principles of order, then a similar claim can be made for the climactic sonority. In terms of definitions previously given, it can well be taken for the symbol of a principle that persuades us not only of its capacity for free choice but also of the rational logic that underlies its choices. In a word, the sonority can be construed as the symbol of a subjectivity that unifies the entire piece, and thereby ensures its intelligibility. This, I will now argue, is the case.

One of the more obvious indications in this prelude that symmetry does not establish its normative status by simple, predictable means is offered by the pedal pattern. The change in the pedal pattern that occurs in connection with the climactic sonority completely differentiates the second half of the prelude from the first. True, the internal pedal pattern of the four phrases of the second half (ABBA') is very nearly as symmetrical as the pattern preceding (AAAA). Still, the two halves are different; and the pedal is not released at the conclusion of the piece.

Likewise, the successive chordal spacings in this prelude are fluid and varied, not rigidly identical. This literal asymmetry, however, can be discounted as a tonal characteristic, one to which Schoenberg called attention when he replaced tonality with a literal conception of pitch relations. Within a framework of traditional practice, which is never violated in this prelude, literal differences of spacing in tonal chord configurations, like those in perspective drawings, are invariably perceived as transparent to less literal, more figurative, overarching structural relationships. Though Western listeners may well sense various literal asymmetries in the spacing of the successive chords, they will automatically "correct" for such differences in the perception of a "higher" tonal logic.

Almost certainly the imperfect symmetry of changes in the melodic direction of the uppermost line contributes to a piquant sense of deviation that could be associated with freedom. Yet an overarching symmetry is maintained. An identical melodic arch is outlined in the corresponding phrase pairs 1-2 and 5-6. Furthermore, the seventh and eighth phrases present almost exactly, except in reverse order, the patterns of melodic direction found in the third and fourth phrases, with the seventh phrase corresponding to the fourth, and the eighth to the third.

I say "almost exactly"; and here, by standards not only of literal structural identity but also of conscious auditory perception, the stipulation "almost" is without question crucial. The deviation from symmetry that occurs with the inversion in the melodic line at the opening of the last melodic phrase (measures 14-15) may be small, but in no way can it be discounted as transparent in effect. By setting the anacrusis G-sharp *below* the next melody note, B, instead of above it as in the third phrase (measures 4-5, where the anacrusis C-sharp is higher than the ensuing downbeat, A-sharp), and then by giving the dotted-eighth-to-sixteenth pattern (B to A) a *downward* direction in measure 15—this is the only time this happens—the prelude allows the dotted-eighth-note B an exceptional prominence not found on the initial first beat of any preceding phrase. This B, of course, can be heard as an effort to reinforce the rather rushed resolution of B-minor in the preceding measure, a reinforcement that has already been initiated, perhaps, by the B that fills in the left-hand sixth on the third beat of measure 13.

This melodic inversion can, in turn, be linked with a series of other changes that occur after the climactic chord, all of which seem to suggest the power of the subjective freedom evoked by that chord to alter what comes after it. From the climactic sixth phrase on, for example, the bass "mazurka" grouping of beats 2-3-1, which characteristically ends each phrase, shows alteration rather than repetition of pitch.

Likewise, up until the climactic chord, the middle voices have done little more than emphasize intermittently the dominant, E, through a crossing of the thumbs, or anticipate themselves through a seemingly irregular pattern of ties. After the climax, however, in measures 13 and 14, the supposedly supplemental middle voices bestir themselves to appropriate the descending line B-A-G-sharp, which culminates, in the next-to-last measure, in the transformation of the rhythmically exceptional, and thus markedly prominent, grace-note A in a middle voice. This latter note, in turn, seems to function as a delayed resolution of these middle voices.

The disruptions of symmetry do not stop here. Because the climactic chord, by exception, presents a dominant (V of II) rather than a tonic at the conclusion of a *consequent* phrase, the resolution of this dominant is displaced, for the only time in the piece, to the opening of the following antecedent.

On the level of the melodic line, this displacement could perhaps be said to last until the hitherto delayed, and final, entrance of B in the top line, on beat 1 of measure 15. In thus breaking through the conventional separations prescribed by the formal phrase marks, the prelude allows rhythmic and metrical asymmetry in the otherwise regularly recurring cadential pattern. And this asymmetry is to some extent reinforced by the exceptional pedal pattern which, as already noted, the sixth and seventh phrases have in common and which, again, tends to clarify the harmony in these measures.

This accelerated pedaling, to be sure, which tends also to atomize the phrases in question, is counterbalanced by the extension of the last pedal marking straight through the end of the final cadence. In other words, the literally asymmetrical length of the final pedal marking can be taken, through its compensation for the truncation of the preceding pedal fields, to reestablish, at least in some rough-hewn quantitative fashion, the claims of symmetrical balance. In addition, of course, the open-ended closing pedal not only reinforces the sound of the final tonic in a quantitative, literal sense but also symbolizes quite explicitly the indisputable claim of the tonic to have the last word.

Here we come, finally, to the principal point made by this first reading: the subsumption of the climax, rendered unmistakable by the very force of the concentrated contrasts it defines, under a more stable, higher order of structure.

Indeed, to what end is all this asymmetrical flourish, shifting, displacement, and reversal undertaken except to underscore some plausibly subjective ordering capacity, as exemplified through the final cadential process in the tonic A, to take action and effect changes that counteract a momentary threat to the intelligible governing authority of the tonic? Even if the asymmetrical melodic prominence given the soprano B on beat 1 of measure 15 "makes sense" as a delayed and thus forceful final attempt to resolve the harmony of the climactic chord persuasively, this melodic B—which is, after all, the dominant of the V triad in A—is by now well out of its own tonal territory. Resolving immediately and propulsively downward to a melodic A, this B is an exception, almost an anomaly. Even as it sounds, it reinforces the governing force of the low tonic A (beat 1, measure 15) that underlies and overwhelms this B, by uniting tonal and sonorous power into a forbiddingly authoritative gesture of conclusion. True, the D underlying the B in measure 15 belongs to the B-minor triad, and thus can also be construed as prolonging or recalling a reference to the latter key. On the other hand, precisely because it appears in conjunction with B, the dominant of V in A, this D projects itself far more immediately as part of the dominant seventh in A.[105] The most that can be said for B on the first beat of measure 15 as the root of a tonality is that we have here an example of a kind of telescoping of two tonalities, in which one, A, clearly predominates as a structural norm.[106]

The exceptional physical rise to the appoggiatura on B, on the first beat of measure 15, is indeed powerful. But it makes sense principally as the sign of a palpable marshaling of energy to effect final closure on A. And what better evidence could we have of the priority of stability over instability, and thus of control over freedom, than the taming of the rhythmically defiant, individually willful grace-note A, through its immediate transformation into a middle-voice tied note, well within the final tonic triads? Could there be clearer metaphorical evidence of subjective control than the yielding by this grace note of its exceptional and striking physical aspects to the superior logical claims of its tonal aspects?

At this point, it is true, the grace note initiates the biggest immediate upward melodic leap in the piece. But the leap measures the tonally stable distance of an octave, and occurs on the tonic, A. Through this double dose of stability—reinforced, of course, by preceding cadential affirmations of A as tonic, and also by the initial rupture of melodic range by the A of measures 3 and 4—the intervening high C-sharp at the climactic moment is emphatically defined as a temporary aberration, a definition that reaffirms its own deference to the governing power of the tonic A. And if even the forcefully defined climactic sonority can mount no more than an illusory threat to the rule of the tonic, how seriously can we take the threat posed by the physically far weaker B in measure 15?

Consider as well the effect we perceive in the resumption of tonal symmetry in the final V–I cadence, made all the more powerful by the contrast of this asymmetrically emphatic grace-note A, and reinforced also by the maintenance of the repeated melodic notes, the rhythm, and the formal phrasing. Is the effect not that of a subjectivity emerging unscathed from the potentially irrational temptations of asymmetry, to exercise its ability, and thereby assert its (rationally grounded) right, to establish the ordered state of symmetry?

Without doubt, the disruptions in symmetry initiated by the climactic chord, however small, are numerous, pervasive, and difficult to discount or ignore. Likewise, the attention this series of asymmetries calls to itself gives a striking symbolic power to the climactic chord, from which that series is perceived as issuing. The chord projects itself as the agent of a subtle yet profound condition of change. Thanks to the presence of this chord, we feel, something happens in the music. Thus the chord effectively symbolizes the power of the freely acting subject to have an impact on its environment.

Yet this freedom is not projected as mere willfulness or whimsy. The subject's claim to the meaningfulness of its freedom is not simply asserted here, as a kind of irrational whistling in the dark. On the contrary, the perceptual opacity (as opposed to transparency) of the changes effected by the climax is fundamentally indebted to the persuasively unified character of the framework in which these changes occur. Certainly the relish we take in following these disruptions is due to our perception of their inextricability from an encompassing structural unity, and also of their indispensable contribution to the tightness, complexity, and interest of that unity.

But even more important, without some governing framework of unity it is unlikely that we would perceive such changes at all, that is, perceive them as meaningful events. Without such a framework, these changes would remain unintelligible. Moreover, freedom itself involves a certain (moral) quality of willfulness, which (as strongly suggested by our experience and by our theoretical reservations about freedom) is subject to irrational abuse. The asymmetries we have noted convey a potential threat as well as a promise. Evoking an image of subjective freedom, they also suggest a capacity for stirring up trouble, for disturbing the equilibrium of the universe, for beginning a descent into chaos.

Such possibilities are palpable in the asymmetries of this prelude; but precisely because our dominant impression is of a governing unity, they are never to be taken seriously. At every moment the prelude is able to persuade us of the rationality of its choices. At no point do we doubt that the ultimate purpose of the asymmetries unleashed by (or through) the climactic sonority is to reassert the subject's ability to discipline its own freedom through rational principles of control, as embodied above all in the tonal force of I.

So thoroughly do principles of unity permeate this structure that it is difficult to imagine entertaining a single moment's doubt of its rational capacity for self-control, even on a first hearing. But if any such doubts were possible, they would certainly be put to rest by the authority of the closing tonic cadence. That authority is persuasive not simply because it rests on an intelligible musical principle but also because its identity and function are so consistent with all that has preceded. The resolution provided by this cadence is utterly compatible with all previously suggested imagery of subjectivity as a principle that controls and determines its own course—imagery that is crystallized in the climactic sonority.

Even in the act of disrupting symmetry, the climactic chord pulls together elements of structure that contribute prominently to tension, such as the moments of rupture in the register, the variability of the pedal pattern, the instability of nontriadic, dissonant sonorities, and the reference to a second tonal area. At the same time, this climax honors certain constancies of symmetry while also extending our perception of the tonic as the principle governing every aspect of this piece. Even asymmetry itself is presented, by way of this chord, as subordinate to tonal kinds of unity.

In doing all these things, the climactic chord provides a powerful focus for our conviction that both the principles of order and the impulses toward freedom in this work emanate from within subjectivity. Again, this conviction seems conclusively confirmed by the final cadence. Rather than suggesting itself as the manifestation of an ordering principle that appears out of nowhere to tame the belligerence of individualized deviations, the final coming to rest on I defines a persuasively subjective gesture. It reassures us, through very powerful figurative means, that subjectivity has the power to resolve its own tensions.

Nor is this all that can be said about the climactic sonority. Rather than treating the potential disjunction between its physical strength and its tonal limitations as a contradiction, this sonority treats the two principles in ways that point clearly to their underlying compatibility, at least in the sense of their susceptibility to rational reconciliation. It is true (as I have labored to demonstrate) that it derives its effectiveness in large part from its success in maintaining the apparent tension between the two conditions. The physically most powerful moment in the prelude is simultaneously perceived as, tonally, the most fragile. Nevertheless, both of these conditions are presented in a manner that leaves no doubt about their common subordination to the same governing set of values. The physical assumption of strength at this moment is no less transient than its suggestion of an alternate tonal center. Hence physical characteristics as well as tonal instability are shown to be secondary in relation to the structural claims of the primary tonic, A.

But, at least within the conventions of Western tonal practice, literal physicality as well as tonal instability are the very stuff of which secondary attributes, *in themselves*, are supposed to be qualitatively composed. Thus, in terms of this first reading, no disjunction is established by the prelude between these two potentially conflicting levels at which the term "secondary" makes sense. On the contrary, the overtones of structural subordination that are never absent from the term "secondary," even insofar as it is used to define a qualitative attribute in itself, are utterly consistent with the relational status implied by this term. A secondary qualitative attribute, by this reading, has secondary structural (or functional) significance. A secondary attribute is secondary. The climax we perceive in this first reading gets its priorities straight, and sets ours likewise.

In terms of the imagery I have just presented here, the climactic sonority has a very powerful figurative significance. By extension, for example, it suggests that even the most physically powerful entity must finally yield primacy of place to conditions of strength that are grounded on rationality. But what is such a suggestion if not the signifier of a world that is fundamentally shaped by principles of rationality?

Let us concede, then, that Chopin's A-Major Prelude, as represented by the identity and effect of its climactic sonority, provides powerful figurative reassurance that the world is at bottom rational. A crucial question still remains. Does this piece also persuade us that its vision of a self-determining subjectivity, operating in a congenial framework of rationality, has status not only in figurative terms but also in reality? I would argue that it does, at least to the extent that any figurative device can—namely, to the extent that the prelude, by this reading, leaves us in no plausible doubt that it is a totally unified structure.[107]

Such unity, granted, may seem first of all to be only a figuratively definable condition. Yet to the degree that the perception of such unity successfully fends off challenges to itself and forcefully persuades us to rely upon its presence (i.e., persuades us that it *is*), powerful counterevidence is provided to the view that structural unity is in some real sense unattainable.

Up to this point it can probably be agreed that the prelude does not readily offer grounds for seriously entertaining such doubts about unity. In saying this I do not deny that the account made thus far of the prelude offers recurrent points of weakness for those who (like myself, in my second reading) insist on scrutinizing the particulars of a general argument. Still, I would be surprised if this account (which conforms to the kind of reception this prelude has been granted in the West for almost a century and a half) seemed in any apparent way useful to arguments that challenged the unified status of the work.

The case for affirming the persuasive impression of unity in this prelude can also be made in considerably more positive terms. One of the most salient aspects of the climactic sonority is its compelling reference to the process of cadencing. And among the factors responsible for the success of this piece in establishing its status as a unified whole, probably none is more important than its projection of a sense of progress toward its final cadence, as a musical symbol of the subjective power to effect closure and thereby to control time and space.

The underlying musical strategy for defining this sense of progress could be said to consist in a progressive definition of the cadence principle itself. In not only alternating half cadences with full ones (except in the climactic sixth phrase) but also grouping all of the cadences into pairs that (again with the same exception) demonstrate the power of I to resolve V, this whole piece could be construed in Paul de Man's sense as posing repeatedly the same literal request for information: "Is *this* how you cadence? Please tell me." For the successive transformations that occur in the final three cadences, in phrases six, seven, and eight, where a challenge is mounted to the principle of the tonic cadence only to be successfully overcome, are sufficient to imbue the final cadence with the authority of a definitive, real, informational answer: "No, *this* is how you cadence."

Now to be sure, the cadence in the climactic sixth phrase seems also to operate on another level of questioning, a secondary level. It seems, that is, to accompany the informational question just posed with a more urgent expression of concern. It asks, "Surely *this* isn't how you cadence? Is there *any* way I can cadence securely?"

But this question, unlike the others, does not in any fundamental sense seem to seek information. On the contrary, it seems to be [!] "merely rhetorical." For as we have seen, the posing of this question, even in terms of the tensions it articulates, is only a temporary event, constituting no real danger and doing no real damage to the authority of such principles of stability as the tonic cadence and structural symmetry. Consequently, in our first reading the force of this question never exceeds that of a figurative or fictitious possibility.

And, indeed, the symmetrically restorative force of the final cadence on I disposes easily of this question. Its response to the worries voiced at the moment of climax—Surely *this* isn't how you cadence; is there *any* way I can cadence securely?—is the following: "Of course that's not how to cadence. *This* is how to cadence. And I'm not going to worry any more. Of course I can cadence securely. Subjectivity always finds an intelligible way to effect closure, to control time and space."

In effect, subjectivity reassures itself of its own real powers to determine the truth, by way of the climactic sonority. Furthermore, though whatever doubts it has expressed turn out to be unwarranted, it does not merely return to the same relatively naive and untested condition of certainty it defined before the climax. In exercising its freedom to pose alternatives, and thus experiencing the doubt and suffering attendant on a recognition of the contingency of happy endings, it has learned something. And precisely through gaining knowledge, it has made something happen, something even more important than simply managing a successful correction of its own tonal course.

What it has learned is that the tonic (along with associated principles of stability), on which it at first uncritically grounded its own sense of value—indeed, its very right to be—is in fact a ground to be trusted. True, the goal it has attained is the same as its starting point; but it now knows that its choice of a goal is correct. This goal is where the subject is *supposed to* end up.[108] In fact it turns out that the free subject has always known what it needed to know. In this respect it is not significantly different from Papageno in his opening song.[109] The difference lies in the self-consciousness of the knowledge possessed. Unlike Mozart's Papageno, the free subject here comes to know that what it knows is real knowledge.

Hence, the tensions to which it has subjected itself have a significance that, in the end, goes beyond the merely temporary, aberrant—and futile. Though they have returned the prelude to the same key and priorities with which it started, they have added the crucial information that these opening assumptions have essential importance. Thus these tensions were not undergone in vain; they can be taken as transformations that effect real progress toward possession of truth. The resemblance here to Hegel's model of *Aufhebung* should be evident. Through a testing of its presumptions against their own antithesis, subjectivity has progressed to a higher level of knowledge—to a stage where it can equate that very knowledge with reality.

It must be added, moreover, that having arrived at a goal it now knows to have real significance [!], the subjectivity that drives this prelude can cease doubting its own powers, meaningfulness, and value. In the end it feels entitled to make the best possible case for its own significance, namely, that its course not only makes sense, and important sense at that, but is actually necessary. True, the goal might conceivably have been reached by some other course—a possibility that will assume importance in my second reading; then again, the music of Mozart and Beethoven, which succeeds so often in projecting its own necessity, also allows the conceivability of other correct courses. Even at the level of a highly individualized phenomenon, Chopin's A-Major Prelude makes a strong case for its own necessity. It allows little ground for doubt that it must be as it is—and thereby that it *must be* (see note 9, this chapter).

The series of questions I have just proposed is modeled directly on de Man's analysis, in "Semiology and Rhetoric," of a poem by Yeats. As it happens, the series also corresponds almost exactly with de Man's analysis of a passage by Proust in the same essay. Within that analysis de Man draws a sharp distinction, to which he attributes "very sizable stakes,"[110] between the figurative devices of metaphor and metonym. The metonym, it will be recalled, defines a relationship of physical adjacence or conventional association (hot dog and mustard). According to de Man, the force of this relationship, which he characterizes as "mere contiguity," never exceeds that of "random contingency."[111]

The metaphor, by contrast, defines a relationship of analogical substitution or exchangeability. This relationship is not merely physical or conventional—attributes that depend on chance—but symbolic, a condition that implies the presence of some underlying, effective, and unifying intelligence. Thus, although metaphorically related elements are equivalent, each also presents significant differences from every other; and these differences allow the possibility of a progressive transformation through the operation of the governing intelligence that gives them force. This possibility of progressive transformation allows metaphor, in de Man's words, "the inner necessity, the 'necessary link,' of a transcendental signification."[112] In other words, metaphorical equivalence, through its fundamentally intelligent capacity to establish unity, has the power to forge an unbreakable link between the literary sign and its ultimate referent in reality. These are indeed "very sizable stakes." Such a power would provide precisely the ground needed for what Jameson calls the reassuring nineteenth-century belief in "the reality of the appearance."

What happens in the passage by Proust, according to de Man, is that the narrator, Marcel, sets up a chain of binary oppositions between the properties of his room and those of the world outside that take on a metaphorical force. "By the act of reading," de Man writes, "these static oppositions are put in motion, thus allowing for the play of substitutions by means of which the claim for totalization can be made."[113]

In this passage, de Man asserts:

> The substitutive totalization by metaphor . . . is said to be more effective than the mere contiguity of metonymic association. As opposed to the random contingency of metonymy . . . , the metaphor is linked to its proper meaning by . . . the "necessary link" that leads to perfect synthesis. In the wake of this synthesis, the entire conceptual vocabulary of metaphysics enters the text: a terminology of generation, of transcendental necessity, of totality, of essence, of permanence, and of unmediated presence. The passage acts out and asserts the priority of metaphor over metonymy in terms of the categories of metaphysics and with reference to the act of reading.[114]

Signifying as it does the possibility of such a momentous metaphysical breakthrough, from the realm of subjective intelligence to the realm of reality, Proust's passage can be said at this level of reading, by de Man's account, to "celebrate the self-willed and autonomous inventiveness of a subject."[115]

So, too, in our first reading of this prelude, the four pairs of cadences—each in itself a hierarchical binary opposition—can be construed as a series of metaphorical transformations, or equivalent substitutes, for a common formula. Even the cadence in the climactic sixth phrase, though deceptive, and thus more akin to a half than to a full cadence, is still a kind of cadence. And this very deviation, in turn, by obviating any effect of endless repetition, assures that the differences among the cadences, and above all, the differences that distinguish the final pair, can be construed as part of a series of progressive transformations, that is, as genuinely significant. True, the complementary tonal oppositions that constitute the pairs of cadences do not evoke the linguistic relation of signifier to signified in quite the same way as do Proust's oppositions between Marcel's room and the open air. Nevertheless, these tonal oppositions also operate initially on this side of the metaphysical divide within the domain of a single language, as pairs of oppositions that can be symbolically unified into a moving totality.

Thus, through the act of listening, these cadences, too, move toward an affirmation that celebrates the power of a free subject to effect closure, to control space and time, and to unify a whole. In so doing they persuade us of rationality—indeed, of intelligibility—as such a powerful principle that it can establish the status and significance of subjectivity in reality itself.

In a sense, through this first reading, Chopin's prelude can be heard as a powerful metaphor for the individual human life, at least as the modern Westerner would like to understand the latter. Moving in time toward a finite end, the music takes an individualized course. As it makes the choices that shape that course, it encounters situations and possibilities that cast doubt on the rightness of those choices, pose threats to its stability and powers of control, and thereby cause it to experience tension and suffering. What follows the last sound is very likely death.

We unquestionably associate a degree of sadness with such perceptions. To the extent that it defines itself through an individual structure, subjectivity recognizes that it is restricted by the very nature of choice (whatever courses may be open to it, it can choose only one) and that the duration of its course is likewise limited. Thus it recognizes that a degree of contingency is built into the very singularity of the existence through which it affirms itself. Moreover, it also acknowledges the theoretical possibility that the forces affecting the kinds and correctness of its choices, as well as its duration, may be contingent, not only in the sense that these forces could emanate from a ground that lies beyond subjective control, but also in the sense that this ground itself might be insufficiently rational to give meaning to the contingencies of subjectivity.

Nevertheless, within the course of its existence, the human subject (as described and exemplified by this prelude) experiences a power to make something happen. Even the audacious tonal gesture of the climactic sonority can be taken to represent not the ignorant bravado of a child but the calculated and admirably daring effort of a free agent—of a consenting adult— who operates in full awareness of both the powers and the restrictions to which it is subject.

On the one hand, this agent asserts its individualistic powers to differ with conventional expectations. Yet on the other hand, when it asserts its individualistic strengths and leaps toward B-minor, it does so with a clear assumption that it will be no less safe than, say, Papageno assumed himself to be. Very much like a baby who trusts it will be caught by its father, this climax exudes confidence in the existence of a framework that will justify its risk. But it acts

more thinkingly than a baby because it has dared to confirm its own knowledge that it can rely upon itself to provide whatever principles of order are
needed to correct its midair mistakes. Trusting in the verifiability of its power
to control its own course, it has dared to define a domain for itself detached
from any (explicit) context of available alternatives, and to test its own
assumptions beyond the epistemological safety net of Papageno's parody of
knowledge. Thereby, it has developed a sense of its own structural identity as
sufficiently stable to justify interpreting its apparently contingent existence as
an unbroken, continuous passage through time that no contingent event can
rupture. Momentarily saddened, as we take it to be, by the transience and contingency of its own action, the subject at its climax considers its efforts more
than counterbalanced by its experience of an exhilarating power to create
meaning in the world—and by the persuasive consistency it discerns between
that experience and the solidity of its own self-definition.

This subject finds satisfaction in the validation of its power to unify itself
so compellingly through principles of rational order as to leave no doubt that
those principles confirm a higher level of being than the merely contingent.
Through the use of those principles, the climax confers a necessity on its very
condition of contingency. Thus the subjectivity represented by the climax in
this prelude can have confidence at every stage of its progress that the apparent contingency of its choices, and of its individuality, affirms a higher order,
a rational order of necessity. The seemingly bad, the dissonant, can be borne
because it is not only subordinate but actually necessary to validate the
claims of an essential rationality.

The temporal progress of individual subjectivity then takes on credible
substance through its ability to ground its own meaning on a timeless order of
being. And this credibility is rendered a certainty by the force with which the
prelude, through its unmistakable unity, retrospectively eradicates all residual
doubts as to the necessity of its individual structure, until even its midcourse
corrections lose their significance as such and become perceived as correct
and necessary choices. Whether subjective individuality makes active
choices or merely accepts the pull of what seems necessary to it, the prelude
tells us, the subject will, through the exercise of its own rational control,
reach a point where it seems to have determined its own course by inarguably
necessary standards.

Given the persuasiveness of the priorities that govern its course on a
moment-to-moment basis, subjectivity in this prelude can safely assume that
the particularities of its choices, and even its seeming or potential missteps,
will eventually be vindicated at the close of its course. Even if it does not at

every moment dispel all sense of the hazards attendant on contingency, it can expect an affirmation at the end that subsumes all such doubts under its own timeless validity. Such a vision offers tremendous existential comfort.[116]

By my first reading, Chopin's A-Major Prelude offers itself as a metaphor for life itself in just such terms. In time (the climactic sonority assures us), the particularities of my course will make sense, to the point where every previous choice and action, including those that evoked anxiety, will seem as if it were *meant to be*. At the end, death itself will come to seem a point of demarcation that allows everything I have done beforehand, including my mistakes and my sufferings, to be understood as having been necessary to confirm the unified shape of the structure represented by my life. And even after my death, the course of my existence will provide evidence of a higher, rational order of being that exists outside of time and that, in turn, gives my existence a secure value and meaning.

In effect, by way of its spokesperson in measure 12, the prelude tells us that "there is something beyond" that gives even the contingencies of freedom a necessity. Even if my freedom allows me to make individual choices that could sometimes be wrong, that freedom is essential because it confirms the merely secondary status of mistakes and the capacity to make them, within a higher order of necessity.

If the subjective freedom—and the suffering—represented by the climactic chord in Chopin's prelude turns out to be limited in its powers to threaten order, and finite in its duration, this is no evidence of its lack of real meaning or value. On the contrary, subjective freedom has demonstrated the reality of its meaning and value precisely through the proper identification and acknowledgment of its own limits. Its limits lie in its contingent aspects, not in the necessary aspects of its ordering principles, principles that give it power. Its limits are *limited*, not *limiting*.

By this reading, freedom is needed to establish the ontological limits of the undeniable contingency of freedom. In fact, freedom shows its own contingencies, like those involved in individual human life, to be not merely tolerable but necessary precisely because they allow us to understand contingency as a principle that answers to a higher necessity. And freedom shows its contingencies to be real contingencies in the sense that they are not something real in themselves but only an aspect of something that *is* real.[117] In a word, the contingencies of freedom and life are essential precisely because they are secondary—because they are no more than secondary.

Forced to choose [!] between itself and necessity (or ultimately even determinism) as the ground of reality, subjectivity by this account opts for a vision that sets limits on the consequences (epistemological as well as moral) of the exercise of its own freedom. Astounding as it may seem from some perspectives, subjectivity attaches so much importance to its ability to demonstrate the rational necessity of its ordering principles that it will agree, finally, to wave away the contingencies of its own freedom. It will agree to do so even if this means denigrating the powers of self-determination that are defined and represented by its freedom—and that are qualitatively (aesthetically) crucial to the enjoyment of the capacity to acquire knowledge.

In the end, subjectivity is more comfortable with a principle that minimizes the significance of the differences between right and wrong, such as determinism, than with one that cannot guarantee the ultimate insignificance of a free capacity to make choices that are wrong. In the end, one could say, given an urgent need to characterize the world order as rational, subjectivity finds it more important that life be by definition intelligible, and thus unmistakably meaningful, than that life confirm our ability to make moral (or aesthetic) choices that may not result in a cognitively demonstrable order. In other words, it seems more safely rational to model one's vision of reality on the verifiably consistent and mechanistically unified structures trusted by cognition than to model that vision on free will, a cognitively open-ended and uncertain moral structure. The unity of Chopin's prelude persuades us that our confidence in the model we prefer is not unfounded.

Chopin's prelude, then, in this reading, offers its own unity as a persuasive guarantee that human life is meaningful, both within its unfolding as a temporal process and also retrospectively, as a complete, stable, unified, and aesthetically satisfying structure. The greatest fears that can be entertained within the course of a life—that suffering is futile, that life itself is a meaningless contingency—will not be realized. The individualities of each course can be assumed to make a real difference. And (to move from Kant to Yogi Berra), in terms of its ultimate ability to establish meaning, a life ain't over even when it's over.

Such a reassuring vision of human life was once more or less guaranteed, in some seemingly literal fashion, by an unquestioning religious faith. In a more skeptical age, however, the possibility remains that such a vision has only figurative status—unless it can somehow be grounded persuasively on reality. This first reading tends to justify precisely such a grounding, by establishing that the images through which subjectivity defines itself are inseparable from a rational condition of order.

Through various powers of unification, above all through its use of the tonic principle, this prelude forges an overwhelmingly persuasive connection between its own individuality and a level of being that we cannot avoid characterizing as reality.[118] In effect, it persuades us to trust in the possibility of leaping through the looking glass of our own figurative language, to accept the themes formed by the structural consistency of our imagery as real, and thereby ultimately to assert the necessity of our own existence.

Now it may well be that all this first reading does is to demonstrate the inescapable dependence of human (or at least, modern Western) ideas about reality on figurative modes of thinking. At bottom, that is, this reading may simply reconfirm a modern Western inability to understand "being" except insofar as being "means."

But it is precisely within the restrictions of our own culture that this first reading attains its greatest persuasiveness. Working within the limits that post-Kantian tradition has set upon the "knowable," Chopin's prelude, in this reading, makes a strong case for the reality of a constant structure that we can call "meaning." By making structural choices that consistently persuade us of their rational intelligibility—and indeed of their necessity—the prelude forcefully persuades us that we have no reasonable alternative except to read in it the meaning it attributes to itself. This meaning is that the prelude has status, as an intelligibly unified structure, and that this status is so unmistakable—so real—that we cannot imagine the prelude as existing in any other form.

By persuading us to read it in this way, the prelude reinforces our inclination to think of meaning itself as something that not only *can* be but *must* be successfully transmitted, and thus of communication not as an impossible or even merely contingent process, but as a necessary one. Even in terms of the modern Western, scientific stipulation that the "real" can be defined only insofar as it is meaningful, the prelude manages to persuade us that the meaningful is real.

But to assert that the meaningful is real is to take a position on the relation of reason to metaphysical reality. Though the prelude presents itself as a symbol for subjectivity at the level of individual human life, it defines itself by way of ordering principles that we can and do construe as having supraindividual validity, that is, a validity existing at a higher level than individual contingency. In this prelude, subjectivity shows its ability to play by rules that are not limited in their general intelligibility by the particularities of individual existence, even if it is only in the latter condition that subjectivity can *show* such an ability. In other words, subjectivity defines here a rationality that can validate itself on a scale far exceeding the particular conditions of individual self-definition, and yet a rationality that nevertheless remains accessible, even congenial, to the workings of subjectivity.

At bottom, what this first reading offers is an account of how Chopin's A-

Major Prelude persuades us to accept the intelligibility of its unity as evidence of a substantive, real rationality. In this first reading, Chopin's A-Major Prelude, like Kant's critiques, rescues the contingencies of subjective experience from potential meaninglessness by evoking a concept of transcendental reason.

A Deconstruction of Chopin's A-Major Prelude: Second Reading

My first reading started with the premise that the climactic effect of the sonority in measure 12 is "essential because it is secondary," that is, because in relation to the entire structure, its significance, along with the means that define its significance, is presented as no more than secondary. There is, however, another way of interpreting the formula "essential because it is secondary" that leads to quite a different reading of Chopin's prelude. One can interpret the phrase to mean that the essential elements of the prelude are precisely those that we characterize as secondary. To put it another way, what is essential to the prelude are the qualitative properties of secondary, marginal, ornamental, or supplementary characteristics (as epitomized by the climax) in themselves.

From this perspective, we would ask whether there are ways in which the climactic chord projects itself not as secondary to some more essential set of norms but as in itself the very norm of what matters in this piece, precisely by virtue of its secondary characteristics. If so, then it might be possible to reverse the hierarchical opposition between the "essential" and the "secondary," and to view those aspects of this piece that reinforce values of stability as secondary in significance, precisely because they are qualitatively (as deemed by conventional standards) essential or primary.

In undertaking such an attempt at reversal, one might eventually undercut the very polarity between notions of the "essential" and the "secondary"—as well as many related polarities, such as "necessary" and "contingent," "real" and "figurative," and conceivably even "logical relation" and "physical identity."

Such a strategy would hypothesize, for example, that the primary function of the climactic chord is not to reaffirm the governing power of tonality but to project a condition of strength that is unsettling and disruptive in as many ways as possible (even tonally). The impression that would emerge would be of a strength that derives its powers in the first instance not from any rationally justifiable basis of superiority but rather from a mere capacity for brute force. Strength of this sort has an arbitrary quality far more consistent with the contingencies involved in physical size, or in culturally specific definitions of power, than with the pull toward universal necessity we associate with a logical conclusion. It is strength of a kind that is more readily imagined as imposed from without on a structure—through the piling up of physical resources, say, or through rhetorical emphasis—rather than as issuing from within symbolically structured relationships.

If the power of the climactic sonority is heard as inhering not in a relativistically defined condition of strength but in a qualitatively contingent one, then even the impact of tonal identity in this chord must be accounted for differently than in our first reading. This impact must be taken to derive principally from some physically or culturally based capacity of music for defining power, to which the connectedness of tonal logic would itself be secondary (though by no means necessarily inessential, in the sense of dispensable). Thus we might explain the presence of V of B-minor at this moment not through its power to reconfirm the superior force of the tonic A but through the immediacy of its sensuous or rhetorical effectiveness as a dramatic gesture.

The term "immediacy" conjures up the specificity of the (physical or cultural) here and now. A climax that operated primarily in the way just described would call more attention to its force as an isolated moment than to its power of reference to other sources of meaning. In this respect it would bear, if not a precise identity, at least a definite resemblance to what Roland Barthes calls a "double sign," defined by Terry Eagleton as a sign that "gestures to its own material existence at the same time as it conveys a meaning."[119]

Such a sign tends to substitute for the transparency of logic (or even of conventional semantic reference) the opaque physicality of the rhetorical or figurative device. One can think of such a sign as tending to pull back from pointing to the world in favor of becoming its own primary "referent"—and thereby revealing the concrete medium as the primary component of the message. This is, as we have already noted, a situation that has become explicit, and sometimes very profitable, in a great deal of contemporary Western culture. To decide whether the climactic sonority in Chopin's A-Major Prelude can plausibly be interpreted as defining this sort of situation, it would be useful to begin by noting some ways in which this sonority seems to call explicit attention to its own sensuous characteristics. But before I do this, I should state clearly that my emphasis, in this second reading, on the possibly primary effect of certain kinds of characteristics does not entail the dispensability of other sorts of characteristics, any more than it did in my first reading. To suggest, for example, that perceptions of physical characteristics may be stronger than tonal perceptions is not to deny that we hear the piece tonally. What I am doing, rather, is asserting that our reading of an event responds to *many* parameters of the latter.[120] The conventions of our reading (or listening) tradition may have conditioned us to ignore some of these parameters as secondary. By trying to isolate those, and by weighing their relative prominence, we may find that some of them play a larger role in our perceptions than we had earlier realized.

The exceptional status of the climactic sonority, it will be recalled, is articulated through qualities of thickness and expanse that emphasize a physical fullness of presence. This sense of a solid, massive physical presence is enhanced as well by the dynamic indication of loudness at this point, by the clarifying effect of the pedal change, and by the fact that the outer notes of this sonority rest on what conventional standards deem the square, stable interval of the fifth (an interval that in other respects is overshadowed in this piece by the sound of vertical intervals recognized as less stable).

This vividly concrete presence, so different from emptinesses elsewhere— several of which I shall take up shortly—calls attention to the climactic sonority not only as the physically most overpowering element in the piece but also as an isolated physical entity. This quality of vivid physicality encourages a perception of this climax, notwithstanding earlier references to B-minor, less as a prepared moment of articulation within an intelligibly cohesive whole than as a sudden, arbitrary, unearned attempt to seize power.

One additional and powerful (though in a literal sense hardly "solid") contribution to this impression of arbitrary self-assertion is provided by what is perhaps the single most readily forgotten aspect of this sonority: its resistance to any physical presentation at all. Chopin indicates that two of the middle notes are to be spanned by the thumb. Whether or not Chopin seriously expected through this fingering to enjoin subsequent interpreters, in the words of his twentieth-century editor, "from the all-too-common arpeggiating of this chord,"[121] the fact is that for many performers, and probably for most women, this sonority simply cannot, and therefore will not, be played as written. When that happens, we have a rather splendid example of an element in a musical text that is not, as deconstructionists love to say, "identical with itself."

For relatively small-handed players like myself, this chord takes on a particularly strong self-contained character; during performance it becomes the dominating element of the piece, for certainly in terms of technical challenge, it is the *only* element in need of conscious attention. Dreading the chord increasingly as we approach it, more often than not (as I have observed in many performances) we will hesitate, and then render it in one or another sort of broken manner.

This breaking of the chord will of itself, in what could be called deconstructive fashion, not only unravel the rhythmic, melodic, and textural symmetries noted in our first reading but also unmake the breaks in symmetry, such as the simultaneous parallel fifths that are delineated in the score. It undermines those qualities of weight, thickness, and fullness within the solid framework of a simultaneously sounded outer fifth that have just been adduced to define the self-contained physical importance of this moment.

And yet all this undermining will not diminish the physicality of the moment, but will rather suspend or even rupture the action undertaken here, allowing us to linger for a moment on this sonority, as if it were governed by a historically authenticated fermata. In other words, the effect will be to evoke even more those arbitrary aspects of the physical—in this case, its absent hardness as well as the contingency of its stuff and its boundaries—that allow this moment to exert such a powerful claim, in itself, on our senses.

But whether or not this chord is broken in performance, its thrust toward self-contained physicality tends to weaken the symbolic power conventionally associated with the hierarchical oppositions of tonal operation. By its own example, this chord draws attention sharply toward parameters of music that we are accustomed to construing more literally than tonality, such as rhythm.

What rhythm defines in this piece is not primarily symmetrical linkage. Symmetry is our term for a device that suggests the presence of a governing constructive intelligence. And for the perception of symmetry, the musical parameter of rhythm by itself in this piece does not seem sufficient. For what rhythm of itself defines in this prelude is only a steady regularity, a pattern of repetition, be it random or inexorable, that is broken at most on two occasions: by the grace-note A in the next-to-last measure; and, at times, by a historically "inadequate" rendering of the climactic sonority.

True, this regularity is multilayered, since the the quasi-mazurka emphasis on beats 2-3-1 appears only in alternate measures. It is also true that this pattern could be construed as the accent, marking, or evidence of a governing intelligence. Nevertheless, just as in the case of open-endedly repeated symmetrical pairs, this multilayered rhythmic steadiness cannot be definitively divorced from a glimpse, at some different or even higher level of perspective, of a mindless regularity. By this I mean a pattern where the "marked" evidence of subjective intention is perceived as dissolving into the pervasiveness of coexisting or contiguous physical patterns—and where pairs of hierarchical oppositions dissolve into an open-ended, infinitely fissionable chain of static, atomized, and adjacent elements.[122] Indeed, within the perspective just suggested, even the grace-note A, which breaks the otherwise rigid rhythmic pattern in this piece, could be taken to be not the bearer of what structural linguistics calls "significant" difference but merely an insignificant statistical deviation.

This line of argument does not stop here. One of the ways in which the climactic sonority disrupts symmetry, as noted in my previous reading, is by encouraging the perception of the sixth phrase as more of an antecedent than a consequent. This effect is produced through a variety of means, both tonal and physical, which together give the phrase the instability conventionally associated with an antecedent. Now antecedent structures in tonal music tend to have a distinct and especially appealing character. This character can readily be explained in tonal terms, as the feeling of excitement generated by movement toward the magnetism of a tonal goal. Baroque and Classical compositions capitalize repeatedly on the structural force of such tonal propulsiveness. No doubt, as "emic listeners" or educated tonal "insiders" (see p. 168), we still tend instinctively to explain the attractive, even titillating, character of antecedents primarily in tonal terms. We tend to hear antecedents on the same level as we do consequents: that of tonal logic.

Yet there is a qualitative difference between antecedents and consequents, which a number of nineteenth-century Romantic composers relished exploring in their music. Tonal consequents are resistant to being perceived as anything but primarily tonal, or logical, in meaning. Antecedents, on the other hand, want to have more fun. The very language one can use to describe the effect of antecedents (here, "appealing," "exciting," "magnetism," "attractive," "titillating," and "relish") is language that without effort can be taken to describe a primarily physical effect. In short, whereas consequents tend toward a relational level of meaning, antecedents may very well tend toward a sensuous one.

Certainly, once one has focused one's attention on the quality of excitement provided by antecedents, it may very well occur to ask whether that excitement stems primarily from the magnetic attraction toward a goal, or from the magnetism of the moment itself. To argue that at some level the tonal goal must be present for the dynamic to work is not necessarily to answer the question asked. The question is not whether the tonic is "inessential," but where to locate the essential character of the antecedent.[123]

One plausible means of pursuing this last question is to see what happens if one dwells on the sensuous capacities of antecedents. Precisely this experiment lay at the heart of many Romantic and post-Romantic styles, including those of Wagner and Mahler. Certainly a question raised prominently by the stylistic effect in each of these cases is whether the logical necessity of consequents is necessarily to be taken as prior to the temporal contingency of sensuousness; or therefore, whether the logical force of the term "prior" is necessarily [!] to be considered prior (but in what sense?) to its temporal force. (Again, the specter of infinite linguistic regress looms large in our ability to formulate such a question.)

Such questions are unsettling. If we once concede that coming first in time defines the archetypal condition of "priority," we will eventually be forced to reconsider some of our most cherished assumptions about the ontological status of rationality. True, we finite creatures may derive some comfort from defining "being" as an essentially temporal rather than abstract (say, logical) condition. (We may have the finitude and contingency of temporality, we can tell ourselves, but those are the very characteristics of reality.) Yet such comforts are apt to seem small if they entail a corollary acknowledgment that the supratemporal (say, logic, or for that matter, God), in its lack of a concrete physical presence—and thus of an ability to be *temporally* prior—is nothing more than a figurative construct, that is, an illusion.

Never mind that the figurative power of precisely such an image—that of the atemporality of the real—brought us tremendous reassurance in our first reading. In our present reading, this vision is not so reassuring. What good does it do us for the temporal to be real if that's all there is? Here the comforting ways of thinking through which, under the pressures of contingency, we regularly redefine the "real" to mean something abstract begin to find themselves severely tested.

It may seem that nothing could be further from a Wagnerian ambience of style than Chopin's A-Major Prelude. Yet once the climactic sonority allows us to perceive a formally plausible consequent as an antecedent, it begins to undermine the distinction between antecedents and consequents. This in turn raises doubts about the character and basis of the priority conventionally assigned to consequents. It opens up other conventionally defined polarities to reexamination. Again and again, it heightens sensitivity to the sensuous sorts of power that can be so palpably associated with antecedents. In fact, once attention is drawn to the physically distinctive, unstable character typical of antecedents, our reading begins to recognize the possibility that weight in this prelude is concentrated not on closings, nor on the logic of closure, but on physically based definitions of strength, including the thickened or opaque forms of language involved in rhetorical figures and rhetorical techniques of emphasis. With this recognition all the assumptions, priorities, and conclusions of our first reading begin to unravel.

Some of the shifts in orientation that might be set in motion by identifying the climactic phrase as an antecedent can be indicated through a series of questions. If, at a moment of particular prominence, an antecedent can be substituted for a consequent, and instability for stability, then which is really prior in importance? What standard should be used for properly identifying each—tonal or physical? Should the same standard be used for both antecedent and consequent? If not, what force does the supposed opposition of these two functions have? If so, is there any substantial difference between them?

If at a moment of prominence a cadence on V of II can be substituted for a cadence on I, is resolution necessarily the primary function of a cadence? Or is the *function* of the cadence actually secondary in significance to its *shape* and *gesture*? Could the normative form of a cadence be noncadential in terms of conventional tonal function? Is the *use* of a cadence less important than the *mentioning* of a "cadence," and, if so, in what sense?[124] Should a cadence be understood as an unprivileged configuration that, like other musical elements, defines itself primarily through the characteristics of its sensuous identity? To go on, is I necessarily the normative key of a cadence? Does the quantitative prevalence of cadences on I in this prelude actually outweigh the physical effect of V of II at the climactic moment? Which of these cadential keys is "really" primary? Is *either* of them really primary?

Facetious as it may seem to question the identity of the primary key in this prelude, this question has considerable force from a perspective that, even provisionally, grants only secondary status to the conventions of tonality. Though by conventional standards this piece must be called the Prelude *in* A, the key of its final tonic, instinctively I myself identify this piece as the Prelude *on* E (and a number of others have told me they agree). Part of this impression may stem from the strong undercurrent of emphasis in this piece on the note B (though not in a major-mode context), which is the dominant of E. But most worth noting, perhaps, E is the pitch on which the prelude begins.

In opening up to doubt the conventionally assumed priority of consequents to antecedents, the climactic sonority increases our sense of the forcefulness of many other opening gestures in the prelude. We become more attuned to the kinds of power offered by destabilization, and concomitantly reluctant to dismiss such kinds of power on the grounds of their secondary logical status.

On a simple level, for example, we become inclined to perceive the absence of pedaling on the initial upbeat of every phrase as a device that limits the domain of the preceding cadential tonality, and gives a clarifying, albeit physically achieved, prominence to each of those initial notes. On a considerably more complex level, we may begin to perceive the very opening gesture of the prelude as an element richer in its resources for defining weight than we had previously supposed. What I am including in the opening gesture is the first four pitches of the piece, which can be construed as delineating the following three intervals: the opening melodic sixth (right hand), the ensuing vertical sixth (both hands), and the melodic second that follows (right hand).

In terms of our first reading, this initial configuration is a throwaway gesture, an opening gambit of such obvious (in)significance as to pose no obstacles to our perception of it as a structurally "transparent" entrance to the real business of the prelude. Such a characterization does not, however, do full justice to our perception of the force in this opening gesture. In fact, if we take the opportunity to stop and consider our reactions to this gesture—and this kind of stopping is strongly recommended by deconstruction—we become aware of numerous elements of both physical and relational power that give this moment great resonance, and could even be construed as making it the most commanding gesture in the piece.

What significance shall we attribute, for example, to the fact that the first two intervals delineated in the prelude are a major sixth, and, in terms of pitch, the identical sixth? Is it possible that we are being encouraged to consider the major sixth—or even the physical pitch relation of E and C-sharp—as more important to the structure of this piece than the interval of the octave? More important, even, than the tonic octave A-A? The latter, after all, is presented explicitly in only two phrases, between the outer voices in the second, and as both a melodic and vertical element in the closing phrase; whereas the opening major sixth, E-C-sharp, is replicated vertically at the start of phrase 3 (measure 4) and at the end of phrase 4 (measures 7-8, outer voices), melodically and vertically at the start of phrase 5 (measures 8-9), and melodically, at the top of the melodic range over a crescendo marking (measure 11), just before the moment of climax.[125] Moreover, from the beginning of phrase 5 (measure 8) to the end of phrase 6 (measure 12), the sixth between E and C-sharp involves three separate registers that together span four octaves.

From the standpoint of conventional tonality, this sixth gives us no reason whatsoever to waste one second's thought on its degree of importance, or, for that matter, on its specific tonal meaning. Yet if we are to explain its suggestion of itself as structurally a somehow definitive gesture, its tonal aspects cannot safely be ignored.

Let us assume, for the moment, as tonal interpretation would encourage us to assume, that the vertical configuration of the sixth on the first beat of the first full measure plays a more important role in the tonal construction of the prelude than does the melodic sixth that immediately precedes that beat.

Even so, what tonal identity—what Roman numeral—is to be assigned this hollow sixth? Tonal logic works by way of triads, but we have here only two notes. What note is missing to complete the triad? What is "meant" by this hollow sixth? (Here is an instance where we can speak as comfortably as the poststructuralists of intention as "situated" in a text without invoking the mysterious mental processes of Chopin himself.)

One might suppose, from the immediate subsequent appearance of a dominant-seventh chord on E, from the later emphasis in measures 7 and 8 on the second inversion of A, which fills in the same outer sixth interval of E and C-sharp, from the tonic harmonization of the melodic sixth in measure 11, and even from the prominence of the A $\frac{6}{4}$ triad on the second beat of the penultimate measure, measure 15 (though here C-sharp is not the topmost note of the sonority), that the "reference" of this opening first beat is to the second inversion of A. The "missing" note would then be the tonic, A. What this would amount to is "reading" the tonic A, at this initial moment, as a "nonoriginary origin," or trace, or absent determinant. One might reinforce this reading figuratively by identifying the first melodic gesture in measure 1 (C-sharp to D) as an "échapée"—that is, as an ornament or figure that literally connotes escape.

Or is the "missing" note "really" G-sharp? This is the note that is struck to fill in the corresponding sixth at the opening of the second half of the piece, in measure 9. Is the resultant C-sharp-minor triad in measure 9 "meant" literally here? Is this nontonal key to be construed here as a metaphorical equivalent of I? Or is its literal configuration "supposed to be" tonally inaudible? Can we be sure that this G-sharp is "only" ornamental?

Perhaps G-sharp, in the role of leading tone, is merely displaced onto this measure as a belated arrival from the middle voices of the third phrase (measures 5 and 6), where its conspicuous absence intensified the reference to B-minor wrapped in the dominant-seventh chord on E? Or maybe, in the same role, it is used to anticipate the third of the unambiguous dominant-seventh chord that enters on the following beat (measure 8, beat 2). In either case, do the elements of this sonority "actually" inhabit different temporal dimensions? What relation is defined here between literally physical and symbolic conditions of identity? Is this an example of an identity divided against itself? Who will answer such questions definitively, or at least to our satisfaction? The ghost of Chopin?

It seems obvious that the main point to be made about such questions does not lie in the particular technical response one makes to them. Indeed, an answer to such questions we have not yet even considered is that the initial hollow sixth can be filled interchangeably by an (absent) A or G-sharp or by a (present) empty space. All three solutions make tonal sense of a kind, as can

be verified by trying all three alternatives in actual performance. Consequently, it may even be the case that the seemingly secondary yet actual hollow sixth at this point has a more normative or essential status, and a more primary constructive force, than any theoretical but absent triad.[126]

This undecidability points to what seems to me the principal importance of
the questions I have raised: the very possibility of asking them. There is a palpable quality of poignance, and a concomitant effect of power, in this opening
stress on the sixth that derives from its very ability to project the ambiguity of
its primary meaning. And without the possibility of any definitive logical conclusion to the dilemma it produces, this interval is unavoidably perceived as
having a weight that is at bottom qualitatively physical and contingent.

As our focus on the opening of this phrase is increased, we become more
aware of an element of arbitrariness or contingency in the following, so-called
consequent phrase. On one level this phrase clearly functions as a tonic
"answer," in root position, to a preceding dominant-seventh "question." Yet its
almost Stravinskyesque rupture of expectation with respect to register—a rupture that will be taken up again and expanded in the approach to the climax—
emphasizes the contingency of actual, physical location and of "mere contiguity." Thus the melodic progression from the top note B, at the end of the first
phrase, to A at the end of the second, can be heard figuratively as the tonally
"sensible" progression of descent from the supertonic to the tonic. But it can
also be heard literally as the melodic progression 2 to 8, that is, as a physically
atomized ascending melodic seventh from which the reassuring "corrective"
force of tonal logic has been removed. As a result, this initial tonic triad, the
only one with both its melody and root on A until the final two sonorities of
the piece, nails down nothing in the sense of providing definitive closure for a
persuasively whole antecedent-consequent unit. The suggestion of a perceptible shift in weight from closing to opening gestures remains in force.

Furthermore, the same sort of shift seems particularly evident in the phrases
that follow the climactic sonority and end the piece. By now *beginning* a pair of
phrases (measure 13) with the tonal *resolution* of a cadential progression, in B-
minor, the prelude in the wake of the climax seems openly to encourage the
perception of such a shift. And the same tilt toward the opening portion can
be heard within each of the last two phrases individually. In part this impression stems from the leap downward to the low B and A at the opening of the
bass line in each phrase (measures 13 and 15). Rather than edging toward
some sense of completion, each of these phrases drops anchor, so to speak, at
the very outset. By figurative extension, all of the preceding phrases can be
heard likewise, as staking out a stable position on which the succeeding few

beats merely rock and reverberate. But in part this impression of a shift stems also from an increase in instability in the second half of the penultimate and closing phrases. This aspect of the closing phrases will be discussed later in this chapter (p. 128). In the case of the seventh or penultimate phrase, some of this second-half instability can be attributed to the replacement of the repeated-note pattern in the middle voice (and the accompanying accelera-tion of harmonic rhythm) with the exceptional downward progression B-A-G-sharp, which absorbs the note B on beat 2 of measure 13 into a movement toward the tonic A on beat 3.

Though this absorption provides an increase in momentum that on one level heightens the effect of counterbalance in the final appearance of I, it also undermines the stability of the resolution on B required by the preceding grand gesture of the climactic chord on V of II. Since a clean triad on B-minor never recurs after the second inversion on beat 2 of measure 13, this absorption into the middle voices smothers the possibility of a resolution on B commensurate in weight with the preceding climactic challenge. In effect, this process calls into question the necessity and authority of cadential resolution by question-ing the very possibility of cadential resolution, a point to which I shall return shortly. Indeed, I would venture that the single most striking impression left by this prelude is the instant onset and totality of the tonal capitulation conceded in the last three beats of the seventh phrase (measures 13-14).

And yet at the same time, even the naturaling of A to produce the "real" tonic in the middle voice on beat 3 of measure 13 does nothing to counteract the sense here of unraveling toward a greater degree of instability. True, this A will be taken up again on a supposedly higher level of structural coherence. But at this moment the A appears only in passing, as it hurtles down to the incomparably unstable force of the leading tone G-sharp. All this heightening of instability in the latter half of phrase 7 sharpens the perception of a shift in weight away from closing toward opening gestures, and not only within this phrase itself. By a kind of backward displacement of symmetry, these processes reinforce our inclination to construe the climactic chord itself as an ante-cedent or beginning gesture.

In a way that is particularly dramatic, moreover, the middle-voice progres-sion in measures 13-14 points, as toward a ghost limb, to a progression that is evoked (though not literally present) in the immediate approach to the cli-mactic sonority. I have in mind an imaginary bass-line progression of A, G-natural, F-sharp, which would parallel the actual B, A-natural, G-sharp progression in phrase 7, and which could easily replace the actual progression of A, A, F-sharp in the bass line of phrase 6 (measures 11-12). The fact that this G-natural does not make an actual appearance in no way detracts from the qualitatively poignant sensation produced by its "trace" at this moment.

Indeed, this absence may lend power to that sensation, a possibility that opens up some deconstructionist sorts of questions on a fascinating scale of potential linguistic regress. For example, what would the relative strength of "absence" suggest about the domain and character of the powers provided by "presence"? Is absence a condition that, by pointing to the limits of presence in a physical sense, reasserts the relative priority of figurative standards for assessing weight? Is absence more a figurative, symbolic condition than a physical one? Is absence less limited than presence by the immediacy of physical concreteness—and thus better able to draw us away from the gravitational force of the contingent toward some realm of necessity?

Such questions, it should be noted, have a relevance that goes beyond the literal condition of absence, to every evocation of a potential alternative. The strategy suggested to me by Rufus Hallmark, for example, turns on the inability of even a physically full sonority, the climactic sonority, to exclude all thoughts of its possible replacement. By this formulation, physical presence, even in the absence of absence, impresses upon us the contingency of its actual configuration.

That the thrust of such questions about absence and presence is to undercut the very distinctions defined by such polarities should begin to be evident. In this connection, it may be worth noting that Lukas Foss is said to have included the "phantom" third-beat G-sharp of measure 11 in an orchestral rendering of this prelude.[127] Comparison of such a rendition with one of the prelude "as written" would, at least in one instance on one epistemological level, allow listeners to test for themselves the relative powers of present and absent alternatives.

The very concept of a powerful absence, which amounts to the presence of a "trace" element, has still other repercussions for our perception of configurations extending in both directions from the climactic sonority. Is it possible, for example, that the opening sonority of measure 5 gains force from the refusal of the third phrase to produce F-sharp, the dominant of B-minor, until the second beat of measure 5? To ask this question is to turn our attention still further backward to that projection of strength we saw in the hollow sixth of the very first measure.

True enough, the "phantom" pitches in both these latter instances may seem odd candidates for the category of "trace" in one important sense. In both cases the "missing" pitch can be shown, with at least some plausibility, to point toward an actual pitch that comes later, rather than before. The "missing" F-sharp on beat 1 of measure 5 is supplied in the following two beats of that measure; the "missing" note in the opening sixth may "really" be the G-sharp that opens the second half of the piece, in measure 9.

It's one thing to speak of a "trace" in situations that point to the disappearance of some earlier presence. But what kind of trace points to something yet to come? Doesn't such a usage undermine not only the meaningfulness of the term "trace" but also its association with a shifting of weight back toward openings? In a way it does. But acknowledging this sudden new reversal in our perception of priorities does not leave us in full repossession of the simpler, more conventional hierarchy of antecedents and consequents that we persuasively confirmed in our first reading. What it leaves us with is a heightened sensitivity to the indeterminacy and contingency of (in this case musical) signs and language.

What we begin now to acknowledge is that the force of a trace, or absent presence, is not restricted by ordinary conceptions of time as a unidirectional, forward-moving process. That is because this force is set in motion not by any metaphysical condition of being in "the music itself" but by, and in relation to, a reader. Readers superimpose numerous absent presences on concrete signs in the act of interpretation, and thereby allow signs to have meanings on a number of temporally different levels. In relation to a reader, one can speak plausibly of "traces" in a sign or structure that refer to events occurring after the fact as well as before it. For that matter, a trace can also point a reader toward a simultaneously occurring effect, and toward configurations that seem to define themselves outside of time.

Such diverse and seemingly contradictory temporal conditions and relationships are held together all the time in the sense that we make of signs and texts. The playing of "Hail to the Chief" as John Kennedy's coffin rested on the steps to the Capitol building, for example, was perceived by many Americans at the time as an excruciatingly powerful moment. Why? As a trace, this song pointed back in time to Kennedy's former power as well as forward to the many ways in which his presence would from then on be missed. It also pointed to the ongoing power within the American concept of "presidency"; and it provided a degree of comfort by suggesting the invulnerability of that concept, and its power, to mere temporal contingencies. The pain evoked by this moment involved a coalescence of meanings involving a variety of relationships to time, some of them contradictory.

Or to take some less exceptional examples, the injured Bill Buckner's muff in the tenth inning of the sixth 1986 World Series game caused suffering to Boston Red Sox fans through its simultaneous evocation of the errorless play by Buckner's imagined replacement that never took place in real time (though it should have). An angry suburbanite "sees" in the uncut lawn next door (actually, it was mine in Chicago) an "ideal" vision of a lawn, along with future declines in property value, "undesirable" new neighbors, and such "timeless" values as the Protestant ethic and the sanctity of private property. On close analysis, it seems clear, the interpretation of any sign involves a capacity to entertain in a single moment the contradictions of presences and absences or traces that define numerous relationships to time. In a culture sensitized to Einstein's equation of mass and energy, such an observation should not come as a surprise.

Once we focus on the ability of a trace to derive its force from a variety of temporal conditions, the kinds of observations we made in our first reading of Chopin's A-Major Prelude are apt to undergo some alteration. Thus, in our present interpretation of the prelude, every consequent, "beginning" with the climactic gesture itself, becomes readable as a variant of antecedent. And in turn, every opening becomes conceivably analyzable as always already the aftermath of some other construct—a construct that is sometimes physically absent rather than present, and that sometimes appears after (or simultaneous with), rather than before, its own aftermath or consequence.

Such readings, it should be evident, have considerable potential relevance to interpretive processes and problems beyond the scope of this prelude. The fluidity I have just suggested between the functions of "antecedents" and "consequents," for example, has a clear counterpart in the fluidity suggested by deconstruction betwen the functions of "signifier" and "signified." In both cases, our attention is drawn to the open-endedness and indeterminacy through which we define meanings.

The perception of such multidirectional connections tends in turn to confirm the deconstructionist assertion that a text is not to be construed as a self-identical physical object, existing in some inarguable condition of reality, but rather as an aggregation of elements in a process of signification, which operates in numerous relations to temporality conceivable by the interpreter. It encourages us to look on sonorous structures, such as this prelude, as force fields involving many different interpretational processes, and yielding many possible meanings or readings.

Concomitantly, this perception discourages us from attributing to the pattern of temporal progression toward a goal the capacity to establish a single, unmistakable meaning for a structure. Rather than attesting to the meaningful necessity of such a course, we will now be more inclined to recognize individual structures as merely contingent arrangements of sound, drawn from among many other possible sounds and arrangements.[128] And we will be more alert to meanings defined by patterns other than unidirectional progress, such as the tilt toward openings that we have been discussing in the seventh phrase.

A comparable tilt "backward" in the final phrase, with its attendant definitions of such terms as "stability" and "weight" and various other parameters of meaning, remains to be discussed. But I cannot turn to this closing phrase without first acknowledging certain effects of the pedal indications that follow the climactic sonority. There is a persuasive argument to be made that the presence of the pedal on the first beat of measure 13, under the bass-note B, establishes the identity of the B-minor triad *throughout* this measure as a stable root-position chord, rather than as an unstable second inversion from beat 2 on. Precisely the same argument can be made, moreover, with respect to the initial bass A of the final phrase, in measure 15. Such arguments would tend to strengthen the view of our earlier reading that the last two phrases of this prelude—especially the last one—provide a definitively weighty resolution.

Yet whether the pedal at these moments produces effects that are essential or secondary in relation to the overall structure of this prelude remains a question that is as "undecidable" as it is interesting. Either theory entails at least some results that are consistent with this second reading. True, if the effect of the pedal is construed as essential, then the lingering first-beat chordal roots will lend stability to the latter parts of measures 13 and 15.[129] But by the same token, an increased emphasis is placed on the disruptions in symmetry and the atomization caused by the sudden and unprecedented changing of the pedal on the first beats of measures 12 and 14. This emphasis, as just noted, would weaken the force of the low B in measure 13 by cutting it off at the start of measure 14, thereby destabilizing the entire phrase at its endpoint. But this destabilization would in turn enhance the clarity, prominence, and isolation of the climactic sonority, an effect that would support my present reading.

In the same way, if the effect of the pedal is perceived as essential, it would be difficult to deny that the holding of the pedal through the final two measures of the prelude maintains the presence of the pitch B—by way of the melodic B that starts measure 15—that was so prominently struck in the bass line on the first beat of measure 13. Now the melodic B that starts measure 15 can readily be heard as the delayed appearance of the expected cadential gesture that was displaced at the end of phrase 6 by the climactic sonority. Moreover, in its specific tonal identity, this B can be heard as a goal that forcefully challenges the structural hegemony of the tonic, A. Thus, if taken as essential, the pedal indications in the last four measures can be heard as maintaining B as a solid presence and force not only on the opening beat of the last two phrases but also through most of phrase 7 and through the whole of phrase 8.

But in the final phrase, of course, the lingering presence and force of that B can hardly be called stabilizing factors. If the pedal keeps B audible throughout the final phrase, it also sustains the low A struck at the start of measure 15. In this way the pedal permits B, if only as a literally physical trace, to cloud the consonance of the final cadence on A, in much the same way as earlier cadences of the prelude were clouded by the pedal.[130] The clouding by B in this final cadence, together with the lack of significant difference between this effect and earlier effects of clouding, tends to weaken the functional authority of the "real" tonic, A—thereby emphasizing the contingency of its tonal authority—when A is presented as a supposedly inarguable point of final destination. In short, the perception of weight is shifted backward, from the closing A to the penultimate B.

This is the case if the effects of the pedal are considered essential. To my own ear, however, the force of actually striking the bass-line F-sharp on beat 2 of measure 13, and subsequently the bass-line E on the same beat of measure 15, distinctly overrides the nominal lingering authority of the pedaled low notes B and A on the first beats of those respective measures. For me, this struck force limits the effect of the pedal to secondary importance and gives the second inversions of the triads in question—B-minor and A—a momentary but memorable and undeniable priority over the corresponding root positions of those triads, as they are initially suggested (though not conclusively realized) in measures 13 and 15. In other words, I would point to the prominence of the struck second inversions in measures 13 and 15 as evidence of tonal instability in the concluding two phrases, and hence as a device that throws emphasis back onto the weight of the opening portion of each phrase—an emphasis that is underscored by the pedal markings themselves![131]

Putting the pedals aside now, such a shift toward antecedents seems to me corroborated, though in a somewhat different way, by the destabilizing effect of the grace-note A in the latter half of the very last phrase, measure 15. As the only indisputable deviation from rhythmic regularity in this entire piece (given the ability of at least some players to produce the climactic sonority without breaking it), this tonic-note A cannot help but call attention to itself; thereby, one would suppose, it must reinforce the identity and authority of the tonic, A, as defined in the concluding cadence.

Yet this prominence of the pitch A is not necessarily to be equated with the concept of "weight" in all of its senses. At this crucial moment in the structure, for example, considerable uncertainty is projected onto the primacy (and reassuring intelligibility) of A as a tonic by at least three structural elements. These are the extraordinary brevity (and thus extreme precariousness) of the middle-voice A, underscored by its status as an ornament; the emphasis thrown, by the ensuing involvement of this same note in a tie, on the striking of the middle-voice C-sharp (beat 2 of measure 15); and the bottom-line E (also struck on beat 2 of measure 15), which constitutes a marked anomaly to a number of previously established patterns of symmetry.

This relatively low E strikes me as jarring on two accounts. First, it constitutes the only instance in the prelude where the initial low note of the 2-3-1 mazurka pattern is not repeated at least once; even the second-beat F-sharp of measure 13, which provided an immediate model for this low E, is repeated once, on the third beat of measure 13. And second, it occurs in a metric position (third-to-last beat of an even-numbered phrase) that, except in the climactic sixth phrase, had previously been used to emphasize at least relative tonal stability. By precedent, therefore—and to compensate for the departure from precedent that has just taken place at the climax—we have a strong expectation that on the second beat of measure 15 the tonic triad will appear over its root, A. The low E that in fact appears on this beat thus calls particular attention to an unstable configuration of the tonic, its second inversion.

Of course, the "more normal" root position of the triad follows immediately, thereby appearing to confirm the status of this E as an anomaly. But the root position follows almost as an afterthought. It does not appear quite soon enough to preclude a hint, enhanced no doubt by the lingering overtones of the final melodic B through the clouding of the last pedal, that the final cadential gesture has no more powers of closure than did the cadence on A at the midpoint of the piece (phrase 4, measures 7-8)—which also took up the six-four position.

For that matter, the six-four triad in phrase 4, like the root-position A triad in phrase 2, at least provided a certain stability of sonority that comes from immediate repetition. In both these instances, one could hear the three successive statements of the same chord as effecting an intensification of stability. Even in the sixth phrase, the climactic sonority, though it shattered the pattern of repetition, maintained an intensification. By contrast, the metrically awkward shift to the root-position tonic on the last beat of measure 15 offers no stability or even an intensity of conviction. In this shift from E to A one almost imagines the bass line starting to stack up the folding chairs while the speaker, in the treble clef, is still pounding his fist.

This is hardly the same as a tying up of loose ends or a resolution of tension.

To me, in fact, this shuffling on the second beat of measure 15 clearly conveys the notion that the supposedly archetypal consequent of this piece, its final cadence on the tonic A, may not be an implicitly intelligible principle of closure. From the perspective just described, certainly, the final tonic cadence seems no more capable of nailing down closure than was the initial tonic cadence in phrase 2. In both places, if only for a moment, the contingency of sonority has outwitted the claim of a closing tonal logic to necessity.

Indeed, the contingent power of sonority may also be conceded in this final phrase by its resort to quantitative emphasis as a means to secure the status of A. Of the twenty-one notes struck in the final phrase, no fewer than nine—almost half—are A's. These span four octaves, and in the passage from the first to the second beat of measure 15, three A's are struck by the right hand with exceptional rapidity. As in the repeated C-major triads that conclude Beethoven's Fifth Symphony, one gets a whiff here of excessive protestation. If the tonal authority of A is indisputable here, why the need to dwell on it so literally?

There would, of course, be less need if this last phrase were not so busy, in the ways just described, mounting physical challenges to the tonal authority of A. And these challenges have particular force because, rather than pitting themselves against A, they co-opt A itself into their operation. In such a context, the device of quantitatively reinforcing A poses a symbolic threat to the priority of logic associated with that note.

Likewise, these A's, in their physical particularity, project an effect of qualitative uncertainty that tends to undermine their tonal effect of self-assurance. We have already noted in this connection the belated appearance of the root position A on the third beat of measure 15, as well as the brevity and immediate suppression of the grace-note A.

Both of these instances involve A in the interval that, by tonal logic, should be the most solid in the piece, namely, the octave. Yet the outer octave on the third beat of measure 15 comes across as an afterthought. And whatever doubts we may have about the performance of the climactic sonority, there can be no question that the octave A involving the grace note is broken. Might this literal breaking not suggest some larger sense in which the tonal power represented by the octave has been broken? Looking at the ways in which physical and symbolic definitions of power continuously come together and separate in a kind of dance during this last phrase, one senses that the piece itself remains undecided, up to the very end, as to its best strategy for securing the supremacy of A.

But in hedging its bets, the piece calls attention to uncertainties that weaken the force of A in the very act of trying to strengthen it. Like the accused man who argues, "I would never have killed my wife, and anyway, I was out of town," the prelude wants to have its A both ways: primarily as the bearer of symbolic tonal power, and primarily as a physically powerful pitch. The combination of these two sources of power may seem like an easy wish to grant; making them both "prior," however, is problematic. The more the music tries to argue both cases, the more it clarifies the weaknesses of each in relation to the other, to the point where both are fatally undermined, and no significant difference can be discerned between them.

Such a dual collapse can be observed even in the last sonority. Ostensibly four A's can be heard in this last chord. Yet two of them, the low A (from measure 15) physically sustained by the pedal and the middle-voice A physically sustained by the tie, have already begun to die out. The other two are given a physical position of prominence at the outer ends of the struck sonority, at a perceptible distance from the two struck inner notes. By stacking its A's in four vertical registers, and by giving this triad the wide expanse of an open position, the piece should leave an unclouded final impression of A as in every way the fundamental element of the piece. Yet the sonority projects markedly less volume and fullness than does the climactic sonority; in a reading that does not automatically assume the priority of the logical to the physical, these characteristics may well signify weakness rather than resolution. And the open position of this sonority can very well be heard as emphasizing not its outer octave A but the struck sixth in its upper two voices—an interval that has been prominent throughout the piece and that, of course, turns attention away from the final cadence to the opening sonorities of the piece.

From the perspective of the interpreter, shifting the projection of weight in this piece from closings to openings has the effect not only of undermining the authority of cadences but also of undercutting the complementary differences that relate pairs. This, in turn, increases the perceptibility of individual components as discrete, self-contained units—precisely the condition that, at the start of this second reading, we attributed to the climactic sonority. Whatever *physical* evidence of strength may be produced through definitions of self-containment, the entire process just described entails a weakening of the basis for perceiving unity in this prelude as a whole. This sort of weakening leads to conclusions in our second reading that are very different from those formed in our first: about the symbolic power of subjectivity in this prelude, about the conceptions it presents of essential and secondary elements, and about the relationship it ultimately suggests between intelligibility and reality.

To clarify the nature of these differences, let us return briefly to the first tonic cadence, in the second phrase, at measures 3 and 4. Earlier I asserted that this cadence nails down nothing. Neither, however, does it generate any further action. As a unit of intelligibility, the portion of the piece that ends at this cadence requires nothing further to complete itself.[132] In actuality, of course, the music carries on in a way that is conventionally quite intelligible.[133] Yet what happens after this first cadence, like the very fact that the piece does continue, has an undeniable contingency.

Let us leave aside, for the moment, the possibility that the conclusion of this piece will force a retrospective reevaluation of the entire preceding musical course as musically necessary. Short of such an eventuality, the contingent progress of this piece produces no evidence of its ability to define itself as an unmistakably unified structure. To begin with, even as the piece makes certain compositional choices, one has an acute (though seldom analyzed) sense that at every moment other, equally intelligible choices could be made.

Thus we can extrapolate from examples already cited a perception that every vertical space could have been filled in differently. Every melodic line could have turned in a different direction. Like the V of II chord at the climax, many (or perhaps any?) harmonies could have been replaced by others. Much of the effect in all these instances stems from the ways in which the differences, conflicts, and absences presented by the prelude call our attention to a simultaneous possibility of "otherness." Sensitizing us as it does to all these contingencies of its structure, the prelude cannot exclude the idea that some change in that structure might give it an aspect or degree of unity that it presently lacks.

On a larger structural level, also, each phrase can be imagined as ending in some other way. Each pair of phrases could lead to some other pair. The whole piece could conceivably end later than it does, or sooner. Nothing in the way the piece is structured discourages us from imagining these hypothetical alternatives. In some ways, as in the constant introduction and petering out of appoggiaturas, the piece draws explicit attention to the possibility of alternatives. But above all, it is structured throughout in ways that tantalize us with a sense of "what if?"—as in "what if things were different?"

The definition of structural contingency on such a relatively large scale is not conducive to the perception of a tightly integrated whole. This is not to deny that the elements and segments in question have a plausible relation to each other. But plausible relationships are not of themselves sufficient to define a condition of wholeness. Nor is it to deny that these components have a common stylistic identity. Indeed, the structure of this piece may well be heard to confirm, many times over, the consistency of stylistic identity in this piece. But stylistic consistency is likewise not sufficient to justify interpreting this piece as a unity—say, as the complete realization of internal premises—rather than as a fragment. To persuade us of its status as a unified structure, this piece, just as in our first reading, must establish its control over a domain in which something happens. Or even better, it must establish itself in some way as a force sufficiently powerful to make something perceptible happen.

Only by defining its identity in relation to some persuasively coherent action can the piece establish the unmistakability of its existence as a unified entity. Yet there are many ways in which it could be argued that nothing really happens, or is made to happen, in this piece. Whereas in our first reading the return of the tonic A, and associated principles of stability, could be taken to signify arrival at a higher level of knowledge, in our present reading this sameness could be taken for evidence that the prelude signifies [!] no capacity for producing change or difference, and hence no indisputable capacity for signifying at all. At most what it signifies, in other words, is the contingency of successful signification.

In a tonal sense, for example, though hints of B-minor appear from time to time, no modulation is ever fully completed; that is, no real breakthrough is effected from the tonic A to some other primary key area.[134] Furthermore, however much the sense of the antecedent-consequent relationship is undermined, the broad physical regularity characteristic of antecedent-consequent structure is rigidly maintained, both at the level where the pairs seem atomized into a series of single, contiguous fragments and at the level of pairing. At both levels the regularity of phrasing is in a formal sense maintained. At the atomized level, the rhythm is, with one (or possibly two) exceptions, totally repetitive. And at the paired level, although the replacement of I with V of II at the climactic moment interrupts the series of functionally identical cadences and thereby asserts a capacity to make a significant change or progress, reference to the cadential shape or gesture of resolving a dominant triad, however hollowed of functional force this gesture may be, is consistently maintained— even at the moment of climactic disruption.

It could even be said that the regularities of the antecedent-consequent shape are maintained so rigidly as to preclude any real action. The maintenance of the antecedent-consequent outline throughout the piece dismantles the promise of engagement-and-resolution that gave Classical periodic structure—now no more than a trace here—its significance as a vital constructive force. This piece does not share the tendency of the Classical style, particularly in developmental types of sections, to break propulsively through the static preening, the Alphonse-Gaston act, of antecedent and consequent in order to establish a resolution that is "metaphorically" related to an exposition, in any structuralist or poststructuralist sense of the term "metaphor." One finds here no quasi-Classical resolution that could be construed as a symbolic replacement on *any* level for a premise, much less on some higher level of knowledge or reality. Instead, on a large scale this piece does nothing more constructive (as opposed to "deconstructive") with its antecedent-consequent structures than line them up as yet another series of ongoing adjacencies. In a sense this piece is *all* premise. But a premise without the possibility of resolution has far more in common with a meaningless concept than it does with a persuasively unified whole.

Almost certainly the brevity of this piece can be cited as corroborative evidence of its inability to make something happen. And yet, even within this brief span, the various atomized series it lays out from the perspective of our second reading are open-ended and, to use Jameson's term again, "infinitely fissionable." In this piece, as in other short pieces by Chopin, we have what Leonard Meyer has characterized as the sense of alighting in the midst of some ongoing process[135] (a formulation not too far, incidentally, from Derrida's "always already").

But if a hierarchical system of paired oppositions is dissolved into a string of what Jameson calls "dual inequalities," all equally marginal in relation to a nonexistent center (in this case the deconstructed tonic), then we have reason for arguing, in de Man's terms, that the "internal necessity" and symbolic intelligibility of metaphorical parallelism is secondary in our text, as we are now reading it, to the "mere contiguity" of metonym. One thinks in this second reading of the "additive" solution that Jameson claims Flaubert found for the concrete definition of a space empty of subjective presence.[136] Certainly the symbolism of the self-resolving musical subject that Adorno describes so problematically, and yet so usefully, as present in Beethoven's developmental process is not present here.

And yet—there remains the climactic outburst, so similar to the "burst of 'affect'" that Jameson discerns in Flaubert's evocation of a "musty smell," and that Jameson calls "the only genuine *event*" in the entire passage.[137] Surely the subject can be said to break into the empty space at this moment and begin to shape it, by giving it a center.

But does it? Let us disregard the physical sense in which, for small-handed players like me, this moment itself suggests forces beyond the control of subjectivity, or even, by some literal analogy, the breakdown of subjective identity. The clearest way in which we could point to a powerful subjective presence, either real or figurative, in the climactic sonority would be by demonstrating persuasively its ability to effect change and make something happen in the music that follows it, and thereby to shape its own course. The fact that the climactic sonority itself cannot break through the peak of range established in the preceding measure does not bode well for its power to make a difference. This small but telling sign of impotence is swiftly reinforced by the clear inability of the climax to sustain the force either of its tonal field or of its physical mass. Nor is this all. Caught up as it is in an ever-widening network of perceived reversals, along with processes of undermining and collapse, the climactic sonority affects our impression of the final measures in a way that deconstructs its own self-assertion: it undercuts the force of the very changes it seems to bring about.

For from one perspective, the momentary self-assertion of the climactic power can be heard as yielding to the superior force of numerous patterns. These would include the repetition of melody notes, rhythm, and formal phrasing; the resumption of the V-I antecedent-consequent pairing; and the return, at the very end, to three successive statements of the same basic triad. Measured against the massively established prominence of such repetitive patterns, all other changes could be heard as mere secondary phenomena, of no more consequence than the accidental wrinkles on a surface. Perceived in this way, such changes could not obscure the extent to which the music seems clearly to back away from its own challenge at the moment of climax, or the extent to which it decides on returning to something like the "obsessional evocation of the 'concrete'" that for Roland Barthes seems to conjure up the randomness of a reality that is no longer construed as intelligible.[138]

From this perspective, what takes place after the climactic sonority is not appreciably different from what took place before it. No power is demonstrated here by the climactic sonority to effect significant change. The sonority may *appear* to effect some changes. Its even more forceful evocation of randomness, however, no longer permits us an uncritical belief in what Jameson calls the "reality of the appearance."

From a second perspective, the climactic gesture can be heard as giving way to a cadential gesture, which successfully imposes its force and gets the last word, even though the functional authority of its tonic identity has been hollowed out through extensive processes of self-questioning. Thus, even if the intermittent resurfacing of B in the final two phrases suggests some residual powers of subjective freedom, these notes yield even as they appear to the superior claims of a cadence on I. And this cadence, it must be acknowledged, is not of the climactic chord's making. It is not subject to the control of that chord. It does not issue out of that chord in any way that could persuasively symbolize the self-determining powers of a rational subject. Rather, in ways very much like the music that follows the climactic outburst in Chopin's E-Major Etude, Opus 10, number 3,[139] this tonic simply assumes its right to exist, and resumes its place in the piece as if the climax had never happened. So much for the hypothesis that the climactic sonority symbolizes the power of subjectivity to make something happen.

The authority of the tonic in the closing phrases derives not from any dynamic internally generated by the climax but from a principle external to the piece itself. This tonic, and above all the final tonic cadence, is simply and inexorably required by convention. What must be maintained at all costs, even if the force of logic fails to verify its own priority, is the conventionally sanctioned authority of the pitch A. This requirement explains as well as anything why G-natural does not appear in the progression leading to the climactic sonority, or for that matter, anywhere in the piece. To lower the leading tone of A would pose a dangerously real threat to the hegemony of this key. A convention intent on consolidating its force cannot risk yielding anything like such a degree of power to representatives of subjectivity.

From the point of view of subjectivity, one can surmise, it makes no difference whether the superior force to which the climactic outburst yields in the final portion of the piece is that of randomness or inexorability. Both are equally indifferent to subjective needs and aspirations. From both perspectives, then, precisely as "the final Flaubertian cadence confirms" in Jameson's analysis, the bid for power by Chopin's putative subject in the climactic sonority seems "doomed in advance to failure."[140] The musical occurrences, or nonoccurrences, that follow the evocation of subjectivity in the climactic sonority are not the consequence of that evocation. At most they take shape as its aftermath—or, more accurately perhaps, in its wake.

Conceivably, the final cadence could try to justify the cultural conventions on which it rests as themselves intrinsically rational. This is a well-known tactic in Western culture. But this cadence would not know how (as who would?) to demonstrate the validity of such a proposition. From a subjective standpoint, in this reading, the tonic triad by itself represents no relevant principle of rationality. From this standpoint, this triad could be exchanged for another; its "necessity" is contingent. More compelling, in my judgment, than any such attempt at rationalization is the likeness of the final tonic cadence to what Jameson calls "the seemingly aimless rationalizing and logical 'car,'" which follows the "burst of 'affect'" in Flaubert's passage and which, by Jameson's account, "offers the very symptom of a cause-and-effect logic running wild and consuming the universe."[141]

What Jameson describes in this formulation seems close in spirit to an observation made by de Man in his second reading of the passage by Proust. "Figures [of speech]," writes de Man—and, ominously, it is the humanly empowering figure of metaphor that he has in mind here—"are assumed to be inventions, the products of a highly particularized individual talent, whereas no one can claim credit for the programmed pattern of grammar. . . . Yet our reading of the Proust passage shows that precisely when the highest claims are being made for the unifying power of metaphor, these very images rely in fact on the deceptive use of semi-automatic grammatical patterns."[142] If there is genius in such a text, de Man might almost be saying, it is above all the genius made possible by an impersonal, culturally defined, suprasubjective system—a system much like tonality, as it has been characterized in the present reading.

De Man's use of the term "deceptive" in this context brings us directly back, both literally and figuratively, to the force of the cadence delineated in our climactic sonority. From a subjective point of view, the worst fears represented by the instability of this chord are subsequently realized by the energy that is suddenly gathered in the exceptional elevation[143] and determination of the melodic B that opens measure 15. Whereas in our earlier reading this B could be dismissed as no more than a passing, minor, or secondary threat to the governing status of the tonic A, in this reading, where the priority of cognitive necessities can no longer be assumed, it takes on urgency as the last chance for subjectivity, now reduced to a freedom of mere self-affirmation, to counteract the threats to subjective control posed by ontologically persuasive principles of both randomness and inexorability. Indeed, on some levels of reading, this B could be persuasively construed as one last attempt by subjectivity to secure a gesture of closure in B-minor that is commensurate in power both to the climactic sonority itself and to the subsequent cadence on A. A strong gesture of closure in B-minor is crucial for validating the risk taken by the climactic sonority, and more particularly, for validating the character of that risk as a symbol of subjective freedom. And note that this B is now in the top voice rather than a middle one.

But this insistence on B projects itself as a tactic of desperation. The very location of the B in the top line exposes its vulnerability to the superior power of the low A against which it is pitted. This B is the exception that confirms the norm—but the norm is no longer felt to be determined by subjectivity. "No more nonsense," says the prelude to this B. "Your tactic has failed, you have lost the game, the power of subjectivity has been tried and found wanting. You have no power over your destiny. If some stronger force wants to step in and bring this charade to a close, it will do so."

The hopes of subjectivity, even as a figurative symbol of power, are now all but dashed. The grace-note A tries to keep those hopes alive. But its force is a diminished one, not only by Beethovenian standards of defiance, but even in relation to the metrical stability and length of preceding anticipatory tied notes in this prelude. Whereas in our earlier reading, subjective control was able to effect a *taming* of this gesture, what we have now is more a *laming* of it; upon asserting itself, the gesture immediately gives up the ghost and yields to a superior force.

However much life may seem to be left in this grace note, it is swiftly stifled and absorbed by a tie into the texture of the tonic chord. Its fate evokes images of the truncation of subjectivity not dissimilar to those evoked by the beheading that closes the fourth movement of the *Symphonie Fantastique*,[144] or by the closing moments of *Til Eulenspiegel* and *Petrushka*. The final self-assertion by this grace-note A offers to subjectivity no hope in the reality of either its freedom or control; at most, it gives the consolation of Galileo's *sotto voce* outburst, "E pur si muove."

Even the overtones of the last melodic B, which linger through the pedal and yet die within the final tonic triad, cannot overpower the final A triad. At most they can confirm the superior force of an order of things that can, if it wishes, coexist indefinitely with disorder—just as it can defy logic by giving the tonic triad the tonally capricious form of a second inversion at the very onset of a final resolution. The workings of such an order are unfathomable to subjectivity, and therefore beyond its secure control, even in its most rational modes of operation.

Earlier in my second reading (p. 132) I left open the possibility that the conclusion of the prelude could "force a retrospective reevaluation of the entire preceding musical course as necessary." As in my first reading (p. 110), such a feat would make the prelude enormously attractive as a metaphor for individual human life. By figurative extension, such a powerful conclusion could persuade us that death itself comes not as just another in a series of contingent, contiguous, and often painful events, but as the completion of a process that transforms the preceding life into a unified, significant whole.

For such a strategy to work, the final cadence of the prelude would have to project itself as such an unmistakably successful conclusion as to persuade us of the necessity of all that preceded. To effect such a reading, the final cadence would have to persuade us that life progresses indisputably toward its own validation. It would have to have sufficient authority to dispel a particularly disquieting image: that of life as a contingent structure on which any or no event, including death, may or may not confer a persuasively coherent shape.[145] But to the extent that the final cadence of this prelude has been shown to reveal its indifference to subjective aspirations, it represents no subjectively significant destination or process of closure. Hence, the pattern of repeated cadences presented in this prelude cannot be interpreted in this second reading, as it was in my first, as a series of metaphorical transformations that demonstrate the symbolizing power of a subjective intelligence to establish what de Man calls a "necessary link" with metaphysical reality.

In this second reading, the figurative relationship that this pattern of repeated cadences projects is not that of metaphor, which implies an underlying intelligence with the power to symbolize, but that of metonym, which implies nothing more than an arbitrary, nonlogical condition of physical or conventional adjacence. What this pattern projects, in other words, is precisely the metonymical condition of "mere contiguity" described by Jameson and de Man in their respective second readings of the passages by Flaubert and Proust. "In the . . . characteristic afterthought [to the 'burst of "affect"']," Jameson writes, "the process of infinite fission and metonymization returns with a vengeance."[146] De Man writes similarly of Proust, "The passage from a . . . structure based on substitution, such as metaphor, to a . . . structure based on contingent association, such as metonymy, shows the mechanical, repetitive aspect of grammatical forms to be operative in a passage that seems at first sight to celebrate the self-willed and autonomous inventiveness of a subject."[147]

Thus, also, in our second reading of Chopin's prelude. To sustain the illusion that it has come to a close in the sense of having really settled something, Chopin's prelude "forgets" what it must—and what my own two readings have, up until this very moment, slipped over as rapidly as possible. It must forget that the power to effect closure, and to ground space and time on an intelligible center, not just in figurative but also in real terms, is not demonstrably within subjective control.

In terms of my first reading, the forgetting, and hence the illusion, works. In terms of my second reading, however, the processes by which the prelude tries to sustain the illusion of "transcendental signification" are no longer persuasive. Since the changes that subjectivity tried to bring about by way of the climactic chord did not secure it any real power, we are still back at the level of structure I had come to acknowledge just before I said, "And yet"[148]—a level I described as an additive string of atomized units. Indeed, we have never left it. At the end of the piece we remain in an additive or "infinite[ly] fission[able]" time and space, which the merely contiguous, metonymical cadences can at best articulate or measure but cannot control or transform. In our second reading, what de Man calls the "rhetorical seductions" of metaphor no longer work.[149]

The notion of an ineffectual "rhetorical seduction" is extremely helpful in clarifying the nature of the "very sizable stakes"[150] that de Man discerns in analyses of this kind—especially if we recall that the term "rhetoric" has traditionally been associated not only with the concreteness of figurative language but also with the desire to persuade—and to persuade through intonation and gesture as well as through the cleverness of a figure of speech.

In a way, my entire second reading is based on the premise that the primary source of power in this prelude is rhetorical emphasis, grounded on the physical concreteness of musical signs. This second reading argues at bottom that through rhetorical emphasis, the prelude attempts to project meaning onto its own physical aspect, and thus to persuade us that physical existence is meaningful. But in so doing, the prelude exposes the arbitrariness of its own rhetorical strategies as well as the tenuousness of the connections it can suggest between physical existence and any sort of meaning at all. To avoid conceding the absence of any implicit necessity in its claims to meaningfulness, and thereby collapsing into a condition of brute physical existence, the prelude tries to establish the significance of its configuration through the seductive illusions of rhetorical emphasis.

And in large measure, my second reading takes the prelude at its word, for even my second reading treats the prelude as a significant structure rather than as a brute physical object. Nevertheless, in subjecting its rhetorical strategies to the pressure of "such sizable stakes," the prelude, in this reading, exposes the real limitations of the rhetorical domain.

Let us return briefly to the pattern of cadences presented by this prelude. In a sense it makes no difference to my second reading whether we think of these cadences in pairs or singly. Rocking back and forth almost mechanically between V and I chords, the questions repetitively posed by the string of cadences can all be heard as "merely" rhetorical. "Is *this* how you cadence?" each asks skeptically. They ask expecting no real answer, for no answer can be expected from a final cadential process that exerts its force through arbitrary rather than intelligible means, be they random or inexorable in character.

Ironically, only the urgency of the question posed by the dramatic deceptive cadence at the climax projects any hope of obtaining a real, informational answer. But the information that the climactic sonority can hope to receive from such an arbitrary cadential process cannot be substantial. In fact, the answer it does receive is equivalent to a confirmation of the impossibility of obtaining any secure information about reality at all. Nor is this answer even a direct consequence of the question posed by the climactic sonority, since this answer appears purely at the whim of a conventional force that answers to no one.

"Surely *this* isn't how you cadence," the climactic sonority asks. "Is there *any* way I can cadence securely?" And the answer provided by the final cadence, through the arbitrary rather than the logical aspects of its force, is, "Right. That's not how you cadence. What you're doing isn't cadencing at all." "Right," that is, not because one sort of cadence is really correct, or even makes more sense than another, but because, whatever subjectivity would like to believe, in reality it makes no difference *what* form a cadence takes. There is no indisputably right way to cadence. Even the tonic is at bottom a sound with no necessary truth value (or even meaning).

But the climactic sonority asks something else as well. "Is there *any* way I can cadence securely?" And here it does find an answer: "No." The answer is underscored by the two remaining cadential gestures, which cannot reproduce even the smooth "2-3-1" chord repetitions that closed every phrase before the climax. It is as if they no longer have the energy to sustain any illusions that the cadences before the climax might still have harbored.

Here, at last, we come close to real information. But the knowledge thus provided, like the final cadence itself, is hollow. In contrast to the conclusion we drew from our first reading, this answer says that subjectivity cannot guarantee its own power to effect closure, unify a whole, or control time and space. In effect, this answer confirms the inability of the subject even to make contact with any intelligible principle of reality, much less to secure intelligibility as a fundamental component of reality. Even the urgent informational question posed by the climactic sonority collapses finally into the merely figurative domain of the rhetorical. About all that subjectivity has left to rejoice in, at this point, is that its most pessimistic images have no more demonstrable a basis in reality than does rhetoric at its most seductive.

By now tremendous differences should be apparent between my two readings. Virtually every argument, conclusion, and image suggested by my first reading has a conflicting or incompatible counterpart in the second. Several of these are particularly worth mentioning.

My first reading found in Chopin's A-Major Prelude evidence for the argument that the precise communication of meaning is not only possible but at bottom guaranteed by the essentially universal rationality of linguistic structures. By this formulation, communication is not a contingent process but an absolutely reliable one. In contrast, my second reading, by emphasizing the contingencies that affect the articulation, transmission, and perception of meanings, opens up the possibility that communication need not, and conceivably cannot, be successful. This is not the same as denying either the existence or the possibility of meaning; nor is it the same as categorically rejecting the possibility of communication. It should be noted, again, that this second reading does not characterize the prelude as meaningless. Rather, just as the first reading designates the precise signifying powers of unified structures as the theme of the prelude, so, too, the second reading designates the meaning (or theme) of the prelude to be the contingency of meaning.

Again, by my first reading, Chopin's prelude can be taken as a metaphor for individual human life in a number of comforting ways. Projecting itself as unified to the point where every structural choice seems necessary, the prelude evokes an image of each life as a structure that is not only meaningful but necessary. This it does mainly by successfully subsuming the contingent aspects of individuality under a universal principle of reason. By contrast, my second reading perceives the prelude as nothing more than a contingent structure, open to many pressures and possibilities in the course of its construction, and enjoying no ontological privilege in its particular physical state. By this formulation, individuality is not a condition rendered real and meaningful through its subsumption under universal rational principles, but simply one possible condition that may or may not have meaning.

Neither the sound nor the logic of Chopin's structure is taken by the second reading to establish itself as in any sense necessary. In this respect, it should be noted, the second reading denies any significant difference between sound and structure. By metaphorical extension, the prelude, in this reading, recognizes the possibility that the course of every human life may be nothing more than an aggregation of contingent circumstances, conditions, and events. From this view, the necessity each life would wish to impute to itself—and in particular to its suffering—is characterized epistemologically as an illusion. Acknowledgment is made of an inability to guarantee that either human life or human suffering has any real meaning. And without some such guarantee, the possibility remains open that when it's over, it's over. Indeed, from the perspective of the second reading, it is possible to conceive of life as merely a series of contiguous events on which no single event, not even death, has a verifiable power to confer a unified shape.

My first reading hypothesizes a subjectively congenial polarity between necessity and freedom, in which necessity was prior. In a way, each reading finally undercuts the significance of the differences between right and wrong choices, but each does so differently. My first reading does this, insisting all the while on the possibility of a "right" interpretation, in the sense that it accords a higher level of being to (cognitive) reason, the underlying principle of "right," than to the contingent level of physical existence at which right and wrong choices are made. My second reading does this because it can find no epistemologically secure ground for distinguishing between the two kinds of choices. Placing greater weight on the contingencies of freedom than on necessities of order, the second reading nevertheless, through its inability to establish a conclusive difference between right and wrong, gives cause to doubt the meaningfulness of a faculty of choice, such as freedom. Thus, whereas the first reading upholds both necessity and freedom, the second undercuts the distinction between these two poles of traditional (Western) rationality, and thereby holds out the possibility that rationality itself has no status in reality.[151]

Finally, contingency is the principal qualitative attribute of the characteristics we have here called "secondary." Contingency—the possible absence of existence—is the only condition of existence that the second reading is willing to recognize. From the standpoint of the second reading, contingency may be all that there is. Thus, on the one hand, the contingencies of the individualized structure are not validated as necessary; and on the other hand, the governing force of tonal logic, and of rationality itself, for that matter, cannot be verified as more than hypothetical or contingent possibilities.

It is in this sense—the sense that contingency is all we can know to "be," and that contingency thus has the best ontological claim of all conditions—that the second reading can characterize the climactic chord as "essential because it is (qualitatively) secondary." To use such a formulation is not to concede the reality of any timeless and necessary "essence," access to which would make this second reading impossible. By this second reading, humans can have no knowledge that goes beyond the contingent to what could be cognitively accepted as the essential. They can know only a world in which secondary or contingent characteristics alone are knowable—and thus primary.[152]

All of these differences seem to me implicit in the conflicting scenarios of question-and-answer imagery that I have proposed in connection with the cadences of the prelude. Given these conflicting scenarios, it is difficult to resist asking ourselves: Which kind of meaning does Chopin's prelude most forcefully encourage us to confer on its physical configuration? Is it a meaning grounded on rational convictions about the ultimate nature of reality? Or is it meaning that has no more sense of its own ontological security than has rhetorical bravado?

To flatten these questions through truisms about the equal indispensability of rational and rhetorical forms of discourse seems to me to miss entirely the urgency of the existential dilemma posed by the very possibility of asking such questions. I would prefer to suggest that the analysis of Chopin's prelude in terms of question-and-answer imagery presents us finally with the same sort of unresolvable ambiguity that de Man discerns as the central issue in his analyses of the texts by Yeats and Proust. De Man's analyses leave us with the sense of an infinite reversibility, and hence an underlying indistinguishability, between the domains of the cognitive and the rhetorical (or aesthetic), as modes of defining reality. And this seems to be the case whether one defines knowledge in terms of literal, empirical information adduced through the operation of underlying logical principles, or in terms of those underlying principles themselves.[153]

At bottom, as I hope to have exemplified through my treatment of tonal logic and dramatic emphasis, both modes of defining reality operate only by means of the distance from reality provided by parallelism, symmetrical analogy, structural metaphor, nonliteral "correction," and other such figurative means. Thus both the cognitive and the rhetorical can be construed as having a figurative rather than a literal force.[154]

Beyond this observation, however, de Man's analyses leave us in many ways uncertain concerning the priority of the figurative and the literal. Certainly, his apparent readiness to pursue his analysis of Proust's text through an open-ended series of reversals suggests an infinite undecidability as to which of these two levels, the figurative or the literal—or which of his two readings—has priority. Yet again, there is an important sense in which his analysis tilts in favor of the figurative over the literal. The very notion of an indistinguishability between these two seems clearly to confirm the entrapment of subjective intelligence within a figurative level of questioning that can never be sure of reaching metaphysical reality.

So, too, my own readings of Chopin's A-Major Prelude move back and forth between interested evocations of the figurative and the literal. In my first reading, the unsettling effect of the rhetorical question at the climactic moment could not destroy the symbolic capacity for structural unification. This capacity remains figurative, yet its force is so powerful that in the end it persuades us to accept its understanding of its own theme as true.[155] Embodying in its own structure evidence of a capacity to guarantee meaning through unity, the prelude persuades us to accept a continuous progress from structure through theme to reality. In short, the prelude persuades us of its ability to transcend its own limitations and present us with an account of reality itself as intelligible. In this sense, my first reading maintains the priority desired by subjectivity of literal, as opposed to figurative, conceptions of the term "reality."

My second reading, by contrast, honors the power of the explicitly (i.e., more honestly) figurative to provide a more persuasive account than any literal conception could of reality—but of reality only as a condition that is beyond subjective access. Of course, we have no sure way of knowing whether such mutual entrapments of "real" and "symbolic" force, like the indeterminate mingling of A and B in the final cadence, have any grounding in the nature of reality itself. Certainly we have no cognitively secure basis for deciding which kind of conception of reality, a literal or a figurative one, is "really" essential (or secondary).

Likewise, in my first reading, the rhetorical challenge mounted by the climactic sonority never threatens to turn exception into norm, or to equate arbitrary, irrational strength with reality. By contrast, the subjectivity evoked by this sonority in my second reading makes precisely such threats, through the very force of its impotence to break out definitively and irreversibly from the monolithic (and by no means self-evidently rational) conventions of tonality imposed upon it, and through its inability to secure an unmistakably intelligible relationship with any domain outside the one it conjures up for itself.

Thus, in this second reading, subjectivity resigns itself to remaining on this side of the great metaphysical divide and shrinks back into itself, unable to prove, through reference to something other than itself, its own power or meaningfulness in reality. Even in the climactic sonority and its aftermath, as in Jameson's second reading, subjectivity defines itself not as a presence but as a ghost or trace at the very moment it is evoked. Within my second reading, this chord marks, in Jameson's words, "the fitful emergence of the subject . . . with a triumphant, desolate flourish."[156] Unable to sustain the illusion of either its own freedom or its own control, subjectivity can still rouse itself to recall that illusion, but can no longer hope to exert real force in what Jameson calls "a henceforth reified universe."[157]

Conclusion

And yet, perhaps even in this second reading of the A-Major Prelude, subjectivity can be construed, at least in some existentialist sense, as having the last word after all; for even knowing the odds it faces, it *does* rouse itself.

Even if the force of subjective intelligibility cannot be definitively secured

as real, the climactic sonority does succeed in perceptibly reinvoking the earlier resistance to A by B-minor (in the third phrase, measures 5 and 6), and in
intensifying that resistance, which in turn intensified the momentary dissonance that launched the second phrase (beat 1 of measure 3). Through this
progressive intensification, this sonority does maintain a moment of gravity, if
not a permanent center, in the latter half of the piece; and thereby it points to
the principle of a subjectively controlled final closure, even if it cannot reach
it. In effect, even if this climactic sonority cannot functionally demonstrate,
beyond our capacity to doubt, the existence of subjectivity as a powerful and
meaningful force, it does, through its refusal to leave its own energies untried,
preserve the figurative powers of subjectivity as a central theme of the prelude.

Such a capacity for energetic exertion, no matter what hardships it posed,
was by no means honored in all nineteenth-century artworks. According to
Lionel Trilling in *Sincerity and Authenticity*,[158] something like the situation of
subjectivity that I have described in relation to this prelude was reflected in a
great deal of European art over the course of the nineteenth century. Many
characters in nineteenth-century European fiction found their individual
authenticity threatened by the overwhelming forces and conventions of society, and by a seemingly mindless, mechanistic universe. And the response of
many a character, in Trilling's words, was simply "to lie down in his isolation
and die."[159]

By the twentieth century, according to Trilling's account, a need became
explicit "to retrieve the human spirit from its acquiescence in non-being."[160]
But the answers that came to Nietzsche's dread of the "weightlessness of all
things," or as Trilling himself put it, to fears about "the inauthenticity of existence," were hardly reassuring.[161] Freud came to the conclusion, says Trilling,
that "life in civilization is largely intractable to reasonable will,"[162] and that
"the momentous claim which life makes upon us [is] by very reason . . . of its
hardness, intractability, and irrationality."[163]

And yet. This response by Freud did not amount to what Trilling calls "the
great refusal of human connection."[164] Rather it represented the rescue, from a
religion in which Freud no longer believed, of "the imperative actuality which
religion attribute[s] to life,"[165] through the belief that "however harsh and
seemingly gratuitous a fate may be, the authenticity of its implicit significance
is not to be denied, confirmed as it is by the recognition of *some* imperative
which has both brought it into being and prescribes its acceptance, and in so
doing affirm[s] the authenticity of him to whom the fate is assigned."[166]

By this standard, even a structure, or a life, that cannot affirm its power to
make something happen and thereby affirm its own ontological status of unity,

can rescue itself from the despair of unrelieved meaninglessness. "It is this authenticating imperative, irrational and beyond the reach of reason," says Trilling of the grounds for belief that were still left to the post-Enlightenment subject, "that Freud wishes to preserve."[167]

Freud's own death lay a century ahead of Chopin's Prelude in A-Major. Yet even as represented in this prelude—which stems, after all, from a post-Kantian culture that has already moved beyond the optimism of the Enlightenment—the situation of human subjectivity as Chopin presents it may not be so radically different from its situation in Western culture today.[168]

And if the subject that emerges in the climactic chord, and sounds its last echo in the grace note, no longer exhibits a Beethovenian strength of will, neither does it refuse the human connection, or just lie down in its isolation and die.

Instead this subject rouses itself to say, "And yet." And because it does, the attempt in this chord to seize power should not necessarily be heard, in the last analysis, as unearned. Perhaps we should prefer to say, rather, that this gesture gives musical voice to Marlow's description of Kurtz's last outburst, which Trilling quotes so movingly from Joseph Conrad's *Heart of Darkness*: "It was an affirmation, a moral victory paid for by innumerable defeats"; and especially, "Better his cry—much better."[169]

3

Toward a Deconstruction of Structural Listening: A Critique of Schoenberg, Adorno, and Stravinsky

> The highest criticism is that which leaves an impression identical
> with the one called forth by the thing criticized.
> —*Robert Schumann*[1]

> We have always two universes of discourse—call them "physical" and
> "phenomenal," or what you will—one dealing with questions of quantitative
> and formal structure, the other with those qualities that constitute a
> "world." . . . Computational representations . . . could never, of themselves,
> constitute "iconic" representations, those representations which are the very
> thread and stuff of life. . . . Experience is not *possible* until it is organized
> iconically; action is not *possible* unless it is organized iconically. . . .
> The final form of cerebral representation must be, or allow, "art"
> —the artful scenery and melody of experience and action.
> —*Oliver Sacks*[2]

Emotion and meaning are coming out of the musicological closet. The underground passages out of uncritical formalism, which Leonard Meyer began to chart more than thirty years ago, are in the process of being discovered by American musicology at large. This developing critique of musical formalism would be facilitated by a reexamination of what I would like to call "structural listening," a method that concentrates attention primarily on the formal relationships established over the course of a single composition.

The general principle of structural listening has become so well established as a norm in the advanced study and teaching of music, at least in this country, that it is all too easy for us to assume its value as self-evident and universal and to overlook its birth out of particular historical circumstances and ideological conflicts. Likewise, it has become easy to "forget," in Nietzsche's sense, that

148

the object of structural listening, a structure that is in some sense abstract, constitutes only one pole of a more general, dialectical framework in which modern Western conceptions of music have been developed.[3] The other pole—medium—is a historical parameter of music, signifying the ongoing relationship of any composition to a public domain of sound and culture, from the time of its initial appearance up to the present. This pole is defined principally through the presentation of sounds, organized by conventional or characteristic usages, into particular configurations called styles, as objects of a physical yet culturally conditioned perception. The precise nature of the relationship between sound and style is an interesting problem that cannot be given attention here. In the discussion that follows, the terms "sound" and "style," as intertwined aspects of the common parameter of medium will often be treated as more or less interchangeable.

The present discussion, which developed from a much shorter critique in an earlier article, has resulted unintentionally in something very close to a deconstruction.[4] Recognizing a hierarchical opposition between structure and medium as fundamental to the concept of structural listening, I have in effect tried to reverse the conventionally assumed priorities in this hierarchy, to undercut the distinction between its poles by presenting the mode and object of structural listening as a function of (or as a "supplement" to, in Derrida's sense) those of nonstructural listening, and to expose some of the concealed ideological assumptions that the concept of structural listening reflects.[5]

The Case for Structural Listening

The variant of structural listening on which I wish to focus my primary attention is the one developed by Schoenberg and Adorno over the course of their writings. I know of no variant that offers on the one hand a stronger or more broadly applicable defense of structural listening and on the other hand a more explicit basis for its own analysis as a cultural construct. To be sure, the concepts worked out by Schoenberg and by Adorno are not identical. Schoenberg's concept is more narrowly focused on the practical concerns of the composer; Adorno's, on the theoretical concerns of the critic. Schoenberg's philosophy is far more naive; and he by no means shared all of Adorno's emphases or opinions, any more than Adorno witnessed without reservation all of Schoenberg's compositional decisions. Nevertheless, the two men were in very close agreement as to the specifics of structural listening; moreover, Adorno's concept of structural listening, like all of his music criticism, was not only developed in a full and informed sympathy with Schoenberg's enterprise but can in fact be read as a defense of Schoenberg. Thus the limited philosophical justification that Schoenberg provided for structural listening is consistently and persuasively grounded by Adorno's more ample account, and for present purposes the two concepts will be considered as one here. Schenkerian conceptions of structure and perception, such as Felix Salzer's "structural hearing," will not be considered here; hence the "Toward" of my title.

This concept of structural listening, as Schoenberg and Adorno presented it, was intended to describe a process wherein the listener follows and comprehends the unfolding realization, with all of its detailed inner relationships, of a generating musical conception, or what Schoenberg calls an "idea."[6] Based on an assumption that valid structural logic is accessible to any reasoning person, such structural listening discourages kinds of understanding that require culturally specific knowledge of things external to the compositional structure, such as conventional associations or theoretical systems. This includes the twelve-tone system and the constitution of any particular "row," though it does not, and indeed cannot, exclude a cultural familiarity with the dynamic of tonality.[7] In Adorno's formulation, knowing even the name of the composer or the composition in question could muddy the purity of the desired process.[8] Structural listening is an active mode that, when successful, gives the listener the sense of composing the piece as it actualizes itself in time.

The concept of structural listening has complex roots in German musical, cultural, and philosophical traditions, with which both Schoenberg and Adorno felt a strong sense of historical continuity. The origins of the concept can usefully be traced to the final phase of the Enlightenment. Kant himself remained faithful to a representational notion of art and never drew the full range of aesthetic conclusions to which his own work pointed. Nevertheless, his Critique of Judgment, with its conception of disinterested aesthetic pleasure and especially its presentation of aesthetic judgment as a conceptless process involving the metaphor of a structural congruence between faculties, marks a crucial step toward the idealization, in Germany during the next century, of both structural autonomy in art and of music as the highest art. A comparable shift was initiated in the musical domain by the instrumental works of Haydn and Mozart, which served as a powerful catalyst for the rich and paradoxical development of formalistic attitudes toward music in nineteenth-century Germany.

I say "rich and paradoxical" because this formalistic movement was from the start marked by a dialectical opposition and intertwining of values that can be associated with musical autonomy on the one hand and with critical, often even verbal, ways of thinking on the other. Beethoven's music itself can be construed as a self-conscious critique of earlier Classical musical conceptions. Arguing musically for autonomous structural values, sometimes through a physically thick and tonally extrinsic rhetorical emphasis, sometimes through a revisionist treatment of inherited structural conventions, Beethoven succeeded in undermining the abstract security of the very condition of autonomy he sought to establish, and suggested musical structure as at bottom a contingent construct, subject to concrete cultural limitations on its character and significance.

Likewise, the notions of absolute music as developed by such early Romantic figures as Wilhelm Heinrich Wackenroder and Ludwig Tieck, and as treated in the music criticism of E. T. A. Hoffmann, Carl Maria von Weber, and Schumann, are of a rich and concrete sort. Attending (in the case of the three music critics) with considerable detail to structural relationships within music, and at the same time affirming the inseparability of a musical structure from the poetic and spiritual associations and imagery that this structure evoked in the imagination, Romantic writing encouraged a kind of listening that was at once structurally abstract and full of content. The critic Edward Rothstein has suggested to me that we call this mode of listening "metaphorical"; Leo Treitler has called the quality to which it directed attention "narrativity."[9] The word I would use to characterize the Romantic conception of musical structure is "replete."

This twofold conception of musical form underwent something of a crisis in Eduard Hanslick's landmark work, *The Beautiful in Music*, published in 1854. Often construed as a bracing antidote to Wagner's expressive or rhetorical "excesses," Hanslick's restriction of the problem of musical understanding to the purely technical parameters of musical structure can indeed be read as a manifesto for formalistic values of a sort that eventually reached beyond Germany and, by way of what Adorno calls Stravinsky's "phenomenology," right up to the present.[10] For a work that is deeply conservative in spirit—and not just because its concept of aesthetic value points directly back to Kant's third critique—*The Beautiful in Music* proved remarkably prescient.

Yet it should not be supposed that Hanslick renounced altogether the full-bodied or replete character of the ideal of autonomy that had been developed between Kant's time and his own. Asserting that "the domain of aesthetics . . . begins only where elementary [mathematical] relations cease to be of importance," Hanslick argues that what "raises a series of musical sounds into the region of music proper and above the range of physical experiment is something free from external constraint, a spiritualized and therefore incalculable something."[11] This is not so far removed from Schumann's assertion that "if we are to hear a convincing form, music must act as freely as poetry on our conceptual capacities"—or, for that matter, from his praise of Berlioz as similar to "Jean Paul, whom someone called a bad logician and a great philosopher."[12] If Hanslick proposes reducing the musical object of criticism to its phenomenological essentials, he arrives at this point through concepts of the aesthetic and of structure that idealize human cultural and spiritual capacities. If Hanslick encourages a reinterpretation of the musically formal as connoting something essentially negative—say, "mere," or empty, form, form as precisely that in music which does not express—the metaphysical spirit of the German traditions that formed his cultural context can and should still be discerned in his argument as what could be called, in Derridean terms, an important absent presence or "trace."[13]

This intertwining of German intellectual tradition with purely structural values continues to characterize the formalism of Schoenberg and Adorno.[14] It marks an important difference between their aesthetic theories and Stravinsky's, as set forth in the latter's *Poetics of Music*, theories that otherwise converge on a number of more or less characteristic twentieth-century Western musical positions, including a common insistence on the need for some sort of structural listening. Both Schoenberg and Stravinsky, for example, define music as a field for the mastery of nature by culture, the latter of which is valued for its scientific and speculative capacities.[15] Both wish to subject music to a governing, objective, and essentially universal principle of rational necessity, which would counteract the capriciousness of personal self-gratification, prejudice, and taste.[16] Both would (theoretically) support an open-ended variety of musical works, which, so long as they were formally coherent, would have no need to justify their "kind" or existence;[17] the internal necessity *of* the work, so to speak, would sufficiently guarantee for both men the outward necessity *for* it.

Both Schoenberg and Stravinsky celebrate the activity of musical construction and would confine musical meaning within the boundaries of the individual composition, exclusive of contextual relationships and (at least in theory) of intent.[18] Both consider reception and effect extrinsic to the concept of composition—the functionalist craftsman Stravinsky no less than the endlessly explaining Schoenberg.[19] Adorno's position on these matters is similar, though always more complicated. Although he sees no actual way of extricating musical structure from its embodiment of social values, and recoils from the hypostatizing of objects as a symptom of ideological dishonesty, he nevertheless maintains the achievement of a totally autonomous musical structure as a utopian ideal.[20] All three men end by locating musical value wholly within some formal sort of parameter, to which it is the listener's business to attend.

There is a difference, however, in the kinds of formal parameters chosen, which one of my students has characterized rather aptly as the contrast between Platonic and Aristotelian enterprises.[21] It is a difference that weakens, to the point of undermining it, Stravinsky's case for structural listening. Allowing for a civilizing speculative capacity, but disallowing all connection between music and philosophy, and recoiling far more successfully than Adorno from any taint of systematic thought, Stravinsky gives himself over to a spirit of empirical discovery that subordinates logical, or even quasi-logical, necessity to usefulness.[22] Indeed, everything about Stravinsky's musical career, including his relationship to past musical history, the progression of his styles, and the inner ordering of his works, points to the same essentially negative pattern of throwing overboard whatever does not serve an immediate purpose.[23] At none of these levels do we sense any interest in demonstrating that steady continuity through which rational processes, especially those pertaining to logical necessity (as opposed to that which is dogmatic or arbitrarily imposed), might confirm their presence in the concrete world.[24] Nor does Stravinsky's *Poetics*, outside of a single evocative paragraph, offer any concrete, positive guidelines for the achievement of an unmistakably perceptible rationality in music.[25] The formal parameter of music for Stravinsky is simply sound as opposed to expression, that is, sound stripped of meaning;[26] and formal value, as characterized in the *Poetics*, amounts to nothing more than a persuasive impression that a particular combination of sounds "works."

By resting the case for a formalistic conception of music on such persuasiveness, Stravinsky, the arch-foe of Wagnerian rhetoric, forfeits the claim of music to validation by any universal principle of rational necessity. At most, he allows the composition to project a plausible rationale, which suggests no necessary basis for its own validity. For all his talk of "necessity," what the Stravinsky of the *Poetics* values in music is not the conceptual but the qualitative or stylistic attributes of objectivity.[27] For this Stravinsky, and arguably for Stravinsky in a good deal of his composition, music succeeds by attaining an appearance of elegance, control, and "cool" nonexpressiveness. This condition, though in itself not beyond the reach of disciplined criticism, appeals not to the rational faculties (at least as Kant defined them) but simply to what in elitist circles of the modern West—and the *Poetics* is unabashed in its elitism—is considered good taste.[28] The patrician British description of an embarrassing social error as not being "good form" captures the spirit of Stravinsky's formalism precisely. The casual ease with which Stravinsky can cite the "tone" of his own work is in striking contrast to Schoenberg's attitude toward such matters.[29] In effect, Stravinsky redefines musical form to mean style, or even "high style," in our currently fashionable "yuppie" sense. In doing so he transforms music from a potentially universal symbol of integrity into a culturally specialized pleasure, leaving its fate to exactly those arbitrary standards of taste that his formalistic principles of appreciation were designed to escape.[30]

Schoenberg and Adorno try to effect this same escape by distinguishing the formal parameter of music from mere sound or style.[31] Instead, Schoenberg and Adorno define the formal parameter of music as an interconnectedness of structure that is both temporally established, and thus concrete, and also objectively determinable. Consequently, they define structural listening not as a sensibility to chic but as attentiveness to a concretely unfolding logic that can vouch for the value of the music. Practiced in the way prescribed by Schoenberg and Adorno, structural listening plunges us into the middle of what could be called the musical argument, allowing us to understand, from the position of an insider, not just the lines but the totality of the argument as it unfolds. Confronting at every moment the rationale of the composition from its own point of view, so to speak, the listener is ideally to be precluded from exercising negative prejudices or forming adverse judgments on the basis of stylistic uncongeniality or, in a sense, even (within moral limits) of philosophical difference.

Adorno, to be sure, who is in most respects far more preoccupied than Schoenberg with the philosophical and ideological implications of musical structure, is not only prepared but determined to reject music he finds morally offensive, including that of Stravinsky's bête noire, Wagner, and of course, that of Stravinsky himself. Significantly, however, Adorno never sees himself as having to choose between structural and moral value, because for Adorno the two are essentially synonymous; "no music has the slightest esthetic worth," he asserts, "if it is not socially true."[32] From Adorno's standpoint, the virtues of the rationality that structural autonomy represents, and that render autonomy the highest condition of art, are not just logically abstract but historically concrete as well. The more a musical structure approximates the self-contained intelligibility characteristic of logic, the more it can and does free itself from what Adorno sees as the deceptions or falsehoods invariably fostered through social ideology in order to maintain the power of existing institutions.[33] Conversely, the greater the distance of music from the logical paradigm, the greater its entrapment in the special interests served by the conventions of social ideology, and the smaller its claim to the essentially moral condition of aesthetic value. In other words, Adorno's characterization of a philosophical attitude in music as morally offensive is never separable from his perception of grave structural weaknesses in that music.

The concept of structural value offered by Schoenberg and Adorno, like their concept of the structural listening that can discern such value, is at once exacting and generous. Demanding an unflagging intelligent concentration on the part of the listener, these men require of the composer, and more generally of themselves, a no less stringent standard of discipline. The self-conscious consistency, the sense of integrity, and the devotion to logic with which Schoenberg tried to regulate every relationship in his own compositional domain—the inner construction of his pieces, the unfolding of his own stylistic progress, and the preservation and development of past musical tradition as a kind of sacred trust—have probably never been equaled by another Western composer. As in Stravinsky's case, his entire musical career can be read as an enlargement of his own compositional principles, but in a sense that is far more "replete."

And correspondingly, Schoenberg's spirit of self-discipline results in a concept of musical structure, and of structural listening, that is far more positive and concrete in character than Stravinsky's formalism. Just as it is usually possible for any educated and reasonably sympathetic listener to perceive the retention of a capacity for individual expressiveness as a value in Schoenberg's music, so too, Schoenberg refuses in his writings to dehumanize either the individuals participating in musical life or music itself by separating structural rigor from an expressive capacity. For Schoenberg these last two are virtually synonymous: the deepest emotional satisfaction in music arises precisely through the achievement of an intensely expressive structural integrity (which is "independent of style and flourish" and communicable at least to those whose "artistic and ethical culture is on a high level").[34]

Nor does either Schoenberg or Adorno shrink from specifying the concrete musical components of a structure that fully allows structural listening. Although Adorno voices serious objections to the twelve-tone method, which Schoenberg explained so painstakingly and generously to his readers, both men are thoroughly dedicated to the goal of reducing music to a condition of what could be called pure structural substance, in which every element justifies its existence through its relation to a governing structural principle. Hence both advocate the principle of "nonredundancy" in music, a principle with many compositional ramifications, including a rationale for chromaticism and dissonance, which they explore in detail; and both advocate the renunciation of preexisting, externally determined conventions, such as symmetrical phrasing and refrains (which in fact often entail redundancy), as foreign to the generating idea of a composition.[35] Such renunciation, it should be stressed, is not to be confused with the simultaneous acceptance and liquidation—or, to use Hegel's terminology, Aufhebung—of artistically transmitted tradition, which both men demanded in their commitment to historical continuity and responsibility. Furthermore, as a way of distilling structural substance, both men place particular importance on the self-developing capacity of a motivic-thematic kernel, or on what they call "developing variation," a process they often though not exclusively associate with Brahms.[36]

The notion of development represents, of course, a continuation of structural concepts and values that originated in Viennese Classicism. (Actually, Schoenberg, with some support from Adorno, locates its origins in Bach.)[37] This notion was likewise prized by Hanslick, who is cited as a particularly adept practitioner of structural listening in one of the most detailed descriptions that Schoenberg gives of this method.[38] Although Adorno is clearly more sensitive than Schoenberg to the self-negating potentialities of development in post-tonal music, he is even more emphatic than Schoenberg in idealizing Beethoven for his developmental powers; and both men admire Brahms's tendency to transform composition into what Adorno calls "total development."[39]

At its best, Schoenberg's and Adorno's concept of structural listening makes a strong case, and certainly a more consistent case than Stravinsky's version does, for the values it wishes to sustain. Evoking as its ideal the possibility of reasoned musical discourse, and thus by extension the possibility of reasoned discourse itself, among differently situated individuals, their concept does not hold musical form accountable only for the connection of its own elements to a rationally governing principle. In addition, their concept ultimately demands that musical form, through its uncompromising integrity and renunciation of sensuous distractions, contribute indirectly but concretely, as well as metaphorically, to the betterment of society. In effect, Schoenberg and Adorno offer structural listening as nothing less ambitious than a method for defining and assessing the moral soundness of every relationship that bears on music.

It is as a service to just some such ideal, I believe, that we in musicology today would at bottom justify our firm and continuing commitment to various forms of structural listening. And yet, for all Adorno's self-conscious acuity, this concept is not without what Paul de Man might call its areas of critical blindness to its own epistemological weaknesses.[40]

The Case Against Structural Listening

Cultural Inappropriateness

The concept of structural listening imagines both composition and listening to be governed by a quasi-Kantian structure of reason that, by virtue of its universal validity, makes possible, at least ideally, the (presumed) ideological neutrality and, hence, something like the epistemological transparency of music. This assumption of a congruence between the underlying principles of composition and those of listening is what lends force to the metaphor of listening to the musical structure "from within." In actuality, however, in ways that I hope will become clear, the metaphorical listening position that structural listening encourages is less that of Schoenberg's and Adorno's structural insider than that of the externally situated, scientific observer. Indeed, it is very close to that of the empirically oriented (anti)hero of Stravinsky's *Poetics*.

This shift in metaphorical position might at first glance seem too slight to jeopardize the goals of structural listening. Scientific observation, after all, is our cultural paradigm of methodological objectivity. Based on concepts and values that are assumed to be universal, and thus presumably exempt from subjective distortion, such observation seems to offer us the power to focus intensely on a musical object entirely on its own terms. Thus a structural listening modeled on scientific observation might seem to offer us our best shot at a relativistic, ideologically neutral condition of tolerance in music, encouraging society to honor the music of all times and cultures equally, on terms set by the music itself.

But just as Western science has increasingly been criticized as a culturally limited and limiting construct, so, too, there is a strong argument to be made that the terms on which structural listening operates originate far less in universal conditions of music than in our own specific cultural predilections. Even at first glance it seems clear that this method does not lend itself with equal ease to all musical repertories, even in the West. Just as tonal theory has been more fully developed than any other Western system of theory, so, too, structural listening seems to work most smoothly when applied to the "common practice" repertories of Germany and Italy, say, between Corelli and Mahler, which form the basis of the Western canon.

This is hardly surprising, since structural listening is generally conceded to have "arisen" from the tonal canon. But why should this allegedly objective method of perception, which is supposed to concern itself with the structure of individual compositions, be used so regularly to confirm the aesthetic superiority of whole styles, particularly Viennese Classicism, to other styles? (And how, for that matter, does the supposed objectivity of Stravinsky's formal perception, unless his very conception of structure is informed by stylistic prejudices, account for his denigration of Wagner's "symphonicism"?)[41] Why, if all music is equal in the ears of the structural listener, do some styles turn out to be more equal than others? And why (except perhaps to serve our own interests as masters of the specialized training and discourse that structural listening in practice nearly always requires) should we academics suppose such listening applicable to music that falls outside the canon?[42]

In fact, the concept of structural listening is considerably less widely applicable and objective a mode of perception than it seems. The choice of this method, as well as the identity of the music it prefers, reflects our own culturally conditioned stylistic orientation as its users. Like Stravinsky's "good form," what structural listening in all its variants offers us is less the conceptual attributes of objectivity than the stylistic impression of objectivity. Whereas it purports to examine music in terms of an intrinsic and potentially universal musical condition—structural autonomy—the notion itself of this condition is foreign to much, if not most, music. One can of course decide to impose this condition as an ideal on any music one chooses. But before one claims the basis for this ideal as universal and intrinsic, one needs some evidence that the music in question is presenting its own structure as fundamentally autonomous, or as "fixed" in various senses.

A fixed structure is discrete and whole; it has clearly delineated boundaries, which would be violated by any conception of this structure as a fragment. A fixed structure is also unchangeable; its internal components and relationships are presumed to have attained something like a status of necessity that disallows alternative versions. Neither of these conditions can persuasively be called characteristic, even as a projected ideal, of Western art music up until the eighteenth century. It could even be argued that they did not obtain fully until that point in the nineteenth century when improvisation was decisively excluded from the concept of art composition and a compositional ideal of precision arose. I mean here precision not just of pitch (which, somewhat paradoxically, the relativistic tonal notion of "key" had already established to the detriment of mode) but also of notation and instrumentation.

To be persuasively autonomous, moreover, a structure must show some evidence of trying to define itself wholly through some implicit and intelligible principle of unity. In music this requires that a composition have some technique for projecting itself as self-determining over time. Whether or not such a technique is suggested by Schenker's concept of linear organization, with the debatable audibility of that concept, its relative inability to account for the particularities of a musical surface, and its reliance on archetypal musical structures as well as on nontemporal, visual schematics, is not a matter that can be analyzed here.

Development, on the other hand, is widely considered by Western musicologists to be capable of projecting the impression of such self-determination. Schoenberg and Adorno quite openly define structural listening as developmental listening. But as virtually all scholars would concede, very little music, even Western art music, makes use of the technique of development (Schoenberg's perception of Bach's music as in some respects developmental [see note 37, this chapter] is not widely shared. Indeed, Bach's achievement is probably better characterized as the synthesis of a great diversity of generic concepts—concerto, trio sonata, dance, fugue, and so forth—than as structural self-determination.)

In its pure state, moreover, the condition of self-determination, or even the projection of such a condition, would require the renunciation of premises, organizational principles, purposes, values, and meanings derived from outside of a musical structure. Almost no Western music outside of certain Classical and contemporary endeavors has come close to accepting such a condition of renunciation. Up until the end of the eighteenth century, for example, most music was shaped to serve an external social function; and in keeping with deep-rooted mimetic or rhetorical ideals, the dominating paradigm of music throughout this period was music with a text. Furthermore, Western music has been assumed in most periods to owe at least some of its significance to a larger cultural network of extra-musical ideas or stylistically related constructs.

Structural listening looks on the ability of a unifying principle to establish the internal "necessity" of a strucure as tantamount to a guarantee of musical value. At the very least this assumption challenges the spirit of Gödel's theorem. In practice, however, the principle on which structural listening relies more than any other to authenticate value is not one of self-evident rationality but rather one of its own choosing: individuality. Both Schoenberg and Adorno emphasize the responsibility of the conscious individual, whether composing or listening, to clarify actively the internal intelligibility of a structure, a process that, ideally, frees the meaning of that structure from social distortion and manipulation. Even in those instances when Schoenberg and Adorno concede the possibility of an instantaneous intuition of musical value, they attribute such intuition at bottom to a structural integrity in the music; and this integrity can be achieved only through an individualistic "compositional force" (Adorno's words), or through what Schoenberg terms an "originality [that] is inseparable from . . . profound personality."[43] In such respects, both men are deeply committed to the governing status of originating intention.[44]

This is not the same as saying that advocates of even a "replete" structural listening ordinarily reserve their highest praise for the music that is most commonly characterized as individual in the sense of personally expressive—that is, Romantic music. Even the most ardent German advocates of a "replete" formalism are seldom prepared to idealize music that values personal expressiveness over developmental autonomy. Certainly Adorno does not; his greatest reverence is for that metaphorically powerful "moment" of individuality—Beethoven's middle-period style—in which the musical subject, determining its own action through uncompromising objective standards of developmental unity, turns itself into a locus of the universal.

Most of us in the Western musical world, at least until recently, have taken for granted some related inseparability of musical greatness and individuality, which in turn we equate with musical value. Yet even excluding non-Western traditions, it would be difficult to characterize with confidence most art music before the common-practice period through reference to ideals of individuality or even to a dialectic of individual and society. Even chromaticism, which we often interpret as signifying resistance to prevailing social norms, does not seem characteristically to be used by earlier music to place the power of individuality at its own ideological center. We recognize as much when we relegate Gesualdo, who might well have been a cultural hero in Mahler's Vienna, to a pocket of historical eccentricity.

The apparent absence of an individualistic ideal of structural autonomy before the firm establishment of tonality as a cultural norm, together with our own commitment to such an ideal, in my judgment helps account for a certain lack of focus that can sometimes be sensed in our study and teaching of early music, and for a certain uneasiness that stems from the difficulty of distinguishing form from style in early music (see below, the text leading to note 73). On the one hand, given our reluctance to attribute the preservation of certain medieval and Renaissance music to either the overt power or the innate virtue of Christianity, much less to sheer happenstance, we want to assume the primarily structural value (and thereby the "greatness") of the early music we teach. But on the other hand, lacking any noncontextual alternative to ideals of structural autonomy, we sometimes allow the teaching of medieval and Renaissance music, which does not strongly support our own structural biases, to disintegrate into the uncritical presentation of shifting stylistic hall-marks that can be named and dated on an exam.

The absence of a clear ideal of autonomy in early music may underlie the often noted failure of modern scholars to produce a persuasive theory of pre-tonal music (as, indeed, of any primarily texted music);[45] conceivably the very notion of such a theory, at least in any structural sense, is self-contradictory. This absence may also account for a certain hollowness at the core of various encyclopedic surveys of Renaissance music, which seem to offer inclusiveness as compensation for the lack of an aesthetic basis for selecting and evaluating works of this period.

Such problems indicate strongly that structural listening does not encour-age the open-ended sensitivity to diverse sorts of music that it promises. Even as this concept urges us to judge a work in terms of the work's own chosen premises, it distances us from music that exhibits no interest in encompassing all of its own premises. In fact, there are ways in which structural listening can be construed as a cultural violation even of the one style, Viennese Classicism, that not only seems clearly predicated on some ideal of structural autonomy but also appears to have realized this ideal with some success. Not at least until Beethoven began to place rhetorical emphasis on many of his main structural junctures, in effect conceding the intrinsic intelligibility of structural relation-ships as a fiction, does the musical evidence suggest that composers valued active structural comprehension over the Enlightenment ideal, as articulated by Kant, of seemingly artless art.[46]

Even more important, perhaps, is the secondary status that such listening accords to the musical parameter of sound. The ideal of structural listening has made our perceptions and analytical concerns as musicologists almost com-pletely dependent on scores, as if the latter were books. One is tempted to argue that structural listening makes more use of the eyes than of the ears. Cer-tainly, to an important extent, structural listening can take place in the mind through intelligent score-reading, without the physical presence of an exter-nal sound-source. But whereas the absence of concrete sound constitutes a debatable loss in the case of literature, it represents nothing less than a cata-strophic sacrifice for music.

This is a sacrifice that Adorno and even Schoenberg, in certain respects, are actually prepared to make. Although their version of structural listening purports to account for every detail of a concrete musical logic, it depreciates the value of sound with unusual explicitness. Adorno identifies sound as that layer of music which, through its use of such historically conditioned re-sources as technology and conventions, bears the imprint of social ideology

and allows the social "neutralization" of structural individuality. Thus the status Adorno accords this "manifest" (as opposed to "latent") layer is not privileged, to say the least. This explains his impatience with the archeological
restoration of early musical sound to its original "purity."[47] It also helps explain his low estimation of Romantic music, which calls explicit attention
to the opaqueness of its own sound and style. To Adorno this concreteness
signifies not an honest admission by Romantic music of its own social and
ideological concreteness but a capitulation to the power and modes of society—an abandonment of the effort, however quixotic, to define universal individuality in music.

By Adorno's account, in fact, "mature music," which concerns itself with
that "subcutaneous" structure where individual integrity can hope to resist or
even transcend social ideology, "becomes suspicious of real sound as such."
Turning color into a function of total structural interrelatedness, such music
makes color in itself essentially superfluous. Adorno praises Schoenberg's
ascetic "negation of all facades," which he likens to that of late Beethoven,
and projects a time when "the silent, imaginative reading of music could render actual playing as superfluous as speaking is made by the reading of written
material."[48]

Adorno's characterization of Schoenberg is echoed by Pierre Boulez's reference to Schoenberg and Webern as composers "for whom the idea of timbre is
almost abstract, and who never cared at all about the physical conditions of
sound emission."[49] In his writings, Schoenberg himself consistently subordinates the values of sound to those of structure, asserting in what may be the
key passage of *Style and Idea* that the responsible composer "will never start
from a preconceived image of a style; he will be ceaselessly occupied with
doing justice to the idea. He is sure that, everything done which the idea
demands, the external appearance will be adequate."[50] This devaluing of
medium has a direct musical counterpart in the naive certainty of
Schoenberg's later works that the tonal conception of "developing variation"
can sustain its intelligibility in a radically altered context of sound. This
contradiction is often noted, but its implications with respect to the notion of
"medium" have not so far been fully recognized.

The subordination of medium, toward which structural listening leads
more strongly than most of us happily admit, represents one logical resolution
of the dialectical opposition between structure and sound that has for some
time been discernible in Western music, and which has antecedents in a tension between essence and appearance that can be traced back in Western
thought at least as far as Plato. In effect, Schoenberg and Adorno, that quin-

tessential foe of ahistorical abstraction, take the same position as Derrida does when he interprets Aristotle's categories as evidence for the priority of abstract thought over concrete language.[51] Stravinsky, at bottom, draws the opposite conclusion, though in identifying essentially stylistic parameters of music as formal, he obscures the implications of his argument and restricts its usefulness.

But however characteristic this tension may have become in Western music, it has seldom been resolved through depreciating sound. On the contrary, as the anticorporeal bias of doctrinaire religion was left behind, Western composers, including the Viennese Classicists, came to place a high value on the sensuous actuality of their music. By the nineteenth century, as I have just indicated, specificities of instrumental color were considered normally constitutive of a musical configuration; they were among the components that "fixed" the piece as a distinctive, individual "organism." Of course, Romantic music was typically contradictory in its attitude toward instrumental color. On the one hand integrating it into their notion of structure, the Romantics simultaneously emphasized color to a degree where it was bound to call attention to itself and, through the habit of associative listening, to things outside of music (the horns and the forest in Weber's *Freischütz,* for example). But this double-sidedness hardly supports the case for structural listening. On the contrary, to the extent that structural listening encourages concentration on the perception of formal relationships at the expense of maintaining an active (though less easily formalized)[52] sensitivity to sound itself, structural listening constitutes a cultural violation of this and many other styles.

This holds even in our own century if we make a clear distinction between the heirs of Schoenberg on the one hand and those of Debussy and Stravinsky on the other. In fact, the only body of music for which we can be fairly confident that structural listening, in its most consistent sense, does not pose a violation of originating norms is Schoenberg's own. (One might, to be sure, extend this observation to Schoenberg's descendants, including Webern, especially in the sense that the latter "out-Schoenbergs" Schoenberg or, to be more precise, that Schoenberg's ideals constitute an essential trace in Webern's music. Which means, of course, that in Webern's music the "self-negating potentialities of development" mentioned above are fully realized.) But despite its appropriateness to Schoenberg's compositional ideals, structural listening, in its devaluation of sound and style, involves another sort of epistemological limitation, which is nowhere more evident than in the application of this method to Schoenberg's own music. This I shall now discuss.

The Need for Nonstructural Knowledge

> We attach too much and too little importance to sensations. We do not see
> that frequently they affect us not merely as sensations, but as signs or images,
> and that their moral effects also have moral causes.
>
> —*Jean-Jacques Rousseau*[53]

Given Adorno's idealization of structural listening, the actual character of his musical writings might seem surprising. His entire output as a music critic can be viewed as illuminating the irreducibility of the concrete medium of music. Actually, it was only through such criticism that Adorno could fulfill what he saw as the critic's principal obligation: to expose the destructive values of society as they manifest themselves in the public and conventional aspects of music, and to disentangle music from the corrupting power and effects of institutional ideology. This obligation required him to engage in continuous criticism of the musical medium (thereby performing much the same service that he praised in Schoenberg's and Webern's recasting of Bach's instrumentation).[54]

Adorno scorned the very notion of an actual nonideological music. Insistence on the nonexistence of ideology in music was radically different for him from a continuing sensitivity to ideology as a force to be resisted, a sensitivity that he discerned in the uncompromising structural integrity of the late Beethoven quartets and Schoenberg's music. Certainly he was no less adamant than Barthes has been in condemning as a lie any attempt by a musical "sign," so to speak, to hide its own cultural artificiality, and to present itself as either a socially and historically isolated object or an ideologically innocent, neutral, or quasi-natural construct, for "merely" formal analysis.[55] Such self-deceptively nonideological analysis was far more consistent with the spirit of Stravinsky's *Poetics*, which can be shown to project a wide range of ideologically loaded, even antihumanistic subtexts.[56] And, indeed, Adorno's own criticism of Stravinsky's music shows him every bit as sensitive as more recent, unmistakably antiformalist critics such as Terry Eagleton to the chasm that separates narrowly formal intentions from a purely formal character, effect, or significance, whether in art or in criticism itself.[57]

Adorno's constant preoccupation with social ideology, then, led him to a continuous engagement with that layer of music which he least valued, and to the establishment of an ongoing, relatively explicit connection between his own values and those of the various cultures represented in the composition, performance, or reception of the music he discussed. As perhaps the premier practitioner in our century of concrete social and historical criticism, who deplored systems and abstractions, Adorno set an unexcelled example for those figures in current literary debate, such as Edward Said, Fredric Jameson, Marshall Blonsky, and Eagleton, who likewise stress the concrete social and historical responsibilities of criticism.[58]

Furthermore, because Adorno viewed music as a part of a historically open-ended context of concrete social relationships, his principal focus as a critic was not the isolated work but the broader category of style. This, too, encouraged him to develop criticism as a mode of stylistic rather than structural analysis, even when dealing with elements of structure. In fact, what Adorno actually did in his musical writings was stylistic criticism of the highest caliber. By this I mean criticism of a kind that had nothing to do with the mere listing of characteristic musical devices but rather demonstrated the capacity of a rigorously fashioned critical language to analyze style incisively. Adorno's ability to find richly evocative yet succinct and precise metaphorical verbal equivalents for structural and nonstructural elements in music, and thereby to characterize persuasively the cultural and historical significance of both individual works and styles, is masterful, even uncanny.

It is sometimes asked whether Adorno really "knew" music. Frequently he is taken to task for not doing the thing he seems most to require of the listener—structural analysis. Moreover, Schoenberg regularly used charts and diagrams as well as the specialized terminology of academic structural analysis; and Adorno himself identified the ability to "name the formal components" as a sign of competence in structural listening. Yet his criticism rarely offers such signs. Probably this was because, for him, such techniques smacked too much of those anti-intellectual "proceedings in which general demonstrability of results matters more than their use to get to the heart of the matter."[59]

But did Adorno get to the heart of the matter? I would argue that even if we reject vehemently the conclusions that pervade Adorno's metaphorical observations (a possibility allowed by the unusually honest and explicit presentation of his own values), Adorno's thorough familiarity with the music he characterizes as well as the aptness and importance of his metaphors are virtually always confirmed by a reconsideration of the music in question. "The genuine experience of music," Adorno wrote, "like that of all art, is as one with criticism."[60] For Adorno, in fact, no less than for the German Romantics a century earlier, metaphorical criticism of the characteristics, choices, and relationships that embed music in one or another sociohistorical context is not a "supplement," in Derrida's sense, to the possession of detailed structural knowledge but rather the very means of getting to the heart of such knowledge.

Now in a way all of this amounts to saying that the kind of structural knowledge that interests Adorno and the German Romantics alike is culturally concrete, encompassing, or "replete." But here it must be explicitly acknowledged that the concept of replete structural listening is itself a concrete, metaphorical account of perception, not a logical principle. Not only does the concept of replete structure itself point to a condition that is characteristic only of music in certain styles, and thus first to a stylistic rather than to a structural condition. In addition, this concept depends, no less than Stravinsky's chic formalism does, on a culturally defined, stylistic sensibility in the listener for its intelligibility, persuasiveness, and usefulness. This stylistic particularity of replete structural listening as a principle helps explain how this concept can readily be misinterpreted by those of us from outside Adorno's culture and not privy to its stylistic nuance as justifying far narrower practices of structural listening. But the fundamental sense in which Adorno's concept of structural listening as well as Schoenberg's compositional choices were both governed by needs more stylistic than structural in character was something Adorno did not and probably could not recognize—any more than he could assess the degree to which his own aesthetic convictions represented cultural preferences.[61]

Nor, therefore, was Adorno willing, any more than Schoenberg was, to understand the widespread unresponsiveness to Schoenberg's music relativistically, as the reflection of something other than an immature unwillingness or intellectual incapacity on the part of the public to master the technical demands of structural listening (see note 64). Grounding structural listening on a supposedly universal rational capacity, Adorno was utterly unable to criticize as "ideological" the elite social standing and the long years of education that were ordinarily required for the exercise of this capacity. He could not bring himself to characterize either Schoenberg's unpopularity or nonstructural modes of listening as functions of legitimate differences, among listeners, in cultural or stylistic orientation.

This is not to say that Adorno was oblivious to actual characteristics and effects of his or Schoenberg's style.[62] On the contrary, Adorno explicitly considered irreducible stylistic "difficulty" necessary to the structuring and value of both men's work. From Adorno's standpoint, a "jagged physiognomy" did not only signify the resistance of individual usage to the conventions of ideology. It was also needed to preserve the integrity of "subcutaneous" argument from social "neutralization." Such integrity required a refusal by structure to compromise itself by "smoothing over," as Adorno accused Brahms of doing, or by obscuring a dehumanizing contradiction between the rational ideals of structure and the ongoing antirational force of society, as represented in the musical medium.[63]

Where Adorno's self-critical capacity failed him was both in his attribution of a universal necessity to social analysis and the conviction that explained such stylistic choices, and in his inability to imagine alternative, equally honest, stylistic definitions of or solutions to the social problems surrounding music. What drew Adorno to Schoenberg's music was not just its structural idealism but also the ugliness, by conventional standards, of its sound. But while it is true that Adorno valued this ugliness for its "negative" capacity to scorn the ideological blandishments of "affirmative culture," it is by no means clear that he would have been similarly drawn to the jagged qualities of grunge or punk rock or Laurie Anderson's music, much less that anything could have convinced him to view Leonard Bernstein's choice of the popular route as socially responsible. Adorno was sympathetic to Schoenberg's ugliness because he understood its cultural significance. And he understood this significance because he operated within the same set of concrete cultural assumptions, expectations, conventions, and values that Schoenberg did. He could listen to Schoenberg's music with the advantage of an insider's knowledge, not of a universal structure, but of a particular style.

Schoenberg, too, was inclined to dismiss objections to his style as signs of a "childish" preoccupation with pleasure of the senses rather than of differences in cultural orientation; just as form for Stravinsky is sound stripped of meaning, so style for Schoenberg is sound devoid of "idea."[64] In emphatically replacing the aesthetic notion of beauty with epistemological notions such as truth and knowledge as the central philosophical problem of music, Schoenberg revealed in his writings the hope of weaning listeners away from sensuous preoccupation.[65] And yet instinctively he recognized the need to draw the listener inside his own stylistic world. Again and again in his writings he explains the numerous "lost" historical origins of his works, including the tonal system and earlier German compositional techniques, which although literally absent from his works are nevertheless constituent elements in the conception and significance of the latter.[66] One would be hard pressed to find a composer whose work is more fully and clearly characterized by elements of Derrida's "trace"—or for that matter a critic whose intelligibility depends more than Adorno's does on a knowledge of absent subtexts. In both cases, these traces and subtexts consist precisely in ideas and values defined in a surrounding cultural context. They are functions not of a literally present structure but of a more open-ended style.

Both Schoenberg's work and that of Adorno provide massive evidence of the degree to which the communication of ideas depends on concrete cultural knowledge, and on the power of signs to convey a richly concrete open-endedness of meaning through a variety of cultural relationships.[67] Their work supports the thesis that style is not extrinsic to structure but rather defines the conditions for actual structural possibilities, and that structure is perceived as a function of style more than as its foundation. Even in a crude sense I would argue that if we are forced in musical analysis to grab hold of one end or the other of the dialectic between a style and a structure that are always affecting each other, it makes most sense to define the composer's starting point as his or her entrance into a preexisting musical style. Certainly such a notion has large currency in our own culture, where its status as a cliché ("the medium is the message") no doubt accounts in large measure for our perception of Stravinsky as more modern (i.e., less dated) than Schoenberg.[68] And certainly for those who begin interpreting either Schoenberg's or Adorno's work from the vantage point of a stylistic outsider, any relatively abstract, structurally rational argument is likely to constitute not the most but the least accessible parameter of meaning.

This is precisely the situation that confronts us with any culturally distant music. Did medieval music, for instance, once define structurally the value and power of individuality? Perhaps it would be most accurate to say that too much distance from the wealth of associations that once informed medieval usages prevents us from answering this question conclusively. To the extent that our perception of medieval culture and its signs remains what anthropologists call "etic" (that is, external and merely physical) rather than "emic" (that is, internal and literate), we are not in a position to view individualities of structure as signifying much more than a stylistic aberration.[69] (Why are we so much more inclined to apply the name "Mannerism" to early than to recent artistic styles?) Certainly the kinds of medieval musical "structure" that our culture allows us to perceive are nothing like the system of relationships that Adorno's structural listening would have us grasp from within.

Ever since the crystallization of the notion of "Art" in the early nineteenth century, it has become a truism of Western culture that the proper evaluation of any structure as "Art" requires the perspective of time. And in a culture that explicitly allows individuals, such as artists, to alter the conventional cultural meanings of signifiers, some time lapse undoubtedly is required for a full understanding of the altered medium. By this time, however, it has probably already (or more likely, as Derrida likes to say, "always already")[70] become impossible to understand the full import of those changes at the time they were made, or hence, to claim an insider's access to arguments structured within that medium. By this point, as Hildesheimer suggests in his biography of Mozart, crucial aspects of an original significance have become unrecoverable.[71] The listener is already hearing overtones of intervening knowledge and experience, which drown out or "erase" various responses that could have originally been intended or anticipated, while adding others. This condition of difference and delay, which Derrida has termed *"différance,"* calls increasing attention over time or distance to the irreducibility of style, both in its concrete physicality and in the ever-changing face it presents to new contexts of interpretation, as a source of signification.[72] In other words, the more culturally distant the music is, the more inescapably aware we become of its style—of its style as a barrier to understanding, and also as a condition of any structural perceptions we may form.[73]

The overtones of which I speak are in actuality so inseparable from all communication, even within a single culture, as to suggest themselves as essential to the very possibility of communication; without the possibility of misreading, as some poststructuralists have argued, reading itself becomes an inconceivable act. And such a situation seems nowhere more explicitly to obtain than when we are faced with interpreting an object that to most of us seems as directly dependent on the concreteness of a medium as music does, or as powerful in its ability to express, project, or evoke a good deal besides a commitment to its own logic. Invoking our own cultural disposition to label certain music "Art" after a time lapse is no proof of an acquired ability to hear musical structure in its original sense. If anything, the use of this label probably signifies the degree to which we remain excluded as interpreters from the original inner dynamic of most music.

What limits the application of structural listening to Schoenberg's music is not the technical difficulty of this method but its misdirectedness. For most listeners, the barriers of Schoenberg's style, which in many ways seem to simulate a condition of great cultural distance, are simply too formidable to be penetrated and discounted as secondary by a focus on structure. Most listeners stand a chance of becoming engaged by Schoenberg's music only in the sense that by gaining sufficient access to the usages and characteristics of his style they might come to recognize its affinities with their own twentieth-century cultural experience (much as they recognize such affinities when contemporary music accompanies a film).

According to the Russian literary theorist Mikhail Bakhtin, theories of literature that take into account only those aspects of style conditioned by fundamentally formal demands for comprehensibility and clarity, while ignoring the culturally interactive aspects of style, "take the listener for a person who passively understands but not for one who actively answers and reacts."[74] Applied to music generally, such an argument would suggest that structural listening reinforces not active engagement but passivity on the part of the

listener, suppressing an inclination to participate in some sort of active dialogue with music. And applied specifically to twentieth-century music such
as Schoenberg's, this argument suggests that only something akin to "stylistic
listening" would permit contemporary listeners to exercise any prerogatives
they might have as cultural insiders. Such an argument accords with my own
observation that such prerogatives *can* be exercised in relation to twentieth-
century art music, and with considerable insight. As I have noted elsewhere
in some detail, I have found that college students almost invariably write
more perceptively and articulately about the "difficult" contemporary music
they hear at concerts than about any other style of Western art music—once
they have allowed themselves to focus on aspects other than such a composition's structural cohesiveness.[75]

But this is precisely the point. Of all methods, structural listening, even in
its "replete" version, seems the least useful for entering the semiotic domain of
sound and style. Carried to its logical conclusion, this method in all its versions, as an exclusive or even as the primary paradigm for listening, cannot
define much of a positive role for society, style, or ultimately even sound in the
reception of music. Discounting metaphorical and affective responses based
on cultural association, personal experience, and imaginative play as at best
secondary, not only in musical perception but also in the theoretical accounts
we make of such perception, this method allows virtually no recognition to
nonstructural varieties of meaning or emotion in the act of listening. Since
these are, of course, precisely the varieties favored by the overwhelming
majority of people, structural listening by itself turns out to be socially divisive, not only in what it demands but also in what it excludes or suppresses.
Such divisiveness by no means necessarily serves the best interests of music.
Indeed, to the extent that structural listening brackets off the intuitive appre-
hensions of music that even specialists have, it unnecessarily limits the benefits of musical education, a point to which I shall return in my conclusion.

Stylistic knowledge *is* to some extent intuitive, but this is by no means a
fatal epistemological liability. To say this is only to admit the inarguable—that
the very act of getting to know music begins with an extra-rational apprehen-
sion of sound—and also to argue that all of the musical knowledge we acquire
is (or ought to be) a process of confirming, modifying, or rejecting that appre-
hension through rational modes of thought. In other words, the rational sub-
stratum of musical knowledge rests finally on some act, choice, or principle
that is not itself rationally demonstrable.

It has been argued that this is the condition of all knowledge.[76] I find this
argument persuasive; but even if one does not, there can be little question that

in music, where we begin with a sound that can to some extent be analyzed into a style and a structure, intuition is epistemologically valuable and in many respects indispensable. Certainly without such intuition (honed always by fact) there would be no hope of distinguishing responsibly between music that resists ideological deception and music that selfishly refuses to participate in the discourse of society. No amount of formal analysis by itself could ever arrive at a rational basis for making such a distinction. And yet the distinction is worth making, or at least attempting.

But this is not all. To place emphasis in listening and analysis on sound and style as prior to musical structure does not absolve the serious critic from a need for rigorous, self-critical discipline in the development of critical methods or of a critical language. Such an emphasis does not remove the historical responsibility of trying to sort out the meaning and values that may have been initially imprinted or subsequently imposed on a composition, even if, as I believe, this can be done only through some sort of dialectical interaction with the present, history being "now" as well as "then." Likewise, such an emphasis does not remove the need for an exacting examination of one's response to the parameter of medium as a function of one's own tastes and prejudices—even though it is probably the case that the inescapable blindness of which Paul de Man has written is more than anything else a blindness to our own stylistic limitations and their effects on our knowledge. Nevertheless, although such an emphasis does entail the fullest possible recognition and analysis of one's own cultural predilections, it does not justify a capitulation to one's own biases, or a refusal to attempt sympathetic entry into an unfamiliar stylistic domain.

Nor, on the other hand, does a stylistic emphasis absolve the serious critic from what I see as an ongoing obligation to seek carefully reasoned ways of investigating and assessing the social and moral significance of the values discerned in music. The desirability of cultural relativism ought not to condemn us, even at the level of theory, to a positivistic tolerance for totalitarian musical styles and practices. It should not exclude us from confronting head-on the moral issues posed by Wagner's music or from giving thought to the overtones of prejudice in the Bach Passions or even *The Magic Flute*. Moreover, such an emphasis should not blind us to the wide-ranging implications of diverse compositional choices, whether these choices involve an uncritical acceptance of extant conventions and conditions or a total, even narcissistic disregard for either the needs of an audience or a public interest in music. It should not render us unwilling to analyze the implications, both literal and symbolic, of the metaphorical characterizations to which disciplined criticism leads us. And although such an emphasis does question an uncritical reverence for structural autonomy, or even complexity, as self-justifying virtues, it does not deny the importance of trying to understand as fully as possible the ongoing dialectical interaction between stylistic means and possibilities on the one hand and structural choices on the other.

Such an emphasis does require a constant effort to recognize and interpret relationships between the elements of a musical configuration and the history, conventions, technology, social conditions, characteristic patterns, responses, and values of the various cultures involved in that music. And such an effort almost invariably requires a willingness to recognize at least the possibility of some positive value in the kinds of immediate, though often diffuse and fragmented, sense that sound and style have for nearly all musical listeners. This is a recognition that Adorno and even Schoenberg, despite his wistful desire to be liked and even despite various efforts to defend his own intuitions, cannot permit.[77] In part they cannot permit it because judgment on grounds of style, without attempts to understand associated particularities of argument, can be abused to justify an unlimited irrationalism in human interaction. Though I dispute the priority of structure in communication, I do not deny the notion of structure or the value of efforts to give a rational account of the dialectic between medium and structure—if, that is, those efforts are morally as well as intellectually rigorous in the sense of being genuinely self-critical. For otherwise the possibility of another abuse arises: stylistic biases that are denied rather than confronted can smuggle their way into ostensibly rational objections to structural logic. This, too, is a form of irrationalism.

But there is a second reason for the refusal of Schoenberg and Adorno to assign positive value to the musical medium. A medium, as the word implies, tends to elude the possession, control, and to some extent even the conscious awareness of any single individual who makes use of it. Thus, valuing the medium of music tends to remove the individual from the center of music. Such a tendency in turn makes clear the vulnerability of music, and music criticism, to a condition of communicative contingency and, even worse for these men, of what I might call moral indeterminacy. The inability to countenance such moral indeterminacy may be the greatest intellectual weakness of their position.

A willingness to entertain moral indeterminacy in music criticism involves not just a recognition of the incompleteness of any single interpretation, which Adorno, in his exquisite sensitivity to the dynamic character of history, surely has. It also involves acknowledging the possibility of limits on one's own moral certainties.[78] In music criticism this means acknowledging the potentially positive as well as negative aspects of human experience that enable every listener, culture, and generation to interpret, and even to perceive and identify, differently the particular elements through which metaphorical distinctions are formulated between something called "structure" and something called "style." This means acknowledging the ability of any listener to regard as highlighted "foreground" elements of music that others have dismissed or ignored as inconsequential "background." And it therefore means acknowledging the possibility of legitimate differences in the ultimately moral values that can be ascribed to the same music. It is precisely this sort of eternal indeterminacy that constitutes the poststructuralist concept of "text." (There may even be some cultural significance to the choice of opposing metaphors, in this connection, by Adorno—and Schenker—on the one hand, and the poststructuralists on the other: whereas for the former the principal bearer of meaning is the subcutaneous layer, not the surface, of a construct, for the latter, interpretation focuses on the foreground rather than looking through it.)

But in any event, it is precisely such indeterminacy that Schoenberg tries to forestall by marking certain musical voices "*Hauptstimme*" (principal voice) or "*Nebenstimme*" (principal subsidiary voice). Such a tactic is tellingly futile, for even such explicit stage directions cannot guarantee that the listener will be able, even with strenuous effort, to share the composer's own perception of a structure. The struggle of humans to live together is thoroughly pervaded by honest as well as dishonest differences in the perceptions on which interpretations are built.

The reluctance to acknowledge such indeterminacy characterizes and limits not only Schoenberg's and Adorno's concept of structural listening but also the many versions of this concept that focus more narrowly on supposedly "fixed" musical structures. This limits the capacity of current formalistic educational methods to develop a new paradigm for the relationship between musical responsibility and society. As one counterbalance to such limitations, the poststructuralist perspective is surely useful, and it is interesting to note that Roland Barthes has given explicit attention to the reintroduction of affect into both musical listening and performance.[79] And it may well be a recognition of such limitations that has led an increasing number of Western composers in recent years to reject ideals of structural autonomy, and to concentrate instead on a redefinition of the musical medium as replete with connections to many elements in the cultures of the twentieth century.[80]

In concluding, I would like to note a few of the ways in which my own education in structural listening has convinced me of its limitations. My first second language was Roman numerals. In my college harmony course, use of the piano was forbidden. Whereas scoreless listening was unheard of in my university education, soundless keyboards were fairly common.

As a music major I was required to take a course on Beethoven and pressured to take a seminar on Bach; only nonmajors were advised to study Italian opera. Performance was never a matter for serious intellectual analysis in my education (except as it pertained to the authenticity of early performance practice). In numerous seminars on early music I transcribed reams of manuscripts, of which I never heard a note or discussed the musical value. As a music major, and later as a teacher, listening to scratched and otherwise dreadful monophonic recordings, I developed a strategy of listening that I have never entirely shaken, whereby I mentally "correct" for inadequacies of sound or performance that distract from my structural concentration. These experiences, if not universally shared by musicologists of my generation, are not, I believe, altogether exceptional.

Yet I am not at all sure that any of this structural discipline has made me a more competent listener than my brother, who travels eight hours a week to the opera houses of New York to hum the tunes and listen to certain sopranos. I'm not even sure that the composers whose works I teach would necessarily prefer me as a listener.

I have heard it argued that structural listening is beneficial because it requires repeated listenings to the same work. But even if repeated listening is considered an unqualified good—in fact, it may exact some cost in terms of a living musical culture—does structural listening really produce the illusion of an ongoing active process of composition? Or does it rather confirm the passivity implicit in Barthes' sense that "'being modern' [is] but the full realization that one cannot begin to write the same works once again"?[81] To this sad finality that Barthes associates with the analysis of closed "works," he opposes the "pleasure" of enjoying the open-ended "text."[82] Is it the "plot" or the sensuous moment that draws us back again and again to the same music? (Are we more likely to revisit an Agatha Christie mystery novel or an Alfred Hitchcock movie [not to mention an Astaire-Rogers musical]?) Are there not ambiguities and dynamics in music of which we structural listeners, as well as ordinary listeners, are in some fundamental sense aware, but to which we alone do not allow ourselves, at least in our professional mode, a full response?[83] Is it not significant that I, today, with all my specialized training, find myself virtually illiterate with respect to the principal musical media of my own culture, those of electronic audio and video?

If the Western dialectic of structure and medium is still with us, should we

not be trying in the classroom to develop intellectually rigorous ways of analyzing sound and style as well as structure? Is it not possible that encouraging
less dependence on the score when we listen, and on ways of perceiving that
the score itself suggests, might help us to develop new and richer ways of
speaking about music? And might not such an expanded language enhance
even our conception of how structure operates, and what it signifies, in music?

In the end, the concept of structural listening, despite the rigorous consistency with which Schoenberg and Adorno sought to define it, is deeply flawed
by inconsistencies between what it promises and what it delivers. Designed to
protect music as a preserve of individual integrity within society, and thereby
ultimately to contribute to the betterment of the individual's position within
society, this concept in Schoenberg's and Adorno's version begs off its social
responsibilities no less than the stylistic snobbishness of Stravinsky's formalism does. Because they make no effort to overcome the cultural narrowness of
their own convictions, the distinctions Schoenberg and Adorno draw
between "replete structure" and medium can be used to justify the same results
that Stravinsky's doctrine encourages: the adherence to a positivistic and
socially narrow concept of form by numerous practices of structural listening
that fall between the extreme positions represented by these masters.

Only some music strives for autonomy. All music has sound and a style.
Only some people listen structurally. Everyone has cultural and emotional
responses to music. These characteristics and responses are not uniform or
immutable but as diverse, unstable, and open-ended as the multitude of contexts in which music defines itself. And yet, the world of knowledge opened
up to us by acknowledging the bases of this indeterminacy as the foundation
for our concept of music is far more encompassing than the domain that the
supposedly universal principle of structural listening can hope to control
without violating or exceeding itself. For whereas a restriction of knowledge
to determinate structures provides no access to crucial aspects of music as it
takes part in history and as it is actually experienced, an admission of those
aspects as the starting point of musical knowledge precludes neither a concomitant analysis of structure nor an extension of rational thinking to an
ever-greater area of that domain of experience where the significance and
value of music are ultimately, and continuously, defined.

All of us who study music are caught in the Western dialectic. To an extent,
all of us in the West who study anything are caught in that dialectic. Against
the values we can protect by insulating abstract modes of thinking from the
contingencies of concrete experience, we have to measure the risk, well symbolized by Schoenberg's paradoxical career, of coarsening through over-

refinement our sensitivity to other responsibilities of knowledge. But music offers a special opportunity to learners, for it confronts us always with the actuality of a medium that remains stubbornly resistant to strategies of abstract reduction. In this respect, it provides an ideal laboratory for testing the formalistic claims of any knowledge against the limits of history and experience. To ignore such an opportunity is to handicap musical study needlessly, and to consign music itself to a status of social irrelevancy that it does not deserve.

4

The Closing of the American Dream?
A Musical Perspective on Allan Bloom,
Spike Lee, and Doing the Right Thing

In general, everyone wants to be scientific and at the same time
to respect the dignity of man.

What happens to poetic imagination when the soul has been subjected to a
rigorous discipline that resists poetry's greatest charms?
—*Allan Bloom*[1]

At what could be called the decisive moment in Spike Lee's 1989 film, *Do The Right Thing*, a young man named Mookie picks up a garbage can and hurls it through the window of the restaurant where he has been working, thereby galvanizing the people around him into mob violence, which destroys the restaurant—and the restaurant owner's dream.[2] The impact of this act is so powerful that it has broken through the fictional boundaries of film to stir up passionate controversy in the American public itself. Was Mookie's act reasonable? The response of viewers to this question has borne out Lee's prediction, "This film is gonna make people pick sides."[3]

Controversy has become increasingly characteristic of American public life in the past decade. In the visual arts, acrid debates have arisen over paintings, photographs, and other displays. Among the books and reports that have generated controversy, a number have involved the content and direction of American college education. Those of us involved in college education should be gratified by this situation, for it suggests that what we do matters to people outside the campus. And among recent books on education, none has been used more vigorously both to support and to attack old-fashioned ideals of education than Allan Bloom's 1987 best-seller, *The Closing of the American Mind*. Disturbed by developments in higher education since the late 1960s, Bloom has sounded an alarm that "reason is gravely threatened" in the American university.[4]

As twin objects of contemplation, Lee's film and Bloom's book seem at first glance an odd couple. Apart from the similarity of their dates and of their controversial effect, these works have only one clear resemblance: both are thoroughly and unmistakably, even self-consciously, American. At the surface level of content, this American quality is of course obvious. Lee's film is set on a block in a quintessentially American neighborhood, Brooklyn's Bedford-Stuyvesant (a block that Lee envisions as "a character in its own right").[5] One of the two main characters is given the repeated tag line, "This is America."[6] Allan Bloom's American focus is obvious from his title, through his recurrent preoccupation with the Enlightenment origins and traditional beliefs of this country, down to his final paragraph, which begins, "This is the American moment in world history."[7]

Now ordinarily, a resemblance formed by so few common qualities—stemming from the late 1980s, being controversial, and being American—might seem a slender link to hang an essay on. In this case, however, the resemblance seems significant. Two of the particular qualities shared by these works have an intriguing relationship: the controversial nature of each work appears to be inextricable from its specifically American character. Furthermore, this pronounced sort of association between American identity and controversial character has become typical of our national discourse since the late 1980s, on subjects ranging from the American flag to the U.S. Constitution.

Americans have traditionally viewed their identity as profoundly dependent on the binding force of the Constitution. Yet for some time, the issues that have most fiercely engaged public discussion—free speech, affirmative action, abortion—have involved conflicting interpretations of this document. In recent years, the binding force of the Constitution has been far less in evidence than its divisive capacity. As we make our way through the 1990s, we seem to be approaching a crisis of confidence in it as a basis of national unity. Insofar as we define our national identity in terms of the Constitution, the very essence of being American today seems to lie in controversy.

Most of the constitutional conflicts, and many of the other disagreements through which we currently define ourselves, can be traced to differences over the same fundamental issue, an issue that clearly agitates Americans, sometimes to the point of obsession. I think of this issue as the relationship between definitions of reason on the one hand, and morality on the other. The frequency with which this relationship figures in our public discourse is not surprising, since the groundwork for its emergence as an issue was laid in the very foundation of this country. It is a relationship that invites analysis as a key to understanding not only how Americans think about their national experience but also how that experience has become imperiled. And nowhere has this relationship been crystallized in recent years with greater vividness than in Allan Bloom's *Closing of the American Mind* and Spike Lee's *Do The Right Thing.*

Americans today are preoccupied with the morality of American life. On the whole we more or less assume that morality and reason are at bottom mutually interdependent and inseparable conditions. Without one, we cannot have the other. In addition most of us (even in the academy) probably share a certain commonsense notion of what a moral conception of reason would involve. Though we don't ordinarily articulate it, this notion involves an ideal of reason as an abstract, universal faculty—a faculty that measures all assertions of truth against the single standard of its own principles and guarantees the validity of all assertions that meet this standard.

To such a conception of reason, which assumed a paradigmatic shape and position during the Enlightenment, we can readily attribute America's achievements in two domains from which Americans draw particular pride, modern science and American jurisprudence. Though success in each of these domains has depended heavily on excluding from consideration moral specificities—that is, on disregarding the moral content of historically concrete situations, which can be regarded philosophically as mere "accidents" because they are actual rather than timeless[8]—both have been generally assumed in this country to contribute to the moral good of the human condition. For from this abstract definition of reason has flowed the eradication of many physical hardships,[9] as well as a conception of human beings as abstractly equal creatures, all of whom have the same right to pursue economic opportunity, and none of whom has a right to special favors from the blind goddess of justice.

These physical and legal benefits of abstract reason are precisely such stuff as "the American dream" is made of. And virtually no one on the American scene with clear political or economic power has so far denied the moral necessity of maintaining the ideal of abstract universal reason as a necessary governing force in American life.

Still, Americans disagree. For this conception of reason, as philosophers well know, involves a paradox.[10] Accepting it *as is* does not just require recognizing abstract universality as an ideal formal condition of reason. It also requires affirming the specific content of this conception: its invocation of a single reasonable standard of truth. But belief in the existence of this standard amounts to recognizing at face value the claim of an abstract universal conception of reason to constitute the *only* valid conception of reason. It requires recognizing the claim of the abstract conception to absolute validity as itself absolute, rather than limited. Not everyone is willing to extend such recognition. Some Americans have concluded that the claim of the abstract conception to exclude all other conceptions of reason must be viewed critically, rather than accepted at face value.

Today, doubt is being voiced in many ways, not about the *logical necessity* of an abstract conception of reason, but about its *moral sufficiency*. Troubled that ideals of abstractness by definition exclude reference to the concreteness of life as it is actually lived, a number of participants in the public discourse are now arguing for the validity of an additional conception of reason. In effect, this school of thought is trying to establish a second paradigm of reason as a force in American life, one that can coexist in tension with the Enlightenment paradigm without supplanting it.[11]

According to this second conception, reason cannot be fully defined apart from its embodiment in the contingencies of actual life, which include individual experience, cultural identity, and particular history. From this second perspective, such contingencies are not viewed simply as impediments to reason, wholly beyond its control. They are also viewed as forces so crucial to defining reason in a morally defensible way that if their importance is not acknowledged, the very survival of reason, in *both* of the conceptions presented here, is ultimately jeopardized.[12]

In varying ways, both Allan Bloom's book and Spike Lee's film call attention to the growing insistence in our country on this second conception of reason. And in so doing, each of these works has pressed us to confront the same question that has been emerging from our constitutional debates: Is the American dream, as defined by abstract standards alone, any longer viable? In my judgment, both of these works, though in very different ways, suggest that it is not.

To Allan Bloom it is a self-evident proposition, based on nature,[13] that reason can be defined only at the level of abstract universal principles.[14] At this level, it is not just possible but necessary to see human nature as a single, unchanging, eternal condition, common to all people in all times, regardless of their particular circumstances.[15] Bloom holds the notions of culture and cultural identity in particular disdain.[16] But fortunately, from his perspective, reason allows us to look right through any cultural specifics that divide us and to enter directly into the abstract logical structure of every human argument, no matter when or where it was; reason allows us to enter and take seriously the *content* of that argument, dismissing its circumstances of origin and any cultural peculiarities or prejudices as inessential.[17] Indeed, a major emphasis of this book is on the supreme importance of reading and evaluating texts at the level of content, as opposed to style or motivation, in order to determine "whether they are true."[18] For Bloom, clearly, the content that matters in a text is to be found in arguments or other semiotic structures that make sense at an abstract level of reason. And Bloom implies that philosophy is the highest form of discourse because it focuses directly on intelligibility at this abstract level of reason; as he puts it at one point, "the philosophic experience is understood by the philosophers to be what is uniquely human, the very definition of man."[19]

The viewpoint taken in Bloom's book really allows us only one way of deciding whether Spike Lee's character Mookie acted reasonably when he hurled the garbage can. We must describe, as abstractly as possible, the events leading up to this act and see if they define a convincingly causal chain. It is to honor the rules of Bloom's game that I have thus far provided few particulars in my account of this moment in the film. By those rules, Mookie's act cannot be considered reasonable.

Measured by abstract standards, this act of violence is not a response to a direct stimulus. By legal standards, Mookie's act has no "proximate cause." In an American court, it would not be recognized as an act of self-defense against a threat. At most, Mookie's lawyer could hope to defend him on grounds of mitigating circumstances. But these are grounds that by definition involve a suspension of abstract legal reason. By abstract logical standards, a justification on such grounds would amount to a case of *post hoc propter hoc*—the fallacy of mistaking a chronological succession for cause and effect. When abstract standards are invoked, no problem attaches to judging Mookie's act unreasonable.

Yet this judgment involves a difficulty. Although Bloom never directly admits it, everything about his abstract notion of reason—the indisputable universal validity of its standards, the self-evident (natural) certainty of its processes of verification, its attraction to general laws rather than to concrete particularities—associates it with one specific concept that has dominated Western notions of reason since the Enlightenment. This is the concept of theoretical or cognitive reason, as analyzed most cogently by Immanuel Kant in his *Critique of Pure Reason*.[20] Kant's achievement was to demonstrate that a condition of abstract universal validity can be established reliably through intersubjectively shared structures of cognitive reason. In this way he protected a reliable epistemological basis for resolving scientific and logical problems.

But many human acts, including Mookie's, fall into a domain that is clearly moral rather than cognitive in character. Determining the "rightness" of these actions requires more than the cognitive processes of scientific and even logical verification; it requires moral judgment. Can the two be joined? However justified we may be in demanding that all notions of reason be moral, and that all notions of morality be reasonable, it is far from self-evident that the archetype of theoretical reason on which we have come to rely in modern Western thought has any bearing on moral questions.

Indeed, as Bloom himself explicitly acknowledges, Kant's own work (to a significant extent involuntarily) showed the lack of any necessary connection between scientific reason and the morally good.[21] What Kant did make clear, through the very restrictions he placed on reliable knowledge, was that cognitive standards are reliable only for abstract cognitive problems, and that no amount of logical reasoning, however rigorous, can ever prove the *moral* rightness of an act with scientific certainty. In other words, Kant affirmed the soundness of abstract theoretical ("pure") reason on cognitive grounds by exposing all other concepts of reason to cognitive doubt. In the process he defined a formidable problem for all who would demonstrate that morality and reason are at bottom mutually interdependent and inseparable conditions.

That Allan Bloom recognizes the existence of this problem there is not the slightest doubt.[22] On the contrary, appalled "by generations of teaching that the most instinctive of all questions—What is good?—has no place in the university," he considers the provision of a foundation for making sound moral judgments the most urgent task facing education today.[23] One could readily argue that the principal goal of Bloom's book is to pursue a way out of Kant's dilemma and out of its philosophical aftermath, as defined especially by Nietzsche and thereafter by such figures as Weber and Heidegger. Bloom is aware that as the theoretical standards for knowledge became increasingly rigorous during the Enlightenment, the capacity to know—in the sense of knowing with clear-cut certainty—gained an elevated philosophical (and cultural) importance in the West.[24] He is aware that starting with the Enlightenment, the term "knowledge" became restricted to the relatively small domain of problems that can be convincingly solved through the faculty defined as "cognitive." He is keenly aware that the consequences of this restriction include placing beyond verification the contents of all domains other than cognition, including the truth of moral positions. And he is equally aware that Kant's segregation of domains (in part because it hinged on an ultimately intersubjective condition of universality) in turn set off other consequences in Western thought: a narrowing recognition of abstraction as an accessible, verifiable condition of thought, even in the scientific domain;[25] a widening erosion of claims to universal truth;[26] and a steady rise in viewpoints that recognize the irreducible particularity of human expression, such as historicism and cultural relativism.[27]

Bloom uses a variety of tactics to elude such consequences of the Enlightenment. At times he emphasizes the links of those who helped unravel Enlightenment concepts of reason with thinkers still rooted in conceptions of universal truth.[28] A more pervasive technique is to present positions derived from Enlightenment thought—including the critiques of the Enlightenment launched by Rousseau—in a framework of skepticism that promises to refute those positions.[29] He reinforces this promise by characterizing these derivative positions as merely optional, seductive, artificial, dogmatic, misconceived, risky, or even impossible responses to the latter Enlightenment, rather than as necessary consequences of it;[30] the question, he notes at one point, is whether such results "are necessary or only accidental."[31]

In some ways, Bloom's tactics go beyond evasion to denial. He feels free, for example, to treat as axiomatic the proposition that morality, like cognition, has abstract universal standards.[32] Though confirming the vulnerability of this proposition since Kant, his stance is eerily suggestive of the last-ditch defense in Kant's own "last great statement of liberal Enlightenment,"[33] sometimes paraphrased as "what is necessary is possible." Bloom speaks as if philosophers today are not subject to Kant's epistemological limits, even on knowing things in themselves. Not only does "the philosopher want . . . to know things as they are"; beyond this, philosophers have actual "access to the nature of things . . . by way of thinking about what men say about them."[34] In fact, as will be seen shortly, Bloom does not shrink from proposing an explicit alternative to the post-Kantian direction of Western thought that he calls "the modern impasse."[35]

In short, Bloom pulls out multiple stops to retain the theoretical possibility of judging choices and actions by abstract universal standards of morality. Yet in the end, the "haunting doubt"[36] evoked by Kant is not dispelled.

If anything, Bloom's failure to refute disturbing consequences of the Enlightenment is emphasized by his preoccupation with those consequences. Over the course of his book, Bloom returns repeatedly to the severing of knowledge from morality that began to take place in the philosophy and political theory of the Enlightenment.[37] Again and again, he bewails the displacement of Socratic philosophy, which used reason precisely to address moral questions, by the natural science of the Enlightenment, which defines reason in a way that excludes moral questions.[38] Starting with the high hopes of Enlightenment philosophers to "make the central human good central to society"[39] by defining a domain for reason that could not be challenged by reasonable doubt, Bloom admits that "the moment of the Enlightenment's success seems also to have been the beginning of its decay."[40] He cannot conceal how philosophical analysis of the Enlightenment gradually exposed the theoretical futility of its hopes.

A significant portion of Bloom's book—one that probably did not contribute much to its sales—is devoted to rehearsing the stages of Western intellectual history through which Kant's restrictions on cognitive reason led to the undermining of reason as a convincing first principle in any domain involving human thought.[41] His greatest difficulty is with Nietzsche, whose "contribution was to draw with perfect intransigence the consequences" of what I have called here Kant's legacy and "try to live with them."[42] One need never have read a word by Nietzsche to grasp the size of the problem he poses for Bloom. By his own account, "The history of Western thought and learning can be encapsulated in the fate of Socrates, beginning with Plato defending him, passing through the Enlightenment institutionalizing him, and ending with Nietzsche accusing on [sic] him"; by "him" in this thumbnail sketch (with its odd preference for fused participles), Bloom clearly denotes a conception of abstract universal reason.[43]

"Enlightenment thinkers," according to Bloom, "carried on a war against the continuing threat to science posed by first causes that are irrational or beyond reason."[44] Bloom is evidently also bothered by such first causes, principally because they jeopardize the rational status of the moral domain; for the recognition of such causes makes theoretically allowable a characterization of moral principles as ultimately irrational. Bloom seems less concerned with the effect of such causes on science. It is, after all, the exclusionary elevation of scientific reason that threatens to dethrone philosophy by disallowing its traditional privileged access to moral questions; "both natural science and historicism," notes Bloom, are "the two great contemporary opponents of philosophy."[45]

Still, despite Bloom's dissatisfaction with the moral limitations of science—despite his attack on the "fact-value distinction" and E. D. Hirsch's resultant dislike for "what he terms the antiscientism of the Bloomites"[46]—Bloom's book cannot by any stretch of the imagination be called a no-holds-barred attack on science. For one thing, modern science is a creation of the Enlightenment, a movement that Bloom admires too much to reject outright, in part on political grounds but also because of its direct links to his beloved Socrates.[47] In addition, because he is anxious to preserve the virtues of intellectual rigor for a philosophical conception of theory, Bloom frequently couples allusions to philosophy and to science, thereby encouraging a subtle identification of the two.[48]

Moreover, envy runs imitation a close second as the sincerest form of flattery; and if there is an attitude that most often accompanies Bloom's expressions of animus toward science, it is not recoil but envy. Envy is implicit in his admissions of resentment at science for excluding philosophy from its status of certainty.[49] It is explicit in his anger that natural science—"the Switzerland of learning"[50]—has secured the freedom to pursue its own questions without regard for any actual moral considerations that might force it to serve social needs.[51]

This is precisely the freedom that Bloom defends as critical to the survival of philosophy, and thereby of the Western university.[52] For as long as it can take an attitude of complete disinterest in what Bloom calls "mere life," philosophy can embody and preserve freedom of thought and speech for all academic disciplines.[53] This is what Bloom has in mind when he evokes Socrates' notion that "the greatest good for a human being is talking about—not practicing—virtue (unless talking about virtue is practicing it)."[54]

Bloom's own strategy for repairing the historical rupture between knowledge and morality is to make an end run around the Enlightenment back to Socratic philosophy as a model of study that (by recognizing rather than trying to deny or co-opt the force of irrational impulses) unifies reason and morality.[55] What he succeeds in *giving* us by way of Socrates, however, is not a convincingly rational ground for reintegrating knowledge and morality but merely the license to shift our scientific ways of doing business back to texts that predate the recognition of this rupture in Western intellectual history.

Bloom asserts the existence of rationally defensible moral arguments in Socrates' dialogues that validate an abstract universal conception of reason; but his treatment of those arguments does not bear out this assertion. In part this is a failure of teaching strategy: whereas Plato "insured [Socrates'] influence, not by reproducing Socrates' philosophy . . . but by representing his action,"[56] Bloom himself, for the most part, simply issues reports about Socrates, summarizing or characterizing his views without presenting them for explication or analysis. As a result, Bloom forfeits the persuasiveness that might come from direct demonstration, leaving the ordinary reader to infer the moral quality of Socrates' arguments either from the uses to which Bloom puts them or from Bloom's own standing as an interpreter of Socrates. But even the few extended quotations from Socrates' dialogues that Bloom does provide tend to occur in contexts that raise moral misgivings.[57] Nor are such misgivings stilled by Bloom's presentation of himself, or for that matter Socrates, as an authority, since by Bloom's own admission the very "essence of philosophy is the abandonment of all authority in favor of individual human reason."[58]

Instead of helping the reader to engage in a dialogue with the actual content of Socrates' arguments, Bloom consistently treats those arguments as if their moral validity were already proven. This assumption allows him to present these arguments, in effect, as morally neutral components of a formal structure, susceptible to analysis through techniques no more morally demanding than those of a chemical analysis—or for that matter, of a musical analysis.

Bloom's treatment of Socrates' arguments recalls a tendency described by Bloom himself in connection with Locke's "frank admission of enlightened selfishness"[59] and evident also in such constructs as Adam Smith's Invisible Hand, modern science, and American law: the tendency to neutralize morally questionable impulses by pulling them into a system where morality is simply supposed to take care of itself. In fact, like many enterprises in the British Enlightenment tradition, Bloom's book goes about trying to preserve the rationality of the moral domain by offering it the epistemological invulnerability of an amoral defense. By presenting morality in an amoral fashion, he confers on his own views of morality a quality of disinterestedness readily associated with the objective certainty of scientific knowledge.[60] But far from supporting Bloom's assertion, from early in his book,[61] that moral principles have the same abstract universality as scientific ones, his defense of morality instead emphasizes the moral insufficiencies of scientific certainty, and thus the gap between cognitive and moral requirements of reason.

One could argue, indeed, that Bloom's entire tribute to Socrates leaves behind less promise of an ultimate reunion between scientific and moral principles of reason than does Spike Lee's simple juxtaposition, at the close of his film, of a quotation from Martin Luther King, which rejects violence on principle as intellectually and morally unreasonable, with one from Malcolm X, which defends violence, under certain socially immoral circumstances, as an intelligent, morally justifiable, and possibly even morally necessary act of self-defense.[62]

True, one can imagine an implicit association, on the one hand, between the words of Martin Luther King, perhaps the greatest American dreamer, and some abstract, universal ideal of reason; and on the other hand, between Malcolm X, a pragmatist, and some more concrete, historical conception of reason. Moreover, Lee, in my judgment, offers no synthesis whatsoever of these two starkly contrasting attitudes toward violence. Nevertheless, Lee has carefully chosen passages that present a powerful common feature. In both language and ideas, each of these passages makes a serious attempt to reconcile intelligence and morality. By closing his film with two passages that recognize the importance of this reconciliation, even as they demonstrate its difficulty, Spike Lee makes an effort, at least, to discharge his responsibility to both aspects of the term "right" in his title Do The Right Thing.[63]

Now to deny that an abstract universal conception of reason can by itself provide a foundation for morality is by no means to argue that such a conception
offers nothing of moral importance through its force as an ideal. As it happens,
the moral promise of such an ideal is something that a musicologist is well
equipped to talk about. There is an approach to the study of music that for a
long time has played a dominant role in American liberal arts programs in
music. I have come to call this approach "structural listening."[64] In all of its
various guises, this approach suggests a musical counterpart to Allan Bloom's
philosophical ideal of reason. It suggests the ideal of a musical structure that,
by virtue of its inner logic, gives an abstract universal intelligibility to music.

The lengths to which musical scholars will go to isolate and define such a
structure can be considerable. Thanks to Heinrich Schenker (1868-1935), the
most influential Western musical theorist in this century, it has actually
become possible to regard all but a handful of specific notes in a given composition as mere historical accidents, which it is the musical thinker's business to
remove from consideration.

The ultimate rationale for structural listening, though seldom examined, is
one that Bloom himself implicitly relies on. The idea behind this attitude is
that by concentrating on the abstract logic of structural relations in music, listeners learn to guard against rejecting a composition on grounds of brute prejudice. In other words, by subjecting all music to the same disinterested structural standards of judgment, we allow music in every style, and thus the music
of every culture, at least in theory, a fair chance of social acceptance.[65] This is
an ideal of great symbolic importance to any society that claims an interest in
the moral quality of human relations; and as an ideal, structural listening offers
an important criterion for the judgment of music.[66] Used to the exclusion of
other criteria, however, as it has been for a large portion of our century, structural listening has serious defects.

Unfortunately for this ideal, its advocates have never been able to define a
general principle of musical logic apart from tonality, a historically and culturally specific system of relationships that has been prominent as a first principle
of construction only in Western music, since sometime in the seventeenth
century. This notion of musical logic has been used by Western musicology for
generations to justify excluding non-Western music from the mainstream of
musical study. Thus this equation of structural logic with tonality has imbued
Western musical thought with a quality of restrictiveness—a quality that
should not, however, be mistaken for rigor.[67]

For not *all* tonal structures have been recognized as having a potentially
abstract, universal validity. Most notably, reference to the ideal of structural

listening has been used by musicologists to justify ignoring Western popular music, even the large portion that is unmistakably tonal. We may criticize the structure of such music as too simple to be worth much; or as failing to be fixed in a permanent written form; or as lacking in refinement, or beauty, or originality; or as inadequate in some other way. The objections we cite can be quite varied (exceptions among popular music to any one of these criticisms would not, after all, be hard to find); but almost invariably we couch them in structural terms. As musicologists we have felt free to ignore Western popular music on the grounds that it does not measure up to our structural ideal—and because of our largely unexamined certainty that that ideal constitutes the only possible abstract universal standard of musical value. This is why students in a conventional American music program, even now, are far more likely to study Western art compositions that are not persuasively good than to study Western popular compositions (or non-Western works of any kind) that seem worth admiring.[68]

In short, the ideal of structural listening has encouraged us to do precisely what it set out to prevent: to reject *whole repertories*, not on any persuasive abstract grounds of reason but on the clearly arbitrary ground that we don't find their particular styles congenial. As a result, this ideal has deprived *every* item in those repertories of a fair chance for acceptance on its own individual merits.

At the same time, academic adherence to this structural ideal has also encouraged us to favor certain other categories of music as a block. Take, for instance, European music of the Middle Ages and the Renaissance. Never mind that some items in this repertory are structurally at least as simple as many popular pieces.[69] Most of it doesn't even use the tonal system. Furthermore, the very idea of tonal structure as an abstract principle that can liberate musical intelligibility from a dependence on actual texts or social functions is an idea that begins to take clear shape in Western music history only during the seventeenth century. Very little Western music written before the period we call Baroque has any relation to an ideal of abstract universal structure. Yet, with one or two notable exceptions, such as Schenker and T. W. Adorno, proponents of structural listening have been perfectly willing to include medieval and Renaissance European music in the mainstream or canon of Western musical study.

Why?

For the same reason, I suspect, that Allan Bloom, at the end of a book that consistently elevates philosophy above all other mental endeavors, seems suddenly willing to rank the works of Homer and Shakespeare alongside Plato's dialogues as objects for the highest form of study.[70] Earlier, despite numerous sprinklings of references to works of the Western literary canon,[71] Bloom has granted literature little more in the way of rational force than a useful rhetorical capacity, as described by Aristotle, to purge the mind of passions and make it receptive to abstract reason.[72] Poetry, as Bloom presents it, is a discourse more intrinsically concrete than philosophy since it is far more enmeshed both in the life of a particular time and place and in the actuality of emotions.[73] Bloom all along assumes a conflict between poetry and philosophy, in which he clearly deems the latter superior.[74]

Now, however, Bloom justifies studying Homer and Shakespeare, and by clear implication the entire canon of Western literature, on the grounds that these works meet the philosophical standard of being completely intelligible on the level of abstract universal reason, without regard for their cultural particularities.[75] In effect he makes the same case toward the end of his book for literature as he makes for Western culture more generally toward the beginning: that by virtue of their special content, higher manifestations of Western culture transcend the condition of culture and enter into an abstract state of reason.[76] Yet, coming from an author whose vision of the ideal university, based on standards of abstract reason, wholly excludes the study of literature and all the other arts,[77] this eleventh-hour justification of literature is neither logical nor credible. Given Bloom's pervasive association of the universal with the abstract, it is inconsistent for him to imply, at one point, a direct identity between the immediate meanings and sensuous reality of art on the one hand and "essential being" on the other.[78] Taken seriously, this identification amounts to accepting the historical reversal in epistemological priority accorded the timeless and the actual—a reversal that elsewhere Bloom stubbornly resists.[79] Nor does Bloom's assertion that "the greatest literature addresses the permanent problems of man"[80] engender a persuasively abstract defense of the literary canon. Even assuming we have the ability to define "permanent" problems in a state of isolation, this criterion by itself entails either a simplistic thematic test for literature that cannot account for differences in thematic treatment—i.e., qualitative differences between works—or the negation of all difference between literature and philosophy.[81] Neither situation offers an adequate abstract standard for judging literature; if anything, Bloom's case for the literary canon signals the absence of such a limited standard.[82] Nevertheless, Bloom does not merely insist upon the superiority of the Western canon to all other literature; he vigorously defends this appraisal as evidence for the moral necessity of preserving a single, universal standard of reason. Only such a standard, he argues, gives us a definitive basis for recognizing some cultural systems as superior to others.[83]

If "high" Western culture cannot be acknowledged as the greatest achievement of civilization, then it drops into what Bloom calls the "drab diversity" of a world in which no culture can be judged indisputably better than any other.[84] Bloom argues that such a world would preclude all possibility of making responsible distinctions, choices, and decisions. Surely all of us *would* consider a world without such possibilities not merely amoral but thoroughly immoral.

Without question, Bloom sees fighting against such a world as a primary purpose of his book, beginning with its title, *The Closing of the American Mind*. Bloom's fear is that by rejecting a single abstract standard of reason, Americans are closing not the golden door to the diverse cultures of the world but "the window to [the high culture of] Europe."[85] By recognizing more than one standard for measuring reason, he warns, Americans are renouncing the very capacity to make responsible distinctions. In brief, Bloom's worry amounts to a version of Jürgen Habermas's "legitimation crisis";[86] though I have not found the term "postmodernism" in Bloom's text, his entire book, perhaps fashioning itself on Kant's "last great statement of liberal Enlightenment"[87] could be characterized as a massive assault on the absence of standards (at least outside the natural sciences) that is now commonly associated with the postmodern condition.[88] But Bloom can offer no logical reason for attributing superiority to high Western culture in particular. What his book does suggest, as a far more consistent and plausible basis for this appraisal, is one that Bloom himself emphatically rejects as irrational on the part of other people, namely, an attachment to one's own culture.[89] Almost certainly, it is the clear perception of such an attachment that primarily explains the widespread public association between Bloom's book, which tries to discredit the very notion of culture, and another bestseller, E. D. Hirsch's *Cultural Literacy*, even though Hirsch openly acknowledges the Western canon as a cultural phenomenon—and even though Hirsch (in sharp contrast to Bloom) proposes the study of this canon precisely to achieve *social* goals.[90]

In fact, each of these books, in its own way, exemplifies an almost irresistible tendency by Western ideals of universality to make space within themselves for the rationally justified presence of a socially privileged group. Typically, this tendency to couple universalistic ideals of equality with an attitude of social elitism shows up in an image that has much in common with the Protestant image of an Elect. In Hirsch's case, the imagery of privilege has been associated principally with a sixty-three page inventory of items that closes an appendix entitled "What Literate Americans Know."[91] The journalist Ray Sokolov captures the effect of this list in his charge that

Hirsch's book "equates literacy with a Quiz Kid's command of facts and turns culture into a trivial pursuit."[92]

Hirsch's evocation of imagery related to an Elect is hardly exceptional in any domain of Western culture. That Western music contributes to such imagery should already be evident from the restrictions surrounding the ideal of abstract structure, which is considered universal to all music—as long as it is Western—unless it is popular. Western music has also made more specific contributions to this imagery. As I argue in another chapter, for example, Mozart's opera *The Magic Flute* opens the image of an Elect to question, not only through its plot but also through its juxtaposition of supposedly universal principles of tonal construction with an equal emphasis on the physical quality of actual vocal and instrumental sonorities.[93] The image of an Elect was given an archetypal formulation in George Orwell's novel, *Animal Farm*, through a now-famous rationalization for the relative equality of pigs. Overtones of this formulation are heard often these days, for example, in a reviewer's description of a recent book by John Silber as one which "concedes that all consciences have equal claim to moral authority, but . . . that some consciences are more equal than others."[94]

Images of this kind pervade every aspect of Allan Bloom's book, including his vision of the ideal university. Such an institution, as Bloom conceives it, would exist to support "theoretical men, of whom at best there are only a few in any nation."[95] Its essential disciplines would include only the natural sciences, political science, and, of course, the highest discipline, philosophy.[96] But not *all* philosophy. Although Bloom defends academic freedom of thought and considers the presence of alternative views vital to the university,[97] his own campus would exclude whole schools of thought.[98] In other words, Bloom would limit the university to those populations, subjects, and points of view which can be encompassed in his own image of an Elect. Galileo expressed a similar sentiment when he wrote, "I deem it my greatest glory to be able to teach princes," adding, "I prefer not to teach others."[99]

Why do our idealistic Western conceptions of human universality so often end up in apologias for the privileged? Bloom's book suggests at least two answers. First, however insistently Bloom defines the philosopher as a figure motivated purely by abstract principles,[100] even philosophers seem to find it necessary to work out their logic with arguments drawn from their own cultural experience. Almost invariably, that experience is one of privilege; and almost invariably the case for an Elect is a case for abstract equality within a socially privileged culture to which its advocate belongs. What results in most such cases is a situation that Bloom himself criticizes in others: "Self-serving is expressed as, and really believed to be, disinterested principle."[101] That is to say, self-interest is mistaken for abstract principle. What Bloom fails to see is just how well this description fits his own position.

Of course, *anyone* who is not rigorously self-critical is likely to overestimate the significance of the culture that is most familiar. This is the irrational aspect of cultural attachment that Bloom himself fears when he complains that "the firm binding of the good with one's own, the refusal to see a distinction between the two, a vision of the cosmos that has a special place for one's people, seem to be conditions of culture."[102] But where a culture has been shaped around ideals of universality, the temptation is especially great to mistake the *universalistic content* of those ideals for a *universal status* and therefore to ascribe universal significance to one's own culture—even to the point of automatically disdaining all cultures that do not view universality in the same way.[103]

This brings us to the second apparent reason for the elitism in Western conceptions of universality, which is actually the obverse of the first. Those arguing for an Elect find it hard to grasp the relationship of their own universalistic ideals to cultural experience that is different from their own. Operating wholly within the boundaries of their own cultural experience, they lack the very thing that Bloom most urges: a basis of comparison that would allow them to retain "the awareness of other possibilities,"[104] that is, to gauge the significance of their abstract universalistic ideals for those who live outside their own cultural boundaries.[105]

Thus, again and again, defenders of the image of an Elect fail to understand that their ideal of the culturally transparent human, so to speak, can be (mis)taken for a reality only by those who already operate within the circle of equality assumed by this image, or who at least are not separated from it by insurmountable obstacles erected by the privileged. People who live with a constant awareness of their cultural differences from those within that circle do not readily envision the human condition as exclusively abstract.[106]

To be sure, as the history of the Enlightenment clearly demonstrates, an emphasis on abstract principles works well to discredit hereditary claims to social privilege in favor of an abstract ideal of equality based on merit.[107] But if recognition is not given also to the concrete aspects of existence in a society, then the concept of abstract merit comes all too easily to replace heredity as a new excuse for entrenched and unearned privilege. Used alone, abstract ideals of judgment cannot take into account the ways in which real circumstances disadvantage entire groups of people and thereby thwart dreams of success through individual effort. From this abstract vantage point it becomes easy to see cultural identity as a logically superfluous, socially embarrassing, or morally degrading burden, borne only by those who deserve to fail.

In a report issued in 1988 entitled "Humanities in America," Lynne Cheney, the chairman of the National Endowment for the Humanities, asserted that "questions . . . about gender, race, and class. . . . are, of course, legitimate questions, but focusing on political issues . . . does not bring students to an understanding of how Milton or Shakespeare speaks to the deepest concerns we all have as human beings."[108] This assertion assumes that gender, race, and class are mere accidents that do not affect our deepest concerns as human beings. It helps perpetuate a vision of the *real* American as a genderless, raceless, and classless person whose particular identity does not involve stubbornly inerasable deviations from the supposedly transparent, invisible, or nonexistent cultural norms of the American Elect.

Self-evident as Cheney may have considered the truth of her statement, it is not persuasive. It is one thing to give priority to the notion of the abstract reasonable person as a legal paradigm. Without question, an abstract universal conception of reason offers tremendous benefits as a political ideal: the great promise of the American political system has always depended on maintaining the real force of that ideal as a fundamental principle of government.[109] It is quite different to argue that the concrete cultural aspects of identity are extrinsic to one's essential humanity—including one's capacity to reason.

By focusing *Do The Right Thing* on a cross-section of people in a way that is never unmindful of their concrete cultural situations, Spike Lee seems to be arguing that cultural identity in fact *is* one of the deepest concerns that we all have as human beings. And not just a negative concern, though his film points unequivocally to irrational aspects of culture and their immoral effects. Clearly Lee does not view the mere possession of a culture as any sort of social liability since, as he demonstrates with emphasis and persuasively through the characters in this film, everyone's identity has an irreducibly cultural aspect.[110]

Nor does he support any presumption that the social exclusion of any group must be attributed, in the first instance, to some moral inferiority in the specific culture of that group. If anything, the meticulous detail through which Lee presents the cultural experience of his characters implies a disinclination to dismiss any whole culture out of hand.[111] But most important, through this detail he is able to suggest that unless the Elect are immersed in the particulars of an unfamiliar culture, they will tend to reject that culture wholesale, out of mere discomfort or stylistic uncongeniality, long before they get to the point of understanding many of the specific structures through which that culture reasons, and thereby condemn everyone within that culture to the same social fate, without a hearing.

In short, Lee's film argues that *only* by granting an unfamiliar culture some provisional acceptance and real attention—by engaging in a dialectic with it—do we put ourselves in a position to perceive differences of thought and action among individuals in that culture, and thus to consider individuals on their own merits. And in this way he suggests that the culture of a disadvantaged group, if carefully examined, can be especially useful in clarifying the essential contribution of concrete culture to a moral definition of reason.

Thus, besides allowing abstract legal interpretations of Mookie's act when he throws the garbage can, Lee painstakingly constructs a series of events and experiences, all inseparable from the concrete cultural experience of his characters, which taken together provide a second perspective on that act. From this second perspective, the decisive moment in the film is defined not as the throwing of the garbage can but as the killing of another young man, Radio Raheem, the owner of a very large and loud boom box, by two policemen.[112]

From this perspective, it becomes possible to think of Mookie's act as reasonable, and perhaps even as morally justified. For Lee does not shrink from examining the moral questions opened up by this second interpretation. Instead, he suggests here a standard of morality in terms of which the reasoning that leads to Mookie's act can be understood and judged. In effect, Lee suggests that acts which can plausibly be understood as efforts to alleviate real suffering have a claim to moral status. He does not present this definition of morality as either definitive or comprehensive. But in part for that reason as well as for other reasons, as I hope to show presently, he does succeed, in my judgment, in offering a morally plausible conception of reason as a faculty that cannot and should not be entirely severed from the actuality of life.

In a sense, Bloom recognizes such a conception when he writes, "We have to have reasons for what we do. It is the sign of our humanity and our possibility of community."[113] For Lee, the notion of community offers a positive aspect, not only within a culture but also, as suggested by his quotation from Martin Luther King (see note 62, this chapter), through the image of a human community. For Bloom, on the other hand, seeking to alleviate suffering within one's own community is a proper goal only for a "vulgar morality" that encourages the dangerous irrationality of "moral indignation."[114]

But is it the parochialism of a communal perspective that bothers Bloom? Or is it simply the desire to interfere with suffering? One potentially important clue appears in Bloom's assertion that "human nature must not be altered in order to have a problem-free world," and that "man is not just a problem-solving being . . . but a problem-recognizing and -accepting being."[115] Whether or not this assertion can be justified logically, it can certainly be seen as part of a pervasive tendency on Bloom's part to trivialize suffering.

To be sure, Bloom is emphatic in characterizing philosophy as a tragic discipline in its determination to confront and accept human suffering. "True openness," he writes, "means closedness to all the charms that make us comfortable with the present."[116]

Bloom repeatedly demands risk as a sign of good faith that the spokesmen for a position are after something more than their own immediate comfort. Of one group, for example, he observes, "if one of their proposals entailed a sacrifice of freedom or pleasure for them or their class, they would be more morally plausible."[117]

And yet Bloom proposes nothing whatsoever in the way of a risk that he himself would accept in order to further his ideals. He does acknowledge academic tenure as a free lunch (which Socrates may have done well to avoid); but this line of argument fizzles out without any recommendation for the abolition of tenure.[118]

Risk, to be sure, Bloom advocates—but always from a position of protection. Comfort is to be disdained—but only by other people, people who are weighted down by social disadvantages of gender, race, or class from which Bloom is insulated. This subcontracting of suffering and risk has lately become a fashionable stance in our country; consider, for example, a recent article in the *New York Times Magazine* by Professor Joseph Epstein, entitled "The Joys of Victimhood."[119] Epstein, like Bloom, believes that the disadvantaged in our society have a moral obligation to accept suffering without complaining. And also like Bloom, Epstein is utterly certain that the disadvantaged take actual joy from the moral superiority conferred by their suffering.[120]

Taking this position has allowed the privileged in current American society to defend a number of cultural prejudices. From their own perspective, these defenders are merely trying to reverse an unfair condition of gross cultural bias toward the disadvantaged—"affirmative-action elitism"[121]—just as Bloom presents himself as a kind of lonely outpost sheriff, fighting to salvage a system of fairness that by now all the rest of us have knocked down and left behind in our race to be first in favoring the underprivileged. In reality, such people are defending a status quo that has served them well and is still very much with us. What they are doing is simply putting old wine into new bottles, giving the same old forms of American prejudice a new kind of intellectual respectability. In effect they are insisting that such prejudices, like the division of people into winners and losers, are required in hardball games of logic, played strictly by the amoral standards of abstract reason. As one 1989 *Newsweek* article on George Bush observed, "It is easy to play by the rules so long as you own the playing field."[122] Not that some rather spectacular reversals haven't occurred along the way—for example, in the transformation of the term "special interests" to denote not the already privileged but those still struggling for social equality.

Positions such as these are rarely expressed with regret; far more common is an attitude of moral indignation. Bloom's own moral indignation sometimes shows up simply in his vehement emphasis on the needs of the already privileged, as opposed to his virtual silence on the needs of the underprivileged.[123] This aspect of Bloom's argument recalls a column Miss Manners once devoted to criticizing the bad etiquette with which we hustle the rich into giving money to charity. Both may have a point, but is it a point worth emphasizing?

Bloom's contempt for moral indignation in others contrasts sharply with his sympathy for those "young men who passionately desir[ing] political glory and believ[ing] they have the talent to rule . . . [have] burned with that special indignation a man reserves for wrongs done to himself."[124] Bloom would support this "special indignation" by contrasting the irrationality of most communities, in which ordinary indignation is generated, with the rationality of philosophers, who form "the real community of man."[125] Too often, however, his own expressions of indignation strike a mean-spirited tone that mutes the persuasiveness of any logical justification. One perceives this tone, for instance, in attempts at clever locutions, such as George Will's allusion to a new "compassion industry," or Bloom's own phrases "flabby ecumenism," "culture leeches," and "conspicuous compassion."[126]

This mean-spirited tone is especially striking in Bloom's references to the university, which "began in spirit," he tells us, "from Socrates' contemptuous and insolent distancing of himself from the Athenian people."[127] And although throughout his book Bloom implicitly treats philosophers as the only thinkers mature enough to confront reality without illusion, he also blesses society for supporting a condition of "eternal childhood for some" (i.e., college professors), who prevent the beauties of "the theoretical life [from] collaps[ing] back into the primal slime from which [it] cannot re-emerge."[128] Bloom says he has never doubted that this life "was anything other than the best one available to me," and he immediately adds, "Never did I think that the university was properly ministerial" (that is, that it should minister) "to the society around it."[129]

Bloom's coarsened sensitivity to the suffering of others offers little reassurance that a university built to his specifications of reason would in any sense be a force for moral good. And such doubts are reinforced by Bloom's insistent imagery of college teaching as a quasi-sexual initiation of the young by the more experienced.[130] Until recently, he observes, "superior experience was always one of the palpable advantages that teachers had over youngsters who were eager to penetrate the mysteries of life." But now, he laments, "this is no longer the case."[131] Surely there has always been another source of superior experience on which adults could draw to teach the young, namely, a longer familiarity with suffering. In this, except for references to the philosopher's unique lack of illusions about the contingency of life and death,[132] Bloom shows little interest.

Most of us could agree with Bloom's assertion that the college years should provide "an atmosphere of free inquiry . . . [that] exclude[s] what is not conducive or is inimical to such inquiry."[133] Not everyone would agree, however, that protecting such an atmosphere requires excluding from education all reference to social reality or to "mere life." Moreover, there are some of us who would also see the four years of a college education as a unique opportunity in which to help the young to develop a conscience.[134] Indeed, we might well consider ourselves successful if we could teach our students to ask this one question of themselves: *who stands to suffer as a result of what I consider reasonable?* Asking this question, of course, cannot by itself guarantee that we end up doing what is morally best. But given the rigorous standard of self-criticism it implies as a condition for promoting our own self-interest, it seems to me a good point at which to begin the examined life.[135]

In fairness we should concede that by focusing our attention on the relationship between reason and morality, Bloom is at least asking the right question. But how could a book so preoccupied with morality turn out to be so mean in spirit? Something about Bloom's answer must be wrong.

It's interesting to note that Bloom himself periodically affords a glimpse of another approach to addressing this relationship, as when he speculates that the "loss of self-consciousness" in science "is somehow connected with the banishment [in the Enlightenment] of poetry."[136] Is it possible that the best answers to Bloom's question, and incidentally the best model for higher education, can be found in the study not of philosophy but of poetry?

Such an idea is bolstered unintentionally by a larger aspect of Bloom's argument. Bloom's conception of morality depends at bottom on what could be called an "either/or" conception of reason. This gets him in trouble because neither of the alternatives he offers—either accepting his definition of reason or abandoning reason altogether—leads to an ironclad, scientifically certain code of moral principles. In fact, whatever choice we make, it seems that the determination of moral goodness in our modern world ends up finally not in the abstract realm of cognition but in the concrete realm of the aesthetic.

To admit this would clearly distress Bloom, even if we took poetry as representative of the aesthetic realm. But it would positively infuriate him if our aesthetic model were music, a medium that Bloom scorns because it "is not only not reasonable, it is hostile to reason."[137] However great Bloom's devotion to high Western culture, he cannot bring himself to equate the powers of Bach or Beethoven with those of Sophocles, Dante, and Shakespeare, or even to talk substantively about Western art music, though he has a great deal to say about the morally debilitating aspects of rock music.[138]

Bloom obviously agrees with "Plato's teaching that music, by its nature, encompasses all that is today most resistant to philosophy."[139] Furthermore, he identifies the interest of modern philosophy in music with two figures, Rousseau and Nietzsche, who played a decisive role in unraveling Enlightenment reason (and, by extension, Socratic philosophy).[140] Thus we can be quite sure that he would reject out of hand any attempt to counter his vision of the university with a model of education based on the study of music.[141]

And yet I would argue that there are many ways in which methods and metaphors suggested by the study of music could have great educational usefulness. In fact, I would go further. The very characteristics that cause Bloom, and Plato, and, for that matter, Kant, to place music on the lowest rung of abstract reason may well make it the *best* medium for developing a concrete conception of reason. For of all mediums, music, despite its supposedly mathematical abstractness, is arguably the one least separable from actual contingencies of physical existence.[142]

Certainly music is among the most irreducible of mediums. True, all so-called artworks depend on a condition of physical concreteness that is diminished when efforts are made to extract them from their medium. Still, some idea of an original can be conveyed when we describe a representational painting, or make prints, photographs, or copies of any work in the visual arts—just as some core of representational literature is retained when we summarize its plot.

By contrast, the very idea of a Monarch outline of music is ludicrous,[143] and even the most devout disciple of Schenker does not mistake his radical reductions for anything called music. Nor is there any way in which a description of physical characteristics or even of structural functions can convey the particularity of a musical composition. At best such descriptions can provide metaphorical equivalents for the effect of a style, or of a piece, when it is actually heard; *nothing*, however, can be extracted from music that conveys anything of its particularity. Yes, most music can be transposed to a different level of pitch; and many, though not all works, can be transcribed for a different set of instruments, or reduced to a smaller medium, as in a four-handed piano version of a symphony. But even in these instances, an idea of the original can be conveyed *only* through a physical act of realization.

In fact, it can be persuasively argued that music *has* no existence except in those moments when it is physically performed. To the extent that painting and poetry have discarded representational goals in the past century, and thereby made themselves more resistant to summary or reduction, what they have done, in the famous words of Walter Pater, is simply aspire to the condition of music.[144]

In short, music, like individual people, is in the last analysis irreducibly actual and particular. Yet music is not irrational; like individual people, it is not without "its reasons."[145] Thus music can be especially useful in helping us to address questions related to reason that abstract conceptions ignore.

Are there kinds of logical argument that cannot be grasped without an understanding of the particular physical configurations through which they are constructed? Are there reasonable arguments that depend explicitly on the concrete resources of a medium rather than on abstract relationships? What happens when an argument is translated from one particular language to another?[146] What is gained and what is lost when a configuration is translated into another key or medium? What significance should we attach to the ways in which tone and rhetorical emphasis undermine logic, for example, in Bloom's own book? Which is more important to the persuasiveness of an argument, rhetoric or logic? Is the persuasiveness of rhetoric always or wholly irrational? Which clarifies better the meaning of a figurative image (say, the image of an Elect): emphasis on its particular content? or reference to parallel aspects of a larger structure (such as high Western culture)? Can any argument expect to establish its own logic without recourse to the physical and cultural peculiarities of a medium, or a style? Is such an expectation desirable?

Or again, is there any standard by which some musical styles can be judged better than others? Are there musical works that can legitimately claim attention more through the merits of their style than through the individuality of their structure or physical identity? Can style disguise the absence of a coherent structure? Is the possession of a recognizable style enough to justify a piece? Can style alone make a piece intelligible? On what kinds of associations does the recognition of a style depend? Is style a source of intelligibility—or a barrier to it? Is general intelligibility enough to justify a piece of music? Or should music be in some way distinctively individualized?[147] What makes music individual: its structure, or its physical appearance? Which merits the greatest emphasis (or attention): a large-scale argument, a cultural style, a personal style, or an individual detail? How can these be distinguished? Can they be distinguished? Are there ways of distinguishing, yet reconciling, the timeless aspects of music with what music requires in real time?

Most of these are questions that musical scholars, not to mention performers, confront regularly. And most suggest important parallels to types of reasoning, problems, and choices that we encounter regularly outside of music, for example, when we try to evaluate political debates, a puzzling action by a person from a different generation, or virtually any televised message.

But even if we confine ourselves to the high Western culture that Bloom favors, it seems to me that the music of Bach, Haydn, Mozart, and Beethoven offers a tremendous opportunity to learn something about reason. For ironically, though it was Romantic thought that elevated philosophical respect for music, it was during the Enlightenment—a period "almost indifferent to [the] fate" of poetry[148]—that Western art music achieved what many people consider its greatest glory. And even if this music did not succeeed in defining a truly abstract, universal structure, accessible to all people of reason, there can be no doubt that this music draws on and projects the *ideal* of such a structure.[149] To examine how composers go about translating such an abstract ideal into the highly concrete terms of music could greatly illuminate ways in which reason can plausibly be understood as a principle embedded in physical reality—and thereby contribute to the rigor with which we make moral judgments.

This is a source of illumination to which Bloom closes his eyes—and ears. Hard as he tried, after all, Kant could not build an airtight cognitive case for the assertion that judgments of natural beauty point ultimately toward "an interest in the morally good."[150] Rather than consider seeking help in the concrete, cognitively uncertain domain of the aesthetic, Bloom seems to prefer letting stand the divide between reason and morality.[151]

As I understand *Do The Right Thing*, one of its main arguments is that reason cannot in any moral sense be wholly distilled from its embodiment in the actuality of life. Is this argument valid? It seems to me that a student trained to analyze the complex and sometimes unwieldy relationship between musical structure and musical detail would be in a better position to answer this question than a philosopher trained by Allan Bloom would be. At least such a student would be prepared to investigate this question by way of asking others that Bloom doesn't even recognize as existing.[152]

A student trained in any of the arts is, or should be, sensitized to the potentially enormous effect that even small changes in a configuration can make in the projection of meaning. And, in this connection, it seems quite evident that the significance we attribute to Mookie's act of hurling the garbage can is highly vulnerable to particular differences in the way we describe this act.

Just how do we describe this act? In Joe Friday fashion—nothing but the facts, ma'am? Well, just what are the facts? Did the policemen kill Radio Raheem? Or did they murder him? Do we describe, as sparsely as possible, the literal sequence of events preceding this act? Okay, then in what order do we recount events that occurred simultaneously? Do we ascribe causal force to this act, or to any of the events surrounding it? If so, how? Did Mookie's act cause the mob violence? Or was it merely a catalyst for violence caused by the killing of Radio Raheem? Do we provide information about the specific identity or history of the characters, and if so, how much, and what kinds? Is Mookie Everyman? Or is he an African American in his twenties who delivers pizza in Bedford-Stuyvesant? Who makes his living delivering pizza in Bedford-Stuyvesant? Is the restaurant owner, Sal, a flawed though decent employer? Or is he a white Italian, in his forties, trying to maintain a business in a black neighborhood? Are the policemen just policemen? Or are they white policemen? Do we attach importance to any particular aspect of Mookie's act? If so, on what basis? Its position in time? Its causal force? Its symbolic power?

For that matter, do we describe only the act itself? If so, how can we be sure where it begins and ends? Does it begin with picking up the garbage can? With the silence immediately beforehand? With the violence preceding *that*? With racism in America? And where does it end? Has it ended yet?

Questions like these are the staples of artistic analysis because they are the staples of artistic construction. We can be quite certain that questions like these posed immediate and often concrete mechanical problems for Spike Lee as he wrote, shot, and edited his movie.[153] A graduate student of mine, a composer, once told me that questions of this kind attacked her from the moment she set to work each day; she is surely not alone in this respect.

Can pointing to such questions serve any educational purpose besides teaching students to analyze artistic forms? Does a capacity to consider Mookie's act from a multitude of perspectives enhance our ability to evaluate it morally? Or does it paralyze that ability? In his insistence on clear-cut answers, Bloom in effect recognizes as morally responsible only one question concerning Mookie's act: Was it legally justifiable? But does that single perspective offer the most responsible way to evaluate this particular act? Have we a guarantee that every act can be categorically defined as morally right or wrong? Are there not some acts that are best described as morally complex or ambiguous?[154] And even where a moral verdict can be reached, which provides a better basis for making morally responsible judgments and distinctions: knowledge of the particulars that surround an act? or ignorance of these particulars? Which contributes more to moral judgments: a basis of certainty? or an ability to make distinctions?

"The serious life," Bloom writes, "means being fully aware of the alternatives, thinking about them with all the intensity one brings to bear on life-and-death questions, in full recognition that every choice is a great risk with necessary consequences that are hard to bear."[155] These are moving and persuasive words; but their force is gravely undermined by Bloom's simplistic notion of choice. What Bloom demands as a sign of moral responsibility is not just a rigorous effort to make the right choice, but actual right choices.[156] Those of us who doubt our access to an absolute standard of rightness will accept no cognitive guarantees from Bloom for his choices. In the end, we will find his work, including his account of reason, less epistemologically cognitive than *stylistically* cognitive—cognitive in an aesthetic sense through its tone of hard certainty, just as Stravinsky's music strikes us as cognitive because of its spare and astringent "cool" sounds.[157]

Bloom himself, however, does not share these doubts. Thus, to Bloom there is no distinction between trying to make the right choice and making it; if, (and only if) one accepts his single standard of reason, one's choices are guaranteed to be right. Those who refuse his standard will lack certainty about the rightness of the available choices. Consequently, he argues, they will not make any choices; or at most they will make what he calls "no-fault choices," which amount to no choices at all.[158] These are the only alternatives he can envision.

But in fact what Bloom offers is a false opposition. The true alternative to accepting his single, abstract conception of reason is to accept a tension between abstract and concrete conceptions of reason, together with the kinds of relationships, ideals, and moral judgments associated with each.

This tension can be viewed as a dialectical definition of reason in which the cognitive certainty of an absolute first principle gives way to an underlying aesthetic uncertainty in order to preserve the benefits of exerting abstract rigor on the making of concrete moral determinations. But despite Bloom's disdain for modern dialectic, this is no anodyne dialectic that "beginning in opposites . . . ends in synthesis, all charms and temptations united in harmony."[159] Instead, precisely by virtue of resisting synthesis, this dialectic offers itself as a principle for seeking the good that does not shrink from either the intellectual complexity or the need for thickness of explanation (in Clifford Geertz's sense) with which actual experience constantly confronts us.[160]

Accepting this dialectic requires mental capacities incompatible with completeness of conceptual control—for example, a capacity to envision reason in terms of imagery of infinite regress. Thus, on the one hand, one can retain within this dialectic the traditional Western notion that in legal matters, general standards must be conceded a priority over particular circumstances. I myself see no workable basis other than this hierarchy for sustaining a societal framework of fairness and respect for the worth of the individual life (and I do not subscribe to the current deprecation of this framework, as an ideal, in some circles of thought today). But even in the legal domain, and for that matter in the domain of science, one need not insulate one's preoccupation with abstract general rules from considerations of concrete circumstance.

And certainly, the primary status of abstract generality in the legal and scientific domains need not blind us to the epistemological claims of concreteness in one of our principal human commonalities: that each of us comes to consciousness and views the world in a framework of cultural particularity. To admit that no universally acceptable abstract principle can be found for calling one culture superior to another is not the same as arguing that no culture can be found morally wanting. Taking respect for the cultural dimension in each other's lives as a provisional starting point in our moral considerations does not force us to approve of cultures that practice cannibalism or genocide, or cultures that put out death contracts on authors. The absence of an objectively indisputable single standard of reason need not condemn us to renouncing the possibility of any standards of reason.[161]

Those tied to the tail of the tiger called abstract universal reason may typically move too fast to make morally responsible distinctions. But in a situation where "willy-nilly," as Bloom puts it in another context,[162] no abstract first cause retains its binding force, and hence moral questions have no definitive answers, the constant struggle to attain moral responsibility becomes crucially important. In this struggle, a dialectical definition of reason is extremely helpful. Maintaining a universal abstract ideal of reason as a social force keeps the claims of our actual human experience honest. Insisting on the concrete requirements of reason keeps the claims of our abstract universal ideals human.

It would be very easy to dismiss the conceptions of reason I analyze here as a latter-day academic version of counting angels on the head of a pin.[163] Yet everywhere we turn today, even in the popular press, the chief elements of these conceptions turn up in one form or another as a focus of concern and disagreement among Americans. It is intriguing to speculate on a few of the practical effects that might result from honoring a dialectical conception of reason.

Suppose that in the case of certain divisive public issues, Americans decided to recognize a tension between the single solutions available through general laws and the diversity of the particular solutions actually wanted in society. Suppose we tried to find solutions not only by using legal restrictions but also by listening to others—by paying close attention to both lines of argument and styles of rhetoric in conflicting positions, by acknowledging areas where exercising discretion might be more fair than applying an inflexible rule, and by taking seriously the powers of moral persuasion that are available in a society that recognizes cultural differences. The problem of cigarette smoking has lessened in this country not primarily because of laws restricting it or even because people respond directly to narrowly rational messages of cause-and-effect (during the vogue for his book, Allan Bloom appeared on magazine covers wielding a cigarette)[164] but because cigarette smoking has come to be perceived as aesthetically gauche. In circles where this perception has not developed—for example, among certain teenagers and in many countries outside the United States—the habit continues unchecked. Perhaps we might handle some of our other problems better if instead of expecting complete cures through purely legal or scientific means, we adjusted our expectations to the unevenness with which real changes so often occur.

Such adjustments come hard to us. What happened, say, a few years ago, when Barney Frank, a fine Congressman, was pressured to resign, what has happened more generally since the press found itself free to expose politicians' private lives, is what always happens when inquiring minds want to know— and when abstract notions of reason—or for that matter, any general principles—are allowed to govern society unchallenged. We have lost the capacity to "know" when to stop. Once we perceive that some abstract system of laws permits an action, we feel not only free but obligated to take that action, as if it were the only action available. The certainties offered by science create a momentum that becomes an imperative, until we no longer feel entitled to voice moral objections because they lack the certainty of science or law. We lose the sense of our ability to protest effectively against excesses of scientific investigation, even if they poison the atmosphere, or, for that matter, to take a persuasive stand against abuses of free speech on the campus that we know to be morally wrong. We even lose the perception that taste has a legitimate role to play in preserving a distinction between public and private.[165] At most we say, "If it's wrong, let's outlaw it"—or we file a lawsuit. But is the solution by general law the only one we have? Is it always the *right* solution?[166]

Or consider one of the great American bugaboos: the relation between equality of opportunity and equality of actual wealth. Let us admit that only a tyranny can legislate *both* kinds of equality. Should we point toward a single standard of reason to justify the suggestion, which has been made in all seriousness, that sacrificing a generation of welfare poor will teach their children moral responsibility?[167] Is there no moral alternative to such legal tyranny except an unlimited tolerance for greed that turns Donald Trump into an American hero? Is it not legitimate to try and muster moral approval in our society for the essentially aesthetic admission, "I *now* have enough," even though we wouldn't want to specify by law the appropriate moment for this admission?

Or again, suppose we Americans admitted that the abstract ideal of the melting pot has been overtaken by new cultural conditions in American life. Would it be morally irresponsible to admit that even though ideals of abstract identity and merit (and, for that matter, of a common public language) still have crucial importance in our society, some social problems do not respond to inflexible general solutions? Or to argue that although every social group has problems, the problems of the less advantaged have a greater claim to national emphasis than do those of the privileged?

The tension I am advocating between abstract and concrete schools of reason could be helpful in reconsiderations of the college curriculum. There are good arguments for continuing to teach the Western canon, though not in a fashion that totally denies the cultural parameters of that canon. Perhaps the most persuasive of these arguments could be characterized as structural in their concerns; and here I return, finally, to the notion of structural listening. Though as a sole criterion for judging music such notions have serious limitations, as an ideal, functioning in dialectic with more concrete criteria, structural arguments furnish some good reasons for studying high Western art.[168] There are also good reasons for opening the curriculum to a broadened range of studies. For even if we continue to honor the theoretical restrictions on knowledge established in the Enlightenment, the actual world of things worth knowing is a lot bigger today than it was yesterday, and it will be even bigger tomorrow. We can realistically expect to create some overlap among the things our college students study. We cannot, and should not, expect to produce a perfect congruence in their studies, any more than we should expect every professor to master the entire range of knowledge available in his or her field[169]—or every American to be oriented primarily toward Europe. What we can do, finally, in our curriculum, is recognize the ongoing tension between the benefits of standardization and diversification, and do our best to harness that tension.

Obviously, this notion of the college curriculum cannot be managed within the same neat confines as a notion based solely on the traditional Western canon. But then, as Congressman Frank once argued in a campaign slogan,

"Neatness isn't everything." In equally memorable but more haunting words, Judge Shirley Hufstedler has made precisely the same point with respect to the U.S. Constitution itself. Urging against the confirmation of Judge Robert Bork as a Justice of the Supreme Court, she criticized Bork's "quest for certitudes to resolve the ambiguities of the Constitution and of the Supreme Court's role in constitutional adjudication" as well as his "effort to develop constitutional litmus tests to avoid his having to confront the grief and the untidiness of the human condition."[170] If Americans didn't buy the need for "impoverishing certitudes" from Bork, why should we buy it at all?[171]

Without question, recognizing a tension between generalized standards and moral solutions based on particular conditions opens up real possibilities of danger. To the very extent that moral principles resist generalized legislation, they are subject to abuse.[172] And yet, moral doubt is not identical with an incapacity to make moral distinctions. To lack Allan Bloom's certainty and swiftness in passing moral judgment is not the same as conceding that our moral decisions must be "sicklied o'er with the pale cast of thought . . . and lose the name of action" (*Hamlet*, act III, scene 1). Indeed, to the extent that Bloom's certainty defines itself through a rhetorical tone of nastiness, Bloom undermines the moral persuasiveness of his arguments—while also conceding the inability of those arguments to succeed by virtue of abstract logic alone.

There are ways to counter the dangers of moral uncertainty. A generation of Americans educated to recognize these dangers would make a good starting defense. At least some college teachers, through the questions they raise and through their manner of conducting discussions, could help students cultivate a (fundamentally aesthetic) capacity for exercising responsible moral discretion—even if Allan Bloom does deride the concept of "intellectual honesty."[173] Surely our students, and our teachers, are smart enough to distinguish between social threats to free inquiry and calls for social help. To expect anything less from ourselves, it seems to me, is to consign college education itself to the status of a trivial pursuit.

But college teachers are not the only individuals who can help us figure out how to impose morally responsible discipline on ourselves, even if we reject a single standard of reason. Here I return to Spike Lee. Concerning the two quotations that end his film, the one from Martin Luther King rejecting violence, the other from Malcolm X defending it in certain instances, Lee said this in an interview: "I never saw it as an either/or proposition. The whole trick is to have this synthesis, to try to mesh these two philosophical approaches."[174] Whether or not Lee actually offers such a synthesis is debatable; in my judgment, an important sign of Lee's moral self-discipline in this movie is his refusal to offer such a synthesis, presumably because he has not yet found one he can accept.[175] Where he and I agree, however, is that his insistent emphasis on *two* views, at the end, offers more promise of a real synthesis than would the emphatic assertion of a single viewpoint.

But the most important evidence of Lee's moral self-discipline, I believe, shows up in an aspect of his film that is without doubt morally superior to its counterpart in Bloom's book. Since Bloom presents his views as drawn from his disinterested use of abstract universal reason, one might suppose that he would stress the abstract equality of all people. Instead, decidedly concrete patterns of inequality emerge—almost by definition suggesting that only certain types of people have the capacity to be abstract (and thereby undercutting Bloom's insistence on human universality). In particular, many aspects of Bloom's book combine to give an emphatic impression of the collective inferiority of women, minorities, and non-Westerners: his hardline lack of sympathy for women's aspirations with which "nature does not cooperate";[176] the idealization of young males as students, a preference emphasized stylistically not only by Bloom's exclusive use of the male pronoun but also by his extraordinarily extensive use of the terms "man" and "men," to the point of suggesting that the term means not "humans" but "males only" (or, perhaps, that the two are synonymous); his almost unbroken refusal of sympathy in the discussion of black issues on campus;[177] his consistent emphasis on the needs and viewpoints of the privileged; his glorification of Western reason (and culture) over non-Western culture; his disdain for the idealistic impulses of his students toward the poor as signs of nothing more than a sense of "moral smugness."[178] Bloom's mean-spirited expressions are directed entirely at members of these groups, or at those who symphathize with any disadvantaged group;[179] his term "spiritedness" in particular seems to signal a naturally grounded state of privilege that excludes most groups.[180] There can be little doubt that a principal reason for the large sales of Bloom's book was the intellectual patina it provided for many readers' prejudices.

By contrast, Lee carefully and successfully avoids derogatory cultural stereotyping, and for that matter, *all* cultural stereotyping.[181] Even the extraordinary scene in which five characters of various backgrounds hurl strings of highly concrete cultural insults against five different ethnic groups is clearly using cathartic shock and humor to reduce the process of stereotyping to absurdity.[182] Against the full and differentiated cultural context presented in this movie, Lee develops a remarkably large number of individualized characters. Each of these is shown to view the world from a different perspective; and with the possible exception of the two uniformed policemen, no two characters are treated alike by Lee simply because they share the same culture.[183] Characters who appear too briefly to be fully individualized are allowed at least some potentially sympathetic dimension.[184]

Where Bloom insists on clear-cut moral choices, even if they entail stereotypes that hurt both groups and individuals, Lee refuses to stereotype, even if this means leaving moral questions unresolved, in a state of tension. Thus, unlike Bloom, Lee never suggests that some cultural groups have cornered the market on moral answers. Likewise, among his individual characters, not one is presented as unambiguously moral or immoral.

And yet not one is absolved from the explicitly moral questions of responsibility raised by his or her actions. That the film takes a tremendous interest in the notion of moral responsibility is evident not only in the title of the film but also in the character of Da Mayor, who as Lee conceives him has "got some valuable knowledge, if [the kids]'d only listen."[185] The essence of this knowledge he communicates to Mookie in the words, "Doctor, always try to do the right thing."[186] Mookie himself is a main focus of the film's questions about moral responsibility; and Lee leaves no doubt that Mookie often does the wrong thing.[187]

But in fact we are put in a position to ask about everyone in Lee's story: Did this character do the right thing? Nor does the action of any character propose morality as a condition that can further self-interest without a cost—or through the delegation of that cost to others. Without doubt, many of the actions taken by the characters in Do The Right Thing do result in suffering by others. In every instance, however, the character pays a price for his or her own action. Whether or not they do the right thing, these characters at least do their own suffering. "In my eyes," Lee notes concerning the racial divisions in his film, "there are no winners in this one."[188]

Whose work exhibits more moral self-discipline, Bloom's or Lee's? Which work exercises greater self-restraint against the temptations of self-interest? Which uses the resources available to it to make the more persuasive argument for moral conduct? At bottom, which conception of reason produces the morally more responsible results? These are questions to which, even without Bloom's single standard, we can give clear-cut answers.

What I set out to do in this essay was to make a persuasive case that a morally valid definition of reason must recognize the concreteness of actual life as well as the abstractness of general principles. Without including both of these human domains in our theoretical considerations, I have argued, we cannot expect the use of reason to have morally good results.

To the best of my ability I have tried to pursue this argument through the logical ways of reasoning that Allan Bloom advocates and, thus, to engage with Bloom's logic. That is to say, even while questioning the privileged status of an abstract notion of reason, I have tried to model my argument throughout this essay on that abstract ideal, and to focus my attention on the content of Bloom's arguments, rather than on his style, circumstances, or motivations. In some measure I have failed. In the very process of trying to define reason in terms of concrete considerations, I have at times found it necessary to step outside my theoretical arguments, and to use the importance of real life as evidence in demonstrating that importance. In doing this I have at times opposed Bloom's viewpoint by logically untenable means, adducing objections based on real life to counter Bloom's dismissal of real life.

To an extent these contradictions and limitations support my own conviction that certain assertions of deconstruction are dead right: that every viewpoint is bounded by its own peculiar blindness; that every argument is entrapped in opposing forms of language and thought; that every defense relies finally on a process of infinite regress, whereby when stopped by the merits of an opposing argument, we retreat to a more fundamental level of conviction.

But to an extent, also, the limitations of my argument here strike me as sound evidence for the very point I am trying to make: that no argument can be made in terms of abstract logic alone. Though I cannot offer a watertight and definitive logical defense of the attitude I have taken here toward morality, I remain certain that the morality of actual life is a condition that we are all capable of assessing in valid ways. General formulas are important, but they will only go so far in accounting for this certainty; and the absence of a general formula for defending one's argument isn't always a bad thing. There are times, for example, when thoughtful silence may be morally preferable to a defined position—or to a strident tone of omniscience; and silence, like tone, is something musicians know about. On the other hand, silence is rarely a defensible response to the sufferings of others, at least when speaking out offers any prospect of relief.

At the beginning of this chapter I cited both Bloom's book and Lee's film as evidence that the American dream, at it has been traditionally defined, is no longer viable. Bloom's testimony to this effect is that of a hostile witness; nevertheless, he closes his book by doubting how the future will judge our stewardship of what he calls "the American moment in world history."[189] In the end, unable to salvage the American dream through purely abstract standards, he clarifies no less than Lee the distorting effects of such standards on American reality.

Despite the great legal image that Lincoln left us of government of the people, by the people, and for the people, America today is in a moral (as well as economic) sense very largely a nation of "us" and "them." The "us" groups are those of us who feel free, and tend to have the power, to make rules and set standards with potentially terrible consequences that we ourselves will never have to experience. The "them" groups are "other people," the ones who have to bear the worst consequences of rules that they can seldom forestall and, for good cultural reasons, usually didn't want in the first place. One could well argue that the American national motto is in grave danger these days of being changed from "*E pluribus unum*" to "*après moi, le déluge.*"

This danger was brought home to me not long after I started work on this essay, by two items in the same issue of Long Island *Newsday*. The first was in a column by Otis Pike: "In general," Pike wrote, "the capital gains proposal the House passed last week transfers more wealth from average citizens to our wealthiest. This is a continuation of a trend that has been demonstrable in our society for a decade. We also have reduced taxes for ourselves and bequeathed deficits to our children. The saddest part of these inherently immoral acts is that voters want it that way."[190]

The second is from a column by Murray Kempton. "Last winter," Kempton tells us, "Metro North opened the doors of Grand Central Station to be sure that the winds would blow upon its [homeless] sleep-ins as fiercely as on the streets outside." When that remedy didn't remove the homeless from the station, he continues, "Metro North boarded up every cubbyhole and removed most of the benches. . . . These measures have brought about conditions scarcely more comfortable for those who have homes to travel to as for those who don't but, since Metro North spread ammonia on its floors as a terminal discouragement to the slumbrous, Grand Central is all but purged by now. Official references to this success scrupulously describe the homeless contingent thus displaced not as 'ejected' but as 'dissipating.'"[191]

If our marriage to abstract reason has produced not just an Elect team of winners but also the moral malformations these columnists describe, then maybe it is time for us to commit bigamy and add a second standard of reason to our household. No principle of reason can prove its own morality; but any principle, even a principle of reason, when honored so rigidly as to exclude all others, sooner or later becomes the basis of an irrationality that can be used to justify immorality in the real world.[192] Whether we work in classrooms or in boardrooms or in smoke-filled rooms, surely it is time for those of us already inside the American dream to do the right thing, and open up that dream to all Americans.

Allan Bloom might dismiss this suggestions as a mere musical fantasy. But then, as Hamlet also said, "There are more things in heaven and earth, Horatio, than are dreamt of in our philosophy" (act I, scene 5).

Notes

Introduction

1. Rose Rosengard Subotnik, "The Challenge of Contemporary Music," *Developing Variations: Style and Ideology in Western Music* (Minneapolis, 1991), p. 293.

2. Though Cage made reference to old notions of autonomous structure in subjecting his random processes of construction to peculiarly rigid principles of organization, the principles were wildly irrelevant to old notions of controlled composition and bounded results. See, for example, his accounts of random compositional processes in "Composition as Process: 1. Changes," in John Cage, *Silence* (Hanover, N.H., 1973), pp. 21, 25, 26, and 28. Cage describes in painstaking detail processes that few would have the energy to try to replicate and that, by definition, one could never use to duplicate results of any sort.

3. Contrary to a common impression, Brown students cannot fill their four years with any courses whatsoever. Once they have declared a major, the requirements for that major are the same as they would be anywhere else. Outside the major, however, students *are* free to choose their own courses; thus we have a chance to note changes in student interests at a fairly early stage.

4. My own observation over twenty years is that although many students come to college with some experience in performance—lessons, high school orchestra or band, etc.—very few, even among upper-middle-class students at expensive private institutions, have attended live performances of Western art music by professional musicians.

5. One cannot help wondering if the changes taking place even in the rarefied world of performance competitions for young virtuoso instrumentalists, not to mention in conservatory curriculums, do not also reflect an erosion of solid ground under the social category of instrumental music.

6. Even students who are fully literate in Western art music depend increasingly on keyboard and computer to write down sounds. Long gone are the days when Hubert Lamb at Wellesley criticized me for neglecting to turn my dipping pen to the side when making note stems.

7. As a brilliant example of nonspecialized writing about musical structure, I would cite a piece I received in February 1993 from Keith Rosen, then a senior at Brown (now attending Yale Law School), entitled "A Missing Letter concerning Beethoven's Fifth Symphony." Fashioning the conceit of a recently unearthed letter, apparently written by Freud after a visit from Beethoven, Keith uses the language of psychoanalysis to describe the scherzo movement of Beethoven's Fifth as a dream of the first movement. Because Rosen's imagery follows the course of events in the scherzo in an unambiguous way, the connections he makes between the tropes of psychoanalysis and those of the symphony are persuasive; they truly stretch the mind.

8. The list provided here, of course, simplifies; one could conversely point to the abstract structures of Bach's keyboard works and the visual titles often used by the French clavecin school.

An alternate image to that of the pendulum might be that of rise and fall. One could look on the current merging of Western art music into its environment as a return to the conditions in which that tradition arose (see chapter 3, "Toward a Deconstruction of Structural Listening," the discussion surrounding note 45). In terms of this image, the ideal of autonomy (and by extension, the whole configuration of values we associate with the Enlightenment) would be seen as a kind of historical flicker that burned for a while and then faded. This image certainly has some persuasiveness, particularly from our vantage point at the end of a millennium. Or is it part of the human condition to view one's own time as the end of a line?

9. See below, chapter 3, "Toward a Deconstruction of Structural Listening," note 1.

10. Here are two samples, passed on by my students, who can parody the style brilliantly. From a review by Helen Twelvetrees in an undated issue of *Bananafish* (from some time in 1993): "Frans de Waard gets up close and personal with Masami Akita on the *Documentation/Collaboration* LP (Korm Plastics) by Merzbow Kapotte Musiek. Side A's a 20-minute volleyball furnace utilizing tapes by de Waard, Emil Beaulieu and SBOTHI, and the mixing talents of Peter Duimelinks and Masami Akita (the latter also used Transforming Feedback Machines and then mastered the whole thing to DAT). On side B, they take turns processing side A. Makes you wonder what these guys have for breakfast. Leftovers, obviously."

And unsigned, from an undated issue of *Chemical Imbalance Magazine* (again the issue appeared some time in 1993): "When was the last time you put on their version of 'Citadel' off *Teen Babes*? Imagine the energy of that song—its ability to know rock history intimately and reject it like REAL punks (which the [Redd] Kross once were)—have it played in your head by Black Flag being fronted by John Belushi when both were in their prime, and you'll get an idea what the [Dung]Beetle are like. If this were a Dungbeetle America, Primus, the Red Hot Chili Peppers, the Rollins Band, They Might Be Giants, and anybody who's ever been on the cover of *Reflex* magazine would be so ashamed at their inability to be even adequate joke/performance rock they'd hang their heads in shame and swallow a fistfull of lye."

11. See, for example, Lester Bangs, *Psychotic Reactions and Carburetor Dung*, ed. Greil Marcus (New York, 1988); Greil Marcus, *Mystery Train: Images of America in Rock'n'Roll Music*, 3rd rev. ed. (New York, 1990); and Greil Marcus, *Lipstick Traces: A Secret History of the 20th Century* (Cambridge, Mass., 1989).

12. Oliver Sacks, "To See and Not to See," *New Yorker* (May 10, 1993), 59-73.

13. Susan McClary, *Feminine Endings: Music, Gender, and Sexuality* (Minneapolis, 1991), pp. 30 and 19.

14. Susan McClary, "Music and Postmodernism," unpublished typescript, 1988, p. 16.

15. No matter how hard traditional musicologists have tried to tailor their conceptions of music to abstract ideals of music, defenders of those ideals, working in Plato's tradition, have often regarded even the most rigorously constructed Western art compositions as intrinsically irrational and hence unworthy of advanced study. (Allan Bloom may be unusually candid on this matter, but he is not atypical; see chapter 4, "The Closing of the American Dream?" notes 77 and 138-41.) It is ironic that a broadened notion of reason, a notion that would permit music full stature as a "rational" academic discipline, arrives just as the narrowly abstract paradigm of musical autonomy—and the paradigm most palatably "reasonable" to figures such as Bloom—is in decline. (See also below, note 19, on the decline of positivistic musicology.)

Looking on "the aesthetic" as an emotional domain, even philosophers sympathetic to music have more than once surprised me by the difficulty they experience in connecting music with any rational mode of thought; the difficulty lies in a deeply ingrained notion of what rationality is. In my own thought, on the other hand, as the subtitle of the present book indicates, the relation of rationality and music is of critical importance.

16. "Lortzing and the German Romantics: A Dialectical Assessment," *Musical Quarterly* 52 (April, 1976), 241-64. Historically, the "new" view here was the idealistic view of the Romantics, the "old" one the pragmatic view of Lortzing, the commercial theater composer. But even in the mid-1970s, when I wrote this piece, it was also possible to see the Romantics' elitist perspective as socially conservative compared to Lortzing's more popular aesthetic.

17. For me during the 1970s, when I taught at the University of Chicago, scholarship required keeping up with French and especially German musical scholarship in its original languages; part of my pioneer status with respect to Adorno came from reading him in German before most of his work was translated. I largely gave up on this obligation when I lost access to university libraries, and may never fully resume it. Am I alone in the impression that fewer titles in foreign languages now turn up in American musicological scholarship than was once the case?

18. For a clear explanation of this concept see the translator's preface to Jacques Derrida's *Of Grammatology*, trans. Gayatri Chakravorty Spivak (Baltimore, 1976), pp. xiii-xvi. Deconstruction proposes the simultaneous erasure and preservation of a term not as an empty trick, or even a use-less game (such as sitting in a corner and not thinking of a white elephant) but as an image of the way in which we actually think.

19. See also above, n. 15. Again, both positivism and formalism fostered a narrowly abstract conception of reason that implicitly undervalued music in many respects.

20. In its essentials, this is a principal argument of my essay "The Role of Ideology in the Study of Western Music," *Developing Variations*, pp. 3-14.

21. See, for example, the double reading of Mozart's music in "Evidence of a Critical Worldview in Mozart's Last Three Symphonies," *Developing Variations*, pp. 98-112; and the reading of Adorno against the grain in "The Historical Structure: Adorno's 'French' Model for the Criticism of Nineteenth-Century Music," ibid., pp. 206-38.

22. See note 21 above. Before writing the piece on Mozart's symphonies, I subjected them to a time-consuming, detailed analysis that resulted in extensive charts and diagrams. In part because there was a strict page limit on that article, none of this material was incorporated into the published essay.

23. "On Grounding Chopin," *Developing Variations*, pp. 141-65.

24. See below, chapter 1, "Whose *Magic Flute?*" section V, and chapter 3, "Toward a Decon-struction of Structural Listening," p. 162.

25. See note 16, above.

26. See *Developing Variations*, pp. 15-41.

27. This article, "Toward a Deconstruction of Structural Listening: A Critique of Schoenberg, Adorno, and Stravinsky," first appeared in *Explorations in Music, the Arts, and Ideas: Essays in Honor of Leonard B. Meyer*, ed. Eugene Narmour and Ruth Solie (Stuyvesant, N.Y., 1988), pp. 87-122. The most significant change I have made has been to correct my description of Kant's notion of art by changing the term "mimetic" to "representational." See p. 90 in the original version, and in the present volume, p. 150.

28. See "The Challenge of Contemporary Music," *Developing Variations*, pp. 277-82.

29. In Narmour and Solie, *Explorations in Music*, see pp. 90-97; in the present volume, see pp. 151-56.

30. In particular, Mikhail Bakhtin, *The Dialogic Imagination*, ed. Michael Holquist, trans. Caryl Emerson and Michael Holquist (Austin, 1981); and Lionel Trilling, *Sincerity and Authenticity* (Cambridge, Mass., 1972).

31. See "Whose *Magic Flute?* Intimations of Reality at the Gates of the Enlightenment," *Nine-teenth Century Music* 15 (1991), 132-50.

32. On this particular shift in paradigm, see my review of Edward Said's *Musical Elaborations* (New York, 1991), in the *Journal of the American Musicological Society* 46 (Fall, 1993), 476-85.

33. The so-called value crisis, to which I devote considerable attention in my final essay, is

most frequently associated today with Nietzsche, who identified it and drew its consequences. The foundations of this crisis, however, become apparent in Kant, in spite of his massive efforts to circumvent it.

34. In a review of James Q. Wilson's *The Moral Sense* (New York, 1993), Harvey Blume (in the *Boston Globe* [July 25, 1993], B38) criticizes a related argument on terms similar to those I use in chapter 4, "The Closing of the American Dream?" For more on this and related points, see below, note 40.

35. By failure, I must assure philosophers, I mean *not* that Kant was too incompetent to know what he was doing but rather that even Kant, finally, could not do what could not be done—itself, admittedly, an ontologically loaded statement.

36. Robert Winter, "A Musicological Offering," *New York Review of Books* 32 (July 18, 1985), 26. See chapter 4, note 169.

37. In my own life, to be sure, a chronic shortage of time has been a problem only in periods where I had a full-time job (as an academic or, in 1983-85, as a computer programmer). During my years of involuntary unemployment, however, I, like most people I know who have been in such a position, was simply unable, psychologically and emotionally, to make maximum use of the large blocks of time that had become theoretically available to me. It was all I could do to keep my scholarly enterprise going at all.

Whether or not shortages of time particularly plague women academics with growing children, as I suspect they do, I was delighted to see this issue of time and quantity addressed by Shirley M. Tilghman in "Science vs. Women—A Radical Solution," *New York Times* (January 26, 1993), A 23. (This was the second of a two-part presentation of excerpts from a speech to the Olin Conference on Women and the Culture of Science at Washington University in St. Louis on October 21, 1992. This conference had no connection to the John M. Olin Center for Inquiry into the Theory and Practice of Democracy at the University of Chicago, of which Allan Bloom was codirector, or to the John M. Olin Foundation, the underwriter of the Center. I am grateful to James Piereson, Executive Director of the John M. Olin Foundation, for his clarification of this matter.)

Professor Tilghman writes: "I don't believe that science must be practiced to the exclusion of all other human activity. The system I object to confuses quantity with quality. It is not the number of hours you work that determines your contributions to science: it is the quality of your insights and your creativity. The distinction between quantity and quality needs to be continually pointed out, and I suspect that it is going to take women to do it. Most important, we must begin by declaring it loud and clear to our students, who still fear that the two are the same."

Despite these sentiments, I would not be at all surprised if in actuality, Professor Tilghman gives as many hours to her profession as her busiest male colleagues do, and manages to meet her obligations by allowing herself a bare minimum of recreational time. That is my own unhealthy way of life, as it is the way of many academic women I know. It should not be supposed that even the kind of intensive, focused study I recommend can be done on a leisurely, part-time basis.

38. Fredric Jameson, "The Realist Floor-Plan," *On Signs*, ed. Marshall Blonsky (Baltimore, 1985). A second stratum is suggested on p. 380 ("I want to conclude this reading with two very suggestive objections that have been made to it"); and a third on pp. 382-83 ("I had already completed the preceding essay when, returning after an absence of some thirty years to Pound's *Cantos*," etc.).

39. On the use of reason to criticize reason, see Allan Bloom, *The Closing of the American Mind* (New York, 1987), e.g., p. 36 ("What we are really doing is applying a Western prejudice," etc.) and p. 41 ("Such a view requires science. . . . this view simultaneously produces melancholy about science," etc.). This notion figures centrally in Bloom's account of Nietzsche, as it does in the account given by deconstruction.

40. Again, I can imagine no proofs for these propositions sufficiently watertight to meet the cognitive demands of abstract reason for proof. I am always encouraged, however, when I en-

counter an impressive mind making similar arguments. At the annual meeting of the American Association of Law Schools in San Francisco, January, 1993, the plenary session was devoted to "Multiple Cultures and the Law." Speaking there in response to Stanley Fish, among others, Cass Sunstein, a highly regarded professor at the University of Chicago Law School, made an effective and moving argument for the importance, and the possibility, of reconciling the relativism of the postmodernist perspective with values, such as freedom, associated with traditional canons of abstract reason. Sunstein's thoughtful remarks, along with three other texts from the same session—Fish's provocative but glib attack on notions such as the canon and free speech, an appealing argument by Patricia Nelson Limerick for culturally broadened scholarly perspectives, and an amusing introduction by the moderator, Derrick Bell—are all published in the *Journal of Legal Education* 43 (March, 1993), 1–26.

41. Walter Reich, "Erasing the Holocaust," *New York Times Book Review* (July 11, 1993), 34.

42. The text in question, produced by the Nation of Islam, was used in Africana Studies 206 during the 1992-93 academic year by Professor Anthony Martin. Statements on the use of this text by the outgoing president of Wellesley, Nannerl Overholser Keohane, two deans, and the Board of Trustees appear in the alumnae magazine *Wellesley* 77:4 (Summer, 1993), 2. Pertinent letters from alumnae appear on the inside front cover and p. 1. This issue has also received extensive coverage in the Boston press.

43. My own understanding of the American right to free speech is that one cannot be jailed for one's opinions. If tenured professors also have the right not to lose a job for their opinions—a right rarely extended to the untenured—then it seems to me that students have a corresponding right not to be penalized through a low grade for their opinions. Though the latter may in fact happen all the time, some recourse to appeal, involving an effort to invoke dispassionate, general standards of accuracy, ought to be available to students.

44. Spike Lee with Lisa Jones, *Do The Right Thing* [A Companion Volume to the Universal Pictures Film] (New York, 1989), p. 59.

45. Ibid., p. 45.

46. Ibid., p. 32. Lee indicated he might change this decision, but in fact he stuck by it: "It's early, but I don't want anyone to die in the riot. Some people will get hurt. Some will definitely get fucked up, but as of now, no one will be killed."

47. See chapter 4, p. 194, the text immediately following the citation of note 112.

48. See chapter 2, "How Could Chopin's A-Major Prelude Be Deconstructed?", note 168.

1. Whose Magic Flute? Intimations of Reality at the Gates of the Enlightenment

1. Alfred Einstein, *Mozart, His Character, His Work* (New York, 1962), p. 464. A shorter version of the present piece was published in *Nineteenth Century Music* 15 (Fall, 1991), 132-50. A still earlier version was first presented at the conference "The Musical and Verbal Arts: Interactions," Dartmouth College, May, 1988. I wish to thank Professor Richard Kramer of the State University of New York at Stony Brook for his excellent suggestions concerning this essay.

2. Theodor W. Adorno, "Classes and Strata," *Introduction to the Sociology of Music*, trans. E. B. Ashton (New York, 1976), pp. 69-70. Relevant also is this remark from the same book (pp. 21-22): "Time and again [the higher art] . . . would absorb elements of the lower music. . . . *The Magic Flute* . . . would [not] be conceivable without an interaction of what by then were separated spheres. The last instance of their reconciliation, utterly stylized and teetering as on a narrow mountain bypass, was *The Magic Flute*—an instant still mourned and longed for in such structures as Strauss and Hofmannsthal's *Ariadne auf Naxos*." The latter imagery may have influenced Edward Said's description of the "relatively rare" work that "dangles pretty much as pure musicality in a

social space off the edge" (*Musical Elaborations* [New York, 1991], pp. 71 and 72); Mozart's *Così fan tutte* heads this list. But whereas Adorno describes a balance between art and popular musical traditions, Said conjures up the possibility of music that breaks free of all ties to the social world.

3. Letters of October 8 and 9, 1791 (no. 615) and October 14, 1791 (no. 616). See Emily Anderson, ed. and trans., *The Letters of Mozart and His Family*, 3rd ed. (New York, 1985), pp. 969 and 970. Cavalieri was the first Constanze in Mozart's *Entführung aus dem Serail*.

4. H. C. Robbins-Landon, *Haydn: The Years of "The Creation" 1796-1800*, in *Haydn: Chronicle and Works*, vol. 4 (Bloomington, Indiana, 1977), p. 32.

5. Part of the problem in determining the authenticity of modernist and postmodernist structures—and hence one reason for the pervasive preoccupation with charlatanism in our culture—is the suspicion that there *is* no reliable basis of unity that would justify the trouble of making a painstakingly detailed analysis. See note 8 below.

6. I am not aware that the musicological perception of *The Magic Flute* as a unified work is (yet) in serious question, despite poststructuralist and subsequent critiques of unity, and despite long-standing argument over whether Mozart and Schikaneder altered the libretto midcourse. The latter theory, incidentally, along with the theory that Carl Ludwig Gieseke rather than Schikaneder wrote the libretto, is discredited in recent scholarship; see Peter Branscombe's volume in the Cambridge Opera Handbook Series, *W. A. Mozart: Die Zauberflöte* (Cambridge, 1991), especially chapter 5, "The Libretto." (I am most grateful to Professor Neal Zaslaw of Cornell University for giving me early access to this source.)

7. Weber's *Freischütz*, 1821, a work that gained a popular following while aspiring to be high art, probably came closest. But support for this opera among the upper classes, and among intellectuals uninvolved in the cause of German opera, was not as solid (see below, note 94); and the work has never been accorded the same artistic value as Mozart's opera has. One is tempted to say that whereas Mozart aimed at entertaining a specific audience and got (the universality of) art, Weber aimed at art and got entertainment. The difference between the two composers reflects a change in cultural values not unlike the shift toward multiculturalism in American society today. Whereas the cosmopolitan values of the Enlightenment allowed Mozart to enjoy the challenge of unifying diverse styles, by Weber's time the presence of diverse styles in a German opera was coming to signify the failure of Germans to find their own particular operatic voice (see below, note 83). For more on such topics see my "Lortzing and the German Romantics: A Dialectical Reappraisal," *Musical Quarterly* 62 (1976), 241-64. Clearly what we today would call the middle class formed a considerably smaller proportion of the original audiences for *The Magic Flute* than it does in the latter twentieth century.

8. By "text" I mean essentially the score in a form that Mozart would have accepted. I have never accepted either the legitimacy or the possibility of drawing exclusively privileged readings from an author's original intentions. But I have always argued that responsible readers recognize the claims of their chosen text as a structure originating outside their own field of vision, or at least (to the extent that this latter is ultimately inaccessible), the claims implied by the *ideal* of such a text. Responsible readers, by my definition, acknowledge the need to negotiate the dialectical distance between the strictures of their own viewpoint and the discipline of a text as something "other."

9. Søren Kierkegaard, "The Immediate Stages of the Erotic or the Musical Erotic," *Either/Or*, ed. Howard A. Johnson, trans. David F. Swenson and Lillian Marvin Swenson (Princeton, 1959), 1:77.

10. Mozart's well-known letter (no. 412) of June 20, 1781, with its assertion that "it is the heart that ennobles a man," explicitly champions this maxim (see Anderson, p. 747). See also Neal Zaslaw, *Mozart's Symphonies: Context, Performance Practice, Reception* (Oxford, 1989), pp. 526-31.

11. Papageno's props include his birdcage, possibly a metaphor for the entrapment that culture represents for nature at Papageno's level, and his costume of bird feathers. The latter, though not specified in the libretto, is shown in a picture of Schikaneder that appears in the original edition

of the libretto (see Einstein, *Mozart*, p. 464). Likewise his text presents a man with a natural occupation (birdcatcher) and natural drives (for a mate).

12. The tiny references to the dominant, D, in the orchestral introduction (measures 7-8) and at the midpoint of the vocal part (measures 33-34) hardly constitute full-scale modulations, even when the latter version is echoed by the orchestra (measures 35-36). The same can be said for the two references to C, the subdominant (measures 15-16 and 43-44).

13. Kierkegaard, *Either/Or*, 1:80.

14. See the entry "Pastoral" in the *Princeton Encyclopedia of Poetry and Poetics* (Princeton, 1974), p. 603. For a more extended account of the musical tradition up to the early eighteenth century see Ellen T. Harris, *Handel and the Pastoral Tradition* (London, 1980), pp. 1-15.

15. A mistake in punctuation, not caught in the final editing, obscured the meaning of this sentence in its first published version (*Nineteenth Century Music* 15 [Fall, 1991], 134).

16. The term stems from Johann Abraham Peter Schulz, preface to *Lieder im Volkston*, 2nd ed. (Berlin, 1785), vol 1. See, e.g., Max Friedländer, *Das deutsche Lied im 18. Jahrhundert*, repr. ed. (Stuttgart and Berlin, 1902), vol. 1, pt. 1, p. 256. (I am most grateful to Richard Kramer for this reference.)

17. On difference (in Derrida's respelled version), see Jacques Derrida, *"Différance," Margins of Philosophy*, trans. and ed. Alan Bass (Chicago, 1982), pp. 3-27; also Jonathan Culler, *On Deconstruction: Theory and Criticism after Structuralism* (Ithaca, 1982), pp. 95-97; and chapter 2 of this volume, pp. 52-53 and 68-69.

18. On Lacan, see Terry Eagleton, *Literary Theory: An Introduction* (Minneapolis, 1983), pp. 164-70; see also Kierkegaard, *Either/Or*, 1:79.

19. This time lag would conform to Derrida's notion of *différance*, a coinage that connotes both difference and delay; see Culler, *On Deconstruction*, p. 97.

20. Lionel Trilling, *Sincerity and Authenticity* (Cambridge, Mass., 1972), p. 62.

21. Ibid., p. 30.

22. That account, it should be noted, gives clear priority to natural over culturally designed forms of beauty. See especially Immanuel Kant, *Critique of Judgment*, trans. J. H. Bernard (New York, 1951), section 42, p. 142; and below, note 35.

23. I refer here to Mozart's well-known letter (no. 426) of September 26, 1781, to his father concerning Osmin, of *Die Entführung aus dem Serail*, in which he notes that the "passions, whether violent or not, must never be expressed [musically] to the point of exciting disgust" (Anderson, *Letters*, p. 769).

24. This section moves from the new tonic, G minor, to the relative major, B-flat, back eventually to G minor, by way of numerous brief excursions to the subdominant, C minor.

25. Trilling, *Sincerity*, pp. 12-18 and 22.

26. See, for example, ibid., pp. 23-24, 30-31, and 69-70. The phrase used by Trilling is not the "real self" but the "actual self" (p. 31).

27. Ironically, given our preoccupation here with the Queen, Trilling's extreme example of the dangers posed by sincerity to the self is Robespierre; see ibid., p. 70.

28. Ibid., p. 104. Trilling draws here on an analysis by Nathalie Sarraute. The description is of "the artist" (in this case, Flaubert) as someone who, unlike most people, has the occasional chance to elude inauthenticity. It is worth comparing with Allan Bloom's description of "true openness" as "closedness to all the charms that make us comfortable with the present" (*The Closing of the American Mind* [New York, 1987], p. 42). Bloom's "true openness" is that of the philosopher; and juxtaposed with Trilling's account, Bloom seems to be putting forward his own kind, the philosopher, as the unusual human being who can elude inauthenticity; see chapter 4 of this book, "The Closing of the American Dream?" note 116. See also this chapter, note 63, and chapter 3, notes 31, 63, and 64.

29. Trilling, *Sincerity*, p. 94. The full passage reads "a degree of rough concreteness or of extrem-

ity"; and although the notion of extremity does not fit so directly into my argument here, the extreme does share with the concrete an emphatic insistence on its own particularity. Trilling's study remains a profound contribution to the search for authenticity, which, today more than ever, seems to me the most pressing concern in analyses of contemporary Western culture. It is not just that authenticity suggests itself as a kind of value that may still hold in a relativistic world. It is also that the more we acknowledge the dependence of our thought on language, the closer we come to defining ourselves as pure social constructs, with no "self" left over, a prospect widely recognized in postmodernist theory today, and one that I myself find troubling. Adorno's skepticism as to the very possibility of musical experience (i.e., an experience of music rather than of social preconceptions thereof) strikes me a good deal more forcefully today than when I first read it. (See his *Sociology*, pp. 226-27, also 142.)

30. One could locate the realization of these fears even earlier, at the last measure of the Larghetto, when the pulses in the strings suddenly appear decisively on, rather than off, the beat (compare the rhythm of the upper strings in measures 45-46 ("Ich musste sie," etc.) with that of measure 60 ("Hilfe war," etc.).

31. This occurs directly after "der Tochter Retter sein" (will be the daughter's rescuer). Other references to the dominant, F, are even more fleeting, such as the tiny transposed orchestral motifs, reminiscent of the opening of the Jupiter symphony, that frame the last section (measures 63 and 99).

32. Significantly, the only time the Queen sings in ensemble is during the moments leading to her downfall, in the second-act finale.

33. Tamino "[i]st gleich beim Empfange des Bildes aufmerksam geworden; seine Liebe nimmt zu, ob er gleich für alle diese Reden taub schien." (Immediately on receiving the portrait, Tamino has become attentive; his love swells, although to all this talk [that has just preceded] he seemed deaf.)

34. The classic source on this development is M. H. Abrams, *The Mirror and the Lamp* (New York, 1953).

35. See especially Kant, *Critique of Judgment*, sections 6-9, pp. 45-54; and note the emphasis on form in Kant's treatment of beauty in the *Critique of Judgment*, e.g., sections 13, p. 59, and 16, p. 66. Though Kant's notion of form in relation to beauty does not correspond precisely to our own conception of structural form, the two notions involve the same fundamental aesthetic values. To be sure, Kant's implicit emphasis on structural aesthetic values was considerably more forward-looking than his explicit disdain for music as a nonrepresentational art. See also Mary Sue Morrow, "Of Unity and Passion: The Aesthetics of Concert Criticism in Early Nineteenth-Century Vienna," *19th Century Music* 13 (1990), 202-6; chapter 3, "Toward a Deconstruction of Structural Listening," p. 150, following the citation of note 8; and this chapter, note 22.

36. Kierkegaard, *Either/Or*, 1: 82.

37. Mikhail M. Bakhtin, "Discourse in the Novel," *The Dialogic Imagination: Four Essays*, ed. Michael Holquist, trans. Caryl Emerson and Michael Holquist (Austin, 1981), pp. 259-422.

38. Ibid., p. 421 note 66.

39. Ibid., pp. 262-63. Bakhtin's analysis of the novel is richly pertinent to issues raised by *The Magic Flute*. A good starting point for further study is provided by the discussions on pp. 299 and 362 of his book. On opera and prose, see below, note 87; and also chapter 2, "How Could Chopin's A-Major Prelude Be Deconstructed?" note 94.

40. See Bakhtin, *Dialogic Imagination*, for example, pp. 264, 271, 330-31, and especially 296-300. See also below, the discussion linking notes 60-63.

41. When I presented the first version of this essay at Dartmouth, a man in the audience (whom I regret I cannot identify) suggested a graceful formulation of at least one aspect of this idea: "All classes are equally capable of tragedy."

Because of the circumstances in which their country was formed, Americans may be especially prone to thinking of equality simply as an abstract condition that excludes inherited status, without concrete considerations; see chapter 4, "The Closing of the American Dream?," note 107.

Sharply relevant to this distinction, as well as to those drawn in chapter 4 between the ideals of Allan Bloom and of Spike Lee, is Isaiah Berlin's distinction between negative and positive liberty, as analyzed by the historian James M. McPherson. To use McPherson's terms and italics, negative liberty, or "freedom *from*," would be a value of the Enlightenment, and of Bloom; positive liberty, or "freedom *to*," would be associated with nineteenth-century realism, and with Lee. Berlin proposes his distinction in the essay "Two Concepts of Liberty," in his book *Four Essays on Liberty* (London, 1970), pp. 118-72. For McPherson's analysis of this distinction, thoughtfully connected to a distinction drawn by Abraham Lincoln, see his review "Liberating Lincoln," in the *New York Review of Books* 41 (April 21, 1994), 10. See also below, chapter 4, and notes 106 and 107, for another context in which this distinction is useful.

42. Carl Dahlhaus, *Realism in Nineteenth-Century Music*, trans. Mary Whittall (Cambridge, England, 1985), p. 60.

43. Kant, *Critique of Judgment*, section 45, pp. 149-50; the italics are Kant's. Worth thinking about in this connection is Mozart's description of the Piano Concertos K. 413-15 as "a happy medium between what is too easy and too difficult; they are very brilliant, pleasing to the ear, and natural, without being vapid. There are passages here and there from which connoisseurs alone can derive satisfaction; but these passages are written in such a way that the less learned cannot fail to be pleased, though without knowing why" (from the letter [no. 476] of December 28, 1782, Anderson, *Letters*, p. 833).

44. A stylistic description of the *volkstümliches Lied* as it developed in the nineteenth century is provided in my article "Lortzing and the German Romantics," p. 250. Except for the occasional chromatic alteration that would often give later songs an air of sentimentality, many of the same features can be found in Papageno's first song: relatively syllabic text settings, rounded melodic shapes, repeated notes, structural melodic sixths, and more generally, symmetrical construction and textural clarity.

45. Mozart himself makes this clear, in the letter of October 8-9, 1791, when he observes that a joke he played on Schikaneder probably "taught many of the audience for the first time that Papageno does not play the instrument himself" (Anderson, *Letters*, p. 969). Though it may seem that the audience up until this point had taken Papageno for "real," it is clear, on reflection, that what startled the audience was the intrusion of the real world (in the person of Mozart) into a fictional realm assumed to exclude reality.

46. As defined by structuralism, metaphor is taken to involve a relationship of equivalence or exchangeability (say, between [former vice president] Dan Quayle and Alexander Throttlebottom [the vice president in George Gershwin's *Of Thee I Sing*]); as a symbolic relationship, metaphor can be imagined to exist only through the ordering activity of an intelligence. Metonym is taken to involve a relationship of adjacency, whether of physical contiguity or of conventional association (both would be illustrated by the relationship between Dan Quayle and Speaker of the House Tom Foley when they presided over a joint session of Congress). As a literal rather than symbolic condition of connectedness, metonymy can be imagined as existing arbitrarily or accidentally, without the active intervention of an intelligence. That is, it can be imagined as existing in a meaningless state; though even in this formulation, as deconstruction has made us aware, the state of meaninglessness can no more be extricated from an act of imagining than, in the discussion that follows, the literal thrust of Wagner's music can be extricated from the irreducibly figurative status of that music. See also below, notes 48, 87, and 88, as well as the more extended discussion of such terms and intertwinings in chapter 2, "How Could Chopin's A-Major Prelude Be Deconstructed?" (especially note 39).

47. For a corroborative view of the gravedigging scene as a literal evocation of natural sound, see Hector Berlioz, "On Imitation in Music," trans. Jacques Barzun, in the Norton critical score of

Berlioz's *Fantastic Symphony*, ed. Edward T. Cone (New York, 1971), p. 39. Despite his rapprochement with aspects of a realistic aesthetic, Berlioz considered such literal evocations of nature an "error."

48. Thus, as I have suggested elsewhere, the world on Mozart's stage presents itself with confidence as a self-contained, meaningful analogue to the world of the audience; whereas nineteenth-century German opera seems to insist that by drawing the audience into itself, it can force the operatic experience to be meaningful. (See my essay, "Why Is Adorno's Criticism the Way It Is?," chapter 3 in *Developing Variations: Style and Ideology in Western Music* [Minneapolis, 1991], pp. 50-52 and note 9 [p. 314].) For an analogue in the relation between music and words in the operas of Mozart and of nineteenth-century German composers, see below, notes 87 and 88.

49. To the extent that they cast off Mozart's operatic surface of formally meaningful musical relationships in favor of a physically concrete musical surface, Wagner's music dramas invite comparison with later styles of painting, such as Impressionism. Relevant to this comparison, and to the one I draw elsewhere between musical poetry and musical prose (this chapter, note 87) is Dahlhaus's counterparadigm involving musical architecture versus musical language: see Carl Dahlhaus, *Between Romanticism and Modernism*, trans. Mary Whittall (Berkeley and Los Angeles, 1980), p. 69; and my own essay, "Tonality, Autonomy, and Competence," chapter 10, *Developing Variations*, especially note 13. See also this chapter, above, notes 39, 40, and 46.

50. Terry Eagleton, *Literary Theory*, p. 136. See also this volume, chapter 2, note 119, and chapter 3, note 55.

51. Theodor W. Adorno, *In Search of Wagner*, trans. Rodney Livingstone (London, 1984), p. 90. See also this volume, chapter 3, note 55.

52. In the twentieth century, as Adorno, who is preoccupied with this problem, puts it, art accepts the stricture that "in art, nothing shall pretend to be something other than it is," a notion that "shakes up the very concept of art as appearance" (see the chapter "Avant-Garde" in his *Sociology*, p. 181).

53. I use "orchestrated" here in Bakhtin's sense (see the passage from his *Dialogic Imagination*, pp. 262-63, cited above in note 39. In addition to serving the purposes of prose, Wagner's music can at times serve those of representational painting, as in the second-act brawl scene of *Meistersinger*, where fugal techniques conjure up visions of a Breughel painting.

54. Kierkegaard simply assumed that to speak of Papageno as a "child of Nature" is a lie (*Either/Or*, 1:82); his use of the term "child" here is relevant to the critique of Papageno that I am about to develop.

55. The author of the entry on "Pastoral" in the *Princeton Encyclopedia of Poetry and Poetics* concedes the appeal of Edmund Gosse's view that the "pastoral is cold, unnatural, artificial, and [that] the humblest reviewer is free to cast a stone at its dishonored grave" (p. 603).

56. Particularly in the socially self-gratifying sense given the verb "slum" in the third edition of *Webster's* dictionary, "to visit slums esp. out of curiosity or for pleasure"; the second edition defines it, more altruistically, as "to visit slums, as for study." Though the figures in Watteau's painting are not dressed as shepherds and shepherdesses, the vague and idealized landscape bears a clear relation to the pastoral sentimentalizations of its century.

57. The first definition of the noun "natural" in *Webster's* third edition is "one born without the usual powers of reason and understanding: IDIOT."

58. Mozart goes on, "But I don't think that the idiot understood my remark" (letter of October 8-9, 1791, Anderson, *Letters*, p. 969).

59. Nor are we surprised to hear his complaint "Immer still, und immer still, und immer still, und immer still!" ([They're] always [telling me to be] still!) in the Quintet in act II. Kierkegaard (*Either/Or*, 1:77) associates Papageno with "galimatias" (confused and meaningless talk).

60. Bakhtin, *Dialogic Imagination*, p. 295.

61. Ibid., p. 297. See also above, note 40.

62. Ibid., pp. 295-96, italics his.

63. Trilling, *Sincerity*, p. 104; see above, note 28.

64. Ibid.; see above, note 29.

65. Ibid., pp. 93-94.

66. For related issues, see references in the index of my earlier collection, *Developing Variations*, under the heading "temporal characteristics" (taking care to subtract two pages from all index references to endnotes, at least in the first edition).

67. This situation is analyzed at length in chapter 4, "The Closing of the American Dream?"

68. That Monostatos, and women generally, would also remain less than equal in an unchanged order seems obvious, though the scope of this essay does not permit musical analysis of such an argument here. In recent years I have offered Monostatos's aria, no. 13, as one of several pieces that students in my Music 1 course at Brown could analyze for their final paper; this assignment has produced wonderful results, both musical and critical.

On the imagery of "less equal than others," see chapter 4, "The Closing of the American Dream?," note 94.

69. See Mikhail M. Bakhtin, *Rabelais and His World*, trans. Hélène Iswolsky (Bloomington, Indiana, 1984), pp. 1-58 and 273-77. Especially suggestive for the present study is Bakhtin's account of the effect of Carnival on Goethe (pp. 244-57), including the reference therein to "the carnivalesque spirit of Hans Sachs" (pp. 245-46). See also Dan Sabbath and Mandel Hall, *End Product: The Last Taboo* (New York, 1977), pp. 265-67.

70. Einstein, *Mozart*, pp. 466-67.

71. See, for example, R. Larry Todd, "Orchestral Texture and the Art of Orchestration," in *The Orchestra: Origins and Transformation*, ed. Joan Peyser (New York, 1986), pp. 197-202. In the discussion that follows, I will use the term "winds" more or less generically to include all blowing instruments. Supportive of this usage (and suggestive for my argument) is Todd's description, (p. 192) of an instrumentation manual of the latter eighteenth century that presents a "systematic discussion of the ranges and special properties of the winds—without differentiation between woodwind and brass—organized into chapters on flute, oboe, clarinet, horn, bassoon, trumpet, and the human voice."

72. In the formulation of this sentence that appears in the *Nineteenth Century Music* version, the word "that" was accidentally deleted between "nature" and "constitutes" (p. 145).

73. Stravinsky implicitly recognized this bracing effect of other instruments during the period when he avoided the violin. Adorno evokes related imagery in connection with the power of individual pitches in certain dissonant sonorities to maintain their discreteness. See his *Philosophy of Modern Music*, trans. Anne G. Mitchell and Wesley V. Blomster (New York, 1973), pp. 85-86, and also 59. Adorno calls this the power to "dissonate" (p. 86). His original German term is *dissonieren*; see T. W. Adorno, *Philosophie der neuen Musik* (Frankfurt, 1958), p. 84. See also note 79 below.

Interestingly, Adorno connects this phenomenon to the Hegelian process of *Aufhebung* (on which see this volume, chapter 2, note 18). In the English version of *Philosophy* he writes, "In a sound consisting of several tones, dissonance is suspended only in the sense of an Hegelian double meaning" (pp. 85-86). The original German reads, "Im mehrtönigen Klang ist die Dissonanz aufgehoben einzig im Hegelschen Doppelsinn" (*Philosophie*, p. 84).

74. See note 35 above.

75. On Kant see *Critique of Judgment*, section 13, pp. 58-59. Compare also Kierkegaard's admiring view, *Either/Or*, 1:82: "[Papageno's] first aria considered musically . . . is only history in a figurative sense. The chime of bells, on the other hand, is the musical expression for his activity, of which one can only get an understanding through music: it is charming, tempting, entrancing, alluring."

76. Dahlhaus, *Realism*, pp. 29-43.

77. The description here, taken from Dahlhaus, *Realism*, p. 35, is itself quoting from Hermann von Waltershausen's book *Der Freischütz* (Munich, 1920).

78. See measure 97, Adagio, in the overture, and also number 9a at the beginning of the second act, "Der dreimalige Accord" (the thrice-sounded chord).

79. Such a pattern has been characteristic in many ways of Western art since the nineteenth century, for example, in the "tradition of the new." Some examples are cited under the heading of "analogy of difference" in the index to my *Developing Variations*. See also note 73 above, on Adorno.

80. Einstein, *Mozart*, pp. 466-67.

81. Relevant in this connection is Ernst Bloch's "Magic Rattle, Human Harp," in his *Essays on the Philosophy of Music*, trans. Peter Palmer (Cambridge, 1985), pp. 140-45. Bloch asserts that over time, the magic powers once associated with music as an emanation inseparable from a physical instrument gave way to the hearing of music as a discrete symbolic structure. The singer, however, is a "remnant" of the old magic: "*by means of the singer*, the melismatic and even the symphonic elusiveness of music finds itself placed in an operatic scene and the action which this localises" (p. 143, italics his). That is to say, by means of the singer this magic is salvaged and transformed in opera, where "music is attached to the material of its instruments, being the sound and speech of this very material" (p. 144). Bloch concludes (p. 145): "The archaic magic of the object [is replaced by] a kind of intrinsic magic of the material. [This] . . . enables opera music to have its issue in a human world portrayed on the stage and to transform the pan-pipe, or the harp [i.e. singer] into actors; these, however, now *voice human material*. They are serving the music above them—with the limiting ideal of the entire theatre itself as a magic flute" (italics his). See also Roland Barthes, "The Grain of the Voice," *The Responsibility of Forms: Critical Essays on Music, Art and Representation*, trans. Richard Howard (New York, 1985), pp. 267-77.

82. See Arthur Lovejoy, *The Great Chain of Being* (Cambridge, Mass., 1936), p. 288, and chapter 10 generally. On diversitarianism, see ibid., p. 294.

83. Precisely this imagery resonates at the center of discussions today concerning multiculturalism and the educational curriculum. Near the end of an essay entitled "The Battle for American History," for example, Bernard A. Weisberger writes: "I know there are people who defend multiple voices—that's the very point of the multi-centrists—but I think they may mistake cacophony for a democratic chorus. . . . Right now we lack the culture to produce . . . sweet concord." See *Columbia College Today* 18 (Spring/Summer, 1991), 15; and above, note 7.

84. In his *French Instrumental Music between the Revolutions (1789-1830)* (Ph.D. diss., Columbia University, 1950), Boris Schwarz points to a related ideal in France, of "democracy for the qualified." I owe this information to a paper entitled "The Composition of Women in the Paris Conservatory," given by Romy Kozak of Stanford University at the Conference on Feminist Theory and Music (University of Minnesota, June, 1991).

85. Lang also liked to argue (in his graduate seminars at Columbia) that, thanks to its dramatic character, the *Requiem* was Mozart's last opera.

86. In this connection, it would be interesting to see whether the wind sonorities in *The Magic Flute* and the sounds of the wind parts added in Mozart's reworking of Handel's *Messiah* (1789) suggest these two works, in some palpable fashion, as companion conceptions. On the metaphorical distinction between Catholic inclusiveness and Protestant exclusiveness see my essay "Ideology in the Study of Western Music," in *Developing Variations*, p. 12, especially the reference to Robert Bellah in note 8 (p. 302). See also this volume, chapter 4, note 93.

87. Though Dahlhaus insists that realism "was never the dominant style in music at any point in the nineteenth century" (*Realism*, p. 120), he connects "the compositional techniques of musical prose, '*dialogisierte Melodie*,' [and] the sacrifices of stylization to expressivity" (ibid., p. 122) with many operas in the nineteenth and early twentieth centuries. (See also above, note 39.)

There is, of course, a paradox in attributing realism to a musical medium that was itself becoming ever more opaque. In the verbal domain, one associates an immediate and opaque (musical!) richness of language with the relative lack of realism in poetry; whereas prose seems to derive its effect of realism from a transparency that allows language to point away from itself toward a discrete conceptual meaning. Yet the beauty of traditional poetry resided in the tension between its language—its figures, its conceits, its rhetoric—and conceptual ideals of structural coherence; by contrast, the ideal of sensuousness in Romantic poetry could well be characterized as responsive to values of concreteness epitomized in the content and aesthetic of prose. Moreover, prose became a culturally dominant medium precisely as the tension between language and meaning moved toward a condition of collapse, so that realism came to involve less the act of conjuring up a metaphorically alternative world *through* art and more the metonymical embodiment of such a world *in* art. (See above, notes 46, 48, and also 49 [especially on Dahlhaus's counterparadigm].) From this standpoint, it could be said that poetry after the Enlightenment tried to maintain its own possibility by invoking the means of prose; an analogy with abstract and programmatic musical conceptions seems plausible.

For a related model of the relation between music and language during the nineteenth century, see my essay "The Cultural Message of Musical Semiology," chapter 9 in *Developing Variations*, especially pp. 173-89. See also this volume, chapter 2, note 94.

88. Again, this distinction with respect to the relation of opera music to a verbal paradigm of content suggests the distinction made earlier with respect to the relation of opera to its audience (see above, note 48). In both instances, the relevant relationship in Mozart is one of metaphorical equivalence; in nineteenth-century opera, it is one of metonymical contiguity.

89. No. 39 (measures 53-68 and 125-29, both in the winds); and no. 40 (the opening in the strings, and the wind passages at measures 68-70).

90. For Wagner's classic description (using the image of Columbus) of Beethoven's symphonies sailing on a sea of longing toward "the word," see the translated excerpt from Wagner's *Das Kunstwerk der Zukunft* [1850] in Oliver Strunk, *Source Readings in Music History* (New York, 1950), pp. 891-95.

91. Kierkegaard, *Either/Or*, 1:81.

92. Ibid. Contrast Kierkegaard's priorities here with Allan Bloom's Platonic ones (this volume, chapter 4, note 138).

93. Ibid., p. 82. The passage continues, "And consequently its whole trend is to do away with music, while still remaining an opera." It is by invoking a contrast to the Enlightenment principles represented by Tamino that I am trying to emphasize the opposite about this opera—its immersion in the immediacy of sound.

94. Kierkegaard, *Either/Or*, 1:51-53. Hegel himself, who mocked Weber's *Freischütz* while championing Rossini, did not accept the musical consequences of his own historically oriented philosophy. See Dahlhaus, *Realism*, pp. 34-35.

95. Kierkegaard, *Either/Or*, 1:80.

96. Edward Said, in a similar way, attributes to Joseph Conrad a reading of *Heart of Darkness* that Conrad could not have anticipated. "Conrad's self-consciously circular narrative forms draw attention to themselves as artificial constructions, encouraging us to sense the potential of a reality that seemed inaccessible to imperialism, just beyond its control, and that only well after Conrad's death in 1924 acquired a substantial presence." See Edward W. Said, *Culture and Imperialism* (New York, 1993), pp. 28-29; interestingly, Said presents this view in the course of deriving two different possible readings of imperialism from Conrad's work (ibid., p. 25). Though the times and political stakes are different, Said's point here, like mine, seems to be that through "formal devices" (p. 28), certain (good) authors can create the basis for a later reading that does not simply exclude them from a positive claim on their own work; that an author's formal choices can in some instances hold their own as a direct source of meaning in a changing world; that historical change does not

always require us to read older works violently against the grain in order to make a moral interpretation, or to treat an author condescendingly because he or she failed to live forever.

To allow for such a possibility is far different, of course, from insisting indiscriminately that any author can or should control all readings of his or her own works, everywhere and for all time. Certainly this is not Said's position; and likewise clearly, I hope, my own work took shape in no small measure to counter this stance, which until fairly recently dominated musicology. See chapter 2 of the present volume, note 8, for example.

Adorno provides a rich discussion of the relationship between the composer's consciousness, the score, and subsequent readings, and especially of ways in which the work can outstrip the author's consciousness, in his essay "Bach Defended against his Devotees," which appears in Theodor W. Adorno, *Prisms*, trans. Samuel and Shierry Weber (London, 1967), pp. 135-46. Especially relevant are pp. 141 and 143-46. See, for example, p. 141: "Nowhere is it written that the conception that a composer has of his music must coincide with its intrinsic nature, with the objective law peculiar to it"; and p. 144: "The musical score is never identical with the work; devotion to the text means the constant effort to grasp that which it hides." On p. 145 Adorno suggests that where Bach left the choice of instruments open in the *Musical Offering* and the *Art of Fugue*, he sensed a contradiction between his musical ideas and the sounds available for them, and therefore "left his most mature instrumental works waiting for the sound that would suit them." Such images strongly evoke the deconstructionist formulation of a text "not identical with itself." See chapter 2, note 52.

2. How Could Chopin's A-Major Prelude Be Deconstructed?

1. Michel Foucault, "What Is an Author?" *Textual Strategies: Perspectives in Post-Structuralist Criticism*, ed. Josué V. Harari (Ithaca, 1979), p. 153.

2. Of particular interest, in my judgment, is "Listening," published in *The Responsibility of Forms: Critical Essays on Music, Art, and Representation*, trans. Richard Howard (New York, 1985), pp. 245-60.

3. See, for example, Jacques Derrida, *La Vérité en peinture* (Paris, 1978); and Roland Barthes, "Is Painting a Language?" in *The Responsibility of Forms*, pp. 149-52.

4. See Edmundo Desnoes, "Will You Ever Shave Your Beard?" *On Signs*, ed. Marshall Blonsky (Baltimore, 1985), pp. 12-15.

5. It should be noted, however, that from Derrida's own standpoint, any usage of language is in effect "always already" the product of translation; and thus translation is an archetypal process of reading even within a single language. Such a conception seems by definition to encourage musical "translations" of deconstructionist theory. For further information on this point, see the translator's preface to Derrida's *Of Grammatology*, trans. Gayatri Chakravorty Spivak (Baltimore, 1976), pp. lxxxvi-lxxxvii. (Derrida's position here seems in marked contrast to Adorno's insistence on preserving the particularities of a text from social neutralization; yet clearly the two are concerned in this respect with a common domain of issues. See chapter 4, "The Closing of the American Dream?" note 146.) See also Barthes, "Is Painting a Language?" pp. 151-52, where Barthes specifically warns against such notions as "'applying' linguistics to the picture, injecting a little semiology into art history." Barthes's main point is to undercut the distinction between object and method in order to emphasize the involvement of both within an ongoing process of interpretation. From this perspective, distinctions between the "objects" in diverse mediums are not significant. Barthes' argument here seems to me important and appealing. Though I do at times in this essay use the word "application" in precisely the sense he rejects, I am not sure I would want to defend this usage as anything more than a convenient shorthand.

6. The exclamation points that will from time to time appear in brackets in this discussion are

indicators of terms used in full awareness of their dependence on a fundamental contradiction. In the present instance, for example, I express a desire not to be misconstrued even as I make use of a theory, deconstruction, that defines the possibility of misconstruction as inseparable from the possibility of communication. Because I cannot discuss every such instance, I have resorted to this shorthand of exclamation points. The reader will undoubtedly identify many similar instances where I failed to provide this marking. Together, these present and absent exclamation points can be taken to indicate loci at which a deconstruction of my own argument might begin.

7. My comparison of Adorno and Lévi-Strauss appears in "The Historical Structure: Adorno's 'French' Model for the Criticism of Nineteenth-Century Music," which can be found in my earlier book, *Developing Variations: Style and Ideology in Western Music* (Minneapolis, 1991), pp. 206-38. A good starting point for pursuing a comparison of Adorno and poststructuralism can be found in an essay by Rainer Nägele, "The Scene of the Other: Theodor W. Adorno's Negative Dialectic in the Context of Poststructuralism," in *Postmodernism and Politics*, ed. Jonathan Arac (Minneapolis, 1986), pp. 91-111.

8. The piece to be analyzed is Chopin's A-Major Prelude, Opus 28, number 7. I am using the version in the Norton critical score of Chopin's *Preludes, Op. 28*, ed. Thomas Higgins (New York, 1973), p. 18. For the score of the piece itself, see the beginning of section IV.

We begin here a characteristically deconstructionist play with images of infinite regress that will pervade this essay. Here I am saying that deconstruction alleges that no text is to be taken at face value. But why should we take that allegation itself at face value? Why should we believe the assertions of a theory aimed at making us doubt the assertions of all texts? Deconstruction is fully aware of such paradoxes, which are of a kind central to the definition of deconstructionist concerns with language. (To be sure, deconstruction would no doubt question the very term "face value," in the sense that it implies some ontologically constant aspect to a text, which deconstruction itself denies. See also below, pp. 54-55, and notes 27-28.)

Though in the present instance I emphasize limits on the degree to which, in effect, an author can expect to control readings of his or her own text, I am not arguing here for the rejection of all authorial claims on the reader. The tension between the possibilities of disregarding or rejecting an author's own reading, and of privileging that reading, lies at the heart of this chapter; see also this volume, chapter 1, note 96.

9. I discuss some aspects of this notion in *Developing Variations*, chapter 3, pp. 45-47, chapter 9, notes 30-31, and chapter 12, pp. 268-71, especially note 11; see also in the present volume, pp. 106-9, 124, and 132, as well as p. 152, between notes 17 and 18. On the conflation of theme and structure or status, see also this chapter, notes 11, 152, and 155, and chapter 4, notes 10 and 103.

10. Jonathan Culler, *On Deconstruction: Theory and Criticism after Structuralism* (Ithaca, 1982), p. 202. The ghost of Gödel, of course, is never far from such formulations.

11. Revising this essay in 1994, I must confess to weariness at a way in which the term "about" has become overused in the popular media. Take the following, perhaps archetypal sentence from an article by Donna Britt entitled "Advice from a Prude: Play It Safe, Not Sorry," in *Newsday*, July 7, 1994, p. A 34: "Like homicide, AIDS is often about choices." Though the ostensible goal of this sentence, as the title of the article indicates, is to encourage responsible choices, notice how the actual language makes it possible to suppose that homicide is an agentless crime. As my husband says of this sentence—an analysis particularly apt to the present chapter—the subject is absent. Clearly this usage of "about" constitutes a postmodernist attempt to deconstruct older notions of causality, showing them to be overly narrow and simplistic ways of construing reality; and the ubiquitousness of the usage indicates the degree to which our ways of thinking have in fact been altered. No doubt when the term first emerged it had a salutary effect on our critical consciousness; but by now it has lost its edge and become neutralized. In my judgment, a small but significant move toward precision and responsibility in public discourse would result from an extended moratorium on this use of the term "about." In reality we shall have to wait until this

mode of constructing reality becomes unfashionable. See also later in this chapter, p. 79, on President Clinton and Ray Charles. On the conflation of theme and structure or status see this chapter, notes 9, 152, and 155, and chapter 4, note 103.

12. A suspicion will perhaps raise itself here that my perception of a continuity between Romantic and deconstructionist imagery is little too convenient—that either out of naïveté or cynicism I found the theme I needed to find. But does the continuity "really" lie in the "objects" of my examination? Or in my eye as a beholder? The most succinct answer I can give to such a question is my long-standing conviction that the "object" and the "eye" can only be construed together, as part of an ongoing dialectic in which the "eye" is primary[!]. On a broader scale, the most persuasive answer I can give to this objection is the present essay in its entirety.

13. The political parameter of scholarship has been analyzed with great eloquence by Terry Eagleton in the last chapter of his *Literary Theory: An Introduction* (Minneapolis, 1983), pp. 194-217. When I first read this book, at a time when I felt utterly isolated in my academic convictions, I was particularly moved by his assertion (p. 210) that the *strategic* or political conception of reading "means asking first not *what* the object is or *how* we should approach it, but *why* we should want to engage with it in the first place" (italics his).

14. See, for example, Theodor W. Adorno, *Introduction to the Sociology of Music*, trans. E. B. Ashton (New York, 1976), p. 197. Adorno's political objections to both Wagner and Stravinsky are inseparable from his perception of grave structural flaws in their music. See also below, chapter 3, the text cited in note 32. As opposed to breaks in structure, breaks in style or medium, insofar as they reflect inadequacies of society, are unavoidable. (See this chapter, pp. 47-48, text leading to note 17; chapter 3, note 63, and also notes 20, 32, 33, and p. 164, the text leading to notes 54 and 55; and chapter 4, note 146.) Stylistic smoothness can usually be taken as a mark of bad faith, though see Adorno's remarks (concerning Mozart's smoothness) in his *Sociology*, pp. 69-70 (I start chapter 1 with a quotation from this passage). See also ibid., p. 70: "The end of music as an ideology will have to await the end of antagonistic society."

15. See especially his *Sociology*, pp. 202 and 211-12; also 64-65.

16. Martin Jay, *The Dialectical Imagination: A History of the Frankfurt School and the Institute of Social Research, 1923-1950* (Boston, 1973), p. 57.

17. See note 14, above. For a more extended treatment of the relationship between sound and structure in Adorno's theory, see chapter 3, especially notes 33 and 47, and pp. 154 and 161-62.

18. Hegel's term *Aufhebung*, generally translated as "sublation," refers to the dialectical movement of argument, and ultimately of the absolute spirit working itself out in history, from earlier stages of thesis and antithesis into a third stage of synthesis—a stage constituting a new and higher level of the process, at which a new dialectical "triad" can begin. As put by various dictionaries of philosophy, the movement into synthesis "preserves what is rational in [thesis and antithesis], but cancels what is irrational" (see "Hegel" in Antony Flew, *A Dictionary of Philosophy* [New York, 1979], p. 130); that is, "the supreme category (synthesis) of the thought process both cancels the antithesis and retains in a processed form the entire content of previous development" (see "Sublation," *Dictionary of Philosophy*, ed. and trans. from the Russian by Murad Saifulin and Richard R. Dixon [New York, 1984], p. 408). Thus the notion of *Aufhebung* is defined as having aspects both of cancellation (say, annihilation) and preservation (say, transcendence); and dialectical analyses sometimes emphasize one moment or the other. See also this chapter, note 53; and chapter 1, note 73. On Derrida and the concept of *Aufhebung*, see the essay "*Différance*" in his book *Margins of Philosophy*, trans. and ed. Alan Bass (Chicago, 1982), pp. 19-20 (Derrida's own remarks and the translator's addition, note 23).

19. For more of Adorno's ideas about art and utopia see his *Sociology*, pp. 44, 46, 115, 133, 142, 215-17, and 224. The term "utopia" itself does not always appear in these discussions.

20. See "The Historical Structure," cited in note 7, this chapter.

21. In retrospect, a deconstructionist procedure also seems evident in my essay "Evidence of a

Critical Worldview in Mozart's Last Three Symphonies," *Developing Variations*, pp. 98-111. Note also the following sentence, which appears in my essay "Romantic Music as Post-Kantian Critique: Classicism, Romanticism, and the Concept of the Semiotic Universe," *Developing Variations*, pp. 127-28: "It is as if [R]omantic music [like Kant's *Critique of Judgment*] revealed a disjunction between . . . two autonomous yet incomplete modes of comprehension to be inherent in semiotic processes." At the time this was written, I don't think I'd ever even heard of deconstruction. Without in any way proposing my own work as a touchstone for sorting out directions in later twentieth-century critical theory, I myself have come to find in this self-discovery of a deconstructionist perspective strong evidence of a fundamental continuity of concerns between the work of Adorno, who has shaped my thinking in a variety of ways, and deconstruction.

22. John Searle, "The Word Turned Upside Down," *New York Review of Books* 30, no. 16 (October 27, 1983), 78, note 3. Though the quotation is unattributed, Searle himself continues, in the same note, "We cannot, of course, exclude the possibility that this may be an expression of praise in the deconstructionist vocabulary." Searle's inability to resist including both the unattributed quote and his own witticism not only confirms his observation that "deconstruction ha[s] found little appeal among professional philosophers" (which I suppose means analytic philosophers), but also captures a shabbiness of tone that I have often observed, with some sadness, in objections made by analytic philosophers to schools they "know" to be wrong (i.e., that they do not like).

23. De Man's conception of blindness is analyzed at length in his *Blindness and Insight: Essays in the Rhetoric of Contemporary Criticism,* 2nd rev. ed. (Minneapolis, 1983). A shorter piece by de Man will figure importantly in the present essay. This is his "Semiology and Rhetoric," found in *Textual Strategies*, pp. 121-24, a so-called classic essay that I have found wonderfully illuminating and suggestive for the analysis of music. It may be worth noting here that my reliance on de Man took its entire shape before the controversies over his Nazi collaborationism and other matters became public knowledge. The dark side of de Man's career has naturally concerned me since I learned about it. The general problem of evaluating texts by authors who have espoused immoral positions, as in the case of Wagner, has been of importance to me at least as far back as my article "The Role of Ideology in the Study of Western Music" (in *Developing Variations*, pp. 3-14). De Man's case in particular has more recently attracted my attention through its prominence in Edward W. Said's *Musical Elaborations* (New York, 1991), pp. 35-40 and 51, a book I review in the *Journal of the American Musicological Association* 46 (Fall 1993), 476-85. At present I am still working out for myself the implications for scholarship of the unfortunate revelations about de Man's past. See also later in this chapter pp. 74-75, as well as notes 45 and 142.

24. On this joy—Barthes's famous, untranslatable *jouissance*—see especially the article by Roland Barthes, "From Work to Text," in *Textual Strategies*, p. 80. For specific musical associations with this term see Barthes's "The Grain of the Voice" in *Image-Music-Text*, trans. Stephen Heath (New York, 1977), pp. 179 and 183 (the French term is not retained in the translation of this essay that appears in Barthes's *The Responsibility of Forms*, trans. Richard Howard [New York, 1985], pp. 268 ["ecstasy"] and 271 ["enjoyment"]). For more on this term, as contrasted with *plaisir*, see the translator's note in *Image-Music-Text*, p. 9. On Jacques Lacan's role in generating this term see the translator's preface to Michel Poizat, *The Angel's Cry: Beyond the Pleasure Principle in Opera*, trans. Arthur Denner (Ithaca, 1992), p. xiii. See also Eagleton, *Literary Theory*, p. 212, on the topic of pleasure more generally; and chapter 3 of this volume, note 82.

25. The definitive discussion of this notion appears in Derrida's essay *"Différance,"* pp. 1-27 (see this chapter, note 18).

26. Or unless we are utterly unable or unwilling to develop a capacity for entertaining fundamental contradictions in our readings of the world—a capacity that, at least until the arrival of postmodernism as an active American academic movement, has seemed to come much more easily to European than to American schools of thought.

27. A useful (and somewhat surprising) introduction to the relation of "being" and "meaning," as that relation concerns deconstruction, can be found in Jacques Derrida's essay "The Supplement of Copula: Philosophy *before* Linguistics," in *Textual Strategies*, pp. 82-120. This article shows how schools of thought that posit language as prior to thought are caught in the same patterns of infinite regress as those that take a more "essentialist" position. Also worth close attention is the rich, though somewhat opaque, discussion of the relationships between "being," "meaning," and "history" that cluster around the notion of *différance* in Derrida's essay *"Différance,"* pp. 21-27. Differences between essentialist and existential views of reality have had, of course, an enormous impact on the history of Western philosophy. They are central to the tensions in our own century between Anglo-American and Continental schools of thought, and also to many nonacademic conflicts. As they are used to account for the sanctity of life, for instance, the two ways of thinking point toward greatly differing attitudes on vital public issues. See T. M. Scanlon's review of *Life's Dominion: An Argument about Abortion, Euthanasia, and Individual Freedom* by Ronald Dworkin, *New York Review of Books* 49 (July 15, 1993), especially p. 49, where Scanlon contrasts a respect for life based on "the natural (or even divine) creative capacity . . . invested in [life]" with one based on "the creative human capacity . . . invested in defining and living it." See this chapter, note 145.

28. An elegant analysis of this assertion can be found in Umberto Eco's essay, "How Culture Conditions the Colours We See," in *On Signs*, ed. Marshall Blonsky (Baltimore, 1985), pp. 157-75.

29. Barthes, "Is Painting a Language?" p. 150 (italics his).

30. For a thoughtful and more extended treatment of the issues involved here, see Culler, *On Deconstruction*, pp. 132, 199, and 280. See also Derrida, *"Différance,"* p. 11, on the relation between *"différance"* and the "possibility of conceptuality."

31. This assertion bears a certain resemblance to Adorno's vision of subjective integrity as already alienated from itself by the act of articulation through a medium. And, indeed, Adorno frequently uses images such as "trace" and "ghost" to describe the self-protective flight of the subject away from sound toward silence. See, for example, his essay "Arnold Schoenberg 1874-1951," in *Prisms*, trans. Samuel and Shierry Weber (London, 1967), pp. 168 and 170; and my own discussion in "Adorno's Diagnosis of Beethoven's Late Style: Early Symptom of a Fatal Condition," *Journal of the American Musicological Society* 29 (1976), 256 and 270. Of course, there is an important difference in tone between the two usages of "trace." Whereas deconstruction is content simply to point out the supraindividual condition of language, Adorno locates in that condition the grounds for the tragic history of Western society. On the relation between "trace" and consciousness, see the citation to Derrida below, note 53. The notion of "trace," it should be added, also figures prominently in the theories of Mikhail M. Bakhtin. See, for example, *The Dialogic Imagination: Four Essays*, ed. Michael Holquist, trans. Caryl Emerson and Michael Holquist (Austin, 1981), p. 276. See also this chapter, notes 49 and 56, on the so-called death or disappearance of the author.

32. For a complete citation see chapter 4, "The Closing of the American Dream?" note 170.

33. This may sound like the "free marketplace of ideas," and thus seem a tribute to empirical as opposed to dialectical traditions of thought. Yet the empirically oriented departments that for years dominated the American academy (again, until the recent explosion of postmodernist, radically relativistic schools of thought) tended traditionally to "specialize"—that is, to make room only for those who shared the same empirically oriented viewpoint. Just as the very act of recognizing dialectical relationships undermines the priority of empirical premises, so, too, perhaps hiring a colleague with an opposing viewpoint is seen by empirical schools as tantamount to a fatal concession, an act that violates the very principle on which such schools rest and thus calls those principles into question. In any case, the academic tradition based on the empirical ideal of the free marketplace of ideas in actuality operated like a regulated market. The exclusionary effects of this system bear much responsibility for the divisiveness and anger, prominent on American campuses in the 1990s, over "hegemonic" practices.

The underlying epistemological issue is that empirical schools tend to call "truth" (the one and only) what dialectical schools—or at least those that aim at a rigorously self-critical attitude—are more willing to call "a viewpoint." (I grant a problem here; see this chapter, note 63.) The same issue figures centrally in my analyses of *The Magic Flute* and the work of Allan Bloom and Spike Lee, found elsewhere in this volume.

34. What I will argue, in effect, is that although the prelude cannot literally guarantee either the preservation or the overriding importance of a particular original meaning, it can be read as pointing to those and other values of its own culture, as if they formed its content or theme.

35. The version I am using is to be found in the Norton critical score of Chopin's *Preludes, Op. 28*, ed. Thomas Higgins (New York, 1973), p. 18.

36. See, for example, "Romantic Music as Post-Kantian Critique," *Developing Variations*, especially pp. 120-28, also p. 135.

37. Culler ends *On Deconstruction*, on p. 280, by acknowledging the attraction of American deconstructionist criticism to works of "the canon" on precisely such grounds.

38. Is it not through some such pattern of endless reversibility between counterpoint and harmony, etc., that the history of Western art music is traditionally explained? It has for many years been evident that the conflicts dividing musical and musicological schools of thought involved the same issues underlying the conflict between opponents of quotas and partisans of affirmative action—a conflict that has itself exploded into American public consciousness in the 1990s.

39. The example of hot dogs and mustard can be used to illustrate not only physical adjacence and conventional association but also the cultural contingency of the latter. My children's social circles utterly reject this once all-American combination. Instead, they have made a metaphorical substitution of ketchup for mustard, thereby producing a metonymical pair that my own friends find inedible. See also chapter 1, note 46. For clarification of the differences between my essentially poststructuralist treatment of metaphor and metonym in this volume and the essentially structuralist treatment of these concepts in my previous one, see *Developing Variations*, chapter 4, note 12. As originally associated with the syntagmatic (as opposed to paradigmatic) axis of language, the contiguity of metonym was defined in terms of significant sequences or recognized orders of words. From this perspective the image pointed toward the logic of syntax, whereas poststructuralism has consistently emphasized the arbitrariness of contiguity.

40. Eagleton, *Literary Theory*, p. 133.

41. It was Schoenberg's clear grasp of this semiotic condition that led him to label certain voices as "*Hauptstimme*" (main voice)" and "*Nebenstimme*" ([principal] subordinate voice). For in rejecting tonality, Schoenberg had lost recourse to the ingrained Western perception of a "double level of articulation" in music, that is, to the more or less automatic, simultaneous perception of a syntactical background, against which particular usages can be construed as foreground. Charles Rosen is among those who have noted the facility with which a composer such as Haydn was able to play on this assumed distinction to create ambiguities within the particular foreground between theme (main idea) and accompanimental figure (subordinate idea). See Charles Rosen, *The Classical Style* (New York, 1972), pp. 116-17. On the relations of syntax and tone in the perception of verbal meanings, see Oliver Sacks, "The President's Speech," *The Man Who Mistook His Wife for a Hat and Other Clinical Tales* (New York, 1985), pp. 80-84. See this volume, chapter 3, note 79, and also the references to "dual structure" in the index to *Developing Variations*.

42. One begins to sense in this vision the validity of Bakhtin's assertion that the "problem of double-voiced parodic and ironic discourse (more accurately, its analogues) in opera, in music, in choreography . . . is extremely interesting." (*The Dialogic Imagination*, p. 421, note 66.)

43. This is not to deny that deconstructionist critics are as susceptible as anyone else to epistemological assumptions that will characteristically draw them, in a first reading, toward the perception of certain kinds of principles rather of others. It is merely to say that an honest (or at least consistent) deconstructionist will try to resist turning those predilections into the basis of a general theory.

44. See this chapter, note 29, and the text to which it corresponds. Barthes's formulation crystallizes neatly something of the identity—or perhaps more accurately, the inseparability—I am trying to propose here between "being" and "meaning" (see this chapter, note 27 and text to which it corresponds). I have toyed endlessly with the phrase "meaningful physical constancy," to ensure the clarity of what I believe to be my meaning, and find myself coming up again and again against internested paradoxes that confirm my growing suspicions about the limits our language places upon our ability to mean.

Would it be better to say "meaningfully physical constancy"? Or "physically meaningful constancy"? What I do *not* mean to imply is a distinction between a "physically meaningful" constancy and a constancy that is "physically existent though meaningless." Rather, I mean to imply meaningfulness as a condition for being able to speak of physical constancy; in other words, I would doubt the very possibility of defining physical constancy as a condition apart from the interpretive processes that allow such constancy to be perceived as such.

If we cannot define or speak of it, it is meaningless (nonexistent) for us. At most we can speak of physical constancy as a kind of asymptote approached by the convergence of many different interpretations. The practical relevance of such distinctions can be suggested by a few simple examples. Would "Old Ironsides" be more physically constant if every nail had not been replaced? Is there an essential difference, from the standpoint of Jewish observance, between using only tableware that has always been divided into milk and meat categories, and using tableware that at some later point in its existence was divided into those categories? Can we speak of physical constancy in a piece of Gregorian chant that no one "knows" how to perform?

Of course, the notion of "physical existence" is obviously problematical in mediums, such as music, that depend heavily on physical acts of reconstitution. But even in the visual arts, where the physical integrity of the "object" seems paramount, and where acts of interpretation take place mainly in the mind, it is possible to conceive of works, such as certain paintings by Mantegna, that continue to "exist" because they are still perceived as meaningful entities, even though they have literally been destroyed. Especially intriguing evidence for the problematical ontological status of the visual is provided by Oliver Sacks in his article "To See and Not to See," *New Yorker*, (May 10, 1993), 59-73. Sacks describes how a fifty-year-old man, having undergone successful cataract surgery after forty-five years of blindness, recovers the capacity to take in visual stimuli but remains largely unable to see objects. See this chapter, note 55.

45. It can be asked, of course, why I should worry about the moral implications of my actions if, as poststructuralism emphasizes, my text can be dissociated from my authorship and still make sense to a reader. (This is the same issue I raised earlier [note 23] in connection with de Man.) The answer seems to me fairly straightforward. To the extent that my reader and I share a common understanding of language, I cannot be sure that immoral meanings I have projected may not be discerned by and influence my reader.

Granted, this may seem a pigheadedly difficult reversal of assumptions ordinarily made about reading. Nevertheless, it seems fair to say that the unavoidable contingency of communication is not equivalent to its impossibility. That is to say, the unavoidability of some misreading—the inevitable loss of *some* meanings—does not exclude the possibility of some successful communication. Indeed, I will be at great pains in this essay to preserve some value for "original," generally transmittable, abstract structures of argument as a pole in the semiotic process.

A more interesting epistemological question is this: If my texts can be detached from myself, and still have meaning for a reader, where is the meaning? Are we to believe that texts are not "really" semiotically neutral or meaningless objects "in themselves," but rather carry with them some "embedded" (or, as we now say, "inscribed") meaning?

The only answer one can give to such a question is that we cannot know the answer. Because texts are not readable in the absence of a reader (indeed, the text is an archetype of Kant's *Ding an sich*), it can never be established with certainty (either metaphysical or scientific) whether the meaning "really" inheres in the text "itself" or in the actions of the reader.

Given the unavailability of a definitive answer, along with our lack of access to texts "in themselves," and our inability to extricate ourselves from our presence as readers, it seems to me more persuasive, at least in terms of experience, to "locate" meaning in relation to a reader. (Bakhtin's assertion in *The Dialogic Imagination*, p. 293, that "there are no 'neutral' words and forms—words and forms that can belong to 'no one,'" obviously assumes the presence of someone who "hears" earlier cultural imprints on language. Even Blonsky's suggestion [*On Signs*, p. xiv, note 3], in effect, that words can be propelled outward—whether by some instinctive expressive capacity or by the force of preexisting language—without any immediate meaning, implies forcefully that meaning awaits a listener.) See also this chapter, note 56, on the death of the author.

46. See p. 12, note 14, in the translation by Alan Bass of Derrida's article "*Différance*" (the italics are Bass's). Seminal discussion by Derrida of the notion of "supplement" can be found in *Of Grammatology*, pp. 141-57 and 195-229. The latter passage is probably his best-known writing on music. Both passages focus on Rousseau.

47. See Spivak's preface to Derrida, *Of Grammatology*, pp. xxx-xxxiii.

48. The classic poststructuralist articulation of this position appears in Roland Barthes, "From Work to Text," *Textual Strategies*, pp. 73-81.

49. This issue has received considerable prominence through the debate over whether the colorization of films made in black and white should be allowed. Although texts pass beyond the power of authors to control the ways in which they are read, it does not of course follow that knowledge of the author's identity plays no part in the readings that are made. On the contrary, I would guess that most of the conscious readings we give to verbal texts (we make many other readings more or less automatically) are thoroughly preconditioned by our preconceived estimation of the author's importance—or to be more precise, of the author's institutional affiliation. Letters written under prestigious letterheads get taken more seriously than letters that lack such letterheads. The more emphatic either our reverence or our disdain for the source of a communication, the more problematic becomes the process of trying to evaluate the structure and content of that communication "objectively." See also the distinction between structure and style noted in this chapter, note 59; and note 56, on the death of the author.

50. During his unsuccessful interview by the Senate for a position on the United States Supreme Court, Judge Robert Bork invoked the notion of "mere background assumptions" in relation to *Brown vs. Board of Education* (a decision he supported). Unfortunately, the transcripts of those Senate hearings run to seven volumes, and I have given up trying to find a specific reference to these words, which I heard at the time on television. On the notion of experience, see this chapter, note 54.

51. On the relation of deconstruction and close reading see Culler, *On Deconstruction*, pp. 199, 220, and 242ff.

52. As Derrida himself puts it at one point, "The signified concept is never present in and of itself, in a sufficient presence that would refer only to itself" ("*Différance*," p. 11). For related ideas in Adorno's work, see this volume, chapter 1, note 96.

53. Poststructuralist notions of the unconscious are complex and often difficult. (See, for example, Jacques Lacan, "Sign, Symbol, Imaginary," in *On Signs*, pp. 203-9, and Julia Kristeva, "The Speaking Subject," ibid., pp. 210-20.) Derrida notes that "there are no 'conscious' traces" ("*Différance*," p. 21), though clearly many elements of trace would be recognizable if presented to the conscious mind. See also this chapter, note 31. For the music historian, a simple but useful example of a trace might be the role played by traditional tonality in Schoenberg's post-tonal music. Though absent, tonality clearly plays a variety of conceivable (and even perceivable) roles in Schoenberg's middle and late periods. From Schoenberg's own perspective, those roles were substantially subject to his own conscious control. Deconstructionists would have far less interest (or

none at all) in Schoenberg's conscious intentions toward tonality. On the other hand, this notion of tonality as a historical trace bears a clear relationship to the view provided by the Hegelian notion of *Aufhebung*, whereby tonality is simultaneously negated and preserved through a historical process of transcendence. See this chapter, note 18; also this volume, chapter 3, pp. 155-56 and 167, especially the reference to note 66.

54. The characteristic reference by Continental schools of philosophy to concepts of experience seems to be a primary reason for their dismissal as "mere metaphysics" among self-styled "scientific" modes of thought, notwithstanding the paradoxes involved in equating metaphysics with knowledge grounded on a respect for experience. The lengths to which the epistemological rejection of experience can reach were brought home to me a few years ago when, working as a computer programmer, I attended a seminar on hospital administration at the University of Chicago Graduate School of Business, a very scientifically oriented institution. When a student proposed counterevidence, based on the "case method," to one speaker's argument, the professor in charge of the seminar sputtered in indignation, "The case method? The *case* method? Why that's—that's like arguing from experience!"

Yet recourse to our own cultural experience forcefully persuades us of the insights to be gained from the notion of "nonoriginary origins." For instance, does the poverty of an American inner city "result" from the limited education of its occupants? Or do the limits of that education "result" from the poverty of its occupants? Experience seems to have shown the social impotence of theories and programs that postulate *any* "first cause" for the configurations of misery in the American inner city. Far more persuasive, I would argue, is a vision of that misery as the "result" of conditions affecting each other in a dialectical pattern (the infamous "endless cycle of poverty") that can never be traced back to a principle or event without numerous identifiable preceding causes of its own.

55. Barthes's essay "Listening" is of great value in trying to analyze this sort of process. Vivid support for an image of perception and interpretation as distinct moments is provided by the work of Oliver Sacks. See this chapter, note 44, and also Oliver Sacks and Robert Wasserman, "The Case of the Colorblind Painter," *New York Review of Books* 34 (November 19, 1987), 30. I discuss the latter briefly in *Developing Variations*, p. 327 (note 8 to chapter 7). See also this chapter, note 45, on Kant's *Ding an sich*.

56. This denial is integrally related to poststructuralist notions of the death or disappearance of the author. For classic presentations of such notions see Roland Barthes, "The Death of the Author," *Image-Music-Text*, trans. Stephen Heath (New York, 1977), pp. 142-48; Foucault, "What Is an Author?" especially pp. 143-45; and Barthes, "From Work to Text," pp. 78-79. See also this chapter, notes 31, 45, and 49.

57. My own opinion is that the American social experiment with abstract definitions of text has proven the best-known solution to date for the ambiguities of the sign we call "Jew"—better than the particularistic solution represented by Israel.

This is not to deny that the idea behind the establishment of Israel points toward a valid pole of human perception: the view that cultural particularities define a solid and opaque rather than structurally "secondary," transparent, and thus discountable aspect of human experience. (On the equality of these poles, see above, pp. 59-60. Ironically, though both Jews and Arabs make concrete, particularistic claims on the Holy Land, Arabs might emphasize an abstract aspect of the Jewish claim. They might argue that for Jews this land played a metaphorical role, in that any number of other places could have served just as well; whereas the Arab claim, a metonymical claim of proximity [in the structuralist sense described above, in note 39], could be satisfied by this place alone. An Israeli counterclaim would involve insisting on the importance of specific symbolic—i.e., mentally defined—metaphorical meanings as opposed to the wholly arbitrary character of physical proximity [in the poststructuralist sense of metonymy]. The terms involved here are very similar to those that will emerge in my analyses of the Chopin prelude. See also this volume, chapter 4, note 125.)

I believe that the poles of both abstract generality and concrete particularity should be honored as significant moments in the Western dialectic of human interpretation. I certainly would not argue that the generality of the abstract ideals of reason developed in the European and American Enlightenment leads inevitably to a respect for ideological pluralism (for more on this point, see chapter 4, "The Closing of the American Dream?," e.g., note 83). I do suggest that grasping the dialectic of text at its moment of generality, and insisting upon the priority of that moment, has so far provided the safest living conditions in history for Jews. Clearly this strategy, at least as left to operate on its own, has not worked so well for other groups at risk in American society. Here again, the ongoing deconstruction of conflicting positions seems to me useful, though I cannot envision a fair solution that negates either side of the dialectic.

58. J. D. Salinger, by contrast, has shown through his efforts to protect his publicly available correspondence from use by other authors that he does not yet concede such futility.

59. I am largely bypassing here detailed consideration, with respect to art, of a relationship that I discuss in other contexts of this essay, one to which I have given a good deal of attention in the past. I refer to the relationship between abstract, underlying, quasi-logical structures and the concrete "surfaces" articulated through culturally particular signs. (This latter is a textual aspect that I myself associate with the notion of style. It is typically cited to distinguish the logical from the figurative or the artistic. It is this aspect that would discourage enlightened English teachers [unlike those of my youth] from demanding the précis of a poem.)

60. For insight into aesthetic aspects of *Ulysses*, I am indebted to Theodore Burtness, a first-rate amateur Joyce scholar from Centerport, N.Y.

61. In this connection it may be useful to recall that the English words "authentic" and "author" do not appear to stem from a common linguistic root—though today (as Derrida would surely emphasize) we tend to treat them as if they do. Issues related to those raised here are examined by Walter Benjamin "The Work of Art in the Age of Mechanical Reproduction" (1936), in *Illuminations,* ed. Hannah Arendt, trans. Harry Zohn (New York, 1968), pp. 217-51. See also Nicholas Kenyon, ed., *Authenticity and Early Music: A Symposium* (New York, 1988).

62. The importance of such "problematization" was brought home to me a few years ago when my family attended a modernized but essentially uncritical performance of *The Taming of the Shrew.* Almost everyone, male and female, to whom I spoke after this performance felt that the time for uncritical acceptance of this work, despite all its linguistic virtuosity and status as a source of commonly known quotations, is over—that, indeed, this work taken at face value constitutes an embarrassment for those hoping to persuade their children to take an interest in Shakespeare. One could make similar observations about racial, religious, or sexual stereotypes perpetuated by such sacred cows as Bach's Passions and Mozart's *Magic Flute.* My own preferred solution to the problems thus raised would be to find a way of problematizing or editing such works, rather than to banish them. I admit fully to the differences in perception evoked by such works. Isn't one of the benefits offered by criticism an enhancement of awareness of the ambiguities represented by these—and arguably by all—artistic endeavors?

63. Such scrupulousness would require, for example, that mere objections to a text, such as those that may have held up acceptance of Frank P. Bourgin's Ph.D. dissertation in the political science department at the University of Chicago for forty-five years, are not based on mere ideological disagreement. (On Bourgin's dissertation see, e.g., Pauline Maier, "The Dissertation That Would Not Die," a review of Frank Bourgin's *The Great Challenge: The Myth of Laissez-Faire in the Early Republic,* in the *New York Times Book Review* [July 30, 1989], 11-12.) Adorno at least tries to clarify his moral basis for equating technical and political judgments of a text. There is a particularly disheartening insidiousness in the traditional American academic practice of rejecting the ideologically different as technically incompetent.

Granted, there is also a danger in admitting considerations of ideology explicitly into the processes of critical judgment. I myself advocate a self-critical ideological sensitivity as an aid to fairness. But self-criticism cannot be ensured; and it would be foolish to deny the terrible powers available to an ideology that gains, in any social arena, unchecked assent to its own correctness. From this perspective it may be better, in the long run, to grant a priority to abstract, scientific ideals of nonideological truth. But such a priority should never be conceded more than a limited and provisional status, and should certainly not be used as a justification for excluding actual ideological diversity. See also this chapter, note 33.

64. For an interesting analysis of this problematical status, not only as defined within academic disciplines but also in relation to the deceptive powers of language and other cultural signs, see Marshall Blonsky's introduction to *On Signs*, for example, p. xx.

65. Eagleton, *Literary Theory*, p. 128.

66. Derrida, *Of Grammatology*, p. 157. The original French reads as follows: "A travers cette séquence de suppléments s'annonce une nécessité: celle d'un enchaînement infini, multipliant inéluctablement les médiations supplémentaires qui produisent le sens de cela même qu'elles diffèrent: le mirage de la chose même, de la présence immédiate, de la perception originaire. L'immédiateté est dérivée. Tout commence par l'intermédiaire, voilà ce qui est 'inconcevable à la raison'" (Jacques Derrida, *De la grammatologie* [Paris, 1967], p. 226).

67. Derrida, *Of Grammatology*, p. 156.

68. Ibid., p. 157. Culler translates this phrase more loosely as "there emerges a law" (*On Deconstruction*, p. 105).

69. See, again, Blonsky's introduction to *On Signs*, p. xiv, note 3, and also the citation to de Man, this chapter note 142.

70. Eagleton's presentation of Lacan's theory of language and desire is helpful in deciphering this aspect of Derrida's work; see Eagleton, *Literary Theory*, pp. 167-68.

71. One can, of course, also read this concluding sentence as a direct reference to the nonoriginary status of language itself; but acknowledging that status amounts to conceding the radical provisionality of knowledge. See also this volume, chapter 4, note 36.

72. Derrida, *Of Grammatology*, p. 156.

73. On the relation of the transcendental signified to "being," see the discussion of Derrida and Heidegger in Spivak's preface to Derrida's *Of Grammatology*, pp. xv-xvi.

On Lacan's characterization of the phallus as the "transcendental signifier," see Eagleton, *Literary Theory*, p. 168. According to Eagleton's account, the phallus "is not in fact an object or reality, not the actual male sexual organ; it is merely an empty marker of difference, a sign of what divides us from the imaginary and inserts us into our predestined place within the symbolic order." Whatever one makes of such imagery, it is interesting to note its hint that male sexuality is a condition sufficiently defined by the existence of desire, even if no appropriate or accessible object for that desire could ever be established. (If the phallus "divides us from the imaginary," does it then follow that it points—and therefore it is?)

74. De Man, in "Semiology and Rhetoric," *Textual Strategies*, pp. 121-40.

75. Jameson, in "The Realist Floor-Plan," *On Signs*, pp. 373-83.

76. Blonsky, *On Signs*, p. ix.

77. De Man, "Semiology and Rhetoric," pp. 130-32.

78. Ibid., p. 131.

79. It may be helpful to have access to the definition of "rhetoric" that I have developed in my own work (initially in "The Cultural Message of Musical Semiology: Some Thoughts on Music, Language, and Criticism since the Enlightenment," *Developing Variations*, pp. 169-94, especially beginning at p. 181). From the start I have understood this term to imply some kind of emphasis applied from outside the structural logic of an argument, which thereby calls attention to its own opaque, figurative, and supplemental status. Though this definition is not central to the present

argument, it is never far from my thoughts here and seems to me compatible with all that is said about "rhetoric" in this chapter.

What is at stake in de Man's reversal here, as will become clear in the ensuing musical analyses, is a questioning of the ontological superiority of logic—and by extension other scientific language—to rhetoric and the language of fiction. Since the advent of poststructuralism, of course, it has become a truism in academic circles that science, and for that matter reality itself, are simply forms of text, and that all texts are constructed or fictional. A related insight, discussed at a number of points in my first collection of essays, can be traced all the way back to the early Romantic conviction—in the wake of the gap left by Kant (despite Hegel) between subject and object—that subjective fantasy was more persuasively true than was objective fact. An ingenious version of this conviction is offered by Janet Malcolm in her essentially postmodernist study of biography (in connection with Sylvia Plath), "The Silent Woman," in the *New Yorker* (August 23 and 30, 1993), 138: "The facts of imaginative literature are as hard as the stone that Dr. Johnson kicked. We must always take the novelist's and the playwright's and the poet's word, just as we are almost always free to doubt the biographer's or the autobiographer's or the historian's or the journalist's. In imaginative literature we are constrained from considering alternative scenarios—there are none. This is the way it *is*. Only in nonfiction does the question of what happened and how people thought and felt remain open" (italics hers). See chapter 3, note 78.

80. Quoted in Jameson, "Floor-Plan," p. 376. The original French, given on pp. 375-76 of Jameson's essay, reads as follows: "Cette maison, revêtue d'ardoises, se trouvait entre un passage et une ruelle aboutissant à la rivière. Elle avait intérieurement des différences de niveau qui faisaient trébucher. Un vestibule étroit séparait la cuisine de la *salle* où Madame Aubain se tenait tout le long du jour, assise près de la croisée dans un fauteuil de paille. Contre le lambris, peint en blanc, s'alignaient huit chaises d'acajou. Un vieux piano supportait, sous un baromètre, un tas pyramidal de boîtes et de cartons. Deux bergères de tapisserie flanquaient la cheminée en marbre jaune et de style Louis XV. La pendule, au milieu, représentait un temple de Vesta—et tout l'appartment sentait un peu le moisi, car le plancher était plus bas que le jardin." It may be noted that I have translated the last sentence more literally than Jameson does so as to preserve the presence and placement of Flaubert's hyphen. Though I have not made an effort to do so here, it strikes me that one could interpret the intrusion of this hyphen into the flow of letters as the physical point of entry for Jameson's (non)subject—and conceivably identify it as parallel to the physical lingering commonly produced by the climactic sonority (measure 12) in Chopin's A-Major Prelude, which I shall discuss below.

81. Jameson, "Floor-Plan," p. 373.

82. All of the elements in this account can be found on pp. 373-74 and 380 of Jameson's essay (ibid.). By necessity, not all of the terms in Jameson's rich analysis will be included here, nor will all of those included be analyzed explicitly (the notion of "cyclical" time, for example, makes its presence felt in my musical analysis only by implication). It may be useful to note at this point the blurring of distinction that Jameson imputes to the modern scientific association of the "physical" and the "measurable" (p. 374). In equating these two terms—in effect subsuming the "physical" under the "measurable"—the modern scientific view renders culturally marginal various affective (psychologically experienced) qualities previously assumed as fundamental to the physical. I should also acknowledge at this point that my use of Jameson's argument flattens the complexity of the relationships he proposes between premodernist, modernist, and postmodernist periods. I do so in order to clarify the tension between my two readings of Chopin's prelude, readings that in terms of Jameson's essay can be distinguished as modernist and postmodernist.

83. Ibid., p. 375. Henceforth this phrase will be used without double quotation marks. Jameson indicates by this phrase "the nineteenth-century 'belief' in science and the referent . . . and the way in which belief in reference governs the practices of nineteenth-century daily life and of the nineteenth-century 'realistic' aesthetic." Interestingly, Jameson, as a self-styled radical historicist, links this nineteenth-century "truth-claim" with those of "late-twentieth-century skepticism,"

that is, with the "'beliefs' . . . of late-twentieth-century linguistics and post-structuralism" in the referent as no more than "a myth, a mirage, or an ideology" (all quotations taken from p. 375). Jameson is arguing that these late-twentieth-century movements are reenacting, within a complex dialectical historical process, nineteenth-century realism's demystifications of the referent. But in recommending that we "bracket or . . . estrange" *both* sets of truth-claims (p. 375), he also hints at the stubbornness with which beliefs about the referent "[hover] above the textual apparatus as a ghostly remanence, as the faint after-image of what the text [is] called upon to transform and to suppress" (p. 382). Through such images he seems to suggest that we can, if only in a figurative sense, preserve the significance of the referent—the real world—in our critical activities.

84. Jameson, "Floor-Plan," pp. 376-78.

85. Ibid., pp. 377 ("dual inequality"), 379 ("infinite fission"), and 378 ("marginalized and decentered").

86. Ibid., p. 378.

87. Ibid., pp. 379-80.

88. Ibid., p. 379.

89. Ibid., p. 380, italics his. See also this volume, chapter 4, note 25.

90. Ibid., See also this volume, chapter 4, note 25.

91. Ibid., p. 381.

92. Ibid., p. 382.

93. Ibid., pp. 381-82.

94. Strange as it may seem at first glance to associate Chopin's music with "realism," our scholarly tradition provides a strong basis for doing so. Paul Henry Lang, for example, in the introduction to *The Experience of Opera* (New York, 1971), p. 28, notes that Romantic opera (as opposed to Mozartian opera) "gathers together smaller, interlocking units of shorter breath but corresponding more closely to the dramatic text." In its informal way, this description captures the essentials of a much more ambitious analysis of realism made by Carl Dahlhaus, not so much in his study *Realism in Nineteenth-Century Music*, trans. Mary Whittall (Cambridge, England, 1985), as in his study *Between Romanticism and Modernism: Four Studies in the Music of the Later Nineteenth Century*, trans. Mary Whittall (Berkeley, 1980), for example, pp. 52-64, and also 44-46. Relying on certain restricted standards for musical realism (in *Realism*, p. 60), Dahlhaus characterizes nineteenth-century musical realism as no more than a secondary historical phenomenon. Yet his analyses of musical prose (even in *Realism*, for example, pp. 73 and 96), like Lang's comment, lend support to a view of musical realism as a technique that, like its literary counterpart, shifts away from large, overarching, "generalizable" forms to a moment-by-moment concentration on particular "surface" details, as significant structural moments. (Charles Rosen takes up this theme of increasing density in *Arnold Schoenberg* [New York, 1975], p. 21; a similarly dense and "immediate" surface in prose, as opposed to poetry, is implied in the last chapter of Bakhtin's *Dialogic Imagination*, for example, pp. 271-72, 285-86, and 297-98.) Where such a technique is put at the service of telling a whole story—as in Wagner's music dramas, or in the nineteenth-century novel—an author will need to work on a large physical scale. Chopin's A-Major Prelude can still be heard as a story in miniature (or perhaps as an anecdote within a story). But it is also taking on the dense concentration of a realistic fragment (see this chapter, note 36). Dahlhaus (*Between Romanticism and Modernism*, p. 46) describes "real sequence" as "an expository procedure, a means of elaborating a musical idea which in itself . . . needs no continuation and would not tolerate conventional 'rounding-off' in a closed period." Chopin's prelude seems to be testing the limits to which any continuation or completion other than "real sequence" can still be persuasive. See also this chapter, note 132.

For related discussion see chapter 1, "Whose *Magic Flute?*" note 87.

95. Jameson, "Floor-Plan," p. 382.

96. Actually, my underlying conclusion has been that *both* the cognitive and the moral struc-

tures of reason proposed by Kant are variants of a fundamentally aesthetic structure. A portion of the work that led me to these conclusions appears in my essay "Kant, Adorno, and the Self-Critique of Reason: Toward a Model for Music Criticism," *Developing Variations*, pp. 57-83, an essay based on two years studying Kant's *Critique of Judgment*. This latter study led me, in a way that my close reading often does, to analyze Kant's text as I would a piece of music, sorting out salient themes and investigating the patterns and structures formed by their elements. When I first presented work on Kant, for example at the CUNY Graduate Center in the mid-1980s, I was criticized quite vehemently by some philosophers for treating the Third Critique as a culturally contingent construction—in effect, as an artwork—instead of accepting the meanings it imputed to itself at face value and thereby treating it as a bearer of abstract, necessary, and universal truth. The discovery that Derrida, in *La Verité en peinture*, explicitly proposes interpreting Kant's *Critique of Judgment* as if it were a work of art (see Culler, *On Deconstruction*, p. 184, also 180-81) has given me particular pleasure—even though the critics I mention almost always had an open disdain for Derrida's work itself.

97. Without elaborating on the point, it can perhaps already be seen that this sort of reading points toward the understanding Kant tried to develop, in his Third Critique, of aesthetic judgment as grounded on a universal structure of reason. In effect, my second reading will suggest reversing this hierarchy, by proposing that rational structures themselves are grounded on inescapably contingent aesthetic judgments. Of great relevance to this issue is Terry Eagleton's *The Ideology of the Aesthetic* (Oxford, England, and Cambridge, Mass., 1990); see, for example, the discussion that begins on p. 382. I had not read this book at the time I wrote the present essay.

98. See this chapter, note 79.

99. See the piece entitled "Dream Images (Love-Death Music)," with its opening instruction, "Musingly, like the gentle caress of a faintly remembered music," the eleventh piece in George Crumb's *Makrokosmos*, vol. 1: *Twelve Fantasy Pieces after the Zodiac for Amplified Piano* (New York, 1974), pp. 17-18. I am grateful to Teddy Shapiro, a recent graduate of Brown, for bringing this piece to my attention with a memorable performance and paper.

100. These are not the same thing, any more than acknowledging the relative primacy, or hegemony, of upper-class white male values in American culture today entails considering less privileged values as "inessential" to the structure of that culture (or as worth less in themselves, a question that will be taken up explicitly in my second reading).

101. See the reference to Rosen, *Classical Style*, this chapter, note 41.

102. Scarlatti's claim to inclusion on this list becomes irresistible once one hears the use to which his music is put in Morton Subotnick's *Return*, a piece about the long history of Halley's Comet. (I heard Subotnick give the following explanation of his piece during a summer concert at the University of Chicago in the mid-1980s.) The first half of the piece ends with the return of the comet in 1759, a triumphant vindication of the prediction by Halley (who had himself died seventeen years earlier). To celebrate this high-water mark of Enlightenment rationality—have doubts about the real effects of reason ever again been as low?—Subotnick's music breaks out into a glorious "sampling" of a D-major passage by Scarlatti (1685-1757). In terms of the argument I am making at this point in my essay, it is interesting to note that Subotnick projects the glory of the D-major tonic not through relational means (such as contrast with the dominant) but through a constant reiteration of formulas for defining the tonic, such as the tonic scale and triad, over a steady tonic pedal. And yet it is not the sheer physical massiveness of Scarlatti's D-major that is impressive here. What Subotnick impresses on us is the supreme confidence of a style in which the force of a symbolic system, tonality, was so secure that this force could be invoked by merely uttering one of its symbols—i.e., through mere "reference" rather than "use" (on this distinction see this chapter, note 124).

103. There is an obvious irony here. Haydn, the earliest of the three Viennese Classicists, was throughout most of his life the one most willing to accept a social status of inferiority. Yet of the

three he seems also to have been the most comfortable in his acceptance and exercise of the superior powers attributed by the Enlightenment to rational thought. Mozart, arguing that "it is the heart that ennobles a man," asserted his essential equality to people of rank (letter [no. 412] of June 20, 1781, in *The Letters of Mozart and His Family*, ed. and trans. Emily Anderson, 3rd ed. [New York, 1985], p. 747); and Beethoven essentially got his aristocratic patrons to give him money and leave him alone (see Maynard Solomon, *Beethoven* [New York, 1977], pp. 148-49, and also 146). Yet neither Mozart nor Beethoven seems to have been entirely comfortable with the movement toward an equation of mental powers and social standing. (For more on Beethoven's inconsistent attitudes toward noble rank see Maynard Solomon, "The Nobility Pretense," *Beethoven Essays* [Cambridge, Mass., 1988], pp. 43-55; of special interest is this quote, p. 55, from Ernst Bloch: "Even when the young musician Beethoven suddenly knew or claimed that he was a genius, he was practicing a scurrilous swindle, for he felt himself to be like Ludwig van Beethoven, a person he had not yet become.") Even as the discomforts of social mobility made themselves apparent, one senses in the music a growing uncertainty—especially in Beethoven's emphatic denials thereof—about the necessary status of the superiority conferred by powers of rationality. Mozart and Beethoven seem to have transacted an exchange of the certainties provided by an uncritical acceptance of rational standards—and of social servitude—for the contingencies of critical questioning—and of social independence.

104. An interesting aspect of these two intervals, the horizontal sixth and the vertical fifth, one that I shall not take up again, concerns their literal physical identity. In all three cases—even in phrase 6, where symmetrical parallelism and a need for tonal development would suggest a change—the melodic sixth uses the same three notes: E and C-sharp. Despite accompanying changes in aspects such as rhythm, meter, register, and harmony, the constancy of pitch here is striking. One senses here, in fact, an emphasis on the literal physical identity of pitches, of the kind I analyzed in "Evidence of a Critical Worldview in Mozart's Last Three Symphonies," *Developing Variations*, pp. 108 and 110. On the other hand, the vertical fifths *do* change, from E-B in the first two instances to F-sharp-C-sharp in measure 12. One has here, perhaps, specific musical sites of a polarity between physical identity and logical function.

105. We have here, actually, an example of a characteristic feature in this piece, which will later be discussed in some detail. I have in mind the importance of tonally ambiguous physical spaces, spaces that could be filled in by two or more alternative pitches, thereby pointing toward different triads, all of which make plausible tonal sense. Is the note "missing" between B and D in measure 15 G-sharp or even F-natural (which would indicate V^7 or V^9 in A)? Or is it F-sharp (which would produce B-minor [over A])? Of course we have already encountered a related phenomenon in Rufus Hallmark's hypothetical substitution of I for V of II at the climactic moment. Both instances point suggestively toward the characterization of tonal logic in this piece as qualitatively contingent.

106. The same can be said of the earlier superimposition of B-minor over the dominant E in measures 5-6 (as discussed previously, p. 95). In my second reading, as will be seen, such superimposed elements would not be discounted as secondary but would rather be noticed, and thereby allowed to undermine the stability of their conventionally governing tonal contexts.

The musical technique here is not altogether dissimilar to Beethoven's technique, which will be readily recalled from the moment of recapitulation in the first movement of the *Eroica*, of prematurely or precipitately superimposing the resolving tonic upon a key leading to it. Of course, Beethoven's technique there differs in several noticeable respects. To begin with, the two keys used here by Beethoven, basically V and I, define graded stages of stability within a single tonal center (I) rather than two potentially distinct tonal centers as in Chopin's prelude. Yet on the other hand, it is the tonic rather than the less stable dominant that is at first introduced by Beethoven as functionally secondary (i.e., though I is the goal, it appears initially in the domain of its own preparation). At that, in at least some of its aspects, such as duration, chromatic overtones, and arguably even instrumental color, Beethoven's dominant chord projects a stronger physical presence than does Chopin's B—or even his B and D, if the latter is identified with a B-minor triad as well as with the dominant seventh of A.

107. By this formulation, we are testing the reality of subjectivity by asking whether the unity we perceive really [!] *is*, apart from our perceptions of it. This test assumes that being is prior to meaning. The legitimacy of such an assumption is precisely what deconstruction forces us to reconsider, even as it shows us that such assumptions are inextricable from whatever we say about reality, just as figurative language is. See the closing pages of this section, starting with note 118.

108. The internesting of linguistic usages is especially hard to avoid here. To say it "is supposed to" end up here, or "is meant to" end up here is already to conflate notions of being with notions of intention.

109. See chapter 1, pp. 3-5, the text leading to Example 1.

110. De Man, "Semiology and Rhetoric," p. 136. See also this chapter, p. 140, note 150.

111. Ibid., p. 134. See also ibid., p. 135, where de Man refers to unity "by sheer habit."

112. Ibid., p. 135.

113. Ibid., pp. 133-34.

114. Ibid., p. 134.

115. Ibid., p. 137. See also this chapter, note 147.

116. See also p. 138 in this chapter. In the spring of 1987, at a very low moment in my career, a compassionate graduate student kept me going by defining the achievement of success as the arrival at a point that made everything preceding, however painful or improbable, seem a necessary preparation—that is, necessary to a wholeness of structure. "Write your book, Rose," he said, "and everyone will think your career was supposed to turn out the way it did." This student, whom I greatly admired, was David Bain, a doctoral candidate at the CUNY Graduate Center. In December, 1992, David Bain took his own life.

117. In its sensitivity to the inextricable contradictions, multiple layers, and infinite regress characteristic of language, deconstruction helps clarify the philosophical ironies and inconsistencies of a notion such as "real contingencies."

118. See this chapter, note 107.

119. Eagleton, *Literary Theory*, p. 136. See also this volume, chapter 1, notes 50 and 51, and chapter 3, note 55.

120. Note how the language constructions here ("of an event," "of the latter") already accept the existence of the text apart from the reader, a situation this reading will subject to radical doubt. ("Latter" here refers to "event.")

121. Thomas Higgins, "Notes toward a Performance with References to the Valldemosa Autograph," in the Norton critical score of Chopin's *Preludes*, p. 63.

122. The pattern I describe here, clearly related to the favored tropes of deconstruction, has some suggestive similarities with the image of a truth-wheel, drawn from Anatole France, that Albert Einstein sometimes used to explain the theory of relativity to laypeople. See Arthur Beckhard, *Albert Einstein* (New York, 1959), pp. 104-6. My language here, of course, is drawn from Jameson. See this chapter, notes 83-85.

123. To put the question this way, of course, is to put in stark relief the reliance of deconstruction on images of binary opposition, the usefulness of which, even for purposes of deconstructive dismantling, is now challenged by many postmodernist thinkers. See the following note.

124. On the distinction between "use" and "mention," see Culler, *On Deconstruction*, pp. 119-20, note 5, on a conflict involving Derrida and Searle. Whereas Searle argues that Derrida overlooks this distinction, Culler argues that Derrida contests it. Culler then adds, "The distinction is still useful; among other things it helps us to describe how language subverts it." This comment sums up with admirable conciseness the double-edged role played by binary oppositions in deconstruction. See also Rosen, *Schoenberg*, p. 22 ("[Mozart's] music does not refer to but *conveys* a

traditional system of meaning while it creates a new one" [italics his]); and this chapter, note 102, on D. Scarlatti.

125. Readers can easily verify for themselves the structural pervasiveness of major and minor sixths at a number of points in the prelude: as a rising melodic interval on the notes E-C-sharp at the start, in measures 8-9, and in measure 11; and also as an unfilled vertical interval in the right-hand part, for example, the unfilled C-sharp-A in measures 3-4 and 15-16, as well as the entire right-hand part in phrase 3 (measures 4-6) and in measures 15-16.

126. To test the plausibility of these three readings of the opening sixth on a lay reader, I played all three for my husband; that is, I played the opening first beat as a second-inversion A triad, as a first-inversion C-sharp-minor triad, and as a hollow sixth, and then asked him which was right. After requesting several rehearings of the whole series, my husband decided that the hollow sixth was right. When I asked him why, he replied, "Because that's the way it really is in the piece." Unless we are determined, like certain Romantics, to credit the composer with privileged access to metaphysical truth, it seems to me that my husband's answer points less to the logical necessity of this hollow sixth than to a culturally ingrained tendency to equate the contingency of what is with the necessity of what is right.

127. This information was conveyed to me by graduate students when I presented a version of this paper at Columbia in 1987. It was my understanding that the students had heard this done in a performance; I do not know if Foss has recorded this version.

128. That this shift in orientation will affect the readings made of the prelude as a metaphor for individual life should be evident. One can, indeed, already glimpse in this diffraction of temporal relationships the vision of a world without meaning—that is, of a world where meaning has been diffused, or even dissolved, into a nondirectional, essentially static and abstract continuum of time and space. Readings such as this second one do offer such visions as possibilities, though not as the only possibilities.

129. The students in my seminar on deconstruction in the fall of 1986 at the CUNY Graduate Center argued strenuously for this interpretation of the pedals. It is also the position taken by Higgins in his notes to the critical edition of the prelude, p. 63: "The original pedaling should be preserved . . . [especially because] the fundamental in the bass survives—a crucial value."

130. Here again, absent pitches can be heard to figure as structurally prominent "traces." Is the "missing" note in the right-hand sixth on beat one of measure 15 the F-sharp of the climactic sonority—an indicator of the B-minor triad—or the "anomalous," delayed G-sharp that presented itself on the first beat of measure 9? That it is futile to try and answer such a question definitively seems obvious. The point is that this moment, like many others in the prelude, points to the contingency of the strategies through which tonal logic tries to establish its structural priority.

131. This is a moment of analysis that comes perilously close to infinite regress. If antecedents originally gained weight in this piece precisely by virtue of their instability, and consequents are now being rendered increasingly unstable, does it perhaps follow that the perception of weight rocks back once again, say at the striking of the second inversion on beat 2 of measure 13, to consequents after all? This is the kind of endless movement suggested by de Man's reading of Proust.

132. See again, Dahlhaus, *Between Romanticism and Modernism*, p. 46, on the Wagnerian "musical idea which in itself . . . needs no continuation and would not tolerate conventional 'rounding-off' in a closed period," as cited earlier, in note 94.

133. Again, a reading such as this one does not deny the intelligibility of tonal logic in the prelude; it merely puts into question the priority of that intelligibility in our perceptions of the prelude.

134. To invoke *The Magic Flute* again, one could indeed argue that Papageno's "Vogelfänger" song, which stays close to its G-major tonic, comes closer to real modulation in its brief moves to D (V) than does this prelude. See chapter 1, note 12.

135. See Leonard Meyer's analysis of Chopin's second prelude, excerpted in the Norton critical score of the *Preludes*, p. 79.

136. Jameson, "Floor-Plan," p. 378. See this chapter, note 86.

137. Ibid., p. 380, italics his. See this chapter, note 89.

138. See the passage from Barthes's essay "L'effet de réel" quoted in Jameson, "Floor-Plan," pp. 381-82 (Jameson provides the full citation to this essay on p. 375); also this chapter, note 93.

139. See my essay "On Grounding Chopin" in *Developing Variations*, pp. 161-62.

140. Jameson, "Floor-Plan," p. 379; see this chapter, note 88.

141. Ibid., p. 380; see this chapter, note 90.

142. De Man, "Semiology and Rhetoric," p. 137. His context here is "the grammatization of rhetoric . . . [,] the passage from a paradigmatic structure based on substitution, such as metaphor, to a syntagmatic structure based on contingent association, such as metonymy." On the same page he notes, "Such a deconstruction puts into question a whole series of concepts that underlie the value judgments of our critical discourse: the metaphors of primacy . . . , and most notably, of the autonomous power to will of the self." Such statements can no doubt be used to confirm de Man's unwillingness to stand by the particular fascist sentiments expressed in some of his earlier articles. An outright dismissal of the ideas here would be unfortunate, however, not necessarily in terms of de Man's own biography, but in terms of its potential discouraging effect on inquiries in general into the cultural (i.e., supraindividual) contributions to texts. On such contributions see also Blonsky, Introduction to *On Signs*, p. xiv. See also this chapter, notes 23, 69, and 147.

143. Its elevation is exceptional not in the sense of its occupying the top register of the piece but because, alone among the melody notes that appear on the first beat of each phrase, this one is higher than both the prior and following melody notes. See pp. 98-99 and 100.

144. To me, at least, the fall of the blade just after the reappearance of the *idée fixe* always sounds like the beheading not of the lover in his last moment of sight but of the beloved he sees. This is an interesting musical trope for trying to mark a boundary between signifier and signified.

145. Relevant to this image is the discussion of Ronald Dworkin's notion of "critical interests" in T. M. Scanlon's review of Dworkin's *Life's Dominion*, pp. 48-49 (for a full citation, see this chapter, note 27). As Scanlon presents them, critical interests involve the standards we each set for ourselves that will give our life value beyond the value of desirable experience. Scanlon notes, "People differ in the particular standards that they want their lives to meet . . . but almost everyone recognizes some standards of this kind and many people care greatly about meeting them" (p. 48). He subsequently notes, however (p. 49), "Judgments [by critical standards], in which one views one's life as a whole and asks how best to perfect it, are quite intelligible, but only a few people give such judgments a dominant role in their lives. It is therefore far from clear that what kindness or beneficence generally requires when we are dealing with anyone . . . is that we ask how best to help realize the plan of their life. Perhaps this is what beneficence would require in the case of someone like Friedrich Nietzsche, for whom the realization of a certain ideal was an all-consuming passion. But for the rest of us the idea of doing what is 'in our best interests' may point more humbly in the direction of comfort and reassurance insofar as these can be provided." The trope of living one's life as if one were shaping a work of art was indeed familiar among nineteenth-century German intellectuals, for whom Goethe furnished its paradigmatic example. Though this image is no longer fashionable, the sense among postmodern academics—a sense derived from poststructuralism—that each person experiences his or her life as the construction of a text bears an important similarity to that older trope.

See also Allan Bloom, *The Closing of the American Mind* (New York, 1987), p. 277: "Individuals demand significance for this individual life, which is so subject to accident." Bloom takes the attitude that philosophers alone can rise above this demand of ordinary people. See my discussion in chapter 4, "The Closing of the American Dream?" note 147 as compared to notes 116 and 100.

146. Jameson, "Floor-Plan," 379-80.

147. De Man, "Semiology and Rhetoric," p. 137. See also notes 115 and 142.

148. See this chapter, p. 134, text leading to note 137.

149. De Man, "Semiology and Rhetoric," p. 136.

150. Ibid. See also note 110.

151. Or, of course, the possibility that *traditional Western* rationality has no status in reality; and in fact, readings such as this second one, like so many readings that have developed out of post-structuralist positions, such as feminist ones—and like so many of my own analyses both before and since this one—amount to a critique of traditional Western notions of reason.

152. There is, obviously, a paradox here. Insisting on restricting the domain from which it extracts value to the cognitively knowable, my first reading proves willing, in the end, to "forget" what it "knows" in order to secure what it feels [!] it *must* know. By contrast, my second reading, admitting the contingencies of cognition, nevertheless remains rigorously observant of the restrictions established by critical standards of cognition. The result, of course, is that the second reading asserts that all cognition falls short of its own standards.

There is a related paradox in the very notion of the honesty of rhetorical figures: a figure that admits it is a figure may have more truth value than a figure that claims to be true. It is in this sense that I have sometimes suggested that Romantic music, admitting its contingent or figurative status, is more honest about itself than Classical structures, to the extent that the latter seem to claim the truth status of an autonomous semiotic structure. The latter involves a conflation of structure and content, whereby themes of epistemological status are conflated with the ontological status of an artwork. See notes 9, 11, and 152 of this chapter; and chapter 4, notes 10 and 103.

153. Of course the very differences between "empirical" (or literal) and "logical" (or structural) parameters of knowledge, exhaustively analyzed by Kant, point to an epistemological problem in Western conceptions of knowledge. Empirical knowledge cannot escape the taint of physical contingency; at bottom it partakes of the aesthetic precisely at the level where Kant did not wish to confine aesthetic judgment. Both the figurative and the literal, in other words, depend fundamentally for their understanding on a sense of the thick, contingent opaqueness of the physical. Nevertheless the deeply ingrained traditional Western acceptance of empirical knowledge as governed by higher and more abstract structural relations seems a sufficient ground in the present discussion for linking empirically defined, literal standards of information with cognition rather than with rhetoric. But it should also be noted that my second reading fastens on the inseparability, from an interpreter's perspective, of logic from its concrete representations—on the inseparability, for example, of logical and arbitrary aspects of tonality—as grounds for asserting the contingency of all knowledge.

154. See this chapter, note 152.

155. See p. 142 for both themes and note 152 for references to conflation of theme and status.

156. Jameson, "Floor-Plan," p. 380. See this chapter, note 89.

157. Ibid. See note 89.

158. Lionel Trilling, *Sincerity and Authenticity* (Cambridge, Mass., 1972).

159. Ibid., p. 132.

160. Ibid.

161. Ibid., p. 158.

162. Ibid., p. 159.

163. Ibid., p. 157.

164. Ibid., p. 171.

165. Ibid., p. 157.

166. Ibid., p. 158, italics his.

167. Ibid.

168. In the few years since I first presented this essay, I have had to change my wording here, from "is not so different" to "may not be so different." For while the vision of subjectivity I cite

here remains congenial to what Eric Hoffsten, one of my brightest Brown students, once called my own "raging humanism," I cannot deny that many of my colleagues have moved into a postmodernist perspective that no longer values this vision.

169. Quoted by Trilling, *Sincerity*, p. 133. Since Trilling himself feels obliged at this point to defend Kurtz's own last words from the charge that they are "a characterization of imperialism," I should stress that it is Trilling, not Kurtz, who moves me here. Still, we should not desist from exploring the degree to which Western liberal ideals of the subject are inextricable from Western imperialist ideologies. (And may have been so from their inception: on "the interconnectedness of imperialism and democracy in [ancient] Athens," see Garry Wills, *Lincoln at Gettysburg: The Words That Remade America* [New York, 1992], p. 296, note 2, and also p. 212.) See also my note on Edward Said and Joseph Conrad, chapter 1, note 96.

3. Toward a Deconstruction of Structural Listening: A Critique of Schoenberg, Adorno, and Stravinsky

1. Quoted in Oliver Strunk, ed., *Source Readings in Music History* (New York, 1950), p. 743. The passage continues, "In this sense Jean Paul, with a poetic companion-piece, can perhaps contribute more to the understanding of a symphony or fantasy by Beethoven without even speaking of the music, than a dozen of those little critics of the arts who lean their ladders against the Colossus and take its exact measurements." A slightly different version of the present chapter appeared earlier in Eugene Narmour and Ruth A. Solie, eds., *Explorations in Music, the Arts, and Ideas: Essays in Honor of Leonard B. Meyer* (Stuyvesant, N.Y., 1988), pp. 87-122.

2. Oliver Sacks, *The Man Who Mistook His Wife for a Hat and Other Clinical Tales* (New York, 1985), pp. 120, 140-41.

3. On Nietzsche see Gayatri Chakravorty Spivak's preface to her translation of Jacques Derrida, *Of Grammatology* (Baltimore, 1976), pp. xxix-xxxiii.

4. See "The Challenge of Contemporary Music" in my earlier collection of essays, *Developing Variations: Style and Ideology in Western Music* (Minneapolis, 1991), pp. 265-95.

5. On "supplement" see Derrida, *Of Grammatology*, pp. 141-64, and Jonathan Culler, *On Deconstruction: Theory and Criticism after Structuralism* (Ithaca, 1982), pp. 102-6.

6. See especially Arnold Schoenberg, *Style and Idea*, ed. Leonard Stein (Berkeley, 1984), pp. 120-21 and 377-82, and Theodor W. Adorno, *Introduction to the Sociology of Music*, trans. E. B. Ashton (New York, 1976), pp. 4-5. Schoenberg's reference to "idea" is on pp. 122-23 of his book. (All subsequent references to Schoenberg as an author are to *Style and Idea*; for reasons of space, titles of individual articles in that collection will not be cited.)

7. On the row see, for example, the letter from Schoenberg quoted in Arnold Whittall, *Schoenberg Chamber Music* (London, 1972), p. 46; Theodor W. Adorno, "Arnold Schoenberg 1874-1951," *Prisms*, trans. Samuel and Shierry Weber (London, 1967), p. 167; and Charles Rosen, *Arnold Schoenberg* (New York, 1975), p. 78.

8. See especially T. W. Adorno, "The Radio Symphony," *Radio Research, 1941*, ed. Paul F. Lazarsfeld and Frank N. Stanton (New York, 1941), pp. 128-33.

9. Leo Treitler, "Mozart and the Idea of Absolute Music," *Music and the Historical Imagination* (Cambridge, Mass., 1989), p. 185.

10. On phenomenology see T. W. Adorno, *Philosophy of Modern Music*, trans. Anne G. Mitchell and Wesley V. Blomster (New York, 1973), pp. 136, 139-42.

11. Eduard Hanslick, *The Beautiful in Music*, ed. Morris Weitz, trans. Gustav Cohen (Indianapolis, 1957), p. 66. See also pp. 50, 122, etc., for the notion of "replete" form. For a more recent translation of Hanslick's work, see Geoffrey Payzant, trans. and ed., *On the Musically Beautiful: A Contribution towards the Revision of the Aesthetic of Music* (Indianapolis, 1986). A more scholarly enterprise than

the Weitz-Cohen edition, Payzant's version provides a great deal of useful explanation and supplementary historical material. I have read both editions carefully and compared them to the ninth revised edition of Hanslick's original German version (*Vom Musikalische-Schönen: Ein Beitrag zur Revision der Aesthetik der Tonkunst* [Leipzig, 1896]). Because I find Cohen's translation itself (though it is less literal) clearer and more helpful in understanding Hanslick, I shall cite page references to that edition first, with the citations to Payzant's edition in parentheses. (To the pages cited at the start of this note, the corresponding pages in Payzant's edition are 42 ["Something spontaneous, spiritual, and therefore incalculable"], 30 ["filled" instead of "replete"], and 122 ["fulfilled" instead of "replete"]. The German word translated by "replete" is *erfüllte*, pp. 79 and 213 in the German edition.)

12. Robert Schumann, "A Symphony by Berlioz," in Hector Berlioz, *Fantastic Symphony*, ed. Edward Cone (New York, 1971), pp. 232 (quoting Ernst Wagner), 233.

13. On "trace" see Spivak, translator's preface to *Of Grammatology*, pp. xv-xviii, and Culler, *On Deconstruction*, pp. 94-96 and 99. On Hanslick see Carl Dahlhaus, *Esthetics of Music*, trans. William W. Austin (Cambridge, 1982), pp. 52-57; and also Carl Dahlhaus, *Between Romanticism and Modernism: Four Studies in the Music of the Later Nineteenth Century*, trans. Mary Whittall (Berkeley and Los Angeles, 1980), p. 38: "Hanslick was opposed to metaphysics (though not as independent of Hegel as he claimed to be)."

14. Schoenberg's writings, to be sure, invoke the intellectual tradition far less explicitly than Adorno's do, and his notion of the potential relationships between music and politics is considerably less sophisticated than Adorno's (see especially Schoenberg, pp. 249-50). On the other hand, his exclusion of cultural associations (ibid., pp. 377-78) as well as semantic content (pp. 126-27) from musical autonomy does not differ from Adorno's *ideal* of autonomy, and he considers structure implicitly expressive (see ibid., pp. 257 and 415-16). See also this chapter, notes 34 and 47.

15. See Schoenberg, pp. 253 and 220; and Igor Stravinsky, *Poetics of Music in the Form of Six Lessons*, trans. Arthus Knodel and Ingolf Dahl (Cambridge, Mass., 1970), chapter 2, pp. 23-24 and 27; chapter 3, p. 49, and chapter 6, p. 17. (All references to Stravinsky will be to this work.) In my earlier published version of this essay, I referred to an earlier edition of Stravinsky's *Poetics* (New York, 1960) by the same translators. The two translations are identical, but the pagination unfortunately differs. In the present version, I shall provide chapter numbers for each reference, with the pages for the older edition in parentheses. Where the passage in question may not be instantly identifiable, I shall also provide some key words from Stravinsky's text. (The corresponding references in the older edition to the pages cited above are 2: 23-24 and 28; 3: 50; and 6: 124.)

16. On taste or caprice see Schoenberg, p. 247, and Stravinsky, 3: 54 and 63 (55 and 66) and 4: 73 (75). See also this chapter, notes 28-31. On necessity and objectivity, see Schoenberg, pp. 53, 133, 220, 244, 256, 407, 432, and 439; and Stravinsky, 2: 32 (33: "true solidarity") and 35 (37); 3: 47 (47), 61-62 (64), and 64-65 (67-68); and 6: 127 (133: "freedom in extreme rigor"). See also this chapter, notes 30 and 78. For Stravinsky on structural processes of listening see Stravinsky, 2: 24 (24) and 6: 133-34 (140).

17. For example, Schoenberg, pp. 257 and 285, and Stravinsky, 3: 48-49 (48-50) and 4: 86-87 (90). On necessity, see this volume, chapter 2, note 9.

18. See Schoenberg, pp. 127 and 254 (see also below, note 44); and Stravinsky, 3: 47-48 (48: "utilitarianism," "rightness") and 4: 86 (90: "face value").

19. See Schoenberg, pp. 50, 104, and 135, despite, for example, 215 on comprehensibility; and Stravinsky, 5: 102-3 (106-7: "end in itself") and 6: 131-32 (137-38: "mere opinion," "public taste"), despite 4: 75-76 (78) on usefulness.

20. See my essay "Adorno's Diagnosis of Beethoven's Late Style: Early Symptom of a Fatal Condition," in *Developing Variations*, pp. 37ff.; also Martin Jay, *The Dialectical Imagination: A History of*

the Frankfurt School and the Institute of Social Research, 1923-1950 (Boston, 1973), p. 179. See also this chapter, note 33.

21. Elliot Hurwitt, who was a candidate for the M.A. in music at Hunter when he studied with me.

22. On empirical process see Stravinsky, for example, 1: 4 (4: "do or make"), 7 (8), and 12 (13); 3: 50-56 (51-57), including 53 (54-55: "invent," "lucky find," "stumble upon") and 55 (57: "grub about"); and Epilogue: 140 (145: on the "search for sensation" and its limits). On craft see 3: 51 (53: "*homo faber*"); 4: 75-76 (78); and 6: 132 (138: "converse of improvisation"). See also this chapter, note 29.

23. See especially Stravinsky, 4: 84-85 (87-88), on the use of various sources and materials as needed.

24. This is so despite Stravinsky's shared preference with Schoenberg for "evolution" over "revolution" (see Schoenberg, pp. 91, 270, 409, and passim, and Stravinsky, 1: 10-11 [11-13]). The "beautiful continuity" of history as Stravinsky describes it (4: 71-72 [73-74]) is actually characterized by considerable discontinuity (and not just because, unlike Schoenberg's concept of history, it rejects the notion of progress). Compare also Stravinsky on posttonal chords that "throw off all constraint to become new entities free of all ties" (3: 38 [40]) and 34-35 (36-37, a passage that accepts dissonance "because it's there," so to speak) to Schoenberg on his own relation to tonality (pp. 256 and 283-84). See also this chapter, text leading to note 66. On Stravinsky's open dogmatism see Stravinsky, 1: 5-6, 8 and 16 (5-7, 9, and 18), and 2: 25 (25: "Instinct is infallible"), though see also this chapter, note 78, on Schoenberg's dogmatic certainty.

25. The single paragraph appears in Stravinsky, 2: 37 (39-40), despite a constant emphasis on rightness and on rules that are never specified (for example, 2: 24 [25] and 3: 48 [48], both on "rightness"; and 3: 65 [68-69: "arbitrariness of the constraint," "rules"]).

26. For example, Stravinsky, 2: 42-43 (46), 4: 77 (79), and 6: 125 (130).

27. It is interesting to note that Stravinsky's famous description of the "realm of necessity" that delivers him from the "abyss of freedom" gives a priority over rules to "solid and concrete elements" of sound and rhythm (3:63-65 [66-69]). See chapter 4, on Allan Bloom, notes 67 and 157. The convergence of Stravinsky's empiricism (see this chapter, note 22) and Milton Babbitt's vision of music—specifically, his erstwhile call on universities to subsidize new music as a form of quasi-scientific research—reinforces the sense that these two men share a *style* of objectivity, no matter how different their methods of composition. For Babbitt's proposal see "Who Cares if You Listen?" (1958), reprinted in *The American Composer Speaks: A Historical Anthology, 1770-1965*, ed. Gilbert Chase (Baton Rouge, 1966), pp. 242-43. A substantial portion of this essay, which Babbitt considered entitling "The Composer as Specialist," is reprinted by Piero Weiss and Richard Taruskin in their collection *Music in the Western World: A History in Documents* (New York, 1984), pp. 529-34.

28. For his elitism see, for instance, Stravinsky, 3: 56 (57-58: "acquired culture," "innate taste"), and 6: 133 (139-40). Interestingly, whereas metaphors of taste are usually employed in a derogatory sense by Schoenberg ("spicy" as opposed to functional dissonances, p. 247) and Adorno ("culinary listening," "Schoenberg," *Prisms*, p. 154, and "culinary merits," *Sociology*, p. 126), Stravinsky revels in such imagery ("appetite," "flow of saliva," "kneading the dough," 3: 51 [51-52]; see also 2: 24 [24: "appetite"]; and see this chapter, notes 30 and 78). This difference is consistent with Adorno's characteristic denigration of music as a "consumer" good. See also Pierre Boulez, *Notes of an Apprenticeship*, trans. Herbert Weinstock (New York, 1968), pp. 249-50, on Stravinsky's "hedonism," and this chapter, notes 31 and 68.

29. See Stravinsky, 1: 10 (12). See also note 30. On Schoenberg see this chapter, notes 50 and 64.

30. Especially relevant here is Stravinsky's invocation, 1: 6 (7), "I shall call upon your feeling and your taste for order and discipline." See also this chapter, notes 16 and 78; Adorno, *Philosophy*, p. 140 and passim on Stravinsky and "specialization"; and Schoenberg, pp. 387-88.

31. "The tradition of German music—as it includes Schoenberg—has been characterized since Beethoven, both in the positive and the negative sense, by the absence of taste" (Adorno, *Philosophy*, pp. 153-54). Adorno contrasts this absence of taste favorably with "the primacy of taste" in Stravinsky's music (ibid., p. 154), though he does concede that Stravinsky's taste, as opposed to that of his followers, involves a "power of renunciation" and a "perverse joy in self-denial" (ibid., p. 153). At this moment indeed, though citing Hegel's support for the view that taste is superficial, merely private, and therefore limited in value, Adorno nevertheless admits that "to a very large degree, taste coincides with the ability to refrain from tempting artistic means" (ibid., p. 153). This observation links Stravinsky's taste, at least, with Schoenberg's ascetic antitaste, which Adorno praises for its maturity (see this chapter, notes 48, 63, and 64). It also evokes the refusal of comfort that Trilling (see this volume, chapter 1, notes 28 and 63) associates with authenticity, a term that actually figures in this passage by Adorno (p. 153). (See also this volume, chapter 4, note 116.) At the same time Adorno's reference, however proud, to both positive and negative aspects of the German absence of taste, like his criticism of Schoenberg's lack of discrimination in his choice of texts, as in "Schoenberg," *Prisms*, pp. 162-63, points a bit uncharacteristically to stylistic limitations in Adorno's own culture. See this chapter, notes 61, 63, and 68, and also 77, and pp.166-67, the text connecting references to notes 63 and 64. See also Schoenberg, p. 247, on the "dictatorship of taste."

32. Adorno, *Sociology*, p. 197. See also this volume, chapter 2, note 14. Of interest is Bakhtin's related assertion that "insight also involves a value judgment on the novel, one not only artistic in the narrow sense but also ideological—for there is no artistic understanding without evaluation"; see Mikhail M. Bakhtin, *The Dialogic Imagination*, ed. Michael Holquist, trans. Caryl Emerson and Michael Holquist (Austin, 1981), p. 416, note 65.

33. Though Adorno regularly uses the term "ideology" in its negative Marxist sense, he does specify that "it is not ideology in itself which is untrue but rather its pretension to correspond to reality" ("Cultural Criticism and Society," *Prisms*, p. 32). See also this chapter, text leading to note 20; this volume, chapter 2, notes 14 and 17, and chapter 4, note 146.

34. The quotations come from *Style and Idea*, pp. 454 and 450 (both on Mahler). See also ibid., pp. 75, 215, 254-57, 321, 438; and Rosen, *Schoenberg*, p. 100; and this chapter, notes 43 and 77. Schoenberg's notions here can be contrasted with the formalistic nature of the underlying "appetite" evoked by Stravinsky (1: 24 [24]).

35. For example, Schoenberg, pp. 101, 102, 104, 114-17, 246, 257, 266-67, and 414-15; and Adorno, "Schoenberg," *Prisms*, p. 152 (Schoenberg's music is "structural down to the last tone"), and p. 168 (on "the task of eliminating the apocryphal elements in twelve-tone technique"). Nonredundancy indicates a need not only for avoiding repetition or reinforcement of a pitch, lest tonal hierarchy be evoked, but also for economy, variation, and musical "prose" as well as for historical originality. The analogy with computer imagery is obvious even though the informational value of redundancy is not highly valued from this compositional perspective. On the relation of art and information see the discussion of Yuri Lotman in Terry Eagleton, *Literary Theory: An Introduction* (Minneapolis, 1983), pp.101-2; and Leonard B. Meyer, *Music, the Arts, and Ideas: Patterns and Predictions in Twentieth-Century Culture* (Chicago, 1967), especially chapter 11, chapters 1-3, and p. 262.

36. See Schoenberg, pp. 129, 279, 397, and passim; also Adorno, "Schoenberg," *Prisms*, p. 154. On Brahms see, for example, Schoenberg, pp. 80 and 129. For a full-scale account of this concept see Walter Frisch, *Brahms and the Principle of Developing Variation* (Berkeley and Los Angeles, 1984). On *Aufhebung* see this volume, chapter 2, note 18.

37. See Schoenberg, especially p. 118; and Adorno, "Bach Defended against his Devotees," *Prisms*, p. 139.

38. See Hanslick, p. 125 (82), and Schoenberg, pp. 120-21. See also this chapter, note 61.

39. See Adorno, "Schoenberg," *Prisms*, pp. 160-61; and Rosen, *Schoenberg*, pp. 96-102; the

great respect among musicologists for Schoenberg's *Erwartung* stems largely from its *musical* recognition of these negative potentialities. This seems to be music as self-negated logic or pure "trace," a condition that is no doubt related to its projection of extreme anxiety. On Beethoven, see Adorno, *Philosophy*, pp. 163-64; on total development see ibid., pp. 56-57.

40. Paul de Man, *Blindness and Insight: Essays in the Rhetoric of Contemporary Criticism*, 2nd rev. ed. (Minneapolis, 1983), especially pp. 105ff. Note also Adorno himself, in "Cultural Criticism and Society," *Prisms*, p. 27, on the blindness of cultural criticism.

41. Stravinsky, 4: 79 (81). On judging whole styles, see chapter 4, p. 188.

42. On education as the mastery of a privileged discourse see Robert Scholes, "Is There a Fish in This Text?" in *On Signs*, ed. Marshall Blonsky (Baltimore, 1985), pp. 308-20; and Eagleton, *Literary Theory*, p. 201.

43. Adorno, *Sociology*, p. 74 (on Berg, especially the success of *Wozzeck*); Schoenberg, p. 133, also 454. See especially this chapter, notes 44 and 77.

44. Schoenberg in his writings and letters gave substantial recognition to the subconscious origins of composition. But he also stressed the discoverable structural logic in such origins and the need for conscious control (see, for example, Schoenberg, pp. 92, 217-18, 244, and 423-24). Schoenberg's description of his "mental tortures" in retaining a passage in the first Chamber Symphony that he was not able to justify structurally for another twenty years is remarkable (ibid., pp. 222-23). It is hard to imagine Stravinsky in such a position (though see Stravinsky, Epilogue: 140 [145]: "It seems that the unity we are seeking is forged without our knowing it"). It is also hard to overstate the intimidating effect of this passage on the would-be structural listener. See also Adorno, *Philosophy*, pp. 138-43, and this chapter, notes 18 and 77.

45. See Joseph Kerman, *Contemplating Music: Challenges to Musicology* (Cambridge, Mass., 1985), pp. 71-72.

46. Immanuel Kant, *The Critique of Judgment*, trans. J. H. Bernard (New York, 1951), section 45, pp. 149-50.

47. See Adorno, "Schoenberg," *Prisms*, pp. 142-46. See this volume, chapter 2, note 17.

48. For the entire quotation see Adorno, "Schoenberg," *Prisms*, p. 169. See also ibid., p. 157 (Schoenberg's "is music for the intellectual ear"); and Adorno, *Philosophy*, p. 15 ("Only in a society which had achieved satisfaction [i.e., for the free individual] would the death of art be possible"). For different views of silent reading see Roland Barthes, *The Responsibility of Forms: Critical Essays on Music, Art, and Representation*, trans. Richard Howard (New York, 1985), pp. 264-65; and Jacques Attali, *Noise: The Political Economy of Music*, trans. Brian Massumi (Minneapolis, 1985), p. 32. See this chapter, notes 31, 63, and 64.

49. Boulez, *Notes of an Apprenticeship*, p. 252. Such assertions do not deny Schoenberg's extraordinary coloristic achievements as a composer (often associated with, though by no means limited to, the third piece in the *Five Pieces for Orchestra*, Op. 16, and *Pierre Lunaire*) but rather emphasize that color *as such*, as opposed to color *as structure*, had no place in Schoenberg's theory of musical value. See also Rosen, *Schoenberg*, p. 48.

50. Schoenberg, *Style and Idea*, p. 121. See also ibid., pp. 56, 132, and 240, on sound, and compare Stravinsky, 2: 26 (27), on "the sensation of the music itself" as "an indispensable element of investigation"; and this chapter, notes 29, 64, and also 22.

51. Jacques Derrida, "The Supplement of Copula: Philosophy *before* Linguistics," in *Textual Strategies: Perspectives in Post-Structuralist Criticism*, ed. Josué V. Harari (Ithaca, 1979), pp. 82-120.

52. A notable breakthrough in the formalizing of a technique characteristically associated with medium was the article by Janet M. Levy entitled "Texture as a Sign in Classic and Romantic Music," *Journal of the American Musicological Society* 35 (1982), 482-531.

53. From the *Essay on the Origin of Languages*, quoted in Derrida, *Of Grammatology*, p. 206. Of interest also is the passage about music and poetry in ancient Greece that is quoted on p. 201: "In cultivating the art of convincing, that of arousing the emotions was lost."

54. See Adorno, "Schoenberg," *Prisms*, p. 146; and also this volume, chapter 2, note 14.

55. On Barthes see Eagleton, *Literary Theory*, p. 136, and also pp. 170 and 187. See also this volume, chapter 1, notes 50 and especially 51 (on Wagner), and chapter 2, notes 14 and 119.

56. I have attempted to do precisely this in an unpublished paper delivered at Queens College, New York, November 5, 1986, at the kind invitation of Joseph Straus.

57. See Eagleton, *Literary Theory*, pp. 49, 207, and passim. My own response to Anthony Barone's paper "The Critical Reception of Verdi in Fascist Italy" at the annual meeting of the American Musicological Society in Cleveland (November 8, 1986) addressed the same theme.

58. See, for example, Edward Said, "The Text, the World, the Critic," in Harari, *Textual Strategies*, pp. 161-88; Fredric Jameson, "The Realist Floor-Plan," in Blonsky, *On Signs*, pp. 373-83; Blonsky, "Introduction: The Agony of Semiotics," ibid., pp. xiii-li, especially starting at p. xix, and "Endword: Americans on the Move," ibid., pp. 507-9; and Eagleton, *Literary Theory*, pp. 194-217.

59. Adorno, *Sociology*, p. 195; on "naming the formal components," see ibid., p. 4.

60. Ibid., p. 152.

61. See especially Adorno, "Schoenberg," *Prisms*, pp. 152-53, on Schoenberg's compositional methods as an outgrowth of necessity rather than temperament; and also ibid., p. 154, on Adorno's characteristic equation of nonstructural listening with "musical stupidity." See also this chapter, note 31.

Worth noting, in terms of this argument, is Hanslick's insistence that only themes of a particular kind lend themselves to logical unfolding (*The Beautiful in Music*, p. 125 [82]). Though he compares such a theme to a "self-evident truth" (p. 124 [or "logical axiom," Payzant trans., p. 81—the German is *selbstständige Axiom*, p. 216]), he notes on the same page that the theme can only be conveyed by playing it. Hanslick concedes in his own way that themes that are open to logical unfolding in fact have the concreteness of a particular culture rather than a universal abstractness. Indeed, he explicitly associates the higher, logical type of theme with German orchestral music (overtures by Beethoven and Mendelssohn), as opposed to the "low music hall" themes of opera overtures by Donizetti and Verdi (p. 125 [or "neighborhood pub" themes, Payzant trans., p. 82—*Kneipe* in German, p. 218]). See also this chapter, note 38.

62. See notes 31 and 68. One has to distinguish, of course, between the effect of Adorno's style as cultural ethos and the sensibility that went into the formation of his own personal style. Though Adorno would no doubt argue that the extraordinary care he took in laying out his language so as to avoid falseness amounted to a series of structural decisions, one experiences the integrity of Adorno's writing as fundamentally a matter of style. In this respect he honored in his own work the demands he made on others concerning style (see this chapter, note 63); see also this volume, chapter 4, note 173.

63. On "jagged physiognomy" see Adorno, *Philosophy*, p. 136; on Brahms see his "Schoenberg," *Prisms*, p. 156. See also the latter, pp. 144 and 153; and Adorno's *Philosophy*, p. 133: "Modern music . . . [has] all of its beauty in denying itself the illusion of beauty." An important formulation of Adorno's attitude toward smoothness of style, and its relation to society, utopia, and ideology, appears in Max Horkheimer and Theodor W. Adorno, *Dialectic of Enlightenment,* trans. John Cumming (New York, 1972), pp. 130-31. See also this volume, chapter 2, note 14. In the present chapter see notes 31 and 64, 20 and 33; see also note 62, on Adorno's own style. Of the greatest interest in this connection is Lionel Trilling's characterization of "authenticity" in *Sincerity and Authenticity* (Cambridge, Mass., 1972). See, for example, p. 11 (on the "strenuous moral experience" of authenticity) and p. 94 ("Nowadays our sense of what authenticity means involves a degree of rough concreteness or of extremity."). See also chapter 1 of this book, "Whose *Magic Flute?*" notes 28, 29, and 63-65; and chapter 4, notes 116, 128, and 134.

64. On this whole topic see, for instance, Schoenberg, pp. 235 (on "the childish preference of the primitive ear for colours"), 401 ("an alert and well-trained mind will demand to be told the more remote matters . . . [and] refuses to listen to baby-talk"), and 408 ("Mature people think in

complexes"); on style versus idea see especially ibid., pp. 118 and 120. See also ibid., p. 378, where Schoenberg dismisses culturally associative modes of listening as directed only at "the perfume of a work, that narcotic emanation of music which affects the senses without involving the mind." See also this chapter, p. 166, and notes 29, 31, 48, 50, and 63; and this volume, chapter 4, note 142.

65. For examples of the shift in paradigm see Schoenberg, pp. 38, 101, 256, 283, 380, and 435. See also Carl Dahlhaus, *Realism in Nineteenth-Century Music,* trans. Mary Whittall (Cambridge, 1985), p. 11. On Adorno's derivation from Hegel of the view that truth is the vocation of art, see, for example, the review of Adorno's *Aesthetic Theory* by Raymond Geuss in *Journal of Philosophy* 83 (1986), 734ff.

66. For example, Schoenberg, pp. 49-51, 91, 284, and 288. Schoenberg's notion of "liquidation" (p. 288) is also suggestive in this connection. See also this volume, chapter 2, note 53, on the relation between trace and *Aufhebung.*

67. See especially Blonsky, Introduction, *On Signs,* pp. xvi-xvii.

68. Adorno did indeed recognize this difference in general perception, and scorned it as a mark of intellectual (and moral) inferiority. See his "Schoenberg," *Prisms,* p. 152, on "Stravinsky and . . . all those who, having adjusted better to contemporary existence, fancy themselves more modern than Schoenberg." (See also Boulez, *Notes of an Apprenticeship,* p. 252, where a similar distinction is made between Wagner and Mussorgsky, though not on Adorno's grounds.) Adorno might perhaps have linked Stravinsky more aptly to postmodern culture. See especially Trilling, *Sincerity,* p. 98, note 1, on the end of the alienation and resistance that characterized "modern" art: in "post-modern" culture "the faculty of 'taste' has re-established itself at the center of the experience of art." (The terms "modern" and "post-modern" here are both Trilling's.)

69. That there are grounds for developing a somewhat different definition of individuality from just such a perception, however, is suggested by this observation of Bruno Nettl's concerning (pre-Islamic) classical Persian music from the latter part of the first millennium: "Similarly, individualism, another central cultural value, is reflected in the importance of the exceptional." (*The Study of Ethnomusicology: Twenty-nine Issues and Concepts* [Urbana, 1983], p. 207). I am grateful to Ken Moore, who as a doctoral candidate in ethnomusicology was my student at the CUNY Graduate Center, for calling this discussion to my attention.

70. For "always already" see Derrida, *Of Grammatology,* p. 201.

71. Wolfgang Hildesheimer, *Mozart,* trans. Marion Faber (New York, 1983), pp. 4, 11-12.

72. On *"différance"* see Spivak, translator's preface to *Of Grammatology,* pp. xxix and xliii; Culler, *On Deconstruction,* pp. 95-99; and chapter 2, "How Could Chopin's A-Major Prelude Be Deconstructed?" notes 25 and 52. The concept is defined and analyzed by Jacques Derrida in his *Margins of Philosophy,* trans. and ed. Alan Bass (Chicago, 1982), in the chapter *"Différance,"* pp. 1-27.

73. Strong support for this assertion is provided in Bakhtin, *Dialogic Imagination,* for example, pp. 283-84, 289, 417, and 420-21.

74. Ibid., p. 280.

75. This discussion appears in my essay "The Challenge of Contemporary Music," as does an analysis of various difficulties connected with the mastery of structural listening. See *Developing Variations,* pp. 277-83, especially 281. Of interest in this connection is Herbert Lindenberger's observation in *Opera: The Extravagant Art* (Ithaca, 1984), pp. 226-27, that "modern ballet (even when accompanied by difficult musical scores)" may enjoy a large public today in part "because ballet is sufficiently abstract that audiences do not feel tempted to panic if they fail to understand the 'meaning.'" It would be interesting to compare Lindenberger's notion of abstraction here with the view taken throughout the present essay.

76. See especially Stanley Rosen, *The Limits of Analysis* (New York, 1980), pp. 216-60. I am deeply indebted to the late David Bain, who was my student while a doctoral candidate in music at the CUNY Graduate Center, for calling this book to my attention and, beyond this, for his clarifying insight into every aspect of this essay, especially those issues taken up in my concluding paragraphs.

77. Again, although Schoenberg's acknowledgment of the role played by intuition in music is not to be denied, neither is the uneasy relationship of this acknowledgment to his essentially discursive sense of musical value. See this chapter, note 44, especially on the first Chamber Symphony, and note the exertion needed to defend his response to Mahler (pp. 449-60). Schoenberg justifies this response on grounds, such as Mahler's profound originality and his high level of culture, that for him confirm Mahler's structural greatness. See especially his remarks on p. 454 concerning Mahler's mode of expression, material, and construction. See also this chapter, note 34.

78. See especially in this connection Schoenberg, p. 38, on the reasons for his unpopularity: "An artist . . . knowing that those parts which were found ugly could not be wrong because he would not have written them if he himself had not liked them, and remembering the judgement of some very understanding friends and experts in musical knowledge who have paid tribute to his work, . . . becomes aware that he himself is not to blame." See also p. 218, on the artist's need to be "convinced of the infallibility of [his] own fantasy."

A kind of counterpart to Schoenberg's moral certainty (the term "infallible" connotes moral as well as cognitive certainty) can be found in Stravinsky's flat assertion that "my experience and investigations are entirely objective" (Stravinsky, 1: 7 [8]). On its face, the ability implied here to avoid Kant's subject-object dichotomy and the cognitive dilemmas of the post-Kantian philosophical loop seems nothing short of extraordinary. If, however, one supposes, as I do, that Stravinksy construes objectivity as an aesthetic style rather than as an epistemological condition, the content of his statement becomes oddly plausible (though of course its objective "style" remains quite different from Schoenberg's willing of infallibility). Certainly an aesthetic reading of this statement is congruent with Stravinsky's own easy association of "taste" and "discipline" (see this chapter, note 30).

79. See Barthes, *Responsibility*, pp. 252-60 (on listening) and 269ff. (on performance); and also Louis Marin, "The 'Aesop' Fable-Animal," in Blonsky, *On Signs*, p. 337 and passim. Such a rapprochement in the realm of neurology is a principle theme of Oliver Sacks's book, *The Man Who Mistook His Wife for a Hat*, which concerns itself extensively with music. See this volume, chapter 2, note 41.

80. Compare also the following excerpt from a letter by a contemporary poet, Brooks Haxton, to the *New York Times Book Review* (January 11, 1987), 37: "For various reasons (including the obscure language of certain influential poets) intelligent, otherwise literate people seldom look toward poetry for communication of any consequence. . . . It is an important trend, which limits our access to the poetry of other ages, and thereby weakens one of our deepest connections to past humanity, weakens our ability to imagine others in the present and, more frighteningly, diminishes our faith in the fullness of a human future. The loss of such profound resources involves (together with literary appreciation) the stewardship of all culture and ultimately of the now precarious natural world."

81. Roland Barthes, "From Work to Text," in Harari, *Textual Strategies*, p. 80.

82. Ibid.; see also Eagleton on pleasure in academia, *Literary Theory*, p. 212, and see this volume, chapter 2, note 24, for more on Barthes.

83. See especially in this connection Gregory Sandow, "Secret of the Silver Ticket," *Village Voice* (April 1, 1986), 86.

4. The Closing of the American Dream? A Musical Perspective on Allan Bloom, Spike Lee, and Doing the Right Thing

(The first reference to Bloom's *Closing of the American Mind* in each note will be abbreviated as "Bloom, p. x"; where the attribution is clear, Bloom's name may be omitted. Subsequent references in that note will not repeat the name "Bloom" unless required for clarity. References to endnotes are to notes in this chapter unless specifically marked otherwise.) This essay grows out of a lecture that was commissioned by Wesleyan University as the annual George Jackson Memorial Lecture, which I presented at Wesleyan on October 17, 1989. I wish here to express my gratitude to Professor Neely Bruce and the Department of Music at Wesleyan for giving me the chance to embark on a study that has meant a great deal to me.

1. Allan Bloom, *The Closing of the American Mind* (New York, 1987), pp. 193 and 266. Compare these quotations with the following passages, which might also have served as mottoes for this chapter, all from Max Horkheimer and Theodor W. Adorno, *Dialectic of Enlightenment*, trans. John Cumming (New York, 1972): "Enlightenment . . . is the philosophy which equates the truth with scientific systematization" (p. 85); "Enlightened reason is as little capable of finding a standard by which to measure any drive in itself, and in comparison with all other drives, as of arranging the universe in spheres" (p. 91); and, "So long as art declines to pass as cognition and is thus separated from practice, social practice tolerates it as it tolerates pleasure" (p. 32). See also the quotes from E. L. Doctorow's 1989 commencement address at Brandeis University, cited here in notes 119, 136, and 192.

2. The film *Do The Right Thing*, which appeared in 1989, was produced, written, and directed by Spike Lee; the copyright is held by Universal Pictures. *Do The Right Thing* [A Companion Volume to the Universal Pictures Film] (New York, 1989), by Spike Lee with Lisa Jones, is a useful companion to the film, which includes the script, a journal kept by Lee (mainly before the production), and other notes. It will be referred to hereafter as *DTRT Companion*. On the status of this moment as decisive, see below, note 112.

3. Lee and Jones, *DTRT Companion*, p. 60.

4. Bloom, p. 377; see also p. 312 (on "the foundations of the university"); p. 240 (on the "rejection of reason" by rationalism, quoted below in note 31); and p. 22 (on the "profoundest crisis" of "modern nations"). Though Bloom speaks of "modern nations" here, his concern throughout his book is with the American university in particular.

5. Lee and Jones, *DTRT Companion*, p. 29.

6. See Lee and Jones, *DTRT Companion*, p. 67 [from Lee's journal before the production]: "Certain themes keep popping up in my notes, which is a good sign. I must remember the line Sal always repeats, THIS IS AMERICA. It's key" (emphasis his). See also p. 53: "Any time Sal gets into one of his philosophical moods, he finishes a sentence with 'This is America.' When Black folks are tearing apart his pizzeria, Sal says, 'You can't do this. This is America.'"

7. Bloom, p. 382. See also p. 39 (on the United States as "one of the highest and most extreme achievements of the rational quest for the good life according to nature").

8. Such principles as *stare decisis* and "neutral principles" exemplify this tendency in law, as does the following sentiment: "The point of the First Amendment is that majority preferences must be expressed in some fashion other than silencing speech on the basis of its contents" (Nat Hentoff, "A Startling Triumph for Free Speech," *Village Voice* [July 28, 1992], 19); in other words, the principle of free speech excludes evaluating the specific moral content of actual speech.

9. Though by 1989 it had already become apparent even to many nonacademics that this conception of reason has also created or worsened many physical hardships, including a variety of diseases and environmental destruction.

10. [ON THE CONFLATION OF STRUCTURE (OR STANCE OR STATUS) AND CONTENT.] Throughout this essay, as also in "How Could Chopin's A-Major Prelude Be Deconstructed?" the spirit of Epimenides' paradox will be evident in many references to the difficulty of separating semiotic structures from the contents of their themes. On this topic in relation to literary theory see Jonathan Culler, *On Deconstruction: Theory and Criticism after Structuralism* (Ithaca, 1982), pp. 201-2. See also below, note 103; notes 17, 18, 24, 81, 82, 83, 135, and 142 are among others with a bearing on this issue. In addition, see note 73; and chapter 2, notes 9 and 152.

11. Though readers can no doubt think of individuals or schools of thought that advocate

adopting this second definition of reason *to the exclusion* of the first, I will not examine such viewpoints, which I do not support, for reasons that should become clear to readers of this essay (and this volume). Any such advocacy of mutual exclusiveness simply replicates the inadequacy of the conception of reason that it is trying to replace. In my judgment, this viewpoint is not only logically unnecessary but also morally irresponsible.

12. [ON BLOOM AND A CONCRETE NOTION OF REASON.]

Allan Bloom in fact states fairly early in his book that "experience or passion . . . are the bases of moral reasoning" (p. 61), and at times he insists on the concrete nature of philosophy (see below, note 19). But he does not demonstrate or develop anything by way of these assertions; even at the end of the book, one has little sense of how Bloom would define "moral reasoning" apart from saying it is what Socrates did; see the text that follows note 56, p. 185, this chapter. On the threat of a narrowly held conception of reason to reason itself, see the penultimate paragraph of this essay.

13. [ON NATURE AS BLOOM'S OWN GROUND.]

From the start, Bloom grounds his own positions on nature-as-opposed-to-culture. See, for example, pp. 38 ("Men cannot remain content with what is given them by their culture if they are to be fully human. . . . A culture is a cave. . . . [we] need to know nature in order to have a standard"—Bloom goes on to reject the "dogmatic assurance that thought is culture-bound, that there is no nature"); 51 ("nature is the only thing that counts in education"); 254 (on the autonomy of the university, based on the "quest for and even discovery of the truth according to nature"—see fuller quotation in note 52, below); 264 ("Philosophy is the rational account of the whole, or of nature"); 270 (on Thales and Socrates); 290 ("[Philosophers] took a dare on the peculiar form of reasoning that comes from the natural inclinations"); 349 (on the writings of Kant and Goethe as "mirrors of nature"). Of particular importance are the statements about philosophers on pp. 279 and 179, cited in this chapter, p. 183, at note 34. See also note 19; Bloom, p. 304 (on human nature); and p. 264 (on the Greek pedigree of the notion of nature).

Bloom's later discussion of Plato's cave and the search for enlightenment (the aspiration to "a nonconventional world, to nature, by the use of reason" [pp. 264-65]) emphasizes the need of reason to work at finding nature. He also implies at one point (p. 317) that American academics were naive in their "conviction of the self-evidence of Enlightenment principles to all thinking people." Nevertheless, reason for Bloom is grounded on nature in a self-evident way; note his approval of the rational statesmen of the Enlightenment who "strive for ends grasped by reason and self-evidently grounded in nature. No values, no creative visions are required for them to see what all reasonable men should see" (p. 209).

Of particular importance to Bloom's entire argument is his linkage, early in the book, of nature with a standard that will allow him to judge Western culture as superior to others. See p. 36 ("to believe [one's own way to be the] best . . . is . . . natural"); p. 38 (on the notion, rejected by Bloom, that "thought is culture-bound," on "the need to know nature in order to have a standard," and on the deleterious effects of cultural relativism); and notes 14, 16, 27, and 83.

14. [BLOOM ON REASON AS AN ABSTRACT UNIVERSAL PRINCIPLE.]

See Bloom, e.g., pp. 292 ("The philosophers, ancient and modern, agreed that the fulfillment of humanity is in the use of reason. Man is the particular being that can know the universal, the temporal being that is aware of eternity" [this follows the passage quoted in note 19]); 173 ("Everyone knows that the particular as particular escapes the grasp of reason, the form of which is the general or the universal"); 254 ("the natural community of men and the universality of thought"); 201 ("the universal standards of reason"); 307 ("universal principles of understanding"); 290 ("the philosopher looks at things under the guise of eternity" and "theory look[s] to the universal and unchangeable while understanding its relation to the particular and changing").

Often the thought is stated negatively, within a criticism of philosophers who developed cultural relativism. The following account of a slippery slope appears, for example, in an account of

Nietzsche (p. 203): "Everyone likes cultural relativism but wants to exempt what concerns him . . . But . . . if there is an escape for one truth . . . then . . . becoming, change, history or what have you is not what is fundamental, but rather, being, the immutable principle of science and philosophy." See also pp. 343 (on education and "high-level generalism"); and 200 (on Nietzsche and the descent from universal notions of self). See also p. 179 ("In order to know such an amorphous being as man, Rousseau himself and his particular history are in his [Rousseau's, not Bloom's] view, more important than is Socrates' quest for man in general or man in himself").

Possibly Bloom is drawn to this negative formulation of universal principles because even he feels a bit uncomfortable with the problematical status of positive formulations in our culture. In any case, he states many of his positions in negative terms, as will be seen in the notes that follow.

15. [BLOOM ON THE PERMANENCE OF HUMAN NATURE.]

See Bloom, e.g., p. 304 ("the rebirth of Greece, always possible because of its universality, and the permanence of human nature"); p. 381 ("What is essential about . . . any of the Platonic dialogues is reproducible in almost all times and places"); pp. 20 and 278 (on human nature); p. 283 ("problems are permanent but their expressions are changing"); p. 343 ("permanent questions"); p. 310 ("Our rationalism is [Socrates'] rationalism"); and p. 49 ("the two universalities, of the body and of the soul"). For a negative version, see p. 308 (explicating Nietzsche): "There cannot be, as Socrates believed, the pure mind, which is trans-historical." Bloom's position, here, is with Socrates.

16. [BLOOM'S LINKAGE OF CULTURE AND IRRATIONALITY.]

The root of the problem for Bloom is that "the idea of culture was adopted . . . [as] an alternative to what was understood [by critics of the Enlightenment] to be the shallow and dehumanizing universality of rights based on our animal nature. The folk mind takes the place of reason" (p. 192). See ibid. on "the fundamental conflict between liberal society and culture"; also p. 191 on the tension between the cosmopolitan view of humanity (with its emphasis on universality and rationality) and the particular view (with its emphasis on culture); and 193 (on the tension between culture and science), and, below, note 27 and especially notes 89 and 102.

17. [BLOOM ON DIRECT ACCESS OF ABSTRACT REASON TO THE MEANINGS OF OTHERS.]

See Bloom, p. 376, for his dismissal of language barriers or translations as serious philosophical problems; and especially p. 381 (in connection with the Socratic dialogues): "Such experiences are always accessible. . . . [The Greeks] proved the viability of what is best in man, independent of accidents, of circumstance. We feel ourselves too dependent on history and culture"; for the continuation, see above, note 15. For Bloom's disdain for any sort of cultural hermeneutics, see, e.g., p. 305, on the discovery of Greek "culture," and p. 373, on the modern misreading of Aristotle. See also below, notes 18, 89, 100, 103, 125, and 146.

Interestingly, E. D. Hirsch, Jr., presents essentially the same idea in his book *The Aims of Interpretation* (Chicago, 1976), the fundamental argument of which is that though many kinds of (contextual) significance can legitimately be attributed to a text, a text has only one valid (verbal) meaning, the one intended by the author. (It is this book I denote in chapter 2, p. 69.) Certainly this notion puts Hirsch squarely in the camp of those opposed to Jacques Derrida, who would go so far as to argue that an original text is itself already a translation (see Gayatri Chakravorty Spivak's preface to her translation of Jacques Derrida's *Of Grammatology* [Baltimore, 1976], p. lxxxvii); and there is no school for which Bloom's book exhibits more contempt than Derrida's; see below, notes 42 and 98.

In fact, Hirsch's earlier book may be more compatible with Bloom's thinking than is Hirsch's own recent best-seller, *Cultural Literacy: What Every American Needs to Know* (New York, 1988), even though it is the latter book that has been commonly associated with Bloom's best-seller. For Hirsch's own objections to this association, see Christopher Hitchens, "Why We Don't Know What We Don't Know: Just Ask E. D. Hirsch," *New York Times Magazine* (May 13, 1990), 59. On the other hand, as I hope to show below, this association is by no means altogether accidental or misguided.

18. [BLOOM ON CONTENT AS THE LOCUS OF MEANING.]

Bloom, p. 373. See also the reference to Thomas Kuhn, and to the question "Is science true?" on p. 200; in essence, Bloom objects to Kuhn for analyzing the structure rather than content of science. At times Bloom's notion of "true" becomes a notion of "real," as when he distinguishes between "real" differences involving the content of fundamental beliefs and what amount to pseudo-differences in cultural style (pp. 192-93). See this chapter, notes 10 and 25.

Of special interest concerning content is this remark on p. 308: "What is fascinating for us . . . is that Nietzsche, and Heidegger following him, are the first modern thinkers . . . to take Socrates . . . really seriously as . . . a living opponent rather than as a cultural artifact. Socrates is alive and must be overcome. It is essential to recognize that this is *the* issue in Nietzsche. It is not a historical or cultural question. It is simply a classic philosophic disputation: Was Socrates right or wrong?" On p. 305 Bloom objects to Rousseau's treatment of Plato as a poet [see below, note 74], and to scholars since Rousseau who have "treated Greek philosophers more as natural scientists treat atoms than as they treat other natural scientists"). See also pp. 309 and 312 for his insistence on the philosophical as opposed to cultural function of the university (i.e., of the true or Enlightenment university, p. 309). For a negative formulation, see Bloom's scorn for the notion that "the scholar cannot understand the texts that he purports to interpret and explain [because he comes from a different culture]," p. 308. See also this chapter, note 24.

On the content of literature, see especially p. 374 ("The truth question is most pressing and acutely embarrassing for those who deal with the philosophic texts, but also creates problems for those treating purely literary works. There is an enormous difference between saying, as teachers once did, 'You must learn to see the world as Homer or Shakespeare did,' and saying, as teachers now do, 'Homer and Shakespeare had some of the same concerns you do and can enrich your vision of the world'"). See also p. 375, on Plato and Dante (quoted below, note 98); and note also this statement, p. 63, on old classic paintings: "Without those meanings [conveyed by the subjects of the paintings], and without their being something essential to the viewer as a moral, political and religious being, the works lose their essence. It is not merely the tradition that is lost . . . in this way. It is being itself that vanishes." (This follows the passage quoted in note 73.) Though Bloom's notion of "being" here is somewhat problematical (see below, note 78), he is insisting that both philosophy and literature be read for content. The difference is that only the content of philosophy is imperishable (see below, notes 73 and 75); see also note 146 (on translation), note 10 (on structure and content), and note 81 (on thematic norms).

19. [BLOOM ON THE CHARACTER AND PRIVILEGED STATUS OF PHILOSOPHY.]

Bloom, p. 273. It cannot be denied that Bloom pays homage to the concreteness of philosophy and its rootedness in experience (see above, note 12). See p. 255 ("Concreteness, not abstractness, is the hallmark of philosophy. All interesting generalization must proceed from the richest awareness of what is to be explained, but the tendency to abstractness leads to simplifying the phenomena in order more easily to deal with them") and p. 61, on experience and passion as "the bases of moral reasoning." On experience see pp. 200, 254, and 273 (on everyday crafts). Nevertheless the overwhelming preponderance of discussion emphasizes reason as a transhistorical principle and minimizes "mere life" (see below, note 53). The reference on p. 254 is to the experience of aristocrats, who appreciate the virtues of knowledge for its own sake over utilitarian knowledge (on the latter, see especially pp. 250-51 and this chapter, notes 52, 95, and 126). Where Bloom does praise concreteness and experience, he seems to be championing Greek-based philosophy against the narrowing that occurred in Enlightenment science (see p. 273, on the movement of the philosophers to the university, though Enlightenment philosophers, unlike the ancients, tried to *apply* theory to practice, p. 291). Bloom's note, p. 292, that "everything turns on what the deepest human experience is" forms part of his praise for Enlightenment thinkers for maintaining ideals of universal reason (the continuation of the passage is given at the start of note 14, above). See also below, note 84, on the "gray net of abstraction" (p. 238) in the modern relativistic world.

On the privileged status of philosophy, and its basis in abstract rational thought, see Bloom, e.g., p. 38 ("philosophy . . . is the most important human science"); p. 264 (the passage centered on "the philosophic life is the highest"); p. 271 ("The important theoretical experience . . . is the only thing men surely have spiritually in common" [see this chapter, note 32]). Worth noting are references to the university, e.g., pp. 245, 254, and especially 272 (the entire page, culminating in the idea that the university "exists to preserve and further what [Socrates] represents"). See also p. 290 ("[Ancient and modern philosophers] were perfectly conscious of what separates them from all other men, and they knew that the gulf is unbridgeable. They knew that their connection with other men would always be mediated by unreason," and quotations above in notes 13 and 14); p. 291 ("philosophers . . . have entirely different ends than the rest of mankind"); also note 100, on the philosopher's abstraction; and the quotations on facing tragic reality, below, note 116. For a more negative version of this idea see p. 302 and especially p. 377 on the regrettable dethroning of philosophy as the ruling discipline in the academy, and related notions (involving the envy of science by philosophy), all cited here in note 49.

20. [ON THE COGNITIVE CHARACTER OF BLOOM'S CONCEPTION OF REASON.]

Of interest are passages in which Bloom draws cognitive concepts, such as causality and (non)contradiction into discussions of noncognitive realms, such as those of art or of value-formation. See especially Bloom's linkage of Aristotle's conception of tragedy to the relation of cause and effect (p. 281, quoted below, in note 72). Likewise, note Bloom's observation that Max Weber's philosophy entailed "a new kind of causality—entirely different from that known to natural science," proceeding as it does from the view that "in a chaotic universe, reason is unreasonable because self-contradiction is inevitable" (p. 209). Although Bloom clearly respects the caliber of Weber's thinking, he is not happy with the direction in which it leads. Contrast the passage about Weber with the accounts of Greek philosophy on p. 267 ("nothing that denies the principle of contradiction is allowed to be authoritative"), and p. 264 ("the principle of contradiction guided the discourse of all"). See also below, the last paragraph of note 48. For ramifications of Bloom's cognitive conception of reason—in particular for the essentially aesthetic character of this cognitive conception—see below, notes 21, 60, 67, 134, 151, 157, and 172.

21. [BLOOM ON THE KANTIAN SPLIT BETWEEN COGNITION AND MORALITY AND ITS EFFECTS ON SCIENCE.]

See Bloom's discussion beginning on p. 299, with the observation that Kant agreed with Rousseau that "natural science had read free, moral, artistic man out of nature." Though Kant believed he had turned "David Hume's distinction between the is and the ought from a humiliation for moral reasoning into the basis for its triumph and its dignity" (p. 300), in the wake of his work "the ground of morals and esthetics disappeared" (p. 302).

On the academic effects of Kant's critical philosophy, see p. 300: "The unity of the university is now Kant. These three kinds of knowledge (the true, the good, the beautiful in new guises) are given their domains by the three Critiques, but are not unified by being knowledge of aspects of a single reality." Of great value in this connection is Terry Eagleton's The Ideology of the Aesthetic (Oxford, 1990), especially chapter 3, "The Kantian Imaginary" (pp. 70-101) and chapter 14, "From the Polis to Postmodernism" (pp. 366-417); see also below, note 150.

For the effects of the division between science and morality on science see Bloom, e.g., p. 50 (on "the great theoretical difficulty of modern natural science—that it cannot explain why it is good"), and also p. 345 (on "the difficulties about the . . . goodness of science raised by Rousseau and Nietzsche"). In addition, see p. 150 (Weber "believed that reason and science themselves were value commitments . . . incapable of asserting their own goodness, thus having lost what had always been most distinctive in them"); p. 349, on the separation of natural science and "humane learning" after Kant and Goethe; and p. 175, on Locke's separation of the rational and virtuous man, cited below in note 59. See also below, notes 37 and 157 (on "impoverishing certitudes"), and the text of this chapter that pertains to note 151, p. 200.

22. [BLOOM ON THE EFFECT OF THE KANTIAN SPLIT ON MORALITY.]

See above, note 21, below, notes 37 and 38, and also Bloom, p. 193 ("Freedom is a postulate, a possibility in Kant, not a demonstration; and that remains the difficulty"); p. 301 (on "haunting doubt as to the reality of the realm of freedom"; see also below, note 36); p. 356 ("as scientists, they know that there are no such knowers as ethicists"); and especially pp. 200-201, paraphrasing Nietzsche (quoted in note 84 below). See also this chapter, note 150, on the formal quality of Kant's moral law.

23. [BLOOM ON THE IMPORTANCE IN COLLEGE EDUCATION OF PROVIDING A FOUNDATION FOR MAKING MORAL JUDGMENTS.]

Bloom, p. 326. See also, for example, p. 282 ("The question is how one lives"); p. 378 (on his disdain for "positivism and ordinary language analysis . . . as simply methods of a sort [that] repel students who come with the humanizing questions"); p. 372 (on the "now inadmissible questions" of "old philosophic texts"); and p. 34 ("relativism has extinguished the real motive of education, the search for a good life"); though also below, notes 156 and 157 (and the text of this chapter that pertains to these notes, p. 202).

24. [BLOOM'S CONCERN WITH CONTENT, NOT CULTURAL CONSEQUENCES.]

Bloom's concern is with the philosophical content of this change, not with the cultural consequences, which he dismisses as consequences of an inability to understand the philosophical issues involved, except in the cases of notable modern philosophers (mainly Continental—see, e.g., p. 377, on Nietzsche and Heidegger, and pp. 337-38, on Weber). See this chapter, note 18.

25. [BLOOM ON THE UNDERMINING OF COGNITIVE BASIS FOR COGNITION.]

See Bloom, p. 204 (on " the difficulty of providing a self-explanation for science and a ground for the theoretical life, which has dogged the life of the mind since early modernity but has become particularly acute with cultural relativism"); p. 345 (on "the difficulties about the truth of science raised by positivism"); p. 196 on Nietzsche ("reason recognizes its own inadequacy" [more is quoted below, in note 37]); p. 150, on Weber ("Scientific analysis itself concludes that reason is powerless"); and p. 310 (on the "radical doubt" cast by Heidegger on "modern philosophy and science"). In effect, Kant has failed in his mission "to set limits to pure reason . . . in such a way that reason will submit rationally" (p. 300). (Though Kant himself distinguished between the subjectivity of the aesthetic and the objectivity of the logical, a primary effect of his critical philosophy has been to crystallize the epistemological difficulties of defining a nonmetaphysical objective realm that does not depend for its definition on subjective faculties. On the subjectivity of the aesthetic see Immanuel Kant, *Critique of Judgment*, trans. J. H. Bernard [New York, 1951], section 1, p. 37, note 1.) See also above, note 18, on Thomas Kuhn's critique of science, and below, notes 37 and 38. In *Dialectic of Enlightenment*, Horkheimer and Adorno point often to the absence of a self-critical capacity in science as a devastating cognitive (as well as moral) liability. See, for example, pp. 25 ("Enlightenment has put away the classic requirement of thinking about thought") and 85 ("The notion of the self-understanding of science contradicts the notion of science itself"). This process entails the abandonment of the thinking subject itself to the requirements of science. See, for example, p. 30: "In the end the transcendental subject of cognition is apparently abandoned as the last reminiscence of subjectivity and replaced by the much smoother work of automatic control mechanisms. Subjectivity has given way to the logic of the allegedly indifferent rules of the game, in order to dictate all the more unrestrainedly." This formulation recalls analyses by Jameson, of Flaubert's subject, and by de Man, of Proust's; see this volume, chapter 2, p. 84, notes 89-90, and pp. 136-37, note 142. See also this chapter, note 166, on the totalizing tendency of reason.

26. On the consequences of this erosion from Bloom's perspective, see below, note 84 (on "drab diversity").

27. [BLOOM ON THE RISE OF PARTICULARISTIC VIEWPOINTS.]

On Bloom's reaction to this development see p. 192 ("There is a continuing war between the universality of the Enlightenment and the particularity that resulted from the teachings of Enlightenment's critics. . . . Such criticism provided a philosophic basis for resisting philosophy"); this is followed by a critique of "the concern with particularity." See also p. 202 on cultural relativism: "There is no place for a theoretical man to stand. . . . A cultural relativist must care for culture more than truth, and fight for culture while knowing it is not true. . . . This is somehow impossible . . . the scientific view is deadly to culture." Bloom goes on to argue that precisely in accepting post-Kantian epistemological limitations, cultural relativists deprive themselves of a basis for making any truth-claims about their own culture, and thus for making any value-distinctions between their own and other cultures. (For the importance of this point, see above, note 13, and below, notes 83, 84, and 89.)

For formulations of these ideas in a negative mode, see the passage from p. 203, on Nietzsche, quoted above in note 14, and the paraphrase of Nietzsche on p. 204 ("Hegel made a mistake; he believed there could be a thoroughly rational God, one who conciliated the demands of culture and those of science").

28. See, for example, pp. 292 and 190-91, on Rousseau's links to the Enlightenment.

29. [BLOOM'S SKEPTICAL REACTION TO ENLIGHTENMENT CRITIQUES.]

See Bloom, p. 292 (on Rousseau); pp. 307-8 (on Nietzsche); p. 207 ("The reconstitution of man in Nietzsche required the sacrifice of reason, which Enlightenment, whatever its failings, kept at the center"); and pp. 200-201 (as quoted below, note 84, on how Nietzsche's relativistic conclusions about truth did not entail an equality of ideas). See also notes 22, 30, 31, 42, 43, and 84.

30. [BLOOM'S PRESENTATION OF ENLIGHTENMENT CRITIQUE AS FLAWED.]

Concerning Nietzsche, for example, see Bloom, p. 201 (on those "who in one way or another accepted [Nietzsche's] insight); pp. 307-9, leading to the observation (p. 309), "He was the rage from 1890 on, and hardly any important painter, poet, or novelist was immune to his charm," which echoes an earlier phrase, "For all the charms of Nietzsche" (p. 207); also pp. 192 (on the "artificial notion" of culture) and 38 (on the "dogmatic assurance that thought is culture-bound"); pp. 203-4, on the inability of most critics to maintain the philosophical rigor of Nietzsche (whose own work became cheapened [by deconstruction], p. 379, as noted below, note 42); pp. 203 and 204 (on "the terrible intellectual and moral risks involved" in Nietzsche's "dangerous experiments"); and p. 202 ("this is somehow impossible, and Nietzsche struggled with the problem throughout his career, perhaps without a satisfactory resolution"). At a moment of discouragement, Bloom does speculate that Nietzsche "may not have been right, but his case looks stronger all the time" (p. 51).

31. [BLOOM'S CRITIQUE OF ENLIGHTENMENT CRITIQUE AS UNNECESSARY.]

Bloom, p. 291 ("the overcoming of the distinction between the eternal and the temporal . . . is surely a result of Enlightenment, although it goes counter to the intentions of the Enlighteners. The question is whether it is a necessary or only accidental result"); and compare the dramatic statement near the close of section 2 (p. 240): "Western rationalism has culminated in a rejection of reason. Is this result necessary?" By "reason," Bloom means here his own conception of reason—abstract universal philosophical reason.

32. [BLOOM'S ASSUMPTION OF UNIVERSAL MORAL PRINCIPLES.]

See Bloom, e.g., p. 271 ("The important theoretical experience leads necessarily toward the first principles of all things and includes an awareness of the good . . . they are the same for all men" [more is quoted above in note 19]); p. 40 ("To deny the possibility of knowing good and bad is to suppress true openness"); and p. 179 ("the truth is the one thing most needful; and conforming to nature is quite different from conforming to law, convention, or opinion"). See perhaps also pp. 19-20 ("The teacher's standpoint is not arbitrary . . . [The teacher's] activity is solicited by something beyond him that at the same time provides him with a standard for judging his students' capacity and achievement").

Note also the inverse and negative statements, beginning with p. 39 ("The fact that there have been different opinions about good and bad in different times and places in no way proves that none is true or superior to others"); p. 244 (on Bloom's classmates who went to "state" instead of "great" universities) and p. 143 (on Nietzsche's perception that "the quest begun by Odysseus . . . has come to an end with the observation that there is nothing to seek": "Good and evil now for the first time appeared as values, of which there have been a thousand and one, none rationally or objectively preferable to any other. The salutary illusion about the existence of good and evil has been definitively dispelled"). See p. 208, also on Nietzsche ("philosophy finds nothingness at the end of its quest"); and below, notes 53, 61, 83, 84, 88, 161, and 172.

33. Bloom, p. 300. See this chapter, notes 21, 36, and 40.

34. The two quotations appear, respectively, in ibid., pp. 279 and 179. See this chapter, note 13.

35. Ibid., p. 310.

36. Ibid., p. 301. See also above, note 22. The haunting doubt is unattachable from the self-eroding quality of Kant's own enterprise, to which Bloom alludes, p. 302 (quoted near start of note 21, above); compare my own discussion in chapter 2, in the text pertaining to note 71. In *Dialectic of Enlightenment*, Horkheimer and Adorno describe this quality succinctly: "Kant's critique itself seems a revocation of his own thought" (p. 94). A bit later in the same book, these authors describe the moral limitation of Enlightenment reason equally tersely: "the impossibility of deriving from reason any fundamental argument against murder" (p. 118).

37. [BLOOM ON THE POST-ENLIGHTENMENT SPLIT OF COGNITION AND MORALITY.]

In addition to notes 21 and 22 above and note 49 below, see, for example, Bloom, p. 295 (on Enlightenment's rejection of the "moderate Socratic compromise"); p. 296 ("Natural science very quickly withdrew from the Enlightenment project as a whole"); p. 210 ("what was once generally agreed upon no longer compels belief. One has to go back to Locke and Adam Smith . . . to find *arguments* for the rational moral basis of liberal society"). The latter is one of many statements suggesting that the severance began in the Enlightenment but was not completed in that period; see also below, the quotation cited in note 40. As with Kant's critique, the attempts of the Enlightenment to secure reason are acknowledged by Bloom as having narrowed and thereby hollowed it.

For a statement in a negative vein, see p. 372 ("Natural science asserts that it is metaphysically neutral, and hence has no need for philosophy, and that imagination is not a faculty that in any way intuits the real—hence art has nothing to do with truth"). Note also numerous implicitly negative statements about inferences drawn from the Enlightenment: by Rousseau, p. 197 ("Culture is a synthesis of reason and religion, attempting to hide the sharp distinction between the two poles"), and p. 298 ("Science undermines virtue"); by Nietzsche, p. 196 ("Victorious rationalism is unable . . . to defend itself theoretically and . . . its human consequences are terrible. . . . Reason cannot found religions" [more is quoted above, in note 25]) and also p. 308 ("Belief [in the pure, transhistorical mind] is the fundamental premise and error of science, an error that becomes manifestly fatal in dealing with human things. The method of the sciences is designed to see only what is everywhere and always, whereas what is particular and emergent is all that counts historically and culturally"); by Weber, p. 194 ("Reason cannot establish values"); and see p. 209 (on the implicit admission of post-Weberian thinkers that "their 'rational' system needs a moral supplement in order to work, and that this morality is not itself rational—or at least the choice of it is not rational, as they understand reason"). Negative recognition of the split is also given in connection with the founding of America, p. 28 ("as a result of a great epistemological effort—religion [was assigned] to the realm of opinion as opposed to knowledge"). The passage notes an attendant contraction of "the claims to moral and political knowledge," to the point where it began to appear that "full freedom can be attained only when there is no such knowledge at all."

Also related are negative remarks on the putative self-sufficiency of Enlightenment reason:

p. 73 ("the triumphant Enlightenment rationalism thought that it had discovered other ways to deal with the irrational part of the soul"); and p. 266, on Enlightenment indifference to the fate of poetry; and p. 267 (see below, note 44, on the war waged by the Enlightenment). See also this chapter, note 59. Italics on p. 210 ("arguments") are Bloom's.

38. [BLOOM'S LAMENT OVER THE "FACT-VALUE DISTINCTION" AND AN ASSOCIATED NARROWING OF PHILOSOPHY; HIS ATTACK ON VALUES.]

This severance is prominently associated with "the fact-value distinction" (see, e.g., pp. 30, 39, 327, and also, indirectly, 270, on Aristophanes' parody of Socrates). Characterized by Bloom as "the very precarious, not to say imaginary, distinction between facts and values" (p. 150), this distinction, along with cultural relativism and historicism, is attacked by Bloom as among the worst consequences of Enlightenment thought (see pp. 38-39). It is not just the positivistic modern fact that Bloom deplores (see this chapter, note 46, on E. D. Hirsch). Much of Bloom's book is devoted to an attack on values ("pallid things," p. 61), which replaced the natural ends still sought by the Enlightenment (p. 209, quoted in note 13, above) but have no rational basis; see p. 143, in connection with Nietzsche ("Values are not discovered by reason, and it is fruitless to seek them, to find the truth or the good life"). See also p. 201, on Nietzsche; p. 209, on Weber; p. 326, on the values of students in the 1960s (which "came on the winds [and] . . . were not the product of students' reasoning or study"); p. 327, on the "values with fallen arches" of the 1960s, which came out of old reasoning but were no longer supported by reason; and below, notes 86 and 88, on the crisis in values and postmodernism.

For commonsense purposes, when Bloom isn't attacking the fact-value distinction, he seems willing enough to rely on it (see, e.g., p. 237, "we now take what were only interpretations of our souls to be facts about them").

On the ancient wholeness of the cognitive and the moral see Bloom, e.g., p. 271 (on "theoretical experience" and "awareness of the good"); p. 300 ("Aristotle's human sciences are part of the science of nature"); p. 264 ("philosophy, and with it what we call science, came to be in Greece"); and p. 363 ("Political science goes all the way back to Greek antiquity and has the dubious parentage of Socrates, Plato and Aristotle, all with bad reputations in the land of modern science. . . . Real science does not talk about good and bad, so that had to be abandoned"). See also p. 298 (as a consequence of the Enlightenment, "science has broken off from the self-consciousness about science that was the core of ancient science"); and p. 251 ("Older, more traditional orders that do not encourage the free play of reason contain elements reminiscent of the nobler, philosophic interpretation of reason and help to prevent its degradation. . . . [They provide] images . . . which preserve the order of the cosmos and of the soul from which philosophy begins"). See this chapter, notes 19, 48, and 55.

Though Enlightenment thinkers had hoped to hold science and morality together, they instead separated them, eventually turning philosophy, once the study of the universal and eternal (p. 290), into poetry, a kind of culturally particular discourse (see below, note 74). In part this failure involved inadequate provision for irrational aspects of the soul. See p. 251 on Hobbes and Pascal, and below, note 55. See also pp. 293-98, the analysis of Swift, which discusses breaks in the Enlightenment between the scientific on the one side and the moral and the aesthetic on the other. See also notes 21, 25, 37, and 59, this chapter.

39. Bloom, p. 292; this sentence continues, "and Enlightenment was and remains the only plausible scheme for doing so." See also this chapter, note 47.

40. Bloom, p. 261. See this chapter, notes 33 and 36, and associated text.

41. Including science itself; see above, note 25.

42. [BLOOM ON NIETZSCHE'S CENTRALITY TO POST-ENLIGHTENMENT CRITIQUE OF ABSTRACT REASON.]

Bloom, p. 203; his exact words are "to draw with perfect intransigence the consequences of that idea," the idea being the substitution of a cultural perspective for an abstract universal one, which

I am arguing derives ultimately from Kant's critical philosophy. See also Bloom, e.g., p. 307 ("Here is where Nietzsche enters, arguing with unparalleled clarity and vigor"); p. 229 ("Nietzsche contributed to what he was trying to cure"); p. 379 ("Deconstructionism [a cheapened interpretation of Nietzsche] . . . is the last, predictable, stage in the suppression of reason and the denial of the possibility of truth in the name of philosophy"). See also p. 309 (on Nietzsche's "rigorous drawing of the consequences of what German humane scholarship really believed"), where Bloom leaves a bit of a way out for "serious men"; and p. 51 ("This [the decay of man] is the crisis [Nietzsche] tried to face resolutely: the very existence of man as man, as a noble being, depended on him and on men like him—so he thought"). See also notes 29 and 30, above, on Nietzsche.

43. Bloom, pp. 267-68; the preceding sentence refers to "attacks" by Rousseau and Nietzsche "on Socratic rationalism made in a Socratic spirit." See also p. 308, on Nietzsche and Socrates, quoted above in note 18.

44. Bloom, p. 267. Bloom notes here "the gradual but never perfect success of that war."

45. Bloom, p. 377 (note also the word "dethrone" earlier in the paragraph). See also above, note 19, and below, notes 47 and 49.

46. See this chapter, note 38; and Hitchens, p. 59: Hirsch "dislikes what he terms the antiscientism of the Bloomites ('If there *isn't* a fact-value distinction, then we are in deep, deep trouble')." See this chapter, note 17.

47. [BLOOM'S ADMIRATION FOR THE ENLIGHTENMENT.]

See Bloom, e.g., p. 259 (on the "daring enterprise," "[broad] vision," and "stunning success" of the Enlightenment, of which "the best of the modern regimes—liberal democracy—is entirely [the] product"); p. 293 ("However contrary it may be to contemporary historical wisdom, the leading thread that runs through all the accidents of modern history is the philosophical doctrine of Enlightenment. Modern regimes were conceived by reason . . . and required the reason of natural science in every aspect of their activity, and the requirements of scientific advance largely determine their policy"); pp. 264-65 ("The very term Enlightenment is connected with Plato's most powerful image . . . , the cave. . . . Enlightenment meant to shine the light of being in the cave and forever to dim the images on the wall" [Plato got the image of the cave, of course, from Socrates]); p. 207 (with respect to reason, Nietzsche "is farther away from Plato . . . than was Descartes or Locke"); p. 264 (the quarrel between the ancients and the moderns was "a struggle for the possession of rationalism by rationalists"); and p. 290 ("the theoretical life remained as distinct from the practical life" in the view of the modern philosophers as in the ancient view").

Worth special note are Bloom's assertions that the Enlightenment privileged philosophy: p. 266 ("It is Enlightenment that was intent on philosophers' ruling, taking Socrates' ironies seriously"); and p. 261 (see the quotation on "rare theoretical men" below, note 53). See also p. 209 (on the Enlightenment ideal of the rational statesman); p. 309 (on the Enlightenment university); and above, note 15 (on Socrates' rationalism), note 37 (references in first paragraph), and especially note 39 (the quotation from p. 292 on Enlightenment as "the only plausible scheme") and note 77 (the quotation from p. 267 on poetry).

48. [BLOOM'S CLOSE ASSOCIATION OF PHILOSOPHY AND SCIENCE.]

See Bloom, p. 372 (The important questions "were once also the questions addressed by science and philosophy"); p. 259 (the "goal [of the Enlightenment] was to reconstitute political and intellectual life totally under the supervision of philosophy and science"); p. 377 ("Philosophy once . . . dared to survey the whole, to seek the first causes of things"); p. 264 (connecting philosophy to science by way of the Greek concept of nature); p. 297 (where Bloom appears to use the term "natural philosopher" to mean "scientist"); p. 260 (see below, note 53, on the "rights of science"); p. 271, on "theoretical experience," as quoted above in note 19; above, note 38, on the wholeness of ancient philosophy; and below, note 55 (quote from p. 41 on the theoretical life).

For a defense of science see, e.g., pp. 181-83, where Bloom attacks the anti-Enlightenment notion of science as a manifestation of culture and criticizes the subsumption of the scientist under the category of artist as the paradigmatic object of modern social admiration. See especially p. 182 ("When every man was understood to be essentially a reasoner, the scientist could be understood to be a perfection of what all men wanted to be. . . . [But now] the theoretical life has lost its status") and p. 183 (on the "sinister loss of confidence in the idea of science . . . the idea which was at the foundation of democratic society and *the* absolute in a relativized world" [italics his]); and also pp. 38-39 (on "the suicide of science"). See this chapter, note 20. The brief critique on p. 200 of Thomas Kuhn (mentioned above in note 18) can also be included here. See also below, note 53 and the quotation that pertains to note 136.

49. [EVIDENCE OF BLOOM'S ENVY OF SCIENCE.]

See pp. 347-48 ("The natural scientists were above the battle, an island unto themselves, and did not feel threatened. . . . It was the absolute independence of their work from the rest of the university's activity, and their trust that theirs is the important task, that made them indifferent. They did not share a common good with the rest of us"); p. 302 ("Philosophy, no longer a part of, or required by, natural science, was nudged over towards the humanities and even became just another historical subject. Its claim to the be ruler in the university no longer earned respect. . . . The natural scientist was . . . the image of the knower"); p. 377 ("real science did not need [the classic philosophic books]"); p. 193 (on how science had no need for a notion of culture); above, note 19 (on the dethronement of philosophy) and note 37 (e.g., the reference to p. 372, on how science does not need philosophy or art); and below, note 55 (quote from p. 41 on abandoning scientific certainty). Also of interest is Bloom's note on p. 358, which begins, "Natural science simply does not care. There is no hostility . . . to anything that is going on elsewhere. It is really self-sufficient, or almost so. If some other discipline proved itself, satisfied natural science's standards of rigor and proof, it would be automatically admitted. Natural science does not boast, is not snobbish. It is genuine." This assertion is given concrete form on pp. 350-51, in the anecdote about the president of Rockefeller University ("from which philosophy had recently been banished"), who "with a kind of wink [let his audience] know that in this sea of democratic relativism natural science stands out like Gibraltar. All the rest is a matter of taste. . . . [Natural scientists] have powerful operational measures of competence. . . . [I]nwardly they believe, at least in my experience, that the only real knowledge is scientific knowledge . . . [and] that there are no real standards outside of the natural sciences. . . . [T]he true elitists of the university [i.e., the scientists] have been able to stay on the good side of the forces of history without having to suffer any of the consequences." See also p. 372 (on the deleterious effects of modern science on the humanities) and below, note 134.

50. Bloom, p. 349. Note on the same page his description of the humanist's resentment toward the scientist ("'I can live without you' is the silent thought that steals into one's mind when . . . relations become painful").

51. [BLOOM ON THE WITHDRAWAL OF SCIENCE FROM SERVICE TO SOCIETY.]

Compare Bloom, p. 377 ("Philosophy once proudly proclaimed that it was the best way of life, and it . . . not only dictated its rules to the special sciences but constituted and ordered them") with pp. 296-97 (on the withdrawal of natural science from the Enlightenment project "leaving the human parts of it to fend for themselves. . . . natural science no longer claimed to be able to legislate human laws. . . . instead of being real partners in . . . overthrowing the antiscientific regimes of the past, the scientists became fellow travelers. . . . [S]cience or reason, which appeared now to belong utterly to the natural philosopher, no longer gave the political and moral thinkers any warrant"). One cannot accuse Bloom of sour grapes in the following passage on p. 297, where he goes on to elaborate on the service of science to the Soviet Union, though his insistence on the "passionate concern" of scientists for politics, in the note to p. 358, does seem a bit contradictory. See also below, note 52.

52. [BLOOM ON THE NEED OF PHILOSOPHY FOR FREEDOM FROM SERVICE TO SOCIETY AND THE IMPORTANCE OF THIS FREEDOM TO THE UNIVERSITY.]

See Bloom, pp. 290-91 on the insistence of all philosophers on a distinction between theory and practice ("The vision of the harmony of theory and practice is only apparent" p. 291). On the survival of the philosopher see p. 278 (on the two possibilities open to the philosopher) and p. 279 ("The philosopher . . . loves the truth. That is an intellectual virtue. He does not love to tell the truth. That is a moral virtue"). See also p. 314 ("Socrates thought it more important to discuss justice, to try to know what it is, than to engage himself in implementing whatever partial perspective on it happened to be exciting the passions of the day").

For warnings that service to society threatens the true function of the university see, e.g., p. 254 ("The university . . . must be contemptuous of public opinion because it has within it the source of autonomy—the quest for and even discovery of the truth according to nature. . . . The university must resist the temptation to try to do everything for society[, and] . . . the desire to be more useful, more relevant, more popular"); 274 ("The theoretical life . . . cannot be, or seriously be understood to be, in the city's service); p. 332 (on the "siren calls of the contemporary scene"); p. 252 ("it is necessary that there be an unpopular institution in our midst [the university] that sets clarity above well-being or compassion, . . . that is free of all snobbism but has standards"); p. 314 ("the distance [of the university from society] is based on something true and necessary, the self-confident possession of the kinds of standpoint outside of public opinion that made it easy for Socrates to resist the pious fanaticism of the Athenian people"); pp. 248-49 (on the importance of encouraging "the noninstrumental use of reason"); and p. 251 (on the virtues of "finality as opposed to instrumentality"). See also below, notes 95, 118, 123, and 129; and perhaps also note 59 (on "enlightened selfishness").

53. [BLOOM ON PHILOSOPHY VS. "MERE LIFE"; BLOOM ON FREE SPEECH AS RESTRICTED BY ABSTRACT REASON.]

See Bloom, p. 274 (the statesman's virtues, as opposed to the philosopher's, "are means to the end of preservation, i.e., [in the statesman's case] the good life is subordinate to and in the service of mere life"); and also p. 285 (on the vulgarly courageous who "share the common ground with the philosophers on which something higher than *mere* life rests" [italics his]). See also this chapter, note 19.

On freedom of thought and speech see, e.g., pp. 251-52 ("the university may be said to exist . . . for the sake of preserving the freedom of the mind . . . for some individuals within it"); p. 288 ("Men now owe their clarity about their ends to reasoners. . . . [T]he right to know, of those who desire to know and can know, has a special status"); and p. 267 (linking the Enlightenment "right to be reasonable" and academic freedom).

Bloom's ideas here often involve negative formulations, of how those freedoms become distorted when not spearheaded by philosophical reason—or as he puts it, when restricted rights based on absolute principles of reason turned into unrestricted freedom, an "openness based on history and social science" (p. 29) rather than on reason. See p. 261 ("Freedom of thought and . . . speech were proposed . . . in order to encourage the . . . voice of reason. . . . The authors of *The Federalist* were not particularly concerned with protecting eccentric or mad opinions or lifestyles. . . . [The Enlightenment] project entailed freedom for the rare theoretical men to engage in rational inquiry in the small number of disciplines that treat the first principles of all things"); and p. 260 ("The rights of science [by which Bloom means rational speech] are now not distinguishable from the rights of thought. . . . Freedom of speech has given way to freedom of expression, in which the obscene gesture enjoys the same protected status as demonstrative discourse. . . . [R]eason has been knocked off its perch").

Bloom's discussion, pp. 28-29, of limits intended by the Founding Fathers on free speech ("To their way of thinking there should be no tolerance for the intolerant," p. 29) is similar, though his example is peculiar. Bloom argues that Lincoln, on the basis of the absolute status of the principle of equality, made a majoritarian defense of slavery impermissible speech—but makes no effort to relate Lincoln's stand to the one taken in the Constitution. (For a useful clarification of the relation of Lincoln to the Founding Fathers on this point, see Garry Wills, *Lincoln at Gettys-*

burg: The Words That Remade America [New York, 1992], e.g., pp. 101-3, 118-20, 124, 130, 131, and especially 145-47.)

Bloom's argument, at bottom, is that certain ideas, but not freedom of speech as such, have an absolute status of truth; or to state it negatively, he opposes the notion that "there are no absolutes; freedom is absolute" (p. 28). Thus he contends that the naive assumption that "the truth unaided always triumphs in the marketplace of ideas" came well after the Founding Fathers (p. 28); and that although the Greeks were "more intent than . . . any men before or since on preserving the freedom of the mind. . . . they . . . never let the principle become a dogma" (p. 284). See this chapter, note 95.

54. Bloom, p. 277; the passage by Socrates to which he refers is given on p. 276. See also the quotation from p. 314 on Socrates, given in note 52.

55. [Bloom's return to the Greeks; Bloom on the Greeks' recognition of the irrational.] On the return to Socrates, see Bloom, e.g., pp. 308-10 (leading up to p. 310, "Are Nietzsche and Heidegger right about Plato and Aristotle? They rightly saw that *the* question is here, and both returned obsessively to Socrates. Our rationalism is his rationalism. Perhaps they did not take seriously enough the changes wrought by the modern rationalists and hence the possibility that the Socratic way might have avoided the modern impasse. . . . A serious argument about what is most profoundly modern leads inevitably to the conclusion that the problem of Socrates is the one thing most needful" [italics his]); p. 312 ("contemplation of Socrates is our most urgent task"); and p. 281 (on the "unbroken chain" of Socrates' teaching; see also p. 311, on the breaking of the "thread").

Worth special attention is p. 41, on the two choices Bloom sees for those who, thanks to the scientific view, have become capable of criticizing the scientific view. "Abandon that certainty [of our great knowledge, based on science], and we might be willing to test the beliefs of those happier peoples in order to see if they know something we do not know. Maybe Homer's genius was not so naive as Schiller thought it was. If we abandon this pride in our knowledge, which presents itself as humility [Bloom means as cultural relativism], the discussion. . . . could go in one of two directions: abandonment of science, or the reestablishment of the theoretical life as both possible and itself productive of self-sufficient happiness." The latter is evidently Bloom's own choice; by "theoretical" he means a return to the combination of philosophy and cognition characteristic of the Greeks. See this chapter, notes 19, 38, and 48.

On the recognition of the irrational by the Greeks (as opposesd to its banishment or co-optation [see note 59] by the Enlightenment), see Bloom, e.g., p. 280 ("Socrates had attacked the poets for appealing to . . . passions that make men ecstatic from terror. . . . Reason should be invoked to remind men of the order of things that exists in spite of the accidents that happen to them individually. . . . These passions . . . are more powerful than reason in almost all men"); pp. 266-67 ("Characteristically, Socrates lives with the essential conflicts and illustrates them, rather than trying to abolish them. . . . Socrates, at least, tries to preserve poetry," unlike the Enlightenment, which tried to solve the problem of the tension between reason and imagination "to the advantage of reason, as Socrates wished it could be solved but thought it could not" [see also p. 73, on "triumphant Enlightenment," cited in note 37, and also see notes 74 and 77]); p. 251 (on older orders that recognize that "reason is only one part of the soul's economy," cited in note 38, above); and p. 295 (on the "Socratic compromise," cited in note 37, above).

According to Bloom, Nietzsche, who "restored something like the soul to our understanding of man, . . . the old soul [that] had lost significance in modernity" (p. 207), indicted Socrates because "his rationalism . . . destroyed the tragic sense of life, which inuited man's true situation amidst things" (p. 308), and because his philosophy, which "*demythologizes* and *demystifies* . . . by *disenchanting* the world . . . leads into a void" (p. 208, italics his). Bloom, though certain that the philosopher "is absolutely immune to tragedy" (p. 277), does not seem to agree precisely with this critique. On the contrary, he attributes to the philosopher a unique ability to confront the tragic situation of humanity (also p. 277, see below, note 116), though Bloom's philosopher does not respond, in Nietzsche's poetic way, by a "creative forming of life against the terror of existence, unendowed with and unguided by any pre-existing forms or patterns" (p. 308). Bloom sees a return to Greece as allowing a return to human fullness from a modern condition in which "the animating principle, [the] soul, has disappeared" (p. 193). Hirsch informs us (Hitchens, p. 59), that the original title for Bloom's book was "Souls without Longing." On the page facing the title page, it still retains as a kind of extended subtitle the motto "How Higher Education Has Failed Democracy and Impoverished the Souls of Today's Students"; see below, notes 123 and 130.

Though he does not mention Bloom by name, Jürgen Habermas could certainly have him in mind in this description of the "old conservatives" descended from Leo Strauss: "They observe the decline of substantive reason, the differentiation of science, morality and art, the modern world view and its merely procedural rationality, with sadness and recommend a withdrawal to a position *anterior* to modernity" ("Modernity—An Incomplete Project," in *The Anti-Aesthetic: Essays on Postmodern Culture*, ed. Hal Foster, [Seattle, 1983], p. 14, italics his).

56. Bloom, p. 281.

57. [MORAL MISGIVINGS RAISED BY BLOOM'S USE OF EXTENDED QUOTATIONS FROM SOCRATES.]

See the quotations that appear on pp. 276 and 333. The misgivings in each instance are raised by Bloom's defense of an elite group (a point to be taken up again later): "gentlemen" (p. 277); for the second passage, see the quotation from p. 332 given below in note 126. Though Bloom dismisses moral objections to such positions as symptoms of "an almost impossible public relations problem" (p. 274), he does not persuasively present the moral soundness of those positions as conclusively established. Certainly his case is not helped by the leap in logic (much criticized by reviewers of this book) that makes a simple identification between "advantaged youths" on the one hand and "the greatest talents" and "the more complex . . . nature[s]" on the other, p. 22; see also below, note 123. (Also worth noting is the reference to "the young in democracies" ["unfurnished persons . . . preoccupied principally with themselves"] in connection with the quotation from Plato's *Republic* on pp. 87-88.) Bloom differentiates sharply between the latter sort of self-absorption and that *amour-propre* based on reason that he attributes to high Western culture (p. 41); see below, note 59.

58. [BLOOM'S DIFFERING POSITIONS ON THE NEED FOR AUTHORITY: IN PHILOSOPHY, AND IN THE ARTS AND AT THE UNIVERSITY.]

Bloom, p. 253; see also p. 275 (the elaboration of the idea that with Socrates "the reverence for antiquity is replaced by reason").

But Bloom does invoke the need for authority in other contexts. See p. 247 (on the value of tradition since "some kind of authority is . . . necessary, at least sometimes, for all men. . . . Without being seduced by its undemocratic and antirational mystique, tradition does provide a counterpoise to . . . the merely current, and contains the petrified remains of old wisdom. The active presence of a tradition in a man's soul gives him a resource against the ephemeral, the kind of resource that only the wise can find simply within themselves" [the subject of "being seduced," in the earlier passage, is unclear]); p. 244 ("tradition provides models of discussion on a uniquely high level"); p. 249 (on the "treasury of great deeds, great men and great thoughts required to nourish . . . doubt"); p. 252 (on the virtues of "standards [that] are in the first place accessible to us from the best of the past"); p. 66 (on the value of heroes, despite "Socrates, who liberated himself from Achilles," especially "in America [where] we have only the bourgeoisie").

In short, Bloom does have a reverence for the sort of authority that can be equated with the traditional Western repertory of great works. But though Bloom may have assumed a clear theoretical distinction between the authority of a (universal, abstract) idea and a (concrete, merely actual) repertory, it is a main point in this chapter (see, e.g., note 25) that the two are not so easily distinguished; and in fact Bloom's book is riddled with inconsistencies stemming from a confusion of the two in the case of high Western culture, as I am about to show (see note 70 and the notes following).

Symptomatic is the attitude of reverence Bloom demands at the university, by his own account the seat of intellectual autonomy. He asserts that "the university is . . . informed by the spirit, which very few men can fully share, of men who are absent, but it must preserve respect for them. It can admit almost anyone, but only if he or she looks up to and can have an inkling of the dignity of what is going on in it" (p. 272). Compare this to Jacob Bronowski's image of the university: "The University is a Mecca to which students come with something less than perfect faith. It is important that students bring a certain ragamuffin, barefoot irreverence to their studies; they are not here to worship what is known but to question it" (*The Ascent of Man* [Boston, 1973], p. 360). See also this chapter, note 95.

59. [Bloom on enlightened selfishness.]

Bloom, p. 175. See pp. 175-76, the entire discussion of "the true self" here, involving Locke's substitution of "the rational and industrious" man for the "virtuous" one, who acts on the basis of "self-interest rightly understood," and "beneath [whose] selfishness, of course, lies an expectation that it conduces more to the good of others than does moralism." See also p. 291 ("[The Enlightenment thinkers] were actually Machiavelli's disciples. It was not by forgetting about the evil in man that they hoped to better his lot but by giving way to it rather than opposing it, by lowering standards. The very qualified rationality that they expected from most men was founded self-consciously on encouraging the greatest of all irrationalities. Selfishness was to be the means to the common good, and they never thought that the moral or artistic splendor of past nations was going to be reproduced in the world they were planning"); and p. 166 ("This is the foundation of rights, a new kind of morality solidly grounded in self-interest"). See also notes 37, 38, and 55.

The distance between the notion of "enlightened selfishness" and the philosopher's need to abjure public service is obviously not great. See notes 52 and 129, and also notes 117 and 118.

60. [Bloom's disinterested style of presenting his views of morality.]

In effect, Bloom imbues morality, like his notion of reason more generally (see above, note 20), with a character of cognitive rigor that amounts to an aesthetic style; see also below, notes 134 and 157. Other traditions besides the British have produced variants of this phenomenon. For a well-known example, see Eagleton on the "clinical neutrality . . . [of] Foucault's . . . scrupulously non-judgmental [style], . . . mediated through a distanced, dispassionate tone, a measured, mandarin French serenely unruffled by its own shocking contents" (*Ideology of the Aesthetic*, p. 384). Given the great difference between the enterprises of Bloom and Foucault, their common recourse to a style of objectivity is worth pondering.

In connection with the argument I develop in this essay, it is worth noting that the faculty with which Kant explicitly links disinterestedness is *aesthetic* judgment. See Immanuel Kant, *Critique of Judgment*, trans. J. H. Bernard (New York, 1951), sections 4 and 5, pp. 41-45. (The same discussion emphasizes the interestedness ["highest interest," section 4, p. 43, not to be confused with ordinary selfishness] aroused by *moral* judgment.) See this chapter, note 150.

Though there is an undeniable consistency in Bloom's imagery and attitudes, I will argue that he (like Stravinsky, see note 67), expects hardness of attitude, essentially a stylistic condition, to be taken for an objective rigor of argument. And I will further argue that, in Bloom's case, any illusion of abstract objectivity is marred by a disconcerting personal tone (see note 126).

See also notes 25, 151, 152, and 157 (especially on "meaning-effect"), and note 172.

61. See above, note 32; also notes 53, 57 (on *amour-propre*), note 83, note 84 (on "drab diversity"), note 85, note 86 (on the "legitimation crisis"), note 88 (on postmodernism), and notes 161 and 172.

62. [Texts of King and Malcolm X Quotations used by Spike Lee.]

The quotation from Martin Luther King reads as follows:

"Violence as a way of achieving racial justice is both impractical and immoral. It is impractical because it is a descending spiral ending in destruction for all. The old law of an eye for an eye leaves everybody blind. It is immoral because it seeks to humiliate the opponent rather than win his understanding—it seeks to annihilate rather than to convert. Violence is immoral because it thrives on hatred rather than love. It destroys community and makes brotherhood impossible. It leaves society in monologue rather than dialogue. Violence ends by defeating itself. It creates bitterness in the survivors and brutality in the destroyers."

The quotation from Malcolm X reads as follows: "I think there are plenty of good people in America, but there are also plenty of bad people in America and the bad ones are the ones who seem to have all the power and be in these positions to block things that you and I need. Because this is the situation, you and I have to preserve the right to do what is necessary to bring an end to that situation, and it doesn't mean that I advocate violence, but at the same time I am not against using violence in self-defense. I don't even call it violence when it's self-defense, I call it intelligence."

The film does not provide sources for either passage, nor does Lee provide either the texts or their sources in the companion volume to his film.

See below, notes 112, 174, 175.

63. For more on the ending of this movie, including its relation to the idea of synthesis, see below, notes 174 and 175, and also note 139.

64. See chapter 3, "Toward a Deconstruction of Structural Listening."

65. [KANT ON DISINTERESTEDNESS AND UNIVERSALITY OF AESTHETIC JUDGMENT.]

See chapter 3, e.g., p. 154, text following the citation of note 31. Note that Kant linked aesthetic judgment both to disinterestedness and to universal standards of beauty (see *Critique of Judgment*, end of section 5 and beginning of section 6, both on p. 45; see above, note 60.

66. See below, note 168.

67. [ON OBJECTIVITY AS AN AESTHETIC STYLE.]

On objectivity as an aesthetic style in music, see my discussion of Stravinsky in chapter 3, "Toward a Deconstruction of Structural Listening," p. 153, text centering on note 27, and p. 158, text following note 42.

See also this chapter, notes 20, 60, 151, 157, and 158.

68. Of course, the very problem of how to describe "good" and "bad" points to the service rendered by a notion such as structural listening. Once structural listening is abandoned as a universal abstract standard, one reaches what Bloom would certainly characterize as the slippery slope of unsupported value judgments. See below, note 86, on the "legitimation crisis" of postmodernism and note 88, on "drab diversity"; also this volume, pp. 157-58.

69. [STRUCTURAL SIMPLICITY OF SOME EARLY WESTERN MUSIC.]

I am thinking in particular of certain genres that use repeated phrases, such as dances based on pairs of repeated phrases (e.g., the medieval estampie) and light strophic vocal genres such as the Renaissance canzonetta/canzonet and balletto/ballett (e.g., Thomas Morley's "My Bonny Lass She Smileth"). If one also includes adherence to any conventional scheme of short-span repetition, various additive patterns of structuring, focus on localized musical events or text elements, and restricted tonal mobility—that is, the absence of a large-scale formal pattern, based on modulation—then by the standard of structural listening a good deal of medieval and even Renaissance music can be judged simple.

70. [BLOOM'S ELEVATION OF WESTERN LITERARY CANON TO LEVEL OF ABSTRACT UNIVERSALITY.]

I found particularly jarring the reference to Shakespeare on p. 380, two pages before the end of the book ("Men may live more truly and fully in reading Plato and Shakespeare than at any other time, because then they are participating in essential being and are forgetting their accidental lives"). Though in the course of studying this book intensively I found more references to literature than I would initially have supposed, Bloom's stance on literature left me unprepared for this closing encomium. See below, notes 73 and 74, and also note 77, on the ideal university.

71. [TYPICAL REFERENCES TO LITERATURE AND THE ARTS BY BLOOM.]

Bloom's references to literature are often made to bolster or exemplify Bloom's characterizations of society or social trends. When he suggests that "maybe Homer's genius was not so naive as Schiller thought it was" (p. 41), he is really arguing the need for a return to Greek philosophy. See also the references to Tolstoy, p. 66; Flaubert, pp. 134-35; Baudelaire, p. 205; Shakespeare, pp. 110-11; Thomas Mann, 230-32; Camus, p. 88; and to the Descartes-Pascal literary tradition in France, p. 52. Sometimes he simply refers to insights or capacities without demonstrating them, much in the manner of his references to Socrates (Tolstoy [vs. Erica Jong], p. 229; Dostoyevski, Joyce, Proust, and Kafka, p. 367; also Tolstoy and Stendhal, p. 64). Other references are mere name dropping (Dante, p. 375; Austen, Donne, Joyce, and Proust, p. 65; also the great Western painters, p. 63; for composers, see below, note 138). For a broader basis of respect for literature sometimes allowed by Bloom, see below, notes 72 and 75.

72. [BLOOM ON THE CATHARTIC FUNCTION OF LITERATURE; BLOOM'S HINTS OF OTHER BENEFITS FROM STUDYING LITERATURE.]

See Bloom, pp. 280-81: "The poet, not the philosopher, can treat the passions that are dangerous to philosophy, which Socrates had to his great cost ignored. . . . Aristotle tells the poets they should present heroes who deserve their fates. . . . The effect of such drama would be to make men gentle and believers in the coherence of the world, in the rational relation of cause and effect." (The relation of this formulation to Lee's *Do The Right Thing* invites reflection.) See this chapter, note 141, on music also this volume, pp. 106-10.

Over the course of his book, Bloom does hint at other reasons for studying literature. See, e.g., p. 61 (we require "literature in the grand style" to develop the "refinement of the mind's eye that permits it to see the delicate distinctions among men . . . and constitutes real taste"); similarly, pp. 63-64 (on great literature "with which we sharpened our vision, allowing us some subtlety in our distinction of human types. . . . Without literature, no such observations are possible and the fine art of comparison is lost . . . people become more alike, for want of knowing they can be otherwise. . . . [We get] poor substitutes for real diversity" (compare this to "drab diversity," note 84, below); p. 227 ("Tragic literature is about [awareness and choice of alternatives]. It articulates all the noble things men want and perhaps need and shows how unbearable it is when it appears that they cannot coexist harmoniously" [the beginning of this passage is quoted below at note 155]); p. 244 ("a great university" does not treat literature merely as "a form of entertainment"); p. 266 ("we think there should be poetry classes as well as education in reasoning"); p. 256 ("the antidote [to viewing oneself as powerless in a democracy] is again the classic, the heroic—Homer, Plutarch"); p. 281 ("philosophy's response to the hostility of civil society is an educational endeavor, rather more poetic or rhetorical than philosophic, the purpose of which is to temper the passions of gentlemen's souls. . . . The model for all such efforts is the dialogues of Plato, which . . . [introduce] a new hero [i.e., Socrates]"). See also above, notes 18 (on content) and 58 (on authority), and below, note 136 (including Bloom's linkages, pp. 277 and 281, of philosophy and rhetoric).

73. [BLOOM ON THE CONCRETE CHARACTER OF POETRY AND THE ARTS.]

In this respect, poetry is similar to the other arts. See Bloom, p. 63 (great artists of the past "counted on immediate recognition of their subjects and . . . on their having a powerful meaning for their viewers. The works were the fulfillment of those meanings, giving them a sensuous reality and hence completing them" [the continuation of this passage is quoted above in note 18]). Moreover, whereas Socrates can be the teacher of philosophy (the study of the timeless) "in an unbroken chain for two and a half millennia" (p. 281), the meanings of art "elaborated over millennia" can be "stilled" and vanish "beyond the dissolving horizon" (p. 63). See also pp. 280-81 (though Socrates decrees a conflict between poetry and philosophy whereas Aristotle sees poetry as serving philosophy, both, by Bloom's account, connect poetry to "the terror at what [men] suffer and their unprotectedness in their suffering" [p. 280] as a result of "the accidents that happen to them individually" [p. 280]); also p. 280 ("the philosopher has less need [than the poet] to enter . . . into the drama of history, or to be *engagé*"); p. 268 (Socrates "is the first [philosopher] to have benefited from a dramatic poetic representation of his way of life, which . . . necessitated . . . reflection not only about what he taught but also about the man himself and how he fitted into the city"); and p. 61 (books—the context is literature—provide "a real basis for discontent with the present and awareness that there are alternatives to it"). See also notes 10, 82, 142, and 168.

74. [BLOOM ON THE BATTLE BETWEEN PHILOSOPHY AND POETRY; BLOOM SIDES WITH PHILOSOPHY.]
See Bloom, e.g., p. 207 ("Myths are made by poets"; for Plato this amounts to a "war between philosophy and poetry . . . [since] the aim of philosophy is to substitute truth for myth"); p. 280 ("Socrates heightens the enmity between philosophy and poetry"); p. 281 ("Socrates criticizes poetry in order to encourage it to be an ally of the philosophers instead of the priests"); p. 309 ("[With Nietzsche] the poets won the old war between philosophy and poetry"); and also the priority of the abstract over the concrete on p. 266 ("we agree . . . that children must be taught the scientific method prior to any claims of the imagination on their belief or conduct").

Implying such a battle in a more negative sense, Bloom is clearly unhappy that, thanks to Nietzsche, "the new philosopher is the ally of the poets and their savior, or philosophy is itself the highest kind of poetry" (p. 208)—in effect a historical deconstruction has occurred. See also p. 309 ("even philosophy began to reinterpret itself as a form of art"); and Bloom's apparent disapproval (p. 305) that "Rousseau admired Plato and thought he had deep insight into human things, but rather more as a poet than a philosopher or scientist" (see also note 18, above), though he does not object to Plato's poetic representation of Socrates (p. 268, quoted in note 73, and p. 281, quoted in note 72); and note Bloom's unhappiness at the replacement of the scientist by the artist as a paradigm (p. 182, quoted in note 48) and with the scientists' aestheticizing of philosophy, on pp. 350-51 (above, anecdote in note 49).

Bloom's most genuine expression of his own view of the relationship between philosophy and poetry may well come when he concedes that "nature [i.e., philosophy] needs the cooperation of convention [i.e., literature]" in order to teach students effectively (p. 51). (Even this concession of a role for literature seems weak when one considers his uncompromising rejection, on p. 278 [quoted in note 89], of the nonphilosopher's belief in a unity of nature and convention.) Siding with Socrates against the Enlightenment (see the quotations from pp. 266-67 cited in notes 55 and 148), Bloom accords poetry a grudging acceptance that in no way threatens his supreme regard for philosophy. He considers literature ancillary, at best, to philosophy. See also below, note 136.

75. [BLOOM'S TREATMENT OF THE WESTERN CANON AS ABSTRACT.]
See p. 380 on Plato and Shakespeare (quoted above, note 70), and the negative account of the notion that Schiller "could not understand Homer as Homer understood himself," p. 308. See also the quotation from p. 108 in the text cited in note 80, below; and above, note 18, on content.

76. See especially p. 380 (in note 70, above); also below, notes 83, 84, 89, 103, 105, and 168.

77. [THE ROLES OF PHILOSOPHY AND POETRY AT BLOOM'S IDEAL UNIVERSITY.]
Bloom does allege (p. 254) that in a democracy "the university as an institution must compensate for what individuals lack. . . . and it must concentrate on philosophy, theology, the literary classics, and on . . . scientists like Newton, Descartes, and Leibniz." This differs, however, from his picture of the ideal university on p. 261: "The disciplines are philosophy, mathematics, physics, chemistry, biology and the science of man, meaning . . . political science. . . . This is the academy."

Again, as suggested above in note 74, Bloom appears to show his real hand when he paraphrases the Enlightenment's dismissal of poetry thus: "Enlightenment is Socrates respected and free to study what he wants" (p. 267). Especially in this context, where he pointedly associates Socrates with modern professors of philosophy and science, Bloom makes clear his comfort with such a vision. See also note 55.

78. [BLOOM'S LINKAGE OF POETRY AND "BEING."]
Bloom, p. 380. See also the linkage of painting to "being itself" on p. 63; a fuller quotation appears above in note 18. Bloom's point in the latter instance is that when original meaning

becomes indecipherable (as happens in the arts), that meaning must be acknowledged as no longer existing, that is, it can no longer be said to *be* in the indisputable, immutable way that philosophical truth *is*. In his way, he uses the term "being" here to honor philosophy. In the process, however, by equating the finite existence of artistic meaning with the timeless being of reason, Bloom undercuts (and potentially overturns—i.e., deconstructs!) one of the principal distinctions on which his book is built.

79. [Bloom's usual insistence on priority of eternal to temporal.]

See above, notes 14 (on the eternal and unchanging), 19 and 37 (on the transhistorical), 27, 31 (on "overcoming" the distinction between eternal and temporal), and 74. See also, e.g., Bloom, p. 230 (his contempt, associated with a character in a Donizetti opera, for those who "blur the distinction between [eternity] and temporality").

Perhaps the most striking evidence of Bloom's attitude toward the relation between philosophical timelessness and historical contingency appears on pp. 283-84: "We moderns think that a comparatively minor change, like that wrought by the French Revolution, necessitates new thought. The ancients held that a man must never let himself be overcome by events unless those events taught something *essentially* new." Bloom goes on to identify the ancient resistance to contingency with a tenacious insistence on freedom of the mind: "They were more intent than were any men before or since on preserving the freedom of the mind. This was their legacy to the university." (Italics are Bloom's.)

80. Bloom, p. 108.

81. [Thematic norms for literature suggested by Bloom.]

Other suggestions of thematic criteria include the hardness of life-and-death choices (Bloom, p. 227) and the heroic (p. 66, Tolstoy; p. 256, Homer—and also Plutarch!) Bloom himself acknowledges in negative fashion the actual difficulty of identifying problems as permanent: "One must begin to wonder whether there is any permanent literature [for students today], because there do not seem to them to be permanent problems for them. . . . This is the first fully historical or historicized generation, not only in theory but also in practice" (p. 108).

82. Again, Bloom's difficulty in pointing toward a credible standard for judging literature is exacerbated by his tendency with literature, as with the philosophy of Socrates, merely to assert rather than to demonstrate qualitative judgments; see note 71, above. Much of Bloom's inconsistency here, as should become clear over the remainder of the chapter, stems from his focus on content to the exclusion of structure, in literary as well as philosophical works. This exclusion severely narrows his basis for distinguishing between abstract and concrete aspects of content while also allowing him to confer on content qualities of abstraction more proper to structure. See notes 10, 73, 142, and 168.

83. [Bloom on the need for a single standard to preserve the ability to judge cultures differently; Bloom's argument for superiority of Western standard and attack on cultural relativism.]

"Nature should be the standard by which we judge our own lives and the lives of peoples. That is why philosophy, not history or anthropology, is the most important science" (Bloom, p. 38).

Bloom's argument here, essentially an attack on cultural relativism, is laid out in a winding fashion on pp. 34-43. His general drift is that Western culture has used the epistemology of science, its own principle, to posit the equality of all cultures. This equalization distorts other cultures, each of which by nature (and basically, for its survival, p. 37) insists on its own superiority; and though in a way this process confirms a corresponding Western sense of cultural superiority (since it depends on scientific epistemology), it does so in a way that renders ineffective the very principles that make the process possible.

In teaching, the effect of this process on undergraduates is that "it points them back to passionate attachment to their own and away from the science which liberates them from it. . . . The human sciences want to make [them] culture-beings with the instruments that were invented to liberate [them] from culture" (pp. 37-38). In other words, starting with a natural stance of ethno-centrism, and drawing on the content of Western culture—i.e., science—in order to criticize that natural stance by studying other cultures, undergraduates take back from other cultures a stance of uncritical loyalty as a kind of content for their own culture, now defined in some localized or con-crete way that shuts out the objectivity of scientific abstraction.

Thus far, with all its reversals and blurred boundaries between stance and content, the resem-blance of the argument to deconstruction is unmistakable. Bloom's way out of this impasse is to insist on abstract (scientific) reason as the universal and only principle of truth, grounded time-lessly on nature, a principle that exposes all standards of worth derived from cultural specificity as hollow. In this way reason affirms as natural the assumption by each culture of its own superiority (its "love of inequality," p. 41), while at the same time demonstrating the inferiority of all cultures that use cultural criteria rather than abstract reason as a standard of judgment—that is, all cultures except that of the West. Acknowledging the superiority of the Western cultural foundation and restricting oneself to the abstract Western view of reason gives one the only possible basis for judg-ing all other views. I question this line of reasoning below when I compare philosophical and musicological training as a preparation for evaluating Mookie's actions in *Do The Right Thing* (see pp. 200-201, text pertaining to notes 152-54).

Because of Bloom's insistence on a linear mode of arguing, his nearness at this moment to cir-cular reasoning is especially disconcerting. In fact, the difficulty of following Bloom's argument here suggest the limits of its effectiveness in dealing with imagery of infinite regress and paradox. It can also be connected to a conflation of universality as a theme and as a status (see this chapter, note 103).

See also, for example, Bloom, pp. 61 and 141-47 on value relativism, especially p. 143 (as quoted above in notes 32 and 38), and pp. 202-4 on Nietzsche and cultural relativism, including the paradox (pp. 202-3) that the cultural relativists are doomed, by their own scientific episte-mology, to believe in no culture at all, even their own. Among the many notes that present related material are note 13, notes 16 and 89 on culture vs. science, note 27, note 32 (especially the quotation on one vs. many truths from Bloom, p. 39), note 53 (on freedom of speech), note 84 (on "drab diversity"), note 86, on the legitimation crisis, note 88, on postmodernism, note 105, and notes 161 and 172. Also related is Bloom, p. 247 (on the "really dangerous form of the tyranny of the majority . . . that breaks the inner will to resist because there is no qualified source of nonconforming principles and no sense of superior right. The majority is all there is").

84. [BLOOM'S ATTACK ON "DRAB DIVERSITY" AND FALSE "OPENNESS"; BLOOM ON THE NEED TO PRESERVE A HIERARCHY OF STANDARDS.]

This phrase, used repeatedly by Bloom, seems to turn up first on p. 34, where Bloom claims that Americans have fallen into provincialism and conformity because "out there in the rest of the world is a drab diversity that teaches only that values are relative, whereas here we can create all the life-styles we want." Bloom is mocking what he sees as an American illusion, that openness to a variety of "life-styles" results in "real" (pp. 64 and 192) or "profound" (p. 338) diversity (when, in fact, this openness involves only the "artificial" and "superficial" [p. 192]). For related images see p. 321 (on American "acquiescence in a leveling off of the peaks"); p. 238 (on the gray net of abstraction," produced not by abstract reason but by relativism, which has filtered out "available alternate visions, a diversity of profound opinions" [see this chapter, note 97]); p. 338 (on Weber's view of "great alternatives" vs. "trivial considerations . . . that overgrow and render indistinguish-able . . . profound problems"); and p. 244 (the "great" university "made a distinction between what is important and not important"). See also p. 43 ("To an eye of dogmatic skepticism, nature herself . . . might appear to be a prejudice. In her place we put a network of critical concepts, which were invented to interpret nature's phenomena but which strangled them and therewith destroyed their own *raison d'être*").

Of particular relevance here is the discussion of "openness," pp. 38-42, centered on the assertion, "Openness to closedness is what we teach," p. 39. By this Bloom means that through cultural relativism we teach two things: closedness to absolute standards of abstract reason, which alone allow us to make true distinctions of worth (including the superiority of Western culture, which is based on reason—this means that the teaching of cultural relativism closes our students off to science and abstract truth); and acceptance of the natural, unexamined ethnocentrism of non-Western cultures as a basis of value. (Because such ethnocentrism is not based on abstract reason, Bloom equates it with closedness, p. 37, though seems to approve of Western ethnocentrism not just because Western standards are right but also because such an attitude is natural; see, e.g., pp. 36 and 38, and below, note 103). True or good openness—"the virtue that permitted us to seek the good by using reason" (p. 38)—is presented on pp. 40 and 42. False openness—cultural relativism—is presented on pp. 26, 28 (the move "from rights to openness"), 29, 39 ("openness that denies the special claim of reason"), 40, and 41. See also below, notes 97, 105, and 152, and the text cited in note 116.

For Bloom's insistence that serious relativists preserved a hierarchical view of standards see his account of Nietzsche on pp. 200-201 ("Though the values . . . of good and evil that originate in the self cannot be said to be true or false . . . or justified by the universal standards of reason, they are not equal, contrary to what vulgar teachers of value theory believe. Nietzsche . . . held that inequality among men is proved by the fact that there is no common experience accessible in principle to all. Such distinctions as authentic-inauthentic, profound-superficial, creator-created replace true and false. . . . Everything in Nietzsche is an attack on rational egalitarianism"); and of Weber, pp. 337-38 ("When Weber found that he could not choose between certain high opposites . . . he did not conclude that all things are equally good, that the distinction betwen high and low disappears. . . . The serious intellectual life was for him the battleground of the great decisions. . . . One can no longer present this or that particular view of the educated or civilized man as authoritative; therefore one must say that education consists in knowing, really knowing, the small number of such views in their integrity. This distinction between profound and superficial—which takes the place of good and bad, true and false—provides a focus for serious study"). (See this chapter, note 22 and 29.)

An aspect of "drab diversity" that particularly disturbs Bloom is the "remov[al of] the sense that there is an outside" (p. 249). This evocation of undifferentiated inertia recalls the brilliant imagery of simulators, television screens, and loss of otherness, etc., in Jean Baudrillard's classic description of postmodern life, "The Ecstasy of Communication" (translated by John Johnston, in Foster's *The Anti-Aesthetic*, pp. 126-34 (see especially p. 130, on our move from a "drama of alienation," where otherness is still imaginable, to an "ecstasy of communication [that is] obscene"). See this chapter, note 97.

85. [BLOOM ON THE SUPERIORITY OF EUROPE.]

Bloom, p. 320. See also p. 321 ("We were dependent on Europe. . . . All of our peaks were derivative"); and p. 34 (a scathing dismissal of "interest in the political problems of Third World countries" as opposed to knowledge and love of Europe).

86. [ON THE "LEGITIMATION CRISIS"—THE DIFFICULTY OF FINDING FIRM GROUNDING FOR ANY VALUES.]

See Jürgen Habermas, *Legitimation Crisis*, trans. Thomas McCarthy (London, 1976); the German original appeared in 1973. Steven Connor defines the term as "the fact that there no longer seems to be access to principles which can act as criteria of value for anything else" (*Postmodernist Culture: An Introduction to Theories of the Contemporary* [Oxford, 1989], p. 8). The term is extremely useful, though as Habermas succinctly notes, subject to widely different interpretations ("Modernism," in Foster, *The Anti-Aesthetic*, pp. 14-15, cited in note 55 above). Habermas's own defense of reason ("Modernism," p. 12), like Shelby Steele's argument for American universalism (see "The New Sovereignty: Grievance Groups Have Become Nations unto Themselves" *Harper's Magazine* [July, 1992], 47-54), is undertaken from a far more liberal viewpoint than Bloom's.

Habermas's "crisis" is essentially what I describe earlier in this chapter (pp. 181-83, pertaining to notes 20-40) in connection with Kant's critical philosophy. Kant's division of the mind into three faculties also figures implicitly in Habermas's account of this phenomenon ("Modernism," p. 9, on Weber's "three autonomous spheres" of "science, morality and art"), as it does in Eagleton's (cited above, note 21). According to Eagleton, *Ideology of the Aesthetic,* p. 405, "It is possible to see in Habermas's ideal speech community an updated version of Kant's community of aesthetic judgment" (see below, notes 109 and 150). See also Bloom, p. 314, on "the value crisis in philosophy." Bloom's envy of science (noted above, notes 49 and 51) stems from the absence of such a crisis within the natural sciences; see this chapter, note 161.

87. Bloom, p. 300.

88. [BLOOM'S BOOK AS AN ATTACK ON POSTMODERNISM, ESPECIALLY ON THE DISAPPEARANCE OF HIERARCHICAL STANDARDS AT THE UNIVERSITY.]

Though it is entirely possible that I missed the term "postmodernism" in Bloom's book, it clearly plays no prominent role there. The term "the postmodern condition" has, of course, become well known through Jean-François Lyotard's book *The Postmodern Condition: A Report on Knowledge,* trans. Geoff Bennington and Brian Massumi (Minneapolis, 1984), an influential study much concerned with the concept of legitimation.

In essence a polemic against postmodernism, Bloom's book is rife with imagery on the need for and absence of standards. A great many appear in connection with education, usually at the university. See, e.g., p. 87 (young Americans "can be anything they want to be, but they have no particular reason to want to be anything in particular"); p. 88 (on the need of students today "to avoid permanent free fall"), an image taken up again on p. 143 ("Nietzsche with the utmost gravity told modern man that he was free-falling in the abyss of nihilism"); p. 253 (in a democracy "the university risks less by having intransigently high standards than by trying to be too inclusive, because the society tends to blur standards in the name of equality"); p. 321 (on "openness . . . to 'doing your own thing'" versus the belief that "the university should try to have a vision of what an educated person is"—and the related phrase, "openness in the age of laxity," p. 342); p. 321 (on the disappearance of "the king's English"); p. 305 (philosophy was once "the rational quest for . . . the *one* good political order vs. the plurality of cultures"); and p. 350 (on multiculturalism as "the ultimate trivialization of a trivial idea [C. P. Snow's notion of two cultures] that was just a rest station on a downward slope"). (Italics are Bloom's.)

Especially striking are p. 337 ("the university now offers no distinctive visage to the young person. He finds a democracy of the disciplines. . . . [which] is really an anarchy, because there are no recognized rules for citizenship and no legitimate titles to rule. In short there is no vision, nor is there a set of competing visions, of what an educated human being is. . . . Out of chaos emerges dispiritedness, because it is impossible to make a reasonable choice"); p. 338 (on the attitude "Oh, what's the use?" and the "multiversity smorgasbord"); and p. 372 ("On the portal of the humanities is written in many ways and many tongues, 'There is no truth—at least here'").

Though Bloom, like the French poststructuralists, traces the diagnosis of this condition back to Nietzsche, his attitude toward the postmodern value crisis has far less in common with Barthes's sanguinity than with the "Continental despair" of the Germans (see p. 147). It is not just Nietzsche for whom the loss of an absolute standard was "an unparalleled catastrophe" (p. 143).

For related material see notes 13 (on the standard of nature), 32, 38, 52 (from p. 252, on standards without snobbism and the autonomy of the university), 53 (on free speech), 84 (on "drab diversity"), 97, 104, 135, 158, and 161.

89. [BLOOM'S ATTACK ON NOTION OF CULTURE, ATTACHMENT TO CULTURE, AND CULTURAL RELATIVISM AS BASED ON IRRATIONALITY.]

See especially Bloom, pp. 277-78, where he contrasts philosophers, who cherish no illusions, with "nonphilosophic men," who "hate truth" when it conflicts with the concrete things [in a word, the culture] that they cherish. "The gods are the guarantors of the unity of nature and con-

vention to most men, which philosophy can only dissolve"; that is, the assumption of the necessity and rightness of one's own culture—"the identification of the good with one's own way"
(p. 36)—rests not on reason, where it would be subject to philosophical disputation, but on belief
in an irrationally chosen first cause, on the unanswerable gods. (See above, note 74.)

Admitting that "loyalty versus quest for the good introduced an unresolvable tension into life"
(pp. 37-38), Bloom clearly differentiates the former, as irrational, from the latter, perhaps most
bluntly on p. 269 (Socrates' difficulties are "a result of an essential opposition between the two
highest claims on a man's loyalty—his community and his reason" [see note 114]) and p. 305
("the discovery of Greek 'culture' was contrary to Greek philosophy. And this particular difference, concerning the best regime as opposed to culture, proved fatal to reason"). See also his
remarks, pp. 202-3, on consequences of Nietzsche's position that Bloom considers untenable
("Culture means a war against chaos *and* a war against other cultures. . . . [T]he scientific view is
deadly to culture. . . . Cultural relativism . . . teaches the need to believe while undermining
belief" [italics his]; more of this passage is quoted above in note 27). In other words, cultural relativism encourages replacing dispassionate belief in scientific reason with passionate belief in the
value of a culture; but because cultural relativism is born of scientific reason, such relativism cannot provide a basis for believing cultural values to be true since its own standards of truth remain
those of science. This is a kind of further development of the process analyzed above in note 83.
See also p. 41, where Bloom argues that Romantics refused hard choices about science, described
above in note 55 ("Our shuttling back and forth between science and culture is a trivialized spin-
off from [the Romantic] posture" [p. 41]).

See also notes 13, 16, 37, 83, 88, 116, and the text cited in note 102.

90. E. D. Hirsch, *Cultural Literacy: What Every American Needs to Know* (New York, 1988).
See, for example, pp. xiii-xiv and 143-45, for the way in which an appeal to social ideals frames
this book.

91. [ON E. D. HIRSCH'S "LIST."]
Cultural Literacy, pp. 152-215. Denying that publishing "the contents of our national vocabulary would have the effect of promoting the culture of the dominant class at the expense of minority cultures," Hirsch argues that such a list would constitute "primarily an instrument of communication among diverse cultures rather than a cultural or class instrument in its own right" (pp.
103-4), and notes further (p. 106) that the possibility of making this "vocabulary" available to all
classes and cultures via schooling accounts for a close connection between the rise of modern
democracy and "the great national literate languages"—i.e., literate culture.

The response to this enterprise has, in many quarters, not been what Hirsch wanted. Even the
title of this list—"The List"—conjures up in its very simplicity the tone of arrogant and exclusionary understatement often projected by ads for luxury products (or by programs for the
Harvard-Yale football game, which as I recall them were entitled simply "The Game").

92. [SOKOLOV'S CRITIQUE OF HIRSCH.]
Raymond Sokolov, "Literacy Isn't a Trivial Pursuit," *Wall Street Journal* (August 11, 1987), 22.
The review goes on: "Mr. Hirsch's approach assumes that there is a set of facts that separates the
cultured from the boors. This idea misunderstands the point of literacy, which is to assist curiosity,
to help us be less ignorant. . . . The literate person is greater than the sum of his allusions. He is
someone who wants to read another book." See also Sokolov's follow-up piece, "New Trivia for
the 'Culturally Literate,'" *Wall Street Journal* (January 4, 1989), A5.

93. Chapter 1, this volume. See especially note 86 (on images of Protestantism and Catholicism
derived from Robert Bellah). See also this chapter, note 107.

94. [ON NOTIONS OF AN "ELECT" AND INEQUALITY.]
Leland Miles, review of John Silber's *Straight Shooting: What's Wrong with America and How to
Fix It*, in the *New York Times Book Review* (September 17, 1989), 32. Useful also in this connec-
tion is Shelby Steele's discussion of how the ideals of the American Founding Fathers started life

as "white entitlement" ("The New Sovereignty," pp. 51-53, cited in note 86, above). See also below, note 106; and this volume, chapter 3, p. 158, text following the citation of note 41.

95. [BLOOM'S ELITIST SENTIMENTS CONCERNING UNIVERSITY AND SOCIETY.]

Bloom, p. 260. For similar sentiments connected with the university, see, e.g., p. 21 ("a small number [of students] will spend their lives in an effort to be autonomous. It is for these last, especially, that liberal education exists"); p. 49 (on "better education for the best people," quoted below in note 123); p. 64 (on the need "to intervene most vigorously in the education of those few who come to the university with a strong urge for *un je ne sais quoi*"); p. 148 (on the University of Chicago in the mid-1940s, when "terms like 'value judgment' were fresh, confined to an elite and promising special insight"); and pp. 271-72 ("The tiny band of men who participate fully in this [philosophical] way of life are the soul of the university"; more of this passage is quoted above, note 58, in a contrast to Bronowski). To be sure, Bloom himself argues explicitly that the abstract universal standards he invokes are "free of all snobbism" (p. 252, see note 52, above).

In connection with political life more generally, see p. 258 ("A society based on reason needs those who reason best"); and p. 261 (on restriction of the Enlightenment project to rare theoretical men, quoted in note 53, above).

Relevant also is Bloom's evident sympathy for "the lover of beautiful and useless things [, who despises] . . . many of the same things the philosopher does and is likely to admire the philosopher for his very uselessness, as an adornment. . . . He can take for granted the things that are the ends of most men's strivings—money and status" (p. 250); see notes 123 and 126, this chapter.

96. See above, notes 19 and 77.

97. [BLOOM'S INSISTENCE ON THE NEED FOR REAL ALTERNATIVES AT THE UNIVERSITY; BLOOM ON THE SMALL DIFFERENCES AMONG PHILOSOPHERS.]

On freedom of thought and speech, see above, note 53. On the need for alternatives, see Bloom, e.g., p. 249 ("Freedom of the mind requires . . . the presence of alternative thoughts. The most successful tyranny is . . . the one . . . that makes it seem inconceivable that other ways are viable" [other parts of this passage appear in note 84 and the text cited in note 104]); and p. 238, in connection with thought about eros ("The only way to see the phenomena, rather than sterile distillations of them . . . would be to have available alternate visions, a diversity of profound opinions" [see note 84]). See also note 73 (from p. 61, on the function of books), note 83 (concerning Bloom, p. 247, on the tyranny of the majority), note 84 (concerning p. 338, on Weber's "battleground" and p. 192, on "real" vs. "artificial" differences), note 88 (concerning p. 337 and "competing visions" of education), and note 158 (on "no-fault choices").

Bloom admits, in a somewhat different spirit, that an "admittedly narrow spectrum . . . prevails in the American university" today (p. 355). And he is at pains to emphasize that whatever turn occurred in the history of philosophy in connection with the Enlightenment and its aftermath, the differences among genuine philosophers, old or new, are relatively small. See, e.g., Bloom, p. 271 (the "sense of community is more important for [philosophers] than any disagreements about final things"); p. 310 ("all the philosophers, the proponents of reason, have something in common, and more or less directly reach back to Aristotle, Socrates' spiritual grandchild"); p. 264 (on ancients and moderns, quoted in note 47); p. 290 (again, on ancients and moderns, partly quoted in note 19); and p. 292 (quoted in note 14). See this chapter, notes 113, 114, and 125, on community; and the quotation from p. 282 in note 116.

98. [BLOOM ON OTHER SCHOOLS OF THOUGHT; SCHOOLS DISDAINED BY BLOOM.]

On p. 377 Bloom expresses a somewhat grudging respect for Continental philosophy ("Although reason is gravely threatened, Nietzsche and Heidegger were genuine philosophers. . . . Philosophy is still possible. And on the Continent even now, school-children are taught philosophy, and it seems to be something real"). On p. 369 he expresses regret that "the social science intellectual in the German or French mold, looked upon as a kind of sage or wise man who could tell all about life, has all but disappeared." The note on p. 222 presents Merleau-Ponty and

Sartre more or less positively; likewise, on p. 378 Bloom writes without rancor of existentialism and phenomenology. Several times, Bloom compares German thought favorably to American. See p. 147 ("We have here the peculiarly American way of digesting Continental despair. It is nihilism with a happy ending") and p. 155 (on American "nihilism without the abyss"); and also p. 317 (on the German "theoretical critique of morality" in the early twentieth century).

Otherwise, however, his references to Continental thinkers, and other schools of thought not his own, tend to be derogatory. See, e.g.: p. 352 (on a "laundering operation for radical Left French ideas in comparative literature," on "Sartre, through Goldmann, to Foucault and Derrida," on such "technique[s] of reading" or "framework[s] for interpretation [as] Marx, Freud, structuralism, and on and on"); pp. 379-80 ("Comparative literature . . . [is now] influenced by the post-Sartrean generation of Parisian Heideggerians, in particular Derrida, Foucault and Barthes. The school is called Deconstructionism, and it is the last, predictable, stage in the suppression of reason. . . . [It is] a cheapened interpretation of Nietzsche. . . . This fad will pass. . . . But it appeals to our worst instincts. . . . Fancy German philosophic talk fascinates us and takes the place of the really serious things"); p. 226 (on the French deconstruction and reconstruction of Nietzsche and Heidegger); p. 320 (on comparative literature as "an assiduous importer of the latest Paris fashions"); p. 371 (on the humanities as "the great old Paris Flea Market"—for other derogatory remarks on the humanities, see p. 372, quoted in notes 88 and 128); p. 369 (on "the merchandise being hawked in comparative literature" as opposed to a serious study such as Greek religion); p. 375 (on "Freudian criticism, Marxist criticism, New Criticism, Structuralism, and Deconstructionism, and many others, all of which have in common the premise that what Plato or Dante had to say about reality is unimportant" [see this chapter, note 18, on content]); p. 239 ("nothing for our Marxist, Freudian, feminist, deconstructionist, or structuralist critics to mangle"); p. 65 (on the Frankfurt School's "habit of parading their intimacy with high culture"); p. 225 ("Adorno's meretricious fabrication of the authoritarian and democratic personality types"—Bloom's scathing reference on p. 229 to post-Kantian dialectical synthesis leaves totally out of consideration Adorno's negative dialectic); p. 226 (on Marcuse); pp. 144-46 (on Erich Fromm); p. 327 (behavioralism and postbehavioralism); p. 65 (feminism); p. 378 (on positivism and ordinary-language analysis, quoted in note 23, above); p. 193, on Skinner, Lacan, and Freud; and pp. 30 and 229, on John Rawls.

Noteworthy in connection with Continental philosophy is Bloom's assertion (p. 203) that Nietzsche "tried to apply to his own thought the teachings of cultural relativism. This practically nobody else does," an observation that seems to me to deny virtually the whole domain of Continental thought one of its most distinguishing characteristics—unless perhaps it is Barthes' mood of *jouissance* to which Bloom objects. (On *jouissance* see chapter 2, note 24.) See also this chapter, note 158 (Bloom, p. 228, on "modern philosophy" and "no-fault choices").

99. Quoted in Timothy Ferris, *Coming of Age in the Milky Way* (New York, 1988), p. 96.

100. [BLOOM ON THE PHILOSOPHER AS A MAN OF ABSTRACTION.]

Bloom regularly presents the philosopher, in his professional mode, as a man of pure (i.e., abstract universal) motives. See, e.g.: p. 277 ("The philosopher, to the extent that he really only enjoys thinking and loves the truth, cannot be disabused. He cherishes no illusion that can crumble" [more is quoted above, in note 89]); p. 282 ("only the philosopher does not need opinions that falsify the significance of things in order to endure them. He alone mixes the reality of death . . . into every thought and deed and is thus able to live while honestly seeking perfect clarity"); p. 290 ("The philosopher always thinks and acts as though he were immortal, while always being fully aware that he is mortal. He tries to stay alive as long as possible in order to philosophize, but will not change his way of life or his thought in order to do so" [see also quotations about the eternal from p. 290 in note 14 above); and notes 17, 19, 116, and 125. Contrast Bloom's view of the philosopher with his view of the ordinary individual (Bloom, p. 277 [quoted in note 147, below]).

101. Bloom, p. 236.

102. Bloom, p. 37; see also above, notes 16 and 89.

103. [ON BLOOM'S CONFLATION OF THEME AND STATUS IN WESTERN CULTURE WITH RESPECT TO THE UNIVERSALITY OF WESTERN THOUGHT.]

To compound this temptation, Bloom's single-minded focus on the content of a text as the only parameter impervious to time and change is, of course, so tailored to his own version of Western philosophical content that it does not accommodate even the content of the "great" Western literature all that persuasively. See this chapter, notes 17 and 18 (on content), notes 10, 82, and 83 (on the interpenetration of philosophical and sometimes literary stance and content), and p. 189, especially the text pertaining to notes 76, 81, and 82 (on literature).

As part of his intricate case for rejecting ethnocentrism outside the West (as an irrational impulse) but requiring it in the West (as grounded on reason), Bloom argues: "Cultural relativism . . . destroy[s] the West's universal or intellectual imperialistic claims, leaving it to be just another culture. So there is equality in the republic of cultures. Unfortunately the West is defined by its need for justification of its ways or values, by its need for discovery of nature, by its need for philosophy and science. This is its cultural imperative. Deprived of that, it will collapse" (p. 39). Bloom's focus at this moment is on an idea I, too, consider important, namely, that the American Enlightenment elevated abstract reason in the main "to overcome ethnocentrism" (p. 39). But to make that point he seems to argue that this American view of life alone has abstract universal validity because it alone contains a concept of abstract universal validity. Rather than making such a sweeping epistemological or even ontological claim for the Western viewpoint, Bloom would be more persuasive, in my judgment, if he argued for the enormous social benefit of maintaining a primary place in society for abstract universality *as a powerful ideal*. See note 11, and especially note 109, on Abraham Lincoln.

Again, Bloom seems on pp. 36-42 to want to have things both ways with respect to non-Western cultures. While looking down on these cultures as inferior, and charging that study of them encourages our students to give too much credit to notions of culture, he seems simultaneously to imply that we should learn from these cultures to consider our own the best. His apparent reasoning is that the content of Western culture has allowed it to transcend the condition of culture, so that those participating in (high) Western culture are actually operating free of culture at a level of abstract reason. Here, too, he has managed to transform the content of his ideas into their own epistemological status. See this volume, chapter 2, notes 9, 11, 152, and 155.

104. Bloom, p. 249.

105. See especially p. 249, and more generally the end of note 84, above, on the importance of the sense of "an outside"; and note 97, on alternatives.

106. [ON CULTURAL CONCRETENESS AS A MARK OF SOCIAL MARGINALIZATION.]

Marian Wright Edelman makes this negative aspect of culture clear when she writes the following: "It is utterly exhausting being black in America. . . . While many minority groups and women feel similar stress, there is no respite or escape from your badge of color. The daily stress of nonstop racial mindfulness and dealings with too many self-centered people who expect you to be cultural and racial translators and yet feel neither the need nor responsibility to reciprocate—to see or hear you as a human being rather than just as a black or a woman or a Jew—is wearing" (this passage from *The Measure of Our Success: A Letter to My Children and Yours* [Boston, 1992] is excerpted in the *New York Times Book Review* [August 23, 1992], 13). Deborah Tannen makes a similar point when she complains that "women [don't] have the freedom to be unmarked that . . . men [do]," in "Wears Jump Suit. Sensible Shoes. Uses Husband's Last Name," *New York Times Magazine* (June 20, 1993), 54; see also above, note 94.

107. [ON ABSTRACT REASON AND THE MERIT SYSTEM, ESPECIALLY AS AN AMERICAN CONCEPT.]

This is Bloom's point in arguing for the importance, at the "great" universities, "of some authentically great thinkers who gave living proof of the existence of the theoretical life and whose motives could not easily be reduced to any of the baser ones. . . . They had authority, not based on power, money or family, but on natural gifts that properly compel respect" (pp. 244-45).

The ongoing tendency of Americans to continue opposing European claims of hereditary privilege is brought up in connection to music by Katrina Irving in "Rock Music and the State: Dissonance or Counterpoint," *Cultural Critique* 10 (Fall, 1988), 155 (discussing the work of John Pattison), "American politics [are] seen as a permanent reaction against European politics"; p. 156 (quoting Pattison), "These are the same values praised in the American revolutionary myth, under the names democracy, pluralism"; and p. 156 (citing the work of Ernesto Laclau and Michel Guillaume St. John de Crèvecoeur), "the historical foundations of the U.S. are precisely those which emphasized 'the people' as a community against British rule." The useful idea suggested by this discussion is that while Europeans can come directly to see meritocracy in terms of a privileged class, American ways of thinking have been so profoundly (and perhaps permanently) shaped by the circumstances of the American Revolution that even privileged Americans see themselves reflexively as escapees from European claims of birth. Related to this discussion—and especially to that which now follows—is Isaiah Berlin's distinction between negative freedom (say, freedom from the hereditary claims of a nobility) and positive freedom (say, the freedom of those described by Marian Wright Edelman [see the preceding note] to participate in the mainstream); on this distinction, see chapter 1, note 41, and the text that pertains to it, p. 22. Also related are the distinction between exclusion and inclusion I have derived from Robert Bellah (see above, note 93), and Bloom's implied distinction between metaphorical and metonymical communities (see below, note 125).

108. Lynne V. Cheney, quoted in *Newsday* (October 21, 1988), 98.

109. [ON THE IMPORTANCE AND POWER OF THE ABSTRACT IDEAL AS AN ASYMPTOTE.]

Garry Wills defines the role of the Declaration of Independence for Lincoln in precisely this way, as a kind of socially powerful moral asymptote. See Wills, *Lincoln*, chapter 3, "The Transcendental Declaration" (citation in note 53), especially pp. 102, 109-11, and 120. In chapter 2 of this volume, pp. 57 and 68-69 ("dialectics of text"), I make the same argument for maintaining the conception of an original text as an abstract ideal. Though I cannot imagine such a text as an ontological or even epistemological reality, since no degree of authorial "purity" can remove the reader's own role in defining the text, I believe some such ideal is necessary—though not sufficient—as a means for maintaining what Habermas calls "communicative rationality" ("Modernity—An Incomplete Project," p. 8). See also the discussion of logical and aesthetic factors in Habermas's concept of an ideal speech community, in Eagleton, *Ideology of the Aesthetic*, pp. 402-8 (mentioned in this chapter, note 86).

110. [CULTURAL IDENTITY AS A PREMISE IN LEE'S FILM.]

Speaking at Adelphi University on March 28, 1990, of his then upcoming film, *Jungle Fever*, Lee made it clear that he considers concrete cultural identity an intrinsic aspect of his characters from their inception. This orientation is also clear in the first general notes for *Do The Right Thing* (Lee and Jones, *DTRT Companion*, p. 24, envisioning Black, Italian, and Puerto Rican characters in "a Black neighborhood in Brooklyn") as well as in details of individual character (nineteenth page of photographs, *DTRT Companion*: "I wanted Charlie, the character who gets his car drenched in the johnny pump, to be an Italian"). See also p. 28 of the journal: "The neighborhood will have a feel of the different cultures that make up the city, specifically Black American, Puerto Rican, West Indian, Korean, and Italian American."

111. [LEE'S ATTENTION TO CULTURAL DETAIL.]

Again, the journal is a convenient source of evidence for the strong attention to specific cultural detail in *Do The Right Thing*. Note, e.g., the following: p. 27 (the list of nicknames of jazz musicians and athletes on which Lee will draw for his characters); p. 29 (on the "Mr. Softee Ice Cream truck"); p. 43 (on the famous Italian Americans whose pictures will hang in the pizzeria); p. 83 (on flags as a visual motif); ninth page of photographs (Jon Kilik, line producer, writes:

"There were certain things that Spike didn't want to give up. And perhaps most important was that the film be shot in Brooklyn, on location in Bedford-Stuyvesant").

112. [ON TWO ALTERNATIVE PIVOTAL MOMENTS IN LEE'S FILM.]

That is to say, just as at the end of the film, Lee presents the viewer with two significantly different texts (note 62, above), so, too, he provides a basis for seeing two different moments as pivotal, depending on one's reading of the film. The idea of having his character hurl a garbage can turns up early in the journal (Lee and Jones, *DTRT Companion*, p. 34); in the screenplay itself the moment of this act is marked "*That's it. All hell breaks loose*" (p. 248, italics his). In an article by James S. Kunen entitled "Spike Lee Inflames the Critics with a Film He Swears Is *The Right Thing*" (*People*, [July 10, 1989], 67), Lee is quoted as saying, "I think all of black America threw that can." By and large the press perceived this as the critical moment. The beginning of Kunen's article is typical: "The garbage can sails through the air as swift and silent as hatred itself" (p. 67). This perception was by no means limited to whites. During Lee's lecture at Adelphi, a young African American teenage girl standing near me told her friend that if she could ask Lee one question, it would be how he justified Mookie's throwing the garbage can.

On p. 33 of Lee's journal, on the other hand, as he speculates on what will cause the climactic riot, this act isn't mentioned, even when he decides he will "drop a bomb" on the audience; and on pp. 40-41, he works backward from the throwing of the garbage can to develop a chain of events going back to the earlier moment. In Kunen's article, he explains the throwing of the can by saying "Black America is tired of having their brothers and sisters murdered by the police for no other reason than being black" (p. 67). And in his lecture at Adelphi Lee said, "I don't know whether you can say Mookie *started* the violence. He reacts to the cops killing Radio Raheem— *that's* what started the violence."

See below, notes 174 and 175.

113. [BLOOM'S SKEPTICISM TOWARD MOST PEOPLE'S "REASONS" AND TOWARD THE CLAIMS OF ORDINARY "COMMUNITY."]

Bloom, p. 238. In fact, Bloom immediately undercuts this observation by noting that most words put forth as reasons are not reasons but (in effect) markers of their absence, "nihilism as moralism" (p. 239). (This also undercuts any positive sense that could be attached to the notion of community; see note 114.) For a related statement, see p. 39 (on "the unhistorical and inhuman belief that opinions are held for no reason. . . . Men and nations always think they have reasons"). Bloom accepts only some reasons as reasonable; reasons not based exclusively on the paradigm of universal abstract reason are not to be considered *legitimate* reasons. (The paradigm of these phrases is, of course, Pascal's "The heart has its reasons"; to Pascal, interestingly, Bloom is willing to ascribe an "intellectual intransigence that forced him to abandon science in favor of faith" [p. 37; see also pp. 227-28].)

On good notions of community from Bloom's perspective, see below, note 125 and also note 97.

114. [BLOOM'S LINKAGE OF ORDINARY "COMMUNITY" AND "MORAL INDIGNATION," BOTH NOTIONS OF WHICH HE DISAPPROVES.]

See Bloom, p. 278, speaking of the ordinary community of citizens: "Vulgar morality is the code of this selfish collectivity, and whatever steps outside its circle is the object of moral indignation. And moral indignation, not ordinary selfishness or sensuality, is the greatest danger to the thinker." See also p. 71, in the context of a discourse on the irrationality of music ("Indignation is the soul's defense against the wound of doubt about its own; it reorders the cosmos to support the justice of its cause. It justifies putting Socrates to death. Recognizing indignation for what it is constitutes knowledge of the soul"); and 327 ("Indignation may be a most noble passion and necessary for fighting wars and righting wrongs. But of all the experiences of the soul it is the most inimical to reason"). On "special" as opposed to "moral" indignation, see below, note 124; see also note 139, for a connection to Radio Raheem's death.

Bloom summarizes his antipathy to the notion of (nonphilosophical) communities in his opposition between "community" and "reason," p. 269 (quoted in note 89, above). See also notes 97, 113, and 125.

115. Bloom, p. 229. Bloom's apparent indifference in this context to the solution of social problems (see also this chapter, notes 52, 123, and 129) should be contrasted with his emphasis on the need for the philosopher's right answers (see below, note 156)—as opposed, in another direction, to the "impoverishing certitudes" of the relativist (p. 239, and see below, note 157). See also below, notes 173-75.

116. [BLOOM ON THE PHILOSOPHER'S CAPACITY TO FACE DEATH.]

Bloom, p. 42. See also p. 277 ("It is the hardest task of all to face the lack of cosmic support for what we care about. Socrates, therefore, defines the task of philosophy as "learning how to die"); pp. 273-74 ("Philosophy . . . is austere and somewhat sad because it takes away many of men's fondest hopes. It . . . does nothing to console men. . . . Instead it points to their unprotectedness and nature's indifference to their individual fates. . . . It therefore has an almost impossible public relations problem"); p. 163 ("Unprotectedness, nakedness, unsuccored suffering and the awfulness of death are the prospects that man without illusions must face," and that man is the philosopher, p. 277); p. 285 ("*The* uncompromisable difference that separates the philosophers from all others concerns death and dying. No way of life other than the philosophic can digest the truth about death"); p. 270 (on Swift and the "harsh disproportion between the world most men cling to and the one inhabited by theoretical men"); and p. 282 (on the philosopher's inescapable "fundamental tension with everyone except his own kind"). (Italics are Bloom's.)

See also notes 19, 52, 55, 89, 97, 100, 118, and 129, and 147. Worth noting is the extent to which the first passage quoted here (from Bloom, p. 42) overlaps with a description by Lionel Trilling of the artist as a man of authenticity (*Sincerity and Authenticity* [Cambridge, Mass., 1972], p. 104). See this volume, chapter 1, notes 28 and 63, and also chapter 3, notes 31, 63, and 64. Unlike Bloom's sentiment, Trilling's (derived from Nathalie Sarraute) is in no way self-serving.

117. [BLOOM'S DISDAIN FOR LACK OF SIGNIFICANT SACRIFICE BY OTHERS.]

Bloom, p. 236; the group in question here fits the stereotype of "bleeding-heart liberals," though Bloom doesn't use that term. See also pp. 327-28 and 333-35 on Bloom's disdain for the lack of significant risk or sacrifice by students in the 1960s. Bloom contrasts student morality in the 1960s, based on conscience (p. 326), with Kantian morality, which "always requires sacrifice," which "must always be for itself and not for some result beyond it," and which "requires resistance to the charms of feeling good about it" (p. 325). See also p. 192 (on divorce); and below, note 134 (on conscience), and note 150 (on Kantian morality).

Bloom's disdain here should be compared with his approval of "enlightened selfishness" (see note 59) and of the philosopher's need to avoid serving the public (seen in notes 52, 129, and also 118).

118. [BLOOM'S AMBIGUOUS ATTITUDES TOWARD EMPLOYMENT IN THE ACADEMY AND TENURE, AND HIS UNCLEAR REFERENCE TO MODERN PHILOSOPHERS' RISK.]

Bloom's attitudes toward employment in the academy and tenure are difficult to sort out. On p. 267 he characterizes a tenured university spot as "a free lunch for philosophers and scientists" while also calling it the modern equivalent of precisely the arrangement Socrates wanted. Along these lines, Bloom often emphasizes Socrates' poverty (p. 267)—though also his utter indifference to "honor and luxury" (p. 270)—and his lack of security. See p. 279 ("The ancients had no tenure to protect them and wanted to avoid the prostitution to which those who have to live off their wits are prone") and also Bloom's closing admonition, p. 382 ("One should never forget that Socrates was not a professor") So far, he implies some good in tenure.

At times, Bloom's attitude toward the modern academic situation is stated ambiguously. When he says, p. 272, "One cannot imagine Socrates as a professor, for reasons that are worthy of our attention," it is not clear whether he refers to Socrates' life or his preferences. Likewise, on p. 298, it is not clear whether he disagrees entirely with Rousseau's view that "the knowers who inhabit the academies . . . become easygoing and self-satisfied. The Ciceros and Bacons would not have been what they were if they had been professors."

But most times he seems to suggest that philosophers are better off without academic jobs and tenure. He seems to approve, for example, that "Socrates' reaction to the accusation is not to assert the right of academic freedom to pursue investigations" (p. 265). On p. 279, after noting the ancients' lack of tenure, he switches to the present tense, as if to imply that tenure has not changed the lot of the modern philosopher ("There is no moral order protecting philosophers or ensuring that truth will win out in the long, or the short, run"). He speaks likewise in the present tense of "the basic fragility of [the philosopher's] situation and that of philosophy" (p. 282). And see especially p. 273: "As a result of Enlightenment, philosophers and philosophy came to inhabit the universities exclusively, abandoning their old habits and haunts. There they have become vulnerable in new ways and thus risk extinction. The classical philosophers would not, for very good reason, have taken this risk." Perhaps Bloom refers here to what he would consider the suicidal turn of modern philosophy away from the Socratic model. But he makes no suggestion that philosophers today should quit their jobs to save Socratic philosophy.

In short, Bloom is far more persuasive when he praises the ancients for being "ever mindful of the responsibilities and the risks of their enterprises" (p. 284) than when he invokes "necessary consequences" accepted by (his own kind of) philosopher (p. 228, see note 158, below); see also notes 52 and 129 (on the philosopher's need for social autonomy), 59 (on enlightened selfishness), 117 (on sacrifice), and 134 (on conscience).

All of these references should be compared to Bloom's unambiguous references to his own "unusually happy" career, p. 22, and also p. 245 (cited below, note 129).

119. [ON THE SUBCONTRACTING OF RISK.]

Joseph Epstein, "The Joys of Victimhood," *New York Times Magazine* (July 2, 1989), 21, 39-41. Especially offputting is Epstein's conclusion by way of unearned glory (a technique much questioned in music!) through reference to "the people I know who are seriously handicapped," p. 41.

The attitude I describe was a focus of criticism in the 1989 commencement address at Brandeis University by the novelist E. L. Doctorow, who described the Reagan conservative as "someone willing to pay the price of other people's suffering for his principles" (quoted by Thomas Collins in *Newsday* [November 29, 1989], 67). The original text of this speech is printed as "The Brandeis Papers: 'A Gangsterdom of the Spirit,'" in *Nation*, 249, no. 10 (October 2, 1989), pp. 348-54. See p. 352 for the source of my quotation, and also below, notes 136 and 192, for other excerpts from this speech. It interests me that Doctorow's speech was written in 1989, the same year in which the present chapter first took shape; though his is far more eloquent, our readings of America in that year overlap considerably. (The reprint of this speech is preceded by an interesting account of its publication history, on p. 348; rebuttals of that account were published two weeks later in *Nation*, 249, no. 12 [October 16, 1989], p. 406.)

120. [ON THE SUFFERER'S ATTITUDE TOWARD SUFFERING.]

Shelby Steele's argument to the same effect, in "The New Sovereignty" (cited in note 86, above), makes a different impression because Steele simultaneously acknowledges the grievances involved as real. See, e.g., p. 49 ("on the woeful neglect of women's intellectual contributions," etc.).

121. [BLOOM ON "AFFIRMATIVE-ACTION ELITISM."]

Bloom, p. 332 ("The elite should really be elite, but these elitists were given the distinction they craved without having earned it. The university provided a kind of affirmative-action elitism. There had for a long time been a conspiracy in the universities to deny that there is a problem for the superior individual, particularly the one with the gift and the passion for ruling, in democratic society").

122. Evan Thomas, "Is Bush a True Wasp?" *Newsweek* (September 25, 1989), 23.

123. [BLOOM'S EMPHASIS ON THE NEEDS OF THE PRIVILEGED; HIS VIEW OF COMPASSION.]

A key discussion in this regard appears in Bloom, pp. 329-31, where Bloom argues that democracy has never been receptive to "the aspiration to be number one and gain great fame," even though this is "both natural in man and, properly trained, one of the soul's great strengths" (p. 329). Ancient democracy did not "persuade the proud and the ambitious that the rule of the many is just. . . . [and] the talented young could hope, and sometimes act, without guilt, to gain first place" (p. 330). Christianity "left the inequalities of this world in place" (p. 330); but in the world of the modern democracy, now the only form of government that philosophy can sanction, "the soul cannot find encouragement for its longing anywhere" (p. 330). (This last notion is intriguing if the intended title for this book was "Souls without Longing" [see above, note 55]; it suggests that Bloom envisioned this book as a lament for the passing of an elite that longed to be first. For an additional explanation, see this chapter, note 130.)

Bloom goes on to unveil a "covert elitism" (p. 329) among American students in the 1960s, who no longer dared seek openly to be first. "Much of modern history can be explained by the search for what Plato called spiritedness for legitimate self-expression" (p. 330), he asserts. "Certainly compassion and the idea of the vanguard were essentially democratic covers for elitist self-assertion. Rousseau, who first made compassion the foundation of democratic sentiment, was fully aware that a sense of superiority to the sufferer is a component of the human experience of compassion. He actually was attempting to channel the inegalitarian impulse into egalitarian channels" (p. 330; for his conclusion, on p. 331, see below, note 126). On compassion see also the reference to "a vague, generalized compassion" (p. 200, and below, notes 126 and 178).

Equally notable is a reverie by Bloom on students past (indeed, the students of my own generation). After quoting from a passage he had written in 1965 on "young Americans, that is, some young Americans," students who were "a kind of democratic version of an aristocracy," Bloom recalls that "[After *Sputnik*] for a moment, leveling education was set back on its heels. There seemed to be no time for that nonsense. Survival itself depended on better education for the best people" (p. 49).

Especially important in this context is Bloom's reference to the "optimistic [American] belief that . . . access to the best is not dependent on chance" (p. 49). This contrasts, of course, with the philosopher's unblinking realization of "our dependence on fortune for what little life we have" (p. 282). (See also p. 277 on "accident," quoted below, note 147.) Bloom himself, moreover, has spoken earlier of students "whom circumstances of one sort or another prevent from having the freedom required to pursue a liberal education," say, "at the twenty or thirty best universities" (p. 22). But this is the very moment when Bloom fails to distinguish between circumstances and ability (see above, note 57). Indeed, Bloom openly assumes that those kept from liberal education are "other kinds of students" than the "advantaged youths"—of "comparatively high intelligence, materially and spiritually free to do pretty much what they want with . . . college"—who are "most likely to take advantage of a liberal education," and who "most need education" to perfect their superior talents and protect their complex natures (p. 22).

See also p. 289 ("in antiquity . . . no philosopher believed it feasible or salutary to change the relations between rich and poor in a fundamental or permanently progressive way"); p. 252 (on setting clarity above "well-being or compassion," in note 52, above); and a negative statement, p. 326 ("not to be considered were natural differences in gifts or in habitual practice of the virtues").

Though in theory these ideas can be tied to a morally defensible ideal of merit, the sheer number of these emphatically stated opinions contributes heavily to the mean-spirited tone discussed below (note 126). In such a context, backed up by Bloom's dismissal of the French Revolution (p. 283, see above, note 79), it is easy to think of the philosopher's "immun[ity] to tragedy" (p. 277, see above, note 55) not as an absence of illusions but as social callousness.

See also above, note 95, for other references to elitism, and note 129, below.

124. [BLOOM ON "SPECIAL INDIGNATION"]

Bloom, p. 329. Compare his ideas of other sorts of indignation, above, note 114; and consider where he might locate the indignation(s) roused by Socrates (p. 282).

125. [Bloom's positive notions of "community."]

Bloom, p. 381. For other positive notions of community (they are either "natural" or philosophical), see p. 254 (quoted in note 14) and p. 271 (quoted in note 97). Bloom also speaks approvingly of a community between "authentically great thinkers" at the "great universit[ies]" and their students, a "community in which there is a true common good" (pp. 244-45); and he refers nostalgically to the period of resistance to Joseph McCarthy as "the last time the university had any sense of community" (p. 324). For negative views of community, see above, notes 113 and 114.

Bloom's views of community could well be characterized through reference to the polarity of metaphor and metonym. A good community, for Bloom, is made up of thinkers who are metaphorical equivalents for each other (say, philosophers); a bad one consists of people who happen to be metonymically contiguous (say, members of a culture). Much as it might pain him to have his thought explained through a structuralist or poststructuralist image, it appears that his view of community does assume images of metaphoric equivalence, as a relation based on rational thought, and of metonymic adjacence, as one based on mindless chance. (See above, chapter 2, note 57.)

To be sure, this distinction seems to have limits for Bloom. Since he limits his good "metaphorical" communities entirely to what he would call reasoners, it seems likely that he would not find a rational basis in a community made up of shoemakers—or musicians. Moreover, as an interpreter interested solely in the content of a text, he abhors equally the notions that only another ancient Greek (metonymic relation) or only another poet (metaphoric relation) could understand Homer (see p. 308). From Bloom's standpoint, indeed, "modern scholarship is a failure" (p. 309) because of the historian's resigned, post-Enlightenment conviction that action is prior to thought and, consequently, that only men of action (as opposed to men of reason) can understand Caesar (see below, note 157). But this brings us back to Bloom's metaphorical conception of philosopher and community. For Bloom, the abstract reasoner alone is in a position to understand what matters about others, whatever their historical particularities—the timeless human condition they share. See above, notes 17 and 100; also note 107, on other dualities.

126. [Bloom's mean-spirited tone and language.]

Will's phrase is quoted in Garry Wills's review of Ethan Bronner, *Battle for Justice: How the Bork Nomination Shook America*, in the *New York Times Book Review* (September 10, 1989), 7. For "flabby ecumenism," see Bloom, p. 308; "culture leeches," p. 51; "conspicuous compassion," see p. 331. Compare his remarks on compassion cited in note 123, and see note 178.

Consider also the apparently contemptuous tone of the following examples: p. 330 ("Elitism is the catch-all epithet expressing our disapproval of the proud and the desire to be first"); p. 314 (on the typical American "popular fit of moralism"); and p. 331, his conclusion to the discussion noted above in note 123 ("None of the exquisite thrills of egalitarian vanity were alien to" the students of the 1960s). See also p. 228, on those who face "real questions" (cited below, note 158).

Almost always Bloom could have made the same point without the contempt; quite clearly this tone serves a rhetorical purpose of emphasis that Bloom felt his argument required.

And as in note 123 above, once set in motion this tone affects one's response to locutions that serve an entirely different purpose. See, e.g., p. 250 (on "the lover of beautiful and useless things," quoted above in note 95); p. 41, on "the love of inequality" (see note 83); and p. 195, on our blindness to modern self-satisfaction ("our capacity for contempt is vanishing"). Note also the tone with which Bloom describes one of his greatest satisfactions as a teacher, a night when his students elected to study Plato instead of joining in a student demonstration: "These students were rather contemptuous of what was going on, because it got in the way of what they thought it important to do. . . . They really *looked down* from the classroom on the frantic activity outside, thinking they were privileged, hardly a one tempted to join the crowd" (p. 332, italics his). Compare p. 324: "In the mid-sixties the natives, in the guise of students, attacked."

Sir Kenneth Clark asserts that "the greatest civilising achievment of the nineteenth century

[was] humanitarianism." What came to "[matter] most in human conduct," for most people, was "kindness" (Kenneth Clark, *Civilisation: A Personal View* [New York, 1969], p. 329). Clark goes on to admit that "certain philosophers, going back to Hegel, tell us that humanitarianism is a weak, sloppy, self-indulgent condition, spritually much inferior to cruelty and violence" and that "kindness is to some extent the offspring of materialism" (ibid., p. 330). Still, given the clear Western ethnocentrism of Clark's book (beginning with the title), the contrast with Bloom is noteworthy.

127. Bloom, p. 311.

128. [BLOOM ON THE SCHOLAR AS ADULT AND AS CHILD.]

Bloom, p. 245. Compare this happy image of the philosopher as child with another of the humanities: "But now the grownups are too busy at work, and the children are left in a day-care center called the humanities, in which the discussions have no echo in the adult world" (p. 372).

In the latter usage, Bloom's imagery of disdain converges on that of Adorno and Schoenberg. See above, chapter 3, p. 166, and notes 31, 63, and especially 48, and 64. See also the present chapter, note 142, on the three men's common characterization of the physical parameters of music as childish.

129. [BLOOM ON HIS HAPPINESS WITH PHILOSOPHY AS A NONMINISTERIAL CAREER.]

Bloom, p. 245. (For me this at once evoked the motto of my alma mater, Wellesley College, "Not to be ministered unto but to minister," which I learned only recently comes from the New Testament. Conceivably Bloom chose the word "minister" here specifically to differentiate his mission from a religious one. One also sees a link here to "enlightened selfishness.")

See also p. 22 (on Bloom's happy career, cited in note 118), note 52 (on the need for philosophy to resist the call to public service), and note 123, concerning Bloom's emphasis on the advantaged.

130. [BLOOM'S SEXUAL IMAGERY OF EDUCATION.]

See Bloom, p. 20 (on the "reasons that help to explain the perversity of an adult who prefers the company of youths to that of grownups"). See also the almost orgasmic account of college education in the section "Eros," pp. 133-36, culminating on pp. 135-36: "A significant number of students used to arrive at the university physically and spiritually virginal, expecting to lose their innocence there. . . . [T]his literal lust for knowledge . . . was what a teacher could see in the eyes of those who flattered him by giving such evidence of their need for him. His own satisfaction was promised by having something with which to feed their hunger, an overflow to bestow on their emptiness. His joy was in hearing the ecstatic 'Oh, yes!' as he dished up Shakespeare and Hegel to minister to their need. Pimp and midwife really described him well. The itch for what appeared to be only sexual intercourse was the material manifestation of the Delphic oracle's command, which is but a remainder of the most fundamental human desire, to 'know thyself.' [But now] sated with easy, clinical and sterile satisfactions of body and soul [. . . students arrive] spiritually detumescent. . . . The real moment for sexual education goes by, and hardly anybody has an idea of what it would be. . . . [Now]the humanists are old maid librarians."

Also noteworthy is the discussion on pp. 237-38 of Plato and eros (cited above in note 97) in connection with Thomas Mann's *Death in Venice*: "Plato found a way of expressing and beautifying, of sublimating, perverse sexuality. . . . Plato both enchants and disenchants eros, and we need both. At least in Mann the tradition in which we could refresh ourselves is present, if not exactly alive . . . [via] Aschenbach. But in America that slender thread . . . has broken. . . . Eros is an obsession, but there is no thought about it, and no possiblity of thought about it." (Here one sees a germ of Bloom's final book, *Love and Friendship* [New York, 1993], especially the section excerpted in the *New York Times Magazine* [May 23, 1993], 27 and 83-84, under the title "The Death of Eros." These works are not otherwise cited in the present article.)

Especially interesting is the glimpse that the end of the passage on p. 238 gives of Bloom's purported original title, "Souls without Longing" (see above, notes 55 and 123): "Souls artificially constituted by a new kind of education live in a world transformed by man's artifice and believe that all values are relative and determined by the private economic or sexual drives of those who hold them. How are they to recover the primary natural experience?" Given Bloom's virtual equation of the "natural" with philosophy (see above, note 13)—and given his contempt for the notion of value—it would seem that his souls without longing might well be students who no longer experience the kind of erotic longing that a philosophical education could fulfill.

See also Bloom, p. 305 ("Plato was indeed the philosopher for lovers. . . . In Plato, eros led to philosophy"); p. 375 ("Nietzsche said that after the ministrations of modern scholarship the *Symposium* is so far away that it can no longer seduce us"); and, in a more comical vein, p. 352 ("humanists . . . had been only antiquarians, eunuchs guarding a harem of aging and now unattractive courtesans"). On p. 69 he associates Mozart with initiation.

131. Bloom, p. 107.

132. See above, note 116.

133. Bloom, p. 244.

134. [BLOOM'S QUASI-COGNITIVE DISDAIN FOR THE NOTION OF CONSCIENCE.]

On Bloom's contempt for conscience see p. 326 ("Conscience, a faculty thoroughly discredited in modern political and moral thought . . . made a great comeback, as the all-purpose ungrounded ground of moral determination"). Bloom's quasi-cognitive contempt here for conscience is qualitatively much like the scientists' disdain for nonscientific softness (see Bloom's complaint about the president of Rockefeller University, pp. 350-51, in note 49); but again, his own cognitive stance can be shown, ultimately, to amount to an aesthetic style; see notes 20, 60, 157, and 67.

Once again, bypassing the difficulties introduced into the notion of "moral rigor" since Kant, Bloom simply refers this aspect of education back to Socrates; because of his difficulty envisioning a paradigm for the educational process other than the (quasi-sexual) transmission of content, he excludes promising alternatives, as I now want to suggest. Bloom does, to be sure, refer to the sacrifices required by Kantian morality (p. 325, see note 117, above), a vision that can be compared with Lionel Trilling's notion of moral strenuousness (see above, chapter 3, note 63); but this does not get Bloom around the purely formal character of Kant's moral law or (as I am about to suggest) the fundamentally aesthetic basis of morality since Kant. See below, notes 136, 150, 156, and 172. See also the discussion in this chapter leading up to note 173, on Bloom and intellectual honesty, p. 206.

135. [BLOOM'S DUBIOUS OPINION OF THE WESTERN "SELF" IN CONNECTION WITH TEACHING BY EXAMPLE, AS OPPOSED TO TEACHING CONTENT.]

Bloom's view is that this sort of moral refinement can be gained only by paying close attention simply to the *content* of Greek philosophy. He is very dubious about the kind of self to which my sort of appeal could made. See, e.g., p. 179 (Socrates' "measure of health was not sincerity, authenticity or any of the other necessarily vague criteria for distinguishing a healthy self. The truth is the one thing most needful"); and the attacks on the notion of intellectual honesty cited below, note 173. At best (p. 203), Nietzsche alone tried to apply his own thought to himself (and thereby, one presumes, to give the notion of the self some bracing rigor; see above, notes 30, 42, and 98, last paragraph). But see also p. 200, for an account of how Western notions of the self fell down a slippery slope.

The closest Bloom comes to my notion is in connection with a discussion of Weber, p. 369: "Even when it was most vigorously teaching that values cannot be the subject matter of knowledge, that very teaching taught about life, as shown by once exciting contrivances as Weber's distinction between the ethics of intention and the ethics of responsibility. This was not textbook learning, but the real stuff of life." But Weber's distinctions "hardly held out against the naturally relaxed democratic tendency to say, 'Oh, what's the use?'" [p. 338]).

136. [BLOOM'S REFERENCES TO POETRY AS AN ALTERNATIVE TO PHILOSOPHY.]

Bloom, p. 298; see above, notes 25 and 36, on the absence of self-consciousness in science. See also p. 277 and p. 281 (quoted above in note 72) on the "rhetorical appeal" (p. 277) of philosophy; p. 292 ("There are other experiences, always the religious, and in modern times the poetic, which make competing claims. But it is not immediately evident that their claims are superior to those of philosophy"); and above, notes 74 and 77, on the war between philosophy and poetry. See also below, notes 150, 156, and 172, on the relation of the moral and the aesthetic as presented by Kant.

Relevant to the argument I shall make here are two remarks from Doctorow's 1989 Brandeis commencement address. Quoting in part from Shelley, Doctorow draws together all three of the Kantian faculties when he characterizes all artists as "unacknowledged . . . legislators of created consciousness who from the struggles of their own minds make poems and stories that would contribute to the moral consciousness of their time" (p. 349 of *Nation* version, cited above in note 119). And, nearing his close (ibid., p. 354), "Everything impractical [your teachers] have given you, lines of poetry, phrases of music, and philosophical propositions . . . is terribly practical—in fact, the only means we have of defending the borders of a magnanimous, humanist civilization." See also below, note 192.

137. Bloom, p. 71.

138. [BLOOM ON CLASSICAL MUSIC.]

The single sentence Bloom devotes to Bach and Beethoven, p. 72, not only seems grudgingly terse in comparison with his reference to writers (see above, note 71) but also concerns only the intentions of these composers, not their music. See this chapter, note 142.

An interesting sidelight on the relation of music and passion is provided by Bloom's discussion of an episode from Swift's *Gulliver's Travels*. Bloom's account suggests that Swift viewed music as a totally inward experience that lacked the appeal of poetry to an erotic sensibility: "The only studies are astronomy and music, and the world is reduced to these two sciences. The men have no contact with ordinary sense experience. . . . [Their] absence of eroticism is connected with an absence of poetic sensibility. These scientists cannot understand poetry, and hence, in Gulliver's view, their science cannot be a science of man" (p. 294). Bloom is not explicit about the relation of this distinction to the Platonic distinction he describes between the ecstatic effect of music and the disciplining force of words (pp. 71-72), as when he defines poetry as "what music becomes as reason emerges" (p. 71). (This last formulation cannot help but recall the very different way in which Kierkegaard draws on a similar notion to evaluate Mozart's *Magic Flute*. See chapter 1, this volume, notes 91-94.) See also this chapter, notes 139, 141, and 142.

139. [BLOOM ON MUSIC AND IRRATIONAL ATTACHMENTS.]

Bloom, p. 71. Bloom argues here and on p. 74 that an attachment to rock music signifies an irrational attitude of indignation, the attitude used to justify putting Socrates to death. This view raises intriguing possibilities concerning the role of indignation in the chain of events in *Do The Right Thing* that starts with Radio Raheem's insistence on playing his boom box loudly and moves to his death at the hands of two policemen. (See above, note 114.)

140. Bloom, p. 73.

141. [BLOOM ON THE CATHARTIC FUNCTION OF MUSIC.]

Bloom does, to be sure, say that "for those who are interested in psychological health, music is at the center of education" (p. 72); the ground he offers for this statement is the power of high-minded music—Bach and Beethoven are his examples—to "[satisfy the passions] while sublimating them" (ibid.). But the role he accords music here is exactly that allowed by Aristotle to poetry: to purge the soul of passion so as to ready it for reason (pp. 280-81, see above, note 72). My argument is, rather, that music itself provides a model of reason.

142. [ON BLOOM'S NOTION OF THE CONCRETENESS OF ART.]

For Bloom's notion that *poetry* is concrete in a way that philosophy is not, see above, note 73. Bloom's notion, to be sure, seems tied primarily to the *content* of literature. His association of rhetoric with poetry (p. 281, quoted in note 72) implies a link between content and means, but Bloom seems entirely undisposed to consider that the means and material of art have significance for rationality in any sense. Certainly he makes no distinction, within the means and material of *any* art, comparable to Adorno's (which I analyze above, in chapter 3) between structure and sound.

Bloom's ideas about the concreteness of art seem particularly crude where music is concerned. Earlier in this chapter (p. 187, text pertaining to note 64), I suggested an analogy between Bloom's abstract notion of reason and abstract notions of musical structure. Yet apart from a brief sugges- tion that nobly intended music can give the passions "artistic unity" (p. 72)—and note how even here, Bloom's content-oriented notion of intention is primary—Bloom, himself, never disentan- gles a structural parameter of music from the totality of the physical characteristics that make it, to his mind, a thoroughly irrational medium. Thus, although he complains that "rock music has one appeal only, a barbaric appeal, to sexual desire" (p. 73), he seems to have no idea of other ways in which concrete musical material, even in the classical realm, might operate. Here he differs markedly from the musical professionals Schoenberg and Adorno, though they would obviously agree with him, concerning the beat of pop music, that "never was there an art form so directed to children" (p. 74—compare the references to chapter 3 cited above, in note 128). See also this chapter, notes 10 and 73, and especially 82 and 168, on conflations or inconsistencies in Bloom's ideas of artistic concreteness; and the reference to musical "reasons" that elicits note 145, below.

143. [ON MUSICAL "MAPS."]

Though amazingly detailed "maps" of structurally complex pieces have been collected into the equivalent of musical atlases. One example is by Earl V. Moore and Theodore E. Heger, *The Sym- phony and the Symphonic Poem: Analytical and Descriptive Charts of the Standard Symphonic Repertory* (Ann Arbor, 1949).

144. Pater's exact words are "All art constantly aspires towards the condition of music," from his essay "Giorgione" in *Studies in the History of the Renaissance*, 1873.

145. See above, note 113.

146. [BLOOM VS. ADORNO AND DERRIDA ON TRANSLATION.]

It is interesting to reflect that in the matter of translation, Bloom in a sense sides with Derrida against Adorno. Both Bloom and Derrida would allow freely for translations, Bloom because the reality of a text lies in its abstract content, Derrida because of his perception that all texts are already translations of still other textual elements, and therefore not sacrosanct or inviolate. (On Bloom, see above, notes 17, 18, 19, and 100; on Derrida, see chapter 2, "How Could Chopin's A- Major Prelude Be Deconstructed?" note 5.) Adorno, on the other hand, insisting on the insepara- bility of material from form, writes in such a way as to make unmistakable the violation done the particularity of a text through translation. But the views that are actually allied here are those of the two Europeans. Both understand the indebtedness of the speaker to an outside social world for materials, and both recognize the contribution of those materials to the meanings conveyed by the text. (See the various references cited in this volume, chapter 2, note 14.) Adorno, however, holds on to a vision of individual control over meaning, although he understands that vision to be futile. Derrida accepts that futility as a starting point for the analysis of meaning. Bloom acknowl- edges no problem in transmitting pure meaning that transcends all accidents of material, and rejects as unnecessary the complexities of the arguments advanced by the other two.

147. [BLOOM ON THE ORDINARY INDIVIDUAL'S NEED FOR VALIDATION.]

On p. 277 Bloom comments, "Individuals demand significance for this individual life, which is so subject to accident." Interestingly, in another chapter of this book ("How Could Chopin's A- Major Prelude be Deconstructed?" e.g., p. 139, note 145), I argue that this very desire could be construed as the theme of Chopin's A-Major Prelude. My argument is made through what I believe to be rigorous formal analysis rather than poetic intuition. And my conclusion is that Chopin shows the futility of this hope emphatically—and no less effectively, I would wager, than the philosophers in Bloom's pantheon.

Compare Bloom's view of the ordinary individual and of the philosopher (see notes 100 and 116, above).

148. Bloom, p. 266; on pp. 266-67 see above, notes 37, 55, and 77. See also note 140, on music and Enlightenment critique (as cited on p. 198).

149. [MODELS OF ABSTRACT AND CONCRETE LANGUAGE IN THE SPEECHES OF LINCOLN AND EVERETT.]

A wonderful verbal analogy is supplied by Garry Wills in his characterization of Lincoln's Gettysburg Address: "The compactness is not merely a matter of length. There is a suppression of particulars in the idealizing art of Lincoln, as in the Greek orations. This restraint . . . makes these works oddly moving despite their impersonal air" (*Lincoln*, p. 53, cited in note 53). Clearly here, as in Classical music, the roles of structure and content in defining ideals of abstraction are by no means always distinct from each other. Though Wills's characterization of classicism shares Bloom's emphasis on abstractness, the comparative modesty of Wills's terms and claims makes his description more appealing. One could put it that where Bloom grounds his case for abstractness, an essentially aesthetic quality, on cognitive certainty (or moral dogma), trying to prove he is right—or to shame us into agreeing with him—Wills makes his case by appealing to our aesthetic sensibilities. Wills's comparison of Lincoln's speech with the rich detail of Edward Everett's also has a clear counterpart in music: "Everett, despite his training as a Hellenist, is not really classical in spirit. He speaks unabashedly for the romantic age" (*Lincoln*, p. 54).

150. [ON THE KANTIAN GAP BETWEEN AESTHETIC AND MORAL.]

See Kant, *Critique of Judgment*, section 42, p. 143. Involved in this inability are the gaps between the mental three faculties (cognitive, aesthetic, moral), as presented in Kant's topography of the mind. (See above, notes 21, including references to Bloom, p. 300, and 86; I discuss this topography at length in "Kant, Adorno, and the Self-Critique of Reason," chapter 4 of *Developing Variations*, especially pp. 59-68.)

As Kant presents the three faculties in the third critique, the relations between them are analogical. As concerns the aesthetic and the moral, see, for example (*Critique of Judgment*, section 42, p. 143), his remarks on "the analogy between the pure judgment of taste . . . and the moral judgment." Both, according to Kant, involve purely formal laws (ibid., p. 142). In the case of aesthetic judgment, this means that no universal, substantive laws about what constitutes beauty can be formulated apart from the actual experience of beauty, much less proven. In the case of morality, this means that although the human mind draws on universal moral law in making moral choices, it likewise has no access to the substantive content of those laws—or, as Kant puts it, we take "satisfaction in the mere forms of practical maxims (so far as they are in themselves qualified for universal legislation)" (ibid.).

The purely formal aspect of Kant's moral law, worked out at length in his second critique, the *Critique of Practical Reason*, has caused well-known difficulties for his interpreters and successors. (Thus Bloom's observation, p. 193, that "freedom is a postulate, a possibility in Kant, not a demonstration; and that remains the difficulty." See note 22 above. An old but useful guide to Kant's conception of the moral, particularly as it presents itself in the *third* critique, is H. W. Cassirer's *A Commentary on Kant's Critique of Judgment* [London, 1938]. See, for example, p. 300, where Cassirer analyzes Kant's first Remark in section 57 of the *Critique of Judgment*, pp. 187-89, and also pp. 61-67.) But this common quality of formality is highly suggestive for the argument I make in the present chapter: Kant seems clearly to characterize judgments of taste and moral judgments alike through a parameter, form, that is fundamentally aesthetic.

Attempting to ascribe an a priori universality to both types of judgment, Kant further asserts that both have a disinterested basis (ibid., section 42, pp. 142-43). But moral judgments, as Kant understands them, lead necessarily to "the highest interest" (ibid., section 4, p. 43, see above, note 60), associated by Kant with "moral feeling" (ibid., section 42, p. 143), that is, an interest in the good. Drawing on his own analogy between mental faculties, Kant argues that aesthetic judgment, though in itself neither "based on [n]or producing any interest" likewise "arouses an immediate interest," though only in the case of natural beauty, not in that of art (ibid., p. 142). The interest aroused is a quasi-moral satisfaction in the fact that nature has (apparently) arranged itself so as to allow us the pleasure of beauty—i.e., it has arranged itself "purposive[ly]" (*zweckmässig*), as if with a purpose (ibid., p. 144). Unlike our moral feeling, our aesthetic interest is "free"; it is not necessary or "based on objective laws" (ibid., p. 143). Nevertheless the aesthetic interest in the purposiveness of nature is "akin to the moral" since it is clearly similar to the concern of reason that "the ideas" (which point to domains of rationality, and especially moral law, that are beyond human knowledge) "should have objective reality" (ibid., p. 143)—a concern, ultimately, that the good should be real.

Though Kant argues these points with intense concern for logic, he falls short of constructing a cognitive proof for a convergence of the beautiful and the moral. Interestingly, in terms of Bloom's case, Kant openly admits that this quasi-moral interest in the beautiful is "not common, but is peculiar to those whose mental disposition either has already been cultivated in the direction of the good or is eminently susceptible of such cultivation" (ibid., p. 143). One sees here the basis for the connection Eagleton draws between "Kant's community of aesthetic judgment" and Habermas's "ideal speech community" (see above, note 86, and also note 89); one also sees the familiar pattern of intertwined universality and elitism characteristic in images of an Elect.

Bloom himself, while asserting that moral conduct involves "a disinterestedness incomprehensible to [most men]" (p. 327), shares none of Kant's interest in linking the moral and the aesthetic, except perhaps in that odd moment when he lumps together beauty and wisdom as qualities that do not require "self-overcoming" (p. 327). Though elsewhere (p. 369) Bloom fleetingly suggests that Continental intellectuals might once have acquired a bit of wisdom through their studies, here he appears to view wisdom as an innate quality. One has to wonder whether a view of teaching that honored suffering as well as sexuality might not make some place for wisdom in the educational process as well.

On related issues see this chapter, notes 21, 22, 60, 134, 136, 156, 172, and 173.

151. [BLOOM'S ASSUMPTION OF A DIVISION BETWEEN REASON AND THE AESTHETIC AND ITS PERPETUATION OF THE KANTIAN COGNITIVE-MORAL SPLIT.]

Where music is concerned, Bloom seems locked into the same position as the analytic philosopher who asked me during a job interview, "What in the world could Beethoven's Opus 1 Number 1 have to do with morality?" The correct answer, I discovered, after not getting the job, was "Nothing whatsoever, Sir." Bloom despises analytic philosophy (see Bloom, p. 378). Yet because both of these men use objectivity as an aesthetic style to present a single conception of rationality, they perpetuate similar restrictions in education. See notes 20, 21, 60, 67, 156, and 157.

152. [DRAWING AN ANALOGY BETWEEN BLOOM'S ATTITUDES TOWARD NON-WESTERN CULTURE AND THE AESTHETIC.]

Bloom might counter this assertion by extending his notion of true openness, discussed above in note 84, and also notes 83 and 103, arguing that just as the Westerner should in effect be closed to accepting the viewpoints of the non-West, so, too, the philosopher should be closed to the viewpoint of the arts, in order to make the best use of the abstract reasoning faculty. From his critic's standpoint, this might create problems in terms of Bloom's own formulations, for example, that "true openness is the accompaniment of the desire to know, hence of the awareness of ignorance" (p. 40). But for Bloom this would not be a problem. His narrowly restricted definition of "knowing" precludes the very possibility of learning something from art, or from non-Western culture (see especially p. 34, cited in note 85, above). See also this chapter, note 10.

153. [ON LEE AND MUSICAL IMAGERY.]

Near the start of his journal, after envisioning his script as "circular," Lee notes, "After the climax of the film, I would like to have a coda. This scene could take place the morning after the riot. We see the aftermath. . . . folks seem to have regained their senses. I'll have to think of a way to convey this" (Lee and Jones, *DTRT Companion*, p. 32). Though tied specifically to the unfolding and content of the story, Lee's conception of structure here is musical: he is working out a concrete logic.

154. One chooses the word "best" here with a sinking sense of the degree to which it symbolizes the post-Kantian epistemological impasse between the faculties. Do we mean "most accurately" (cognitive realm)? "most responsibly" (moral realm)? "most elegantly" (aesthetic realm)? Although this essay is intended as a response to that impasse, it makes no claim to have resolved it.

155. Bloom, p. 227. The continuation of this passage is quoted above, note 72.

156. [ON THE "RIGHT" VS. THE "REASONABLE."]

Despite his brief for Socratic dialectic as the only kind that "although drawn forward by the search for synthesis, always culminates in doubt" (p. 229), and his admiring observation that "characteristically, Socrates lives with the essential conflicts and illustrates them, rather than trying to abolish them" (p. 266), Bloom in this book asserts the need for cognitively solid answers that only the philosopher can provide. (For his tolerance of unanswered social dilemmas, and his contempt for the certainties of relativists, see notes 115 and 153. For more on dialectics, see below, note 159. See also notes 158 and 173-75.) Bloom's position here has affinities with a recent debate in early childhood education over the merits of "right" vs. "reasoned" answers. (See, e.g., Janet Elder, "A Learned Response: 'Right' answers give way to reasoned answers" in the *New York Times*, section 4A (Education Life Supplement), (January 6, 1991), 23. Here too Bloom and E. D. Hirsch line up on the same side of the issue. For a criticism of Hirsch's emphasis on content (right answers) as opposed to process (reasoning) in early education, see Joseph Shenker's review of *A First Dictionary of Cultural Literacy: What Our Children Need to Know*, ed. E. D. Hirsch Jr. with William Rowland and Michael Stanford (Boston, 1989) in the *New York Times Book Review* (December 17, 1989), 22. To be sure, here, as in his earlier books, Hirsch's explicit concern is to improve the situation of the unprivileged.

For a similar issue in jurisprudence, see Bernard Schwartz, "Justice vs. Justice," in the *New York Times Book Review* (October 15), 18, 20, a review of James F. Simon's *The Antagonists: Hugo Black, Felix Frankfurter and Civil Liberties in Modern America*. "For Black," Schwartz writes, "the issue on judicial review was not *reasonableness* but *rightness*. If a law was contrary to his own conception of what the Constitution demanded, it did not matter that a reasonable legislator might reach the opposite conclusion" (p. 18, emphasis his). This may sound like Black sides with Bloom; yet, as presented by Schwartz, Black's conception of rightness involved attention to concrete situations, whereas his philosophical opponent, Frankfurter, put paramount an ideal of abstractness.

Differences such as these have a clear analogue in the difference between substantive and formal moral laws that is raised by Kant's concept of morality; see above, note 150. See also below, note 157.

157. [ON "COGNITIVE STYLE"; BLOOM ON "IMPOVERISHING CERTITUDES."]

As opposed to the "hot" melodramatic bombast of Wagner, which Stravinsky despised. See this chapter, note 67, and chapter 3, note 27.

A "cognitive style" has about the same relation to an objective argument as the postmodern "meaning-effect" has to a meaning. (On meaning-effect, see Fredric Jameson, "Postmodernism and Consumer Society" [in Foster's *The Anti-Aesthetic*, cited note 55], p. 119; and, for a slightly different formulation, Fredric Jameson, *Postmodernism, or, The Cultural Logic of Late Capitalism* [Durham, 1991], p. 26.) Meaning-effect can also be tied to Bloom's own disdainful category of "no-fault choices" (see note 158). Thus, in this respect, Bloom's work bears an ironic similarity to concepts he despises.

Also relevant here is Bloom's notion of "impoverishing certitudes" (see also note 171, below). On p. 239, Bloom idealizes philosophical study, which, as he defines it, would "turn our impoverishing certitudes into humanizing doubts." By "certitudes" here, Bloom means not those of the philosopher; on the contrary this passage forms part of an impassioned plea for the urgency of the philosopher's firm ground of belief as opposed to the nihilism of relativists (see also notes 115, 156, and 173). What Bloom labels impoverishing are the moral certitudes of those he criticizes. "It is not the morality of relativism that I find appalling," he writes (also on p. 239). "What is astounding and degrading is the dogmatism with which we accept such relativism, and our easygoing lack of concern about what that means for our lives." At this moment, Bloom's aesthetic mode of certainty turns into moral conviction, for in effect he applies the same argument to relativists that could be applied to himself: that their certitudes come not from cognitive verifiability but from a noncognitive fiat. See Bloom's own gloomy discussion of "Goethe's moment [as] the first where the side of action is taken by theory itself, thus announcing the end of the ancient opposition," and of the post-Kantian insight that "the hidden premise of the realm of freedom is that action has primacy over thought" (p. 303); on this, see also above, note 125. On the split between cognition and morality, see above, note 21. On cognitive styles see above, notes 20, 60, 67, 134, 151, and 173; and also chapter 3 of this book, note 27.

158. [BLOOM ON "NO-FAULT CHOICES."]

Bloom, p. 228. The tone of this entire page is stridently condescending: "Real choices [are] possible only for one who faces real questions. . . . Now, when we speak of the right to choice, we mean there are no necessary consequences. . . . America is moving with the aid of modern philosophy toward no-fault choices." (By "modern philosophy," Bloom does not mean his own brand; see above 98). Bloom's no-fault choices have a clear resemblance to Jameson's meaning-effect (see above, note 157).

On the need for "real" choices and alternatives see above, note 84 (on "drab diversity"), note 97, and the text cited in note 104. Note also the convergence of cognition and morality in a discussion of choice related to Plato, p. 237 ("there is nothing good for man which is not informed by thought and affirmed by real choice, which means choice instructed by deliberation").

See also below, note 172; and note 175, on Spike Lee's refusal of synthesis.

159. [BLOOM'S DISDAIN FOR MODERN DIALECTICS.]

Bloom, p. 229. See also above, note 98, the references in note 156, and even note 83 on Bloom's nonrecognition of negative dialectics and other nonresolving arguments.

160. For the application of Geertz's ideas to musicological study see Gary Tomlinson, "The Web of Culture," *Nineteenth Century Music* 7 (April, 1984), 350-62.

161. [ON THE POSSIBILITY OF MAKING QUALITATIVE DISTINCTIONS WITHOUT AN IRONCLAD FIRST PRINCIPLE.]

The assertion I make here is a source of profound and painful doubt for Bloom. Bloom is preoccupied with the immense difficulty of showing, with philosophical rigor, how standards could be maintained in a world that lacks a universal first principle. This difficulty he identifies, in effect, as Nietzsche's central problem, and almost certainly it is the central problem of his own book. (See also above, notes 86 and 88, on the value crisis in philosophy and on postmodernism.)

At first sight, Bloom's point on p. 39 may seem similar to the assertion I have just made: "The fact that there have been different opinions about good and bad in different times and places in no way proves that none is true or superior to others." But where I would use the term "true" very cautiously, Bloom's explicit argument here is that one set of principles is true, and one only (Western moral principles, based on abstract reason; see the context in which this was quoted, above, note 32, and also notes 83 and 84).

William (Bill) Kristol, a conservative, whose glowing review provides a blurb on the back cover of Bloom's book, made a potentially more open statement than Bloom's at a press conference (televised on C-Span) during the Republican Convention in Houston, on August 19, 1992. Comparing heterosexuality and homosexuality, Kristol said, "There is no contradiction between tolerance and saying that some living arrangements are better than others." He went on to argue that it was in the best traditions of America and even of Western civilization to admit that tolerance does not entail a lack of standards. For more on this point, see below, note 172.

A thoughtful nonacademic friend of mine, having read Bloom's book a few years after it came out, decided that Bloom's thesis of Western superiority had to be right because otherwise Americans would have no legitimate basis for condemning the Iranian death warrant on the author

Salman Rushdie. In a sense this man is arguing for a Kantian "what is necessary is possible": the American viewpoint has to be right because the Ayatollah has to be wrong. Writing before the Rushdie incident, Bloom essentially supported such a view. Arguing that even some cultural relativists embrace universal standards of right and wrong when they criticize the Ayatollah's violation of human rights, Bloom charges that "[these] are persons who want to eat their cake and have it too" (p. 191). Again, my own view is that Bloom's either/or scenario—like his rejection of dialectic—is unnecessarily simplistic. See this chapter, pp. 197-98, text between notes 136 and 137, and above, note 159, and also note 103 (on Bloom's sweeping claim).

162. See Bloom, pp. 20 and 266. In both instances, Bloom implies the indisputability of his own views of education.

163. The scholastic image is not so far removed from the satirical accounts of science described by Bloom on p. 270.

164. [BLOOM AND CIGARETTES.]

See, e.g., the cover of the *Newsday Magazine* of September 20, 1987 (with its cover story "The Blooming of America") or the cover of the *New York Times Magazine* of January 3, 1988 (with its cover story "Chicago's Grumpy Guru").

165. [ON THE DISTINCTION BETWEEN PUBLIC AND PRIVATE.]

See Baudrillard, "The Ecstasy of Communication" (in Foster, *The Anti-Aesthetic* [cited in note 55], pp. 130-31: "We live in the ecstasy of communication. And this communication is obscene. . . . It is no longer . . . the traditional obscenity of what is hidden, repressed, forbidden or obscure; on the contrary, it is the obscenity of the visible, of the all-too-visible, of the more-visible-than-the-visible."

166. [ON THE AMERICAN PENCHANT FOR THE LAW AND THE TOTALIZING TENDENCY OF REASON.]

The columnist Paul Greenberg, writing on the Supreme Court, cites de Tocqueville's observation in *Democracy in America* that "every great question in this society eventually becomes a legal one" (the column, entitled "The Revue Comes to Court," appeared in the *Providence Journal-Bulletin* [January 25, 1991], A18).

Or again from the popular press. Writing of drugs and gangs, Ann Landers asks, "Is this a city problem, a federal problem, a medical problem, an economic problem or what? Any answers out there?" (in Long Island *Newsday* [October 6, 1989], Part II, 6). Can we not conceive of a *moral* problem in our own back yard? At bottom, what is involved here is the totalizing tendency of reason, as described by Kant, for example, in the *Critique of Judgment*, section 25, p. 88: "There is . . . in our reason a claim for absolute totality, regarded as a real idea." Later thinkers have connected this tendency to that absence of a self-critical capacity in science, noted above in note 25. See, for example, the following formulations by Horkheimer and Adorno in *Dialectic of Enlightenment*: "Enlightenment is totalitarian," p. 6; "The great discoveries of applied science are paid for with an increasing diminution of theoretical awareness," p. xi, where "the indefatigable self-destructiveness of enlightenment" is also noted; "Thinking objectifies itself to become an automatic, self-activating process; an impersonation of the machine that it produces itself so that ultimately the machine can replace it," p. 25; and "The more the machinery of thought subjects existence to itself, the more blind its resignation in reproducing existence," p. 27. See also p. 39, on the (unsuccessful) attempt of thinking, in its compulsion, to blot out its own nature, a nature evident precisely in that compulsion. The original German word for "compulsion" is *Zwang*; see Max Horkheimer and Theodor W. Adorno, *Dialektik der Aufklärung: Philosophische Fragmente* [Frankfurt am Main, 1988], p. 45. I am indebted to Steve Taylor, a graduate student in music at Brown University, for helping me decipher this difficult passage.) See also above, note 25, on Jameson, de Man, and automatic mechanisms of reason.

167. [ON THE RELATION OF EQUALITY OF OPPORTUNITY AND EQUALITY OF RESULTS.]

Michael Harrington alluded (with great disapproval) to this proposal, on William Buckley's program *Firing Line*, aired September 24, 1989, on PBS in New York. Bloom himself addresses the issue of equal opportunity vs. equal wealth when he writes, (p. 229), "Kant argued that men are equal in dignity because of their capacity for moral choice. It is the business of society to provide the conditions for such choice and esteem for those who achieve it." He goes on to complain that, with John Rawls's *A Theory of Justice* as a guideline, we have watered down Kant's formula to "Men are equal in dignity. Our business is to distribute esteem equally." Bloom's clear implication should be familiar in terms of the history of notions of the Elect: those who prosper do so because they have proven themselves morally worthy.

168. [ON THE BENEFITS OF STRUCTURAL ARTISTIC STANDARDS.]

On "structural listening," see this chapter, p. 187, text leading to note 64. By structural arguments, I mean those that focus on a complex unification of diverse elements. In terms of all the arts, rather than just music, structural arguments for the canon involve narrativity, linearity, tonality, perspective—all the structural elements now under severe attack as signifiers of oppressive, patriarchal societies. Much of that attack is to be taken seriously—the abstract rationalism of Western society has caused enough damage to warrant a sustained critique.

Yet one need not capitulate completely to this attack. In a clever cartoon entitled "Perspective" (in the *New Yorker* magazine of June 22, 1992, p. 108), Charles Barsotti draws a man putting his arm through a picture of a doorway and saying, "Just another lie invented by dead European white males." But of course these elements are considerably more than that, and can be defended as accomplishments of a very high order. Structural unification points toward interesting artistic skills as well as toward a condition of generality (though not pure abstraction), and thereby to beneficial aspects of generality (general appeal, disapproval of cultural prejudices, and so on). It also offers definite standards of evaluation, something useful that is not readily offered by other aspects of art. Arguments over judging art would be a great deal more instructive, in my opinion, if the merits as well as the limitations of structural criteria were acknowledged. (I myself have designed a course at Brown that examines and debates a variety of standards for judging music, in part because my students have found the structural standard so infuriatingly inadequate [and self-assured], and in part because they have had to acknowledge the difficulty of denying, and matching, its strengths.) See also chapter 2, p. 60, up to note 37.

Craig Owens has made the helpful suggestion that "the phrase *master narrative* seems tautologous, since all narrative, by virtue of 'its power to master the dispiriting effects of the corrosive force of the temporal process,' may be narrative of mastery" ("Feminists and Postmodernism," in Foster, *The Anti-Aesthetic* [cited in note 55], p. 66). Owens's own quotation here is from Hayden White; and although Owens criticizes White for failing to admit that the universality of aesthetic forms is now in question (his second note on p. 78, referring to p. 58), White's words here suggest another sense in which the notion of mastery can be powerfully defended.

But again (see notes 70, 75, and 79, above), Bloom goes unacceptably far in suggesting that the Western canon is to be valued, in effect, as a structure of abstract universal rationality, denying the distinctive concreteness of art in order to make a claim that no art can credibly sustain. There is no reason why Shakespeare's plays should not be studied both in terms of abstract notions of structure (of substantial general interest) and in terms of the concrete society in which they emerged. On art and concreteness, see also this chapter, notes 73, 82, and 142.

169. [ON THE "SUBOTNIK SYNDROME."]

My concern here is more or less the same one that Robert Winter once dubbed "the Subotnik syndrome" ("A Musicological Offering," *New York Review of Books* 32 [July 18, 1985], p. 26). See this volume, Introduction, notes 36 and 37.

170. [HUFSTEDLER ON UNTIDINESS OF THE HUMAN CONDITION.]

Testimony of Shirley Hufstedler to Senate Committee on the Judiciary, September 25, 1987, recorded in the Supreme Court of the United States, *Hearings and Reports on Successful and Unsuccessful Nominations of Supreme Court Justices by the Senate Judiciary Committee 1916-1987*, vol. 14 B, compiled by Roy M. Mersky and J. Myron Jacobstein (Buffalo, 1990), p. 2513 (alternate numbering, p. 2333). Hufstedler, a practicing attorney at the time, was a former secretary of education and federal circuit court judge. When Hufstedler finished speaking, the Chairman of the Judiciary Committee, Senator Joseph Biden, responded, "Thank you, Madam Secretary. Presumptuous of me to make an editorial comment, that was a brilliant statement" (p. 2515/2335). Biden's uncharacteristic act of evaluation was, in my judgment, warranted. For me, Hufstedler's testimony was the highwater mark of the Bork hearings.

171. [ON AMERICAN RESISTANCE TO AT LEAST SOME CONSERVATIVE CERTAINTIES.]

On "impoverishing certitudes" (Bloom, p. 239), see above, note 157. Garry Wills, in his review of Ethan Bronner's *Battle for Justice* (cited in note 126), p. 7, argues that "the coalition that blocked the confirmation of Judge Bork has a better claim to being the moral majority than Jerry Falwell's legions ever did."

172. [ON THE RESISTANCE OF THE MORAL TO GENERALIZED LEGISLATION AND THE CONVERGENCE OF THE MORAL ON THE AESTHETIC.]

See this chapter, note 161, and also notes 20, 21, 36, and 150. Lacking a common absolute standard of rightness, Bill Kristol and I would disagree irreconcilably on how to apply his assertion that tolerance does not preclude standards. Certainly I would not use it, as he did, to deprecate homosexual living arrangements. Are these good-faith differences in the application of moral standards to a concrete situation? This is clearly an instance in which abstract standards of legal equality are of crucial moral importance in tempering an evaluation of the particular that Kristol might designate as a moral evaluation because of its content, but that others might well characterize as aesthetic in its ground—a distaste for a style.

173. [BLOOM ON INTELLECTUAL HONESTY.]

For scornful references to the notion of intellectual honesty see Bloom, p. 201, p. 261 ("that sort of thing [has] nothing to do with the university"), and p. 266. Clearly Bloom's objection here, at bottom, is to the essentially aesthetic character of intellectual honesty. This character is also implicitly acknowledged by the excruciating avoidance of falseness that manifests itself—and with forceful persuasiveness, I would argue—in the style more than in any other parameter of Adorno's work. See above, chapter 3, note 62; and also this chapter, notes 115, 156, and 157.

174. [LEE ON THE ENDING OF HIS FILM.]

David Ansen, "The 'Vision' Thing," *Newsweek*, October 2, 1989, p. 137. Immediately preceding this quotation, Ansen writes, "[Lee] insists that people misunderstood the controversial quotations about violence from Martin Luther King and Malcolm X that end 'Do The Right Thing.'" (See above, notes 62 and 112.) Given Bloom's disdain for both easy syntheses (p. 229, see above, note 159) and "no-fault choices" (p. 228, see above, note 158)—and given his conflicting opinions about the need for alternatives (see notes 84 and 97), solutions, and doubts (see notes 115 and 156, and 157), depending on what is at issue (philosophy, relativism, social problems, etc.)—one wonders what Bloom would make of Lee's ending, either as synthesis (Lee's interpretation here) or countersynthesis (see below, note 175).

With respect to the question of violence in the closing quotes, it should noted that Lee kept to his decision not to kill anyone in the riot he depicted (Lee and Jones, *DTRT Companion*, p. 32; see this volume, Introduction, note 46).

175. [LEE ON THE PROBLEM OF SYNTHESIS AT THE END OF HIS FILM.]

In fact, Lee has provided considerable evidence that he does not consider this dual ending a completed synthesis. His comments on the ending in the *DTRT Companion*, for example, are instructive: pp. 71-72, "I gotta watch it, the ending I'm talking about. I can't let the last scene between Mookie and Sal be too chummy. Remember, Sal has had his business burnt to the ground"; p. 45, "Even if Sal's not a saint, in the end when he sits down with Mookie on the curb, there has to be a sliver of realization on his part. He has to recognize Mookie's humanity"; p. 72, "Mookie instigated the burning of [Sal's] pizzeria. This was his life and Sal should be mad as shit"; p. 74, "Paramount is scared that this film might incite Black folks to riot. Needless to say, I don't agree with them," an observation tied explicitly to the ending of the film (on p. 76): "The president [of Paramount] has big problems with the end of the picture. . . . I've been in discussion with Paramount Pictures about the ending. They want an ending that they feel won't incite a giant Black uprising"; pp. 78-79, "One of the problems of the ending of the film as it stands [after the first draft] is that Mookie is too impartial when the riot breaks out. He has to be on Radio Raheem's side from the beginning, even if he doesn't get physically involved." On p. 80 Lee reports that Paramount has decided not to do the film, and Lee goes to Universal. The epilogue to the *DTRT Companion* concerns itself with the ending of the film: p. 281, "Universal's main concern, just like Paramount's, was the ending. Was it too open-ended?" Lee cites some alternative endings he considered, but on p. 282 he informs us that flying back to New York he kept thinking about "that photograph of Malcolm X and Martin Luther King shaking hands. . . . I had to find a way to tie these two great men into the finale. . . . Both men died for the love of their people, but had different strategies for realizing freedom. Why not end the film with an appropriate quote from each? In the end justice will prevail one way or another. There are two paths to that. The way of King, or the way of Malcolm." In his very last paragraph, Lee suggests that if pressed he would side with Malcolm X; but he does not make that choice in the film itself.

   Also interesting were Lee's remarks at Adelphi on the ending of the film. Lee recounted how he fought "tooth and nail" to keep his ending as opposed to what the film studios wanted. "I refused to say 'This is America. Race and religion don't matter"; he refused, he said, "to have Sal and Mookie embrace over a John Williams score, with 1000 violins swelling." (On the phrase "This is America," as used in the film, see above, note 6; on Adelphi, see note 110.)

   176. [BLOOM'S APPARENT DISDAIN FOR WOMEN.]

   Bloom, p. 130; the entire discussion on pp. 127-33 would anger even women who go out of their way to support many so-called traditional values; see also, for example, the rather sneering throwaway reference to abortion on p. 172.

   177. [BLOOM'S REMARKS ON BLACK ISSUES.]

   See especially pp. 92-93; the comparison of "affirmative-action elitism" with "the superior individual," on p. 332 (see above, note 121) could of course be read as supercilious toward many groups, but comes directly after a description of black students in the 1960s (p. 331).

   178. Bloom, p. 236; see also his remarks on compassion, pp. 330-31, given above in note 123, second paragraph, and note 126 ("conspicuous compassion"). On Europe and the Third World see above, note 85, especially the quotation from p. 34.

   179. See above, notes 117, 123, and 126.

   180. [BLOOM'S BRIEF FOR (MALE) SPIRITEDNESS.]

   See Bloom, p. 129 ("Machismo—the polemical description of maleness or spiritedness, which was the central *natural* passion in men's souls in the psychology of the ancients, the passion of attachment and loyalty—was the villain, was the source of the difference between the sexes"); p. 330 ("democracy . . . is hostile to such spiritedness"); and p. 330 (quoted above in note 123, second paragraph). The unprincipled Regina in *The Little Foxes* by Lillian Hellman admires a similar quality, as when (at the end of the film) she says to her suddenly intractable daughter, "Why, Alexandra, you have spirit after all. I used to think you were all sugar-water." Male sparring certainly plays a role in Lee's film. See, for example, Lee's remarks (in Lee and Jones, *DTRT Companion*, sixteenth page of photographs) on the confrontation between Clifton, the white homesteader, and Buggin' Out: "To me this scene is really about how men, Black and white, test each other's manhood." But the dynamic is not used, as Bloom's concept of spiritedness is, to define a privileged class. See also above, note 123, on Plato.

   181. [LEE'S THOUGHTS ON STEREOTYPES.]

   For evidence of Lee's attitude toward this issue see p. 45 ("I must be careful to avoid stereotypes in *Do The Right Thing*. . . . Only real characters, no types") and p. 33 (on "the way I want to tell the story. It can't be just a diatribe, WHITE MAN THIS, WHITE MAN THAT. The treatment of racism will have to be carried in the subtext until the end of the film"). Though Lee makes clear in the context of the latter quote that his chief interest is in not detracting from a careful and realistic portrayal of racism in America, he is nevertheless setting the avoidance of stereotypes here as a standard for himself.

182. Written versions of these texts are given in Lee and Jones, *DTRT Companion*, pp. 186-87; a longer version of Pino's diatribe against blacks appears under his picture, on the eighteenth page of photographs. For the development of this scene, see ibid., pp. 36 and 60.

183. [LEE'S AVOIDANCE (AND USE) OF STEREOTYPES.]

This one lack of differentiation could be justified by the leveling presence of uniforms; and even the policemen have a humanized aspect toward the beginning when they tell Charlie, the owner of the wet white convertible, to get lost. Officer Ponte's reference to *"these people"* (Lee and Jones, *DTRT Companion*, p. 159, emphasis Lee's) may be a play on Charlie's contemptuous reference to "you people" (ibid., p. 156). By contrast, Lee's failure either to distinguish between the characters of Moe and Josh Flatbush or to give them any sympathetic aspect signals a disappointing lapse in his later film, *Mo' Better Blues*, from the high standard set in *Do The Right Thing*.

184. [LEE'S PROVISION FOR ANOTHER VIEWPOINT.]

For example, the character of Clifton, "a yuppie" (Lee and Jones, *DTRT Companion*, p. 165) who owns a brownstone on the block where the story takes place, is presented pretty much as he might present himself. While he is clearly an object of resentment in this neighborhood, he shows normal politeness; and instead of portraying the stereotyped absentee slumlord, Clifton is shown as the unusual white character who lives in his Bedford-Stuyvesant brownstone. See Lee and Jones, *DTRT Companion*, pp. 165-69. See also the description on the sixteenth page of photographs (ibid.).

185. Lee and Jones, *DTRT Companion*, p. 52; Lee continues, "One of the few kids who does listen is Mookie."

186. Ibid., p. 144.

187. [LEE'S DESIGN OF MOOKIE AS A PERSON WITH FLAWS.]

See especially Lee's notes in *DTRT Companion*, p. 82: "When Jade [Mookie's sister] is giving Mookie a hard time, the one thing she mentions over and over is, 'You're not responsible. You don't take care of your responsibilities.' Mookie wants to know what responsibilities she is referring to. Jade says, 'I didn't stutter. You don't take care of your responsibilities. Y'know what I'm talking 'bout.' Of course we find out later, responsibilities means Mookie's child."

188. Lee and Jones, *DTRT Companion*, p. 60.

189. Bloom, p. 382.

190. "Viewpoints: Rich Get Rich with the Tax Cut for Capital Gains," *Newsday* (October 4, 1989), 80.

191. "Avoiding Subways' Homeless," Ibid., 78.

192. Strikingly relevant to the argument I have made here about the results of an exclusionary notion of reason is the reference in E. L. Doctorow's 1989 Brandeis commencement speech to Sherwood Anderson's "theory of grotesques," whereby "people snatch up a truth and make it their own predominating truth to the exclusion of all others. . . . What happens, says Anderson, is that the moment a person does this—clutches one truth too tightly—the truth so embraced becomes a lie and the person turns into a grotesque" (p. 249 of the *Nation* version, cited above, note 119).

Also worth noting is the following excerpt from a book review, in which I have italicized phrases that could serve as a précis of much of my closing chapter: "[The author] does not long for a return to the all too smug 'atmosphere' that characterized Protestant domination of American education and society. . . . However, he hopes that religious claims can be reintroduced into academic life *now that the coercive universalism implicit in much of modern rationalism has been credibly challenged by a new respect for genuine pluralism and an acknowledgment of the social determinants of knowledge. The truths of scientific investigation have a deserved prestige, but the reach of reason is not limited to one methodology.*" The excerpt comes from a review by Paul Baumann (associate editor of *Commonweal* magazine) that appeared under the title, "A Guide to Moral Crisis within Modern Academe," in Long Island *Newsday*, July 21, 1994, p. B6. The review was of George M. Marsden's book *The Soul of the American University: From Protestant Establishment to Established Nonbelief* (New York, 1994).

Index

Since efforts have been made not to duplicate information, associations should be checked under both names and terms. Occasional references to ideas rather than specific terms are generally indicated by the placement of page numbers in parentheses. Surnames or other abbreviated proper names used in cross-references should be checked against main entries for those names. The term "Prelude" refers, throughout, to Chopin's Prelude in A-Major, Opus 28, number 7. Following this index, a separate inventory provides references to endnotes in Chapter 4 concerning Allan Bloom's *Closing of the American Mind*.

Jonathan Sadler, my undergraduate teaching and research assistant at Brown, was of great help in assembling this index.

"About" as fashionable expression, 44, 79, 227-28n

Abrams, Meyer H., 220n

Absence, 280n (of reasons). *See also* Chopin, Prelude; Presence; trace

Abstract-concrete, xv-xvi, 270n; and American self-critique, 29-30; and Baroque, 93; and Classic vs. Romantic, 30, 35, 200, 289n; examples of (Wills), 289n; and ideals vs. needs, 60; and Israel, 235n; and listening, 176; and musical instruments, 31; and universals, 32

Abstract constants, need for, 69

Abstract ideals (importance or priority of), xxvii, 236n; of artistic value, xlii; in Classical style, 200; of commonality, xliii; of original text, 279n; of universality, 179, 191, 203, 278n; of original text, 279n. *See also* Asymptote; Autonomy; Merit system

Abstract reason. *See* reason, abstract

Accuracy, standards of, 217n

Adelphi University. *See* Lee, Spike

Adorno, Theodor W., xix, xxx, xxxi, xxxiii; and abstract-concrete, 30; and affirmative culture, 167; asceticism of, 155, 166-67, 248-50nn, 288n; and authentic performance, 47-49, 164, 226n; and authorial intention, 226n; and autonomous subject, 47; and Bach, 164, 226n; on bad faith, 228n; on Beethoven, 72, 134; on Berg, 249n; blindness of, 249n; Bloom on, 277n; childhood imagery of, 162, 166, 248n; and conscious individual, 159-60; critical language of, 165; and deconstruction, 43-55, 229n; on dissonance, 223n; on early music, 188; elitism of, 175; and existentialist dilemma, 49, 50; on experience, 220n; on expression, 155, 160; formalism of, 152-53, 155; on freedom and responsibility, 47-48; and history, 47-49, 52-53; and ideology, 154, 159, 161-62, 164, 166, 228n, 248n; on illusion, 222n; and the individual, 47, 172; and intention, 152, 159-60; on Kant, 260n; and Lévi-Strauss, 227n; metaphorical criticism by, 165; and metaphysical despair, 52; on modernity, 251n; on moral and aesthetic, 154-55; and moral and structural, 154, 156; on Mozart, 1, 228n; on musical subject, 160; on mutatis mutandis, 49; and nature vs. culture, 152; on necessity of the work, 152; on neutralization, 48, 162; on phantasmagoria and Wagner, 25; on reason

Inventory of Endnotes in Chapter 4 Referring to Allan Bloom's *Closing of the American Mind*

For views by Bloom on the general topics listed in this inventory, see the page numbers and endnotes (to chapter 4 of this volume) specified. Topics are listed alphabetically and, except for those on the arts, are not grouped together by subject. Topics preceded by an asterisk refer explicitly to universities or teaching. Page numbers refer only to the start of each endnote. A selection of more detailed references to Bloom's ideas appears in the Index.

Rose Rosengard Subotnik is a musical scholar and cultural critic known for her work in critical and literary theory as applied to music. She is a past member of the Department of Music and the Committee on the History of Culture at the University of Chicago, where she was awarded the Guggenheim and American Council of Learned Society fellowships. She is currently professor of music at Brown University. Her previous collection of essays, *Developing Variations: Style and Ideology in Western Music*, was published by the University of Minnesota Press in 1991.